AMERICA'S GAME

AMERICA'S GAME

★ ★ ★ THE NFL AT 100 ★ ★ ★

JERRY RICE
AND RANDY O. WILLIAMS

DEY ST.

An Imprint of WILLIAM MORROW

HarperCollins books may be purchased for educational, business, or sales promotional use. For information, please email the Special Markets Department at SPsales@harpercollins.com.

A hardcover edition of this book was published in 2019 by Dey Street, an imprint of William Morrow.

FIRST DEY STREET PAPERBACK PUBLISHED 2020.

Designed by Michelle Crowe

Part opener photos by Alex Kravtsov, Everett Collection, Mark Herreid, Melinda Nagy/Shutterstock, Inc.

Library of Congress Cataloging-in-Publication Data has been applied for.

ISBN 978-0-06-269291-7

20 21 22 23 24   DIX/LSC   10 9 8 7 6 5 4 3 2 1

CONTENTS

PART ONE
First Quarter (1920–1944)

PART THREE
Third Quarter (1970–1994)

PART FOUR
Fourth Quarter (1995–2019)

PREFACE

August 7, 2010. It is one of the proudest days of my life, and I remember it as if it just happened yesterday.

I am walking up to the podium wearing my new gold jacket, issued only to members of the Pro Football Hall of Fame, in Canton, Ohio, and as I get ready to deliver my induction speech, I stop to look around and reflect on the magnitude of the moment. I think to myself, "I am surrounded by legends. This is living history, and I am part of a team that will live forever: the Pro Football Hall of Fame team."

That day reminded me of the tremendous history professional football has experienced and that I am only a small chapter in the history book. And although I thought I knew a lot of that history (and played a part in a lot of it), the reality is that it was just the tip of the iceberg.

After all the hard work and great success we had producing a best-selling book celebrating 50 years of the Super Bowl, Randy Williams called me one evening with an idea and a challenge. (He knew my weakness.)

"Evening, Jerry. Remember when everyone said the 49ers would not even reach the playoffs after your Super Bowl XXIII win, and yet you guys made it all the way to achieve back-to-back titles?

"Well, how about this?" he continued. "Are you up for the challenge of a literary equivalent?"

"Randy, what are you talking about?"

"First, a book celebrating fifty years of the Super Bowl; now how about chronicling one hundred years of the National Football League? That's football symmetry, my friend."

Just like during my playing days, whenever I had a good season, I always challenged myself to work harder in the off-season and come back to have even a better season. So, of course, I accepted Randy's challenge. Not because I wanted merely to secure another best seller but because I love the sport and wanted to learn even more about the history of the NFL from all those who have touched the game: the coaches, players, and media.

We could explore the great names of the past, such as Red Grange, Sammy Baugh, and Don Hutson, but also dig deeper into many different subjects, such as how the league survived both the Great Depression and the manpower shortage caused by athletes serving in World War II. We could look more closely at and understand how rules and equipment changes impacted the game through the decades. We could share the stories of the African American pioneers who fought to integrate the league, including Fritz Pollard and Paul Robeson, and, later, Kenny Washington and Woody Strode.

We could examine the vital role television played in building the game's popularity. We could also reflect on some of the greatest offensive and defensive units that dominated different periods.

With so many important topics, one of the biggest challenges— while still being respectful to the game, players, and coaches—was limiting it to a single volume. So, Randy and I asked players and fans we'd come across what they'd like to see, and much of that is found in this book.

From my own personal experiences and observations of teammates and opponents, along with players and coaches from long before and after my playing days, this unique book will help fans live through the one hundred years of the National Football League from the inside. What makes this book different from others is that we spoke to people who were involved in some way, whether as a player, coach, executive, or member of the media. They shared their stories, feelings, and even some of their personal photos, which we've included. Like I said earlier, even as a knowledgeable fan, I learned so much more about the game I love by working on this project. The best part was that it did not feel like work!

And I'm sure of one thing: I will be getting another call from Randy with another challenge. Maybe a book about comebacks? (Would I have to return the gold jacket?)

I hope this book inspires you to learn more about the game we all love. I know the work I put in to it made me want to suit up again! The more I spoke with players, I was constantly reminded about how much the NFL means to so many people.

—*Jerry Rice*

ACKNOWLEDGMENTS

This book, like the subject it celebrates, has been a team effort and on the roster are a varied group of talented individuals who brought distinct skills and unstinting support to make the creation of this project possible.

In gratitude to:

Marty Zager, Al Ruddy, John Alexenko, Hugh Dodson, Dan and Yvonne Pane, Jim Glen, Travis Cranley, Dan Finklea, Mark Turner, Al Petersen, Dan Aranguren, Geoff Nathanson, Alex Rice, Craig Cacek, John Grogan, Bob Sharka, Eben Ham, Maureen "Triple L" Dunn, Ciao Jianjie, Danielle Sanchez-Witzel, Jim and Mari Davis, Sabrina Elizondo, Walt Dobrowolski, John and Karen Loesing, Jim Vincent, Gianluca Gasparini, Casey Cawelti, Rob Miller, Lisa Lapeyre-Davis, Mariam Jansyan, Paul Fantazia, and especially Monica Herdoiza.

Anthony Mattero and Jackie Raskin for their sharp, intuitive business skills.

Sasha Marin Taylor for being the bridge of support to everything.

To the talented team at HarperCollins/Dey Street led by Lynn Grady and Carrie Thornton including editor Matthew Daddona whose zeal for shaping sports stories helped make this tome well-rounded. Among the other skilled specialists coming into play here include: Ben Steinberg, Kell Wilson, Imani Gary, Erin Reback, Andrea Molitor, Kyran Cassidy, Robert Smigielski, Nyamekye Waliyaya, Michelle Grove, Ted Kutt, and Jeanne Reina.

Dad, Mom, Susan, Rick, Mark, and Roger—a football-friendly family.

Gary Cypres of the Sports Museum of Los Angeles.

Wayne Wilson, Shirley Ito, and Michael Salmon of the LA84 Sports Library.

The media managers for the individual NFL teams as well as the league office and the assistants who handle the affairs of those now retired from the game.

Peter John-Baptiste and Mike Annarella of the Cleveland Browns; Rich Dalrymple and Jonathan Horn of the Dallas Cowboys; Ben Manges, Deanna Ivey, and Stuart Zaas of the Detroit Lions; Brad Gee and Steve Sanders of the Kansas City Chiefs; Jason Jenkins and Scott Stone of the Miami Dolphins; Josh Rupprecht and Jamaal France of the San Diego/LA Chargers; Terrell Lloyd of the San Francisco 49ers as well as Tony Wyllie and Garrett Campbell of the Washington Redskins for providing images that help convey their franchise's rich history. Charlie Waters for the images from Dallas. Dr. James King for the Ralph Hay-Canton Bulldogs-Jim Thorpe images. Bill Hofheimer and Bob Flanagan from ESPN.

My road crew . . . Mary Knox down in Dallas, Alex Martin in KC, Dan Masonson in NY, Vicky Gates and Vivian Wright in Florida, Doug Ireland in Natchitoches, and Stephanie Peterson in Glendale.

The keepers of the flame—David Baker, Joe Horrigan, Michelle Norris and Jon Kendle at the Pro Football Hall of Fame in Canton, Ohio.

The many journalists and broadcasters who shared their keen perspectives.

Jerry Rice for embracing the challenge and loving the football symmetry of following a best-selling book celebrating 50 years of the Super Bowl with a work commemorating 100 years of the National Football League.

Finally, I would like to convey my appreciation of the many players and coaches whose clear expression for their love of the game resonated in our conversations, and in giving it all they had each Sunday afternoon, year-after-year, decade-after-decade, have provided America with a unique sport.

Thank you.

—Randy O. Williams

In my football career, I was fortunate enough to have two Hall of Fame quarterbacks throw me the ball, and for that I am extremely thankful! But now in my retirement, I have struck gold again with my coauthor, Randy O. Williams. Randy has been like my quarterback and has been a great teammate and partner on our book projects. Without Randy's dedication and total commitment, this book would not be possible, and I am forever grateful to him!

I'd also like to thank our agent, Anthony Mattero, for believing in us, and, of course, a special thank-you to the team at HarperCollins/Dey Street for partnering with us again. Matthew Daddona, thank you for keeping us together and being more than our editor. You helped us tell the stories of all these football greats, from coaches, to players, to the media!

I really have to thank all the players, coaches, executives, and members of the media for sharing your stories with us and helping us to make our book unique and personable. You give our book that competitive edge! I also have to give a special thanks to those who were instrumental in giving an incredible interview, helping us to secure interviews, or granting us rights to use photos. So, thank you, J. B. Bernstein (Barry Sanders), Terrell Lloyd and the 49ers, John

Lynch, Bus Cook (Brett Favre), Sean Morgan (Lawrence Taylor), Jason Jenkins and the Miami Dolphins, and Peter John-Baptiste and the Cleveland Browns.

It wouldn't be right if I didn't thank my longtime manager-agent and friend Sasha Marin Taylor. I appreciate your hard work and for making my life easier.

A special thank-you to Eddie DeBartolo Jr. You are more than the greatest owner in the NFL. You're simply the greatest, and I love you!

To the National Football League, thank you for so many great years and for giving us so much to talk about.

Thank you to the Pro Football Hall of Fame for allowing Randy to visit and look through the archives and for being supportive of our efforts.

I also want to thank my brothers and sisters for their love and continued support.

Thank you to my children for having allowed me to play the game I love, as I know it meant sacrificing time with your father. I appreciate your understanding and love you.

To my fiancée, Tish Pelayo, thank you for being my ride-or-die. I can't imagine mimosa Sundays without you. Your love, support, and understanding mean the world to me.

Lastly, even though they are no longer with me, I would like to thank my parents, Joe Nathan Rice and Eddie B. Rice, for instilling in me the meaning of hard work and dedication. Without them, there is no Jerry Rice.

—*Jerry Rice*

First Quarter

★ ★ ★ 1920–1944 ★ ★ ★

CHAPTER ONE

BECOMING AMERICA'S GAME

The origin of American football goes like this: one cold, misty afternoon in 1823 on the athletic field of a school in the Midlands of England, a young ministry student, William Webb Ellis, decided, with his team down in a soccer match, to suddenly pick up the ball and run with it. This maneuver, maybe emanating from divine inspiration, was completely against the rules of the game, but it became the origin of another: rugby. Why was it called rugby? That was the name of the school where the incident took place.[1]

Ellis died in 1872, unaware of his apparently historic achievement. Around that time, a power struggle for the sport between amateur and professional factions grew so intense that British high society created the Ellis myth as a means of controlling the direction of the game. But it just ended up splitting rugby into two opposing camps.

That story, however, shares something in common with the origin of another popular American sport: baseball. Passed down for generations was the myth that Abner Doubleday invented baseball. In fact, there is no record of Doubleday, a Civil War general on the side of the Union, ever being connected to the sport. In a well-documented life, none of his letters and journals, going back to his days at West Point, even mentions the word. The only real reference tying Doubleday to athletics at all appeared in an 1893 obituary, which stated that he was a man "who did not care for outdoor sports."[2] Doubleday's baseball story illustrates the fact that few sports have a single founder (an exception, perhaps, being basketball's James Naismith). The same goes for football.

Settlers arriving in America brought their sports of soccer and, later, rugby with them. Played freely and shared liberally on these shores, the games became a mishmash of styles—more rugby than soccer and, in most cases, operating without an established rule book. On Saturday, November 6, 1869, Rutgers College edged the College of New Jersey (later to be known as Princeton University), 6–4, in the first college soccer-football game. The game used modified London Football Association rules, in which players could not use their hands. They could advance the ball only by kicking. But unlike typical soccer, with 11 to a side, 25 players per side filled the field. Over the next few years, the physical mayhem of rugby would edge out soccer in terms of early stateside popularity.

Written records indicate that the first rugby match occurred in May 1874, when Harvard University hosted Montreal's McGill University. As the game spread among colleges, common rules were slowly adopted.

However, winning on the road was comparatively tougher for the American patriots of Harvard, Princeton, Yale University, and other Ivy League schools, because even though these games shared a handful of standards, many rules still varied per home field. It was a true home field advantage, with visitors having no choice but to play by their opponents' rules.

That began changing in 1876, at what became known as the Massasoit Convention in Springfield, Massachusetts—the same town where James Naismith would put up a peach basket and invent basketball 15 years later. Yale's captain and halfback, Walter Camp, a soft-spoken yet persuasive 20-year-old with stylish mutton-chop sideburns, began to push for a series of rules that would eventually resemble elements of football as we know it. Some of Camp's proposals included: a system of downs; a line of scrimmage; a direct center-to-quarterback snap; and 11 players to a side. He also sought to further limit debilitating human collisions by prohibiting more than one player from being in motion before the start of a play.

Another change credited to Camp, who would become known as the "Father of American Football," was reducing the length of the field concurrent with downsizing the number of players, from about 140 by 70 yards, inching closer to today's field, which is 120 yards long and 53 1/3 yards wide. Initially, Camp's downs system called for three plays in which to gain five yards.

Though college football would become extraordinarily popular over the next few decades, it was around the early 1890s that the sport saw the arrival of the first professionals. Like Camp, the very first was a Yale alumnus.

William "Pudge" Heffelfinger was a terrific guard who had made Walter Camp's first All-America team (an honor subsequently given annually to the best American college football players at their respective positions) in 1889. A year after graduating Yale in 1891, Pudge was the first player known to be paid to play the game, receiving $500 to join the Allegheny Athletic Association for a face-off against the Pittsburgh Athletic Club. It paid off, as the beefy Heffelfinger made the game-winning play. Muscling through the opponent's line, he jarred the ball loose, picked up the fumble, and rumbled in for the only score as Allegheny won, 4–0. Yes, a touchdown was worth 4 points then.

Play was dominated by pushing, punching, gouging, kicking, choking, flying elbows, and violent collisions. There was no such thing as a "spread offense." And one formation, the "flying wedge," resembled a V-shaped human battering ram, with players interlocking arms and running interference for the ball carrier. (Reportedly, each lineman grabbed suitcase handles sewn into the pants of the man in front of him.[3]) The flying wedge would become a leading cause of not only crippling injuries but also deaths.

Broken arms, jaws, noses, and shoulders were commonplace. But following an alarming number of fractured skulls, broken necks, and extensive internal bleeding—some of them fatal—there arose a public outcry to outlaw the sport. This forced President Theodore Roosevelt into action in 1905. A longtime football fan, Roosevelt carried sufficient influence to force the powers of football to move beyond their brutal nineteenth-century origins and reform the sport—knowing that the president could issue an executive order banning football altogether.

The result was the founding of the Intercollegiate Athletic Association of the United States, which in 1910 would become known as the National Collegiate Athletic Association, or NCAA. As part of dramatic reforms, in 1906 new rules were put in place to spread the game out with different positions stretching the formation and increase success based more on finesse and less on raw, brutish strength in a congested scrum. These included outlawing mass formations such as the flying wedge; establishing a neutral zone called the line of scrimmage before each play; doubling the first-down distance to ten yards; and establishing a penalty system. Regulations encouraging the forward pass would eventually have a huge impact on the game. Though not incorporated heavily during the first few years after its legalization, the forward pass gained widespread usage after teams saw the success that coach Knute Rockne and quarterback Gus Dorais had with it at the University of Notre Dame starting in 1913.

With new, uniform rules to go with its established history, as well as big-city locations and new mass communications technologies such as radio and cinema newsreels, college football flourished in the 1910s and 1920s, with programs stretching across America. Many universities built their own stadiums through fund-raising by supportive alumni. Successful college football teams became a vehicle of local pride for communities and whole regions that otherwise might have been connected only slightly; the game unified them and gave them an outlet for celebrating their place in American society. The season-capping Bowl Games became events that rivaled the baseball World Series in national significance.

Using similar vehicles (though it would take a few decades), the road to professional football's preeminence began in earnest in Canton, Ohio, in 1920, when a young man with a vision shared beers with a handful of fellow enthusiastic pioneers eager to finally make the pro game a success.

CHAPTER TWO

THE NFL KICKS OFF

An understanding of the National Football League is not complete without considering the contributions of George Halas, arguably the most influential figure in the history of professional football.

How important was he to the game? "You can never give him too much credit," according to Joe Horrigan, executive director of the Pro Football Hall of Fame.

Growing up in Chicago and studying civil engineering at the University of Illinois, Halas was a solid athlete. He played receiver and defensive end for future College Football Hall of Fame coach Robert Zuppke, who led his teams to four national titles and helped take the Illini to the Big Ten football championship. One of the early leaders in making intercollegiate sports a growing force, the roots of the Big Ten traces back to 1895, when school executives from the universities of Illinois, Minnesota, Northwestern, Chicago, Purdue, and Wisconsin gathered and created regulations to govern athletics.

After graduating, Halas joined the US Navy for service in World War I. While in uniform, he organized and played football, basketball, and baseball with some very good teams at the Great Lakes Naval Training Station. He showed such promise in the latter sport, given his speed and glove, that the New York Yankees wanted him as soon as the war was over. Upon being discharged as an ensign, Halas reported to Yankees training camp in Florida in 1919 and won the right field job. But during an exhibition game, after roping a fastball off Rube Marquard, a future Hall of Fame southpaw, the speedy Halas was injured while trying to stretch a double into a triple; he jarred his hip and sustained a leg injury from the jolt of hitting the hard dirt in his slide.[4]

Still hampered by a sore hip months later, Halas traveled to Youngstown, Ohio, to visit a Welsh-born sports injury specialist named John D. "Bonesetter" Reese, who, despite having no formal medical training—and not even a medical license—would lend his healing touch to many famous athletes in later years. But the reality was that another, more serious malady ended Halas's baseball career: like so many others before and after him, he had trouble hitting the curveball. In 22 at-bats for New York that summer, the 24-year-old managed just two singles, for a .091 batting average, and whiffing eight times. Even if he'd performed reasonably well, he wouldn't have kept the right field job for long: that winter, while Halas was back in the Midwest, the Yankees landed the game's most fearsome slugger (and also one of its standout pitchers). George Herman "Babe" Ruth would claim the position for the next fifteen years.

Despite the setback, Halas did not give up on baseball, deciding to play for a minor league team in Saint Paul, Minnesota. But when management wanted him to take a salary cut, he turned back to football. He was playing for the independent pro football team the Hammond (Indiana) Pros in 1919 when, based on his reputation organizing the military service sports teams, he was recruited by A. E. "Gene" Staley, the sports-loving owner of a major cornstarch manufacturer in Decatur, Illinois. Many businesses sponsored athletic departments for their employees, and Staley wanted Halas to run the A. E. Staley Manufacturing Company football team.

All in, besides being a player-coach, Halas did his own scouting, recruiting, and signing of players. His handpicked group included: George Trafton, a fine center from Notre Dame; Jimmy Conzelman, a star halfback at Saint Louis's Washington University, and a future coach; running back Guy Chamberlin, an all-American from Nebraska; and halfback Edward "Dutch" Sternaman, a fellow University of Illinois grad.

The next big decision was trying to figure out who the Staley Starchmakers should play. Halas wrote a letter to Ralph Hay, owner and manager of the Canton Bulldogs, a dominating squad in organized ball referred to as "The Ohio League" suggesting they form a league. This led to formative meetings on August 20 and September 17, 1920. Several club owners had been kicking around the idea of forming a league for some time, particularly Hay and a man named Joe Carr, who ran the Columbus Panhandles. But as the Hall of Fame's Horrigan pointed out, "This was in the day when you couldn't just pick up the phone or send faxes or emails; thus it was hard to organize something. In August, only the four Ohio team reps showed up."

That first meeting, though sparsely attended, heightened the participants' awareness of the key issues that needed to be addressed, including astronomically rising salaries; employing college players still enrolled in school; and the problem of pro players jumping from team to team based on whichever one dangled the highest offer. They coined a name for the new entity: the American Professional Football Conference, or APFC. According to a local newspaper, the *Evening Repository,* the representatives had also proposed resolutions to end poaching among teams:

[M]embers of the organization reach an agreement to refrain from offering inducements to players to jump from one team to another, which has been one of the glaring drawbacks to the game in past seasons. Contracts must be respected by players as far as possible, as well as by club managers. The move to abolish com-

petitive bidding for star players is a matter of self-protection for
the magnates, as they have been facing a steady upward trend in
the prices demanded by players of ability, especially those who
have acquired big college reputations.[5]

On September 17, a hot and muggy Friday evening, the second
scheduled meeting was supposed to take place in Ralph Hay's office,
but this time there were so many attendees that it had to be held in
the showroom of his Canton automobile dealership.

As the participants sat on the vehicles' fenders and running
boards while the beer flowed freely, here is what was accomplished
on that historic day, according to the official minutes of the meeting.[6]

The teams represented four states: from Ohio, the Canton Bulldogs, the Akron Pros, the Cleveland Tigers, and the Dayton Triangles; from Indiana, the Hammond Pros and the Muncie Flyers;
from New York, the Rochester Jeffersons; and from Illinois, the
Rock Island Independents, the Decatur Staleys, and the Racine Cardinals. The Massillon (Ohio) Tigers withdrew for the 1920 season.
Four other teams—the Buffalo All-Americans, the Chicago Tigers,
the Columbus Panhandles, and the Detroit Heralds—would join
the league during the year.

The name of the league was amended slightly to the American
Professional Football Association (now acronymed APFA). Stanley
Cofall was elected vice president, while A. F. Ranney became secretary and treasurer. Cofall, a former captain while playing halfback
at Notre Dame, helped create the Cleveland Indians football team.
Ranney was a former player at the University of Akron and one of
the owners of the Akron Pros.

By making Jim Thorpe president, the owners felt it would help
generate more awareness for their new league. After all, professional
football first proved itself a viable spectator sport in the 1910s with
the establishment of the Ohio League. Canton, its premiere team,
featured the legendary Olympic gold medal decathlete and football

star, so the APFA knew the potential was there. They hoped that a better organization, with a legend at the helm, would help it grow.

A membership fee of $100 per team was charged to give an appearance of respectability, but no club ever paid it. Scheduling was left up to the teams, and there were wide variations, both in the overall number of games played and in the number played against APFA member franchises.

The APFA began play on September 26, 1920, with the Rock Island Independents flattening a nonleague team, the St. Paul Ideals, 48–0. A week later, Dayton beat Columbus, 14–0, in the first contest between two teams from the APFA.

This was a start in the right direction, but plenty of kinks would have to be worked out. For example,

Canton Bulldogs owner Ralph Hay and his star player, Jim Thorpe.

Courtesy Dr. James F. King

all the teams were lumped into a single division and did not even play the same number of games. Strangely, in what you'd have to call a lost opportunity, no definitive championship game was held for years. At the end of each season, the team with the best record was simply declared champion without the benefit of a title matchup.

The Akron Pros were the only team that went undefeated that first year, at 8-0-3. And by beating the Canton Bulldogs twice, they were the unofficial champions of the APFA. Fritz Pollard played in the Akron backfield the year before and, as co-coach of the 1920 team, would go down in history as the NFL's first black head coach.

After one year as the Staleys' player-coach, Halas felt that Decatur simply wasn't big enough to support a team, especially one that had no venue of its own. A. E. Staley, the team's owner, reminded George that he was doing it merely for promotional value, so it was agreed in October 1921 that Halas could go to Chicago with the understanding that for one year they must call themselves the Chicago Staleys. Halas, along with Staley's partner at the time, Dutch Sternaman, were off to the City of Broad Shoulders. Staley gave them $5,000 seed money to get started.

Arriving in the Windy City with no place to play, Halas made a deal with William Veeck Sr., president of the Chicago Cubs: in exchange for letting the Staleys play at the baseball team's Wrigley Field (known at the time as Cubs Park), the Cubs would get a percentage of the football gate and concessions. In a whirlwind of activity, Halas not only assumed player-coach-owner-GM duties but also personally distributed flyers to promote upcoming games. Though the Staleys averaged fewer than ten thousand spectators per game, they finished the season with a 9-1-1 record, good enough to win the first league championship of the APFA. In 1922, Halas changed the name of his team to the Chicago Bears, hoping to gain interest by playing off the name of the popular Cubbies. That same year, he also suggested the APFA change its name to the National Football League (NFL).

After the first season, Jim Thorpe was replaced by Joe Carr to head up league operations. From 1921 until his death in 1939, Carr served as president of the NFL, and his significant contribution included seeing the league established in major cities. The Detroit Lions, New York Giants, Washington Redskins, Philadelphia Eagles, and Pittsburgh Steelers were all added on his watch.

Carr had worked previously as the promotional director for Minor League Baseball's governing body. During his tenure, he oversaw an expansion of the minor league system from 12 leagues to 40, operating in more than 250 cities. He would adapt the lessons he'd learned from that sport to his new position with the NFL.

One important rule change he imposed was outlawing players from suiting up for different teams in the same week. He gave teams territorial rights to players within the league, restricted player movement, developed membership criteria for franchises, and insisted that standings were kept so that a true champion could be crowned. (But still there was no championship game.)

Canton, behind a talented group that included five future Hall of Famers (Thorpe, Chamberlin, Joe Guyon, Pete Henry, and Link Lyman), was one of pro football's best teams in 1922 and 1923. The Bulldogs won back-to-back titles, producing a cumulative record of 21-0-3. Overall, some excitement was building, but still the league stood on shaky ground. Teams continued to come and go. And as the pro game tried to make inroads, the powerful and influential college football establishment was pushing hard to squash the NFL before it could get any footing.

In an era dominated by amateur athletics, there was a hailstorm about the sanctity of what the college game did for young men compared with the cheap, money-driven professional sport. Legendary collegiate football coach Amos Alonzo Stagg, then entering his third decade helming the University of Chicago Maroons, called professional football a "menace" and preached that to "patronize Sunday professional football is to cooperate with the forces which are destructive of the interscholastic and intercollegiate football which serve to the upbuilding of the present and future generations."

George "Potsy" Clark, while coaching at the University of Kansas in 1924, warned, "The most serious menace to the game today is professional football. This parasite will soon injure the academic game unless the amateur sports-loving public, especially the college alumni faculties and student bodies, foresee the danger . . . professional football promoters don't care about the high standards and educational values of academic football."[7] Ironically, Clark would go on to a lengthy coaching career in the NFL with the Brooklyn Dodgers and the Portsmouth (Ohio) Spartans/Detroit Lions.

Of course, the new league tread carefully in its dealings with the collegiate game. After all, that pipeline providing a constant flow of young talent was essential to its survival. Fading away were the days when men played with their college team on Saturday and then slyly suited up for a pro game on Sunday. The NFL knew it could not continue that practice. At an APFA meeting in January 1921, the owners adopted a strict rule prohibiting the use of a player still in college. Each club had to post a guarantee of $1,000, which would be forfeited to the league if it should violate the noncollegian law.[8]

The Green Bay Packers didn't make it through the 1921 season without committing multiple infractions, having lured several Notre Dame stars to join their roster. This cost the young men their amateur status and prompted the university to suspend them.

After admitting to having used players who had college eligibility remaining during the 1921 season, Green Bay withdrew from the APFA. However, Curly Lambeau, who had played at Notre Dame under coach Knute Rockne and had founded the Packers after his employer, the Indian Packing Company, agreed to provide backing money, promised to obey league rules and then used $50 of his own money to buy back the franchise. Unfortunately, the even more frigid weather for that region hampered attendance, and Lambeau went broke. Nevertheless, with support from local merchants, who arranged a $2,500 loan for the club, a public nonprofit corporation was set up to operate the team. With that, Lambeau was out as owner but in as player/coach.

But all that aside, over the next few years, the NFL gained popularity. The simple reason? Its talent was getting better.

Ray Davis, a former Howard College (now Samford University) center who had just helped his Portsmouth Spartans to a 6-2-4 record (under coach Potsy Clark) in the NFL for the 1932 season, compared the level of play between college and pro games: "The average first-rate college team would never score on a National League team. And you can bet your bottom dollar that the pros would put the ball across somehow. We are sure that we could lick any college football team in the country."[9]

In 1933, after watching the Chicago Bears defeat the New York Giants, 23–21, in the very first NFL championship game (finally!), sportswriter Chuck Voorhis of the *Charlotte Observer* expressed yet another reason why the league was growing: "The 24,000 fans who turned out in inclement weather for this contest saw some mighty brilliant football. All in all, the professional brand of football tends to create a much more open contest. And 'open' contests invariably produce greater thrills."[10]

Once the NFL realized the game was improving because the players were maturing, they had to convince the fans that it was a better brand of football and to make them feel the partisanship enjoyed by college football. Leading the way would be Washington Redskins owner George Preston Marshall, who was an entertainment promoter first. He viewed football as pageantry and, to that end, put together his own marching band, introduced a team fight song, and staged elaborate halftime shows to draw in women and children.

Another factor playing into the NFL's favor was pure fan economics.

College football tickets were fairly pricey and out of reach for the average fan, whereas seats at an NFL game were comparatively inexpensive. Furthermore, in the era of the six-day workweek, many folks would be working Saturdays. Playing their games on Sunday helped in that regard; but it also hampered the league because some cities prohibited sports on the Christian Sabbath.

The year 1925 saw five new franchises admitted to the NFL: the Pottsville (Pennsylvania) Maroons, who had been perhaps the most successful independent pro team; a new Canton Bulldogs squad; the

Providence Steam Rollers; the Detroit Panthers, featuring Jimmy Conzelman as owner, coach, and tailback; and, perhaps most important, the New York Giants, who were awarded to Tim Mara. The novice owner, who was both a bookbinder and a bookmaker, admitting he knew nothing about football, quipped famously: "I figure an exclusive franchise for anything in New York is worth five hundred dollars." In today's dollars, that would be roughly $7,300.

It was also the year that the Associated Press news service began carrying scores of NFL games on its national trunk wire. Given that newspapers dominated the media then, this proved to be an important PR tool. The NFL also established its first player limit, at 16 players.

This was the year that Harold "Red" Grange, a superstar running back from the University of Illinois, called the attention of the nation's sports fans to professional football.

In a deal negotiated between George Halas and Grange's "agent," a small-town movie theater owner named Charles Cassius "C. C." (Cash and Carry) Pyle, on November 22 Grange signed with the Chicago Bears. Although he'd played his last college game, "the Galloping Ghost" was technically not yet eligible for the pros, because his class hadn't graduated. He dropped out and made his debut on Thanksgiving Day against crosstown rivals the Chicago Cardinals in front of nearly 40,000 fans shoehorned into Cubs Park—at the time the largest crowd in pro football history. Despite the Cardinals keying on stopping the marquee player, including giving him a black eye, Grange totaled 36 yards from scrimmage, added 56 yards on punt returns, and threw six passes. His key contribution came on the defensive side of the ball by coming up with an interception to break up the Cardinals' only real scoring threat of the day.

Number 77 finished his truncated rookie season by scoring three touchdowns over the final seven games. Then he and the Bears went on a lucrative whirlwind barnstorming tour. This series of post-season travel exhibition games designed to help draw attention to the NFL by featuring its new star, would be such a success that the practice of barnstorming reached across sports and would later be used by the Harlem Globetrotters, Negro baseball leagues, auto racers, and other football teams.

The Bears' tour saw them play eight games in 12 days, in Saint Louis, Philadelphia, New York City, Washington, Boston, Pittsburgh, Detroit, and Chicago, reportedly raking in half of the gate receipts. On December 6, at the Polo Grounds in Upper Manhattan, a massive crowd of 73,000 came out to see their team take on Grange and the Bears. Although Chicago won, 19–7, the excitement stirred by just this one game helped to ensure the future of the fledgling NFL franchise in New York.

The new Bears running back was a media sensation wherever he went, and glowing descriptions of his talents spread rapidly across the country, such as this from Grantland Rice, one of the preeminent sportswriters of the day:

"Grange runs as [Finnish track star Paavo] Nurmi runs and [boxer Jack] Dempsey moves, with almost no effort, as a shadow flits and drifts and darts. There is no gathering of muscles for an extra lunge. There is only the effortless, ghostlike weave and glide upon effortless legs with a body that can detach itself from the hips—with a change of pace, then come to a dead stop and pick up instant speed, so perfect in the coordination of brain and sinew."

The Grange-led Bears continued into the new year, traveling through the South and then along the West Coast. On January 16, 1926, more than 75,000 fans poured into the Los Angeles Coliseum to watch them defeat the hometown Tigers.

Joe Horrigan called the Grange signing "the biggest thing that happened in pro football," adding, "It was a clear violation of their own rule! But it will always be forgiven because it did so much for the game. There was nothing that could have brought more attention to the National Football League."

Looking back decades later on a career filled with many accomplishments, George Halas reflected, "I've always thought it was the tremendous publicity generated by the Grange tour that established pro football as a national sport."

The success of the Grange signing showed the owners the power of promoting their game through star power. Now the league was about to expand its roster of heroes.

CHAPTER THREE

SEEING STARS

In order to help make them a success, the nascent National Football League would need to borrow a page from the script that built Hollywood as well as from the playbooks of other sports, and that meant an emphasis on two words: star power.

The NFL began play at the dawn of the 1920s, an era in which even the gangster Al Capone was treated with an air of deference. Influenced by the growing impact of newspapers, radio, and film newsreels, America was becoming a nation that admired celebrities.

Clara Bow, Charlie Chaplin, Al Jolson, and Gloria Swanson graced the silver screens. Dance was king, and pre-Paris Josephine Baker was its queen. Aviator Charles Lindbergh and scientist Albert Einstein were treated like royalty. The glamour couple was the celebrated author of *The Great Gatsby*, F. Scott Fitzgerald, and his witty socialite wife, legendary flapper Zelda Sayre.

In sports, the 1920s was a golden age. Among the superstars was Jack Dempsey in boxing, Bobby Jones in golf, Bill Tilden in tennis, Johnny Weissmuller in swimming, and slugger Babe Ruth in baseball.

There was a great sense of coming prosperity, as Americans' personal incomes improved significantly with a mass migration leaving farm work and moving to industrial centers in and around large cities. As a result, there was more leisure time, and attending sports events was growing by leaps and bounds.

In football, the flourishing college game was closing in on Major League Baseball as America's most popular spectator sport. Leading the charge in espousing that football built not only a young man's physical skills but also his moral character, Notre Dame coach Knute Rockne preached that the gridiron taught the individual to triumph over adversity and attain glory as part of a group endeavor.

JIM THORPE

Owners in the pro game recognized this character trait, and thus the early stars of the National Football League came from the ranks of the college game. For example, the storied Native American player Jim Thorpe had been an all-American at the Carlisle Indian Industrial School, in Carlisle, Pennsylvania, before going on to win two gold medals in the 1912 Olympic Games. Then, beginning in 1915, at the age of twenty-eight, he signed with the Canton Bulldogs of the Ohio League as a player-coach. Just as he'd dominated intercollegiate play, Thorpe crushed professional opponents in leading Canton to several championships, demonstrating time and again that he had all the skills: running, passing, punting, blocking, drop kicking, place kicking, and tackling. (Oh, yes: at the same time, the versatile six-foot-one, 200-pounder spent six seasons patrolling the outfield for the baseball New York Giants and two other teams.)

"Thorpe was a great punter and passer as well as a fine ball carrier," said pioneering college coach Glenn Scobey "Pop" Warner, who founded the football program at the Carlisle boarding school that Thorpe attended. "He was without superior as a safety and could play any defensive back position."[11]

Jimmy Conzelman, a Hall of Fame player-coach and solid runner in his own right, illustrated this point. "[In one game] I saw an opening and started down the sideline. . . . I got about three yards, when Thorpe came along. He didn't try to tackle me. He just hit me with his hip, and I flew over a short fence about six feet away. I thought someone had fired a big shell. The funny part is that Thorpe used his hip in a tackle as often as his arms and shoulders. Jim had a hip that seemed to jump out of joint. Especially when you tried to tackle him. He had both offensive and defensive hips. Those were the times when the cure-all for any football injury was a dab of io- dine and four fingers of bourbon."[12]

Combine that with his unprecedented success winning both the pentathlon and decathlon at the 1912 Summer Olympics in Stock- holm, Sweden, and Thorpe became a living legend, proclaimed "the world's greatest athlete." His being named president of the Ameri- can Professional Football Association in 1920 was a key reason for the new league's successful start. (For more on Thorpe, see chapter 5, "Indians and Eskimos.")

RED GRANGE

The next great collegiate player to turn pro was Red Grange. Facing the defending national champion University of Michigan Wolver- ines on October 18, 1924, the 21-year-old produced a legendary feat. The Galloping Ghost immediately put a charge into the crowd by taking the game's opening kickoff all the way for a 95-yard touch- down. The next three times he touched the ball, he found his way into the end zone on runs of 56, 67, and 45 yards. (All of this hap- pened in the first 12 minutes.) He later added a fifth touchdown and passed for a sixth as Illinois won, 39–14, on that crisp fall afternoon. Grange totaled 402 yards, transforming the humble native of Whea- ton, Illinois, into a national figure.

"This man Red Grange of Illinois is three or four men rolled into one for football purposes," penned the inimitable American writer Damon Runyon. "He is Jack Dempsey, Babe Ruth, Al Jolson, Paavo Nurmi, and Man o' War. Put together, they spell Grange."

Gifted with an uncanny combination of speed, agility, and power—legend has it that he developed his formidable strength from a summer delivery job lugging large blocks of ice up apartment building stairs—the Galloping Ghost ran all over the field.

Alas, a knee injury sidelined Grange for the entire 1928 season. He returned the following year but never regained his unique gallop and uncanny ability to change directions on a dime, leaving defenders rolling in the dirt. From 1929 through his final NFL season, the Bears star's success came primarily on defense. Fortunately, the NFL did not lose a step with the loss of Grange, as a bigger, more formidable running back came onto the scene, took the ball, and ran with it.

ERNIE NEVERS

At Stanford University, where he was a four-sport star, Ernie Nevers was at his best on the football field as a multitalented fullback with exceptional running, passing, and kicking skills.

After college, the ruggedly handsome Minnesotan played for a pro football team in Jacksonville, Florida, but the franchise folded after just two games. That unforeseen development was not as catastrophic as it would have been for your average footballer; in a matter of weeks, Nevers had taken up residence on the pitcher's mound for the St. Louis Browns of the American League. Though he lost twice as many games as he won, the six-foot-tall right-hander pitched three seasons for the Brownies and then spent 1928 and 1929 in the minors with the San Francisco Mission Bells of the Pacific Coast League. He did, however, take his shoulder pads on the road in 1927, playing for the NFL's Duluth Eskimos, a travel team (basically a designated road team that does not have a home field) from his home state of Minnesota. (See chapter 5, "Indians and Eskimos.")

In 1929, Nevers went to work for the Chicago Cardinals. That November, the fullback had a stretch of games that would end in record-setting fashion. On November 6 he led his team to a 16–0 victory over the Providence Steam Roller in the first night game in NFL history. Nevers threw a 30-yard touchdown pass, kicked a 33-yard field goal, and ran for another touchdown.

On November 24 he scored all 19 points in a 19–0 shutout of the Dayton Triangles, running for three touchdowns and kicking an extra point. Then four days later, on Thanksgiving, in a show-down against crosstown rivals the Bears in Wrigley Field, Nevers set an NFL record for points scored by a player in a single game. The 26-year-old claimed all 40 points in the Cardinals' 40–6 victory, rushing for six touchdowns) and booting four extra points. It is a record that still stands today.

How good was the Big Dog? He earned election to the Pro Football Hall of Fame despite just a brief five-year career.

"Ernie Nevers played his position [fullback] by far the best of any player I saw," said his Stanford coach, none other than Pop Warner. "He had a powerful physique; was big and powerful yet very active."[13]

It was no coincidence that the next big NFL star would also be a powerful running back, as that was key to fielding a successful team (just as it is now).

BRONKO NAGURSKI

Born in Canada to parents of Polish Ukrainian descent, the young Bronislau "Bronko" Nagurski grew up, like Ernie Nevers, in Minnesota. As a young man, he toiled in sawmills and other lumbering operations, growing to "timber" levels himself: six foot two.

At the University of Minnesota, he was the first college player ever named all-American at two positions: tackle and fullback. Then in 1930 he joined Red Grange in the Chicago Bears' backfield, which was akin to having renowned bandleaders Duke Ellington and Louis Armstrong sharing the same stage. At a team practice the great Grange discovered painfully what it was like to try to bring down Bronko: "When you hit him at the ankles, it is almost like getting an electric shock," he quipped. "If you hit him above the ankles, you are likely to get killed."

Bronko Nagurski (isn't that one of the greatest names ever for a running back?) killed the NFL as a devastating sixty-minute player through 1937 with his tank-like running, bone-rattling blocking, and sledgehammer tackling. Oh, and he could throw, too.

Wrapping up the 1932 season, playing to determine the best team in the league, the game was still knotted at 0–0 in the waning moments, and the first-place Bears were stymied by the stout defense of the third-place Portsmouth Spartans. From the Spartans' 2-yard line, Nagurski faked a run but fooled the defense as he then suddenly stepped back and tossed a touchdown pass to Grange. Despite opposition protests that Nagurski was not the required 5 yards behind the line of scrimmage, the call stood, and the Bears were champions.

Rule changes made before the 1933 season made it legal to throw the ball anywhere behind the line of scrimmage. So, what did the burly back do when he found himself in the title game that season against an evenly matched New York Giants team? He threw two touchdown passes which proved to be the difference in the Bears' 23–21 triumph, the first championship game under the new alignment of East and West Divisions.

Bronko retired in 1938—if you consider tossing opponents out of the ring as a professional wrestler retirement. His new career proved quite lucrative. For an encore, in 1943 Bronko came out of retirement after five years to suit up as a Chicago Bear, appearing in eight games. In the championship game, on December 26, 1943, he added a final career touchdown by barreling into the end zone from 3 yards out during the Bears' 41–21 rout of the Washington Redskins. Talk about going out in style.

CHAPTER FOUR

HEAD AND SHOULDERS

What would hulking linebacker Khalil Mack think of using tiny, flimsy shoulder pads made of bone and canvas?

Can you imagine Kansas City Chiefs QB Patrick Mahomes throwing a football shaped like a melon 60 yards on a line?

How about Dick Butkus attempting to make a tackle using a "helmet" composed of just a few strips of leather?

I know for me it would be strange trying to run a post route (or *any* pass pattern, for that matter) wearing high-top cleats with those long spikes!

But that is how foot ball (as it was spelled back then) was played in the early days. Let's take a brief look at how the basic gear developed as the game evolved.

Early football, especially coming off the heels of its breaking away from rugby, was a very, very rough sport. Players wore their lost teeth, cauliflower ears, facial scars, and twisted noses as badges of courage. In that first intercollegiate football game between the future Rutgers and Princeton Universities in 1869, the players simply removed their top hats and waistcoats, rolled up their sleeves, and played in their street clothes. For a while, the well-dressed football player wore heavy knit sweaters for protection from blows to the body. That was the extent of padding then.

There was no real impetus for developing protective gear until a public outcry over football-related injuries and even deaths awakened the game's powers that be. (Presumably, President Teddy Roosevelt's threat to abolish the sport if steps weren't taken to reduce the dangers also grabbed their attention.) Suddenly the search was on for a safer approach to football, beginning with those critical rule changes we discussed earlier in addition to incorporating protective equipment into the standard uniform.

A. G. Spalding and Company Sporting Goods was the first to offer athletic equipment. Others, such as Rawlings Sporting Goods Co., sprang up and played an important role in the game's development. It was Rawlings's production head, William Whitley, who developed a combo uniform-padding scheme. His "Foot Ball Armor," as it was marketed, helped usher in a series of developments aimed at safeguarding players.

As far as protecting the skull, you know what these tough guys did at the turn of the century? They grew their hair out. Seriously! They believed that a thick mane of hair would help absorb the shock of collisions. (I wonder what great long-locked players of the modern era, such as Pittsburgh Steelers safety Troy Polamalu and Green Bay Packers [now Los Angeles Rams] linebacker Clay Matthews would think about that theory. If they could go back in time, I'm sure their new teammates would be very impressed with their coiffures.)

In the early 1900s, sporting goods companies sold various styles of "harnesses." These essentially covered the skull and ears and were composed mostly of felt and leather, with ear flaps soon to be added for a total price of about $4. Then, as models appeared that came down over the neck, they were referred to as helmets. Still, many players disdained the use of headwear, and helmets would not be a required article of equipment in college football until 1939 and in the NFL until 1943.

Improvements continued. New features included a padded chin guard, a sweatband on the inside, and increased ventilation. Despite that, most players found helmets hot and heavy and simply chose to continue taking their chances with uncovered craniums. The flattop harness had a serious flaw in that as long as it merely sat right atop the skull, it did not truly protect the wearer, offering a false sense of security.

Through the 1920s and 1930s, headgear did find more helpful components. One major breakthrough was the creation of suspension, whereby fabric inside the helmet was configured in such a way so as to help distribute impact better. In recapping the history of the development of the helmet, a 2000 *Philadelphia Daily News* story said it was the arrival of teardrop-shaped helmets with its new suspension design that allowed "the impact of a blow to slide to one side instead of being absorbed head-on."[14]

In 1939 a model was created by the John Riddell Company of Chicago that would bear resemblance to the current headwear: the plastic helmet. More durable and lighter than those made of leather, the Riddell helmet featured a web suspension inside that allowed the player to adjust it to the shape and size of his head.[15]

After World War II, with helmets now mandatory in the NFL, more technical improvements followed to help make them lighter, stronger, and cooler. There also came a wave of aesthetic changes, none with greater impact than a design made by a player-artist.

Fred Gehrke, an art major at the University of Utah, joined the Cleveland Rams as a halfback in 1940. In the off-season, he worked in the design department of the Northrop Aircraft Company. At the close of the 1947 campaign, Rams coach Bob Snyder asked the running back to put his artistic talents to work in designing a new team uniform to improve morale. Gehrke, who decades later became general manager of the Denver Broncos, painted the distinctive horn design, which proved wildly popular. Before the 1949 season, Riddell manufacturers were able to include the design, with the paint baked on from the inside and showing through the transparent plastic. Gehrke's famous design helped football became far more colorful, as other teams followed suit, coordinating the helmets with the jerseys and pants.[16]

One change that would help distinguish football players from hockey players was the face mask, as players grew attached to the idea of keeping their full set of teeth. The device had been around in some form since the 1930s, including Lucite models, but those kept shattering. In 1955 Cleveland Browns coach Paul Brown, in an effort to save his star quarterback Otto Graham's smile, co-invented the BT-5 face mask with a Riddell Company consultant by the name of G. E. Morgan. *BT* stood for bar tubular and was a single tube-like bar that was usually made from a combination of rubber, steel, and plastic. Made possible by the superior rigidity of the plastic helmet, the tubular single bar soon expanded to double, triple, and a full "birdcage" face mask. The type chosen usually depended on the requirements of the position played. This development gained acceptance throughout the league. Quarterback Bobby Layne, who produced a brilliant Hall of Fame career spent mostly with the Detroit Lions, retired in 1962 and was one of the last players to play without a face mask.

Now reasonably ensured that his nose and teeth would remain intact, and combined with vastly improved suspension and able to divert a blow from any direction, a player no longer had to worry about his head when blocking or tackling—or so was the assumption back then. As a result, a new style of play developed, featuring furious headfirst charges like rhinos.

Combined with lighter protective gear overall, the speed of the game increased. The result was something those helmetless pioneers back in the early 1900s could never have imagined, with serious punishment inflicted on both sides of the ball. Collisions became more intense now that both combatants felt they could rely on their helmets while making a play.

"Making plays" using a football helmet took on an entirely different meaning for the resourceful Paul Brown. In 1956 the Cleveland coach hired an inventor to rig up a radio receiver in the helmet of his quarterback George Ratterman. Instead of shuffling in offensive guards to transmit plays, Brown held a transmitter in his hand, and Ratterman listened over his receiver above the ear pad. The quarterback couldn't talk back to the coach (Isn't that still the case today, with or without a radio?), but the experiment proved short lived anyway due to interference on the frequency. Ratterman, expecting to hear Coach Brown call the next play, would hear instead various forms of chatter—including taxi driver calls to and from their dispatchers—depending on which way he turned his head, like a human antenna. Commissioner De Benneville "Bert" Bell soon banned such devices altogether.

However, radio would make a comeback decades later. In 1995, in a "déjà vu" move, the football helmet went high-tech, as a new rule allowed the quarterback to have a radio transmitter in his helmet, enabling the coach to call in plays without the need for elaborate sideline signals or player shuttles.

Regarding protection for the rest of the body, the first general use of pads began in the 1890s with the introduction of shin guards, pants with quilting on the front of the thighs, and shoulder pads. These primitive shoulder pads were really nothing more than small patches of leather sewn onto the jersey, but their effectiveness would trigger the addition of similar pads for elbows, knees, and thighs.

However, once again, it must be remembered there was a certain macho code at play in those first years.

In the early days of football, it was a game of iron men, with substitutions permitted only in case of injury. And heaven help the occasional player who resorted to the use of homemade pads, for he'd be laughed out of the game as a—you got it—*sissy*.

Shoulder pads were constantly undergoing changes. In one of the more landmark developments, in 1921 legendary college football coach John Heisman, then of the University of Pennsylvania (and, yes, the man in whose honor the Heisman Trophy would be named), created a design that used two layers of heavy white felt, along with a section of hard fiber in between, to protect the shoulder blades and collarbone.

STAYING ON YOUR FEET

Courtesy of Riddell

While developments for protecting the head and the shoulders underwent drastic changes, football shoe design, though no less important, has remained fairly stable. Several excellent kickers, including Rich Karlis of the Broncos and Tony Franklin of the Eagles, both of whom played in the 1980s, preferred to perform barefoot. Yet cleats were key for Hall of Fame running back Barry Sanders to pivot on a dime; they were vital for big offensive tackle Anthony Munoz to keep his legs under him in making a block; and defensive tackle Mean Joe Greene, crouched in his stance, relied on them to get a good push-off for launching into a blocker like Munoz. Of course, as Munoz and Greene grappled, Munoz's Cincinnati Bengals teammate Boomer Esiason (and *every* other quarterback) needed quality shoes to set his feet for optimum passing accuracy potential.

And while Joe Namath dazzled with his white shoes (and quick release), rushing toward the flamboyant New York Jets field general was the Pittsburgh Steelers' hulking defensive end L. C. Greenwood in his flashy gold cleats. But aesthetics always played second-string to traction; otherwise they would be slipping and sliding as if starring in an old Keystone Cops silent movie. On the other hand, if the foot can't slide when the leg absorbs a severe blow, something has to give. Unfortunately, much too often, it has been the knee.

Since the late 1950s, much concern has been expressed over the shoe as the chief culprit in knee injuries. An analysis of game films in the 1960s by the Detroit Lions showed that one-third of their players' injuries were related to the problem of cleats catching in the turf. This was compounded by the fact that 1965 saw the opening of the world's first domed sports stadium, the Houston Astrodome, home of the Astros baseball team. The builders of the so-called Eighth Wonder of the World failed to anticipate that the semitransparent roof would block the sun, causing the grass field to die within a matter of months. For the 1966 season, it was replaced with a synthetic grass carpet known as AstroTurf. It didn't take long before other fields, outdoors as well as indoors, began installing artificial grass. Players discovered that the standard shoe, which has seven cleats, did not provide sufficient traction on plastic surfaces. Manufacturers competed to make the best shoe for it. New models varied but usually centered around the use of either a series of wedge-like protrusions or multiple small rubberized cleats molded as part of the sole and heel.

Naturally, fake grass was not an issue in the early days of the sport, as the football shoe began in the late nineteenth century as a modified baseball shoe with cleats that could better handle the mud. By the 1890s, the first true football shoe with permanent cleats appeared. There was even a version using wood cleats.

In the 1920s, just as the NFL was getting under way, the interchangeable cone-shaped cleat was introduced, but it was not widely used until the following decade. This model of footwear was composed of cleats, five-eighths of an inch long, that screwed onto the sole of the shoe and could be changed quickly if a cleat wore down. A one-inch cleat was available for muddy or wet fields, which was often the case in the Midwest and the Northeast.

However, one team actually won an NFL championship without cleats. Playing on the frozen tundra (Are those two words applicable only to Green Bay's Lambeau Field? Nope!) of the Polo Grounds in the 1934 title game—only the second in NFL history—the New York Giants were trailing the Chicago Bears, 13–3, when the home team switched to sneakers in the third quarter. The equipment change worked, as the Giants rallied.

Largely attributable to superior footing, which led to three late rushing touchdowns, including a 42-yard run by Ken Strong as Bears players futilely lunged after him, slipping on the ice, New York came back for a 30–13 win over previously undefeated Chicago.

Another breakthrough was the brainchild—surprisingly—of the normally conservative coach George Halas. For the 1940 NFL title game, at Washington's Griffith Stadium, his Bears ran onto the field wearing low-cut shoes, in one of the first reported usages of that style, and a radical departure from the traditional black high-top. Chicago picked a good time to introduce them. The shoes clearly provided greater speed and freedom of movement, helping the Bears punish the Redskins, 73–0.

The advantages of the new low-cuts, combined with the growing practice of taping players' ankles to help prevent injury, rendered the old high shoes obsolete. Baltimore Colts quarterback John

Unitas, whose seventeen-year career spanned the late fifties, sixties, and early seventies, preferred sticking with the old high-tops.
Meanwhile, his teammate and fellow member of the Football Hall
of Fame, running back Lenny Moore, added some style to the low-
tops. He was the first player to popularize wrapping his black shoes
completely in white tape, earning him the nickname Spats.

In today's game, regardless of being high- or low-top, the surface
played on, and the technical material on the bottom of their shoes,
footwear represents a platform for players to show their individual-
ism; a chance to express themselves. The issues that players select
to bring awareness to a cause important to them via their footwear
represent dozens of different charitable organizations: from ones
that focus on preventing bullying, to those that support families
impacted by gun and domestic violence. Players will share images
of their cleats and the stories behind them on social media, using
the hash tag #mycausemycleats. It is part of the NFL's *My Cause My
Cleats* campaign, which began in 2016.

Players such as quarterbacks Cam Newton of the Carolina Panthers and the Oakland Raiders' Derek Carr, among many others,
work directly with local artists who use air-brushing techniques to
paint the cleats, as well as with manufacturers Adidas, Nike, and
Under Armour to design their shoes.

The National Football League embraces its history by occasionally having teams dress up in throwback uniforms, made to replicate
a given franchise's original colors and patterns but using modern fab-
rics and, of course, helmets. Despite the fact that today's players are
significantly bigger, stronger, and faster than those from the early era
of NFL football, and the obvious dangers that brings, undoubtedly
with the warrior mentality so prevalent, there would still be more
than a few modern-day football players who would embrace what it
would feel like to play the game like they did "back in the day."

CHAPTER FIVE

INDIANS AND ESKIMOS

For the NFL, still struggling with franchises that came and went—yet at the same time looking to build its fan base—so-called traveling teams were important to the league's early growth.

Throughout the 1920s, a handful of teams spent most of the football season living out of their suitcases, hosting a home contest maybe once or twice every 24 games. These vagabond franchises included the Dayton Triangles, Hammond/Akron Pros, Rochester Jeffersons, and Columbus Panhandles/Tigers. The 1924–26 Kansas City Blues (who changed their name to the Cowboys for the 1925 season before splintering two years later) and the 1926 Los Angeles Buccaneers (then based in Chicago) were also true road warriors. It was sort of a "have cleats and shoulder pads will travel" atmosphere.

Two of the most popular traveling squads were led by a pair of all-time greats. Jim Thorpe was the star of the Oorang Indians, while Ernie Nevers was the face of the Duluth Eskimos. Though he was now thirty-four, Thorpe relied more on savvy from his experience, but still he could physically dominate not only as a runner and defensive back but also excel at punting, drop-kicking, and place-kicking.

"Jim Thorpe was the best man in his position I ever saw. The cleverest man for his weight I ever saw. Jim was as fast, shifty and clever as any lightweight back and yet was heavy enough to play the smashing game and be a power in the interference," said his coach at Carlisle Indian Industrial School, Pop Warner.[17]

Thorpe loved animals, especially dogs, and became friends with a man named Walter Lingo, who was building an empire breeding and selling Airedale terriers out of the small town of LaRue, Ohio. They'd often go hunting together. During one trip, Lingo presented his idea of sponsoring an all-Indian traveling football team as a way to promote his Oorang Kennel Company.

Thorpe became the team's coach-player and recruited as many of his fellow Native Americans as he could, including a pair of his talented Carlisle college teammates, Joe Guyon and Pete Calac. Oorang players came from tribes such as the Blackfoot, Mohican, Winnebago, Mission, Mohawk, Chippewa, Penobscot, Cherokee, and the Sac and Fox Nation, which claimed Thorpe as a tribesman. Instead of Gronkowski, Schottenheimer, and Robustelli, the roster was filled with names like War Eagle, Joe Little Twig, Big Bear, and one of the all-time great names, Long Time Sleep.

Of the 20 games they played over two seasons, only one was played at "home" in nearby Marion, Ohio. With a population of well under a thousand people, LaRue remains the smallest town ever to have been the "home" of an NFL franchise—and likely of any professional team in any league in the United States.

Unfortunately, without much talent, the team did not do well over its two-year run, finishing 3-6 and then 1-10. However, it elevated the concept of a halftime show, with fans most likely cheering louder during the midgame festivities than they did for most Indians gridiron play. During halftime, Lingo not only presented Indian shooting exhibitions and various tribal dances, but also a sort of Indian Olympics involving a tomahawk throw, a knife toss, and handy rope work as a lasso. Thorpe would regularly thrill the crowds by drop-kicking balls through the uprights from midfield. And his teammate Long Time Sleep would, once in a while, wrestle a bear.

Of course, the main event was to feature his dogs whenever he could. His halftime shows would include having his Airedales tracking live raccoons and chasing them up (fake) trees. He'd also have fully trained Red Cross dogs, which went for the whopping sum of $500 (this, at a time when an NFL franchise cost $100, on average!), perform reenactments of bringing medicine to wounded soldiers in the trenches.[18]

But in the trenches of professional football, and for this traveling team in particular, sadly, the biggest play in Oorang's two-year history was a turnover in which Bears owner-coach-player George Halas plucked a Thorpe fumble in midair at Chicago's 2-yard line and raced 98 yards for a touchdown, a record return that stood for nearly a half century.

Another colorful traveling team led by a superstar was to be found up in the northern reaches of Minnesota.

The Duluth Kelleys football team was sponsored by a hardware store—until funding ran out. This shouldn't have come as too much of a surprise to a team that had trouble filling seats because the harsh winters in Duluth, a port city located in northeastern Minnesota, right on Lake Superior, essentially prevented home games being played from mid-November onward. Following a financially unsuccessful 1925 season, the Kelleys were sold to team treasurer Ole Haugsrud for $1 and the assumption of the team's debt.

At the time, Ernie Nevers, an all-American fullback from Stanford, was the most hailed player since Red Grange.

Nevers's most legendary collegiate performance came in the 1925 Rose Bowl against Knute Rockne and Notre Dame, with its legendary "Four Horsemen": quarterback Harry Stuhldreher, fullback Elmer Layden, and halfbacks Jim Crowley and Don Miller. However, he nearly missed the game. Nevers had broken his left ankle before the opening game of the season *and* his right ankle in the next-to-last game. The running back was on crutches until two days before the Rose Bowl. Still, the warrior took the field on game day. Many observers felt he'd be back on the sidelines after the first contact.

Not only did Nevers play the entire game, but he rushed for more than 100 yards. Although Stanford lost, 27–10, even the noted Irish coach was amazed by the gritty young man's performance. "Nevers could do everything," Rockne recalled later. "He tore our line to shreds, ran the ends, forward passed, and kicked."

Despite being heavily coveted by the pro football world, Nevers didn't jump to the NFL right out of Stanford. After college, he played both professional basketball and baseball. However, it did not take a degree from Stanford to see where the real opportunity lay. After being dazzled by the huge sums he saw the Galloping Ghost was pocketing on barnstorming tours through his agent C. C. "Cash and Carry" Pyle, Nevers was amenable to similar offers.

And it was Haugsrud who won. They'd been high school classmates in Superior, Wisconsin, and after visiting Nevers in Saint Louis, where he was pitching for the Browns, the Duluth owner snared the Big Dog by offering him the princely sum of a reported $15,000 plus a good chunk of the gate. What's more, Haugsrud agreed to officially change the club's name to Ernie Nevers's Eskimos.[19] But the powerful running back would be tested due to all the games that had to be played in order to pay for the hefty contract.

With the help of such stellar teammates as fellow future Hall of Famers Johnny Blood and Walter Kiesling, Nevers would be up to the task, and then some. In 1926, his first year as a pro football player, the Eskimos played 29 games—all but two of them on the road—in 117 days, including one stretch of five games in eight days. The team was nicknamed the Iron Men of the North, and no one was more durable than Nevers. Incredibly, he missed a total of just 26 minutes all season, and that was only because doctors had ordered him to sit out a game after he was diagnosed with appendicitis. But with Duluth trailing 6–0, Nevers couldn't stand to watch from the sidelines any longer. Disregarding the medical directive, he ran back into the game, threw a 62-yard TD pass, and kicked the extra point to give the Eskimos a 7–6 win.

The team's star held up better than did his work clothes which took a beating from the constant travel. As Nevers once explained: "Sometimes we used to take two showers after games. The first one would be with our uniforms on. Then we'd beat them like rugs to get some of the water out, throw them into our bags, get dressed, and catch a train."

The Eskimos wore a distinctive white-and-midnight-blue uniform that featured their logo—an igloo, naturally—on the front, in homage to their home city. They were one of the first NFL teams to even have a logo. To further promote the team, when traveling, they wore their distinctive heavy, white wool overcoats, despite playing just two games at home, such as it was, up in cold Duluth.

What that great barnstorming journey of 1926 accomplished, in effect, was nothing less than allow a struggling league, with 22 franchises in big and small markets, to survive a challenge from the rival American Football League and its star: none other than Red Grange. (An upstart league formed by Grange and his agent Charles Pyle, the AFL folded after just one season).

After leaving Duluth as player-coach following a 1-8 record in its second season, Nevers would go on to play for the Chicago Cardinals. In his first season, 1929, he easily led the league in both touchdowns (with 12) and total points scored (85). The following year, he ran into the end zone six times, and in 1931, his final season, his eight touchdowns were second only to Green Bay tailback Johnny Blood. Nevers would hold a variety of coaching positions throughout the 1930s before eventually leaving the game. But his warmest football memories appear lodged in the igloo of his Eskimos.

"When I turned pro and joined the Duluth Eskimos in 1926,"

he reflected, "we barnstormed after the regular season. We went from September to January, and from Maine to Texas to the Pacific Coast. In all, we played twenty-nine games, and we had only sixteen men on the squad. If the coach took a man out of the game for a substitution, he got mad. That's how much we loved it."

CHAPTER SIX

SNEAKERS, SLAUGHTERS, AND GOING INSIDE

Shortened dimensions, dangerous walls on the edge of the playing surface, modified rules, playing indoors on a "field" designed for hockey, and finally a disputed play that proved to be the difference maker—the 1932 NFL playoff game changed the league forever.

Eight teams made up the league that season, pared down from ten the year before. The Chicago Bears and the Portsmouth Spartans finished tied for first place, with 6-1 records. (Six Bears' games ended in ties, while the Spartans fought to ties four times.) A decisive game was scheduled to be played at Wrigley Field on Sunday, December 18.

However, a blizzard had left the Windy City up to its hips in snow. George Halas didn't want to postpone the game until the following week, which would conflict with Christmas and hurt the gate receipts. The impromptu title game promised badly needed cash for both squads, particularly for the small-market Spartans, deep in debt and not far from folding. So the Bears' owner, who had stepped down as coach after the 1929 season but would return to the sidelines and lead his squad to the NFL title in 1933, arranged for the contest to be played indoors at Chicago Stadium, home of the National Hockey League's Blackhawks. The action would take place on "turf"—in reality, a layer of dirt, tanbark, and animal droppings provided by a circus that had just left town. Not only was the playing field odoriferous, to put it mildly (reportedly, the stench of the manure donated by the performing elephants caused at least one Chicago player to get sick to his stomach), but also the field had to be shrunk to 45 yards wide and 60 yards long, with the end zones less than 10 yards deep and boarded by the hockey rink's dasher boards.

Due to the unusual playing dimensions, special rules were adopted for the game:

- Kickoffs were made from the 10-yard line.
- Only one set of goalposts was used and placed at the goal line for extra points only; field goals were banned.
- When a team crossed midfield, it was immediately set back 20 yards.
- For the first time, in-bounds lines, or hashmarks, were drawn 10 yards from either sideline, so that the ball could be moved there after each out-of-bounds play.

History books often record that indoor football was born on September 9, 1968, when the Houston Oilers of the American Football League became tenants at the Houston Astrodome for the start of their ninth season. But, no, the first indoor football game actually took place, purely through necessity, thirty-six years before.

The Bears were heavily favored, as they had two major advantages, starting with a smothering defense that had posted seven shutouts during the season. But also, the Spartans would be without their best player, quarterback Earl "Dutch" Clark. The NFL's leading scorer was not in the building, having accepted an off-season basketball coaching job at his alma mater, Colorado College. Clark was already at work there, and the college president would not permit him to miss his duties in order to play in the unscheduled title game.

Still, for the first three quarters, Portsmouth gave Chicago all it could handle. Despite the temptingly short distances to "pay dirt," players repeatedly lost their footing on the makeshift turf as they tried to run, and so the teams headed into the final quarter locked in a scoreless tie. That's when Chicago's Dick Nesbitt picked off a pass and returned it into the Portsmouth red zone.

Two runs by Bronko Nagurski bought Chicago a first down at the 2-yard line. The big halfback, who finished second in the league in yards rushing, with 533, was stopped for no gain on his next two carries, setting up a controversial play that would have major ramifications for the game's future.

Taking the snap, Nagurski faked a run, then backpedaled and threw a pass to Red Grange in the end zone for a touchdown. Potsy Clark, the Spartans' coach, argued that the play was illegal because the prevailing rules stated that forward passes had to be thrown from a point at least 5 yards behind the line of scrimmage. The referee, however, ruled that Nagurski *had* obeyed the 5-yard rule, thus allowing the TD to stand. The conversion made it 7–0, and Chicago added a safety to win, 9–0.

It was a historic game that resulted in several permanent rule changes, including: (1) placing goalposts on the goal line; (2) moving the ball in 10 yards from either sideline; (3) the forward pass was made legal from anywhere behind the line of scrimmage; and (4) structurally the league would now be divided into two divisions, with the winners to meet in an annual championship game.

All of these changes proved smart moves with immediate payoffs, as evidenced by the seasonlong buildup leading to the first true NFL championship game the next season. In that game, played at Wrigley Field, with George Halas back as head coach after a three-year absence, the Bears would edge the New York Giants, 23–21. It was a much more open contest that heightened the movement and excitement of football. Fittingly, the 1933 title game came down to the last very play.

Out of options, the Giants completed a desperate pass to running back Dale Burnett near the Bears' 5-yard line. Only one man stood between him and the goal line: wily veteran Red Grange.

Seeing that Burnett had a teammate nearby, the Galloping Ghost made a distinctive tackle to preserve the Bears' victory.

"I tackled Dale high so he could not lateral," Grange explained afterward.

The next season's title game, a rematch between the Bears and Giants, would make history for a different reason: a wardrobe malfunction.

Back in early November, the Giants had their hats handed to them in Chicago, getting whipped by the Bears, 27–7.

Having lost last year's crown to Chicago and now suffering this midseason embarrassment, the Giants were keen on gaining any advantage they could to settle the score, or at least some of it.

On December 9, 1934, the site of the NFL championship game, New York's Polo Grounds, was in poor condition. The heavy, freezing rain from the night before had left the playing surface slick with ice, and temperatures were in the single digits.

It was like a hockey rink out there, so captain Ray Flaherty told coach Steve Owen of a similar situation during a game when he played at Gonzaga University and that wearing sneakers saved the day. Owen was willing to give it a try. However, it was a Sunday, and almost all sporting goods stores were closed. By the time a Giants assistant found some usable shoes at a nearby college, there were ten minutes remaining in the third quarter, with the Bears ahead, 13–3.

Owen called a timeout as his players changed into new footwear. While the Bears were sliding around, New York grinded out 27 points to win 30–13 over previously unbeaten Chicago, making it known forever as "the Sneakers Game."

The Bears would not hibernate for long. Halas retooled the well-worn T-formation he'd been using for more than 20 years and honed it to perfection (with much input by coaches Clark Shaughnessy and Ralph Jones). It would all be on display in the most lopsided game ever, titlewise or not, in NFL history.

On December 8, 1940, in the NFL championship game, Chicago, behind quarterback Sid Luckman, slaughtered the Washington Redskins, 73–0, to earn the franchise its fourth league title. Not only did 36,034 fans at Washington's Griffith Stadium suffer through the debacle, it also happened to be the first football game ever carried on network radio. Famed sportscaster Red Barber called the play-by-play for more than 120 stations on the Mutual Broadcasting System.

The Bears' crushing Washington was a real team effort, as 10 different players scored touchdowns! The Redskins committed nine turnovers, and Chicago scored on three interceptions returned for touchdowns.

Washington owner George Preston Marshall had cause to reflect afterward on how he might have contributed to his team's all-time embarrassing defeat. He'd inflamed the Bears' players with public comments he'd made on November 17, after the Redskins defeated Chicago in a controversial 7–3 game.

After Coach Halas protested in vain for an interference call against Washington on a potential touchdown pass from Luckman

Controversial and influential: Washington Redskins owner George Preston Marshall.

Courtesy Washington Redskins

to running back Bill Osmanski that could have changed the game's outcome, several newspapers quoted Marshall calling Halas and his Bears "front-runners, quitters. They're a bunch of crybabies. They fold up when the going gets tough."

Never one to miss an opportunity to fire up his team, Halas shrewdly used those words against Marshall by posting the articles on the clubhouse bulletin board, so that all of his players saw the demeaning quotes. Apparently, it helped motivate an unrelenting Bears attack that will unlikely ever be matched: a 73–0 victory in a title game.

CHAPTER SEVEN

THE PICK 'EM GAME

Walking off the field before a sparse crowd at the Baker Bowl, Philadelphia Eagles owner Bert Bell sighed as he watched the Green Bay Packers, loaded with stars such as Don Hutson, Clarke Hinkle, Arnie Herber, and Johnny Blood, celebrate their 13–6 season-ending victory. His team had lost its fifth straight game to finish the 1935 season with the worst record in the NFL. It didn't exactly come as a shock, given that the Eagles ranked dead last in offense and next to last in defense. But now, after several poor years, he at least had reason for optimism that he could improve his franchise's fortunes, thanks to a bold concept he'd pitched his fellow owners at a meeting the previous May.

Bell's idea? To hold an annual draft at which NFL teams selected college players in an inverse order of their finish the previous year. Thus, the club with the worst record in the league would pick first, in each round, while the reigning NFL champion would get last dibs. Until now, players had been able to sign with any club. Open signing tended to make the strong stronger and the weak weaker. It was one of the reasons that perennial powers such as George Halas of the Bears and Tim Mara of the Giants hesitated at first to adopt this concept. But they came to see that the league would have trouble surviving unless there was a system in place that allowed each team to have an even chance to bid for talent.

The idea came to Bell when he made a trip to the University of Minnesota in the hopes of signing the Golden Gophers' two-way star fullback and linebacker Stanislaus Kostka. Before the draft was instituted, that's how it was done: teams' management would descend upon college campuses to negotiate with the preeminent players.

The best players in the country, like Kostka, wanted to play for the best teams and to make more money. And the teams that played better made more money and could thus pay those players even more, which only increased the incentive to sign with a perennial winner. Bell's theory was that the NFL was like a chain—only as strong as its weakest link—and his Philly team had been a weak link for too long. Coming back empty-handed, again, after having failed to land the much-needed Kostka, Bell hatched his idea that would change team sports forever.

The first NFL draft began in a casual atmosphere at the Ritz-Carlton hotel in Philadelphia on February 8, 1936. Absent was the group of jersey-wearing, face-painted characters who provide their own versions of the Bronx cheer in response to their favorite team's selections. Also yet to make their appearance were stacks of fact-filled binders on which to judge the available talent as each of the nine rounds played out.

Instead, the names of 90 eligible collegiate players were written on a blackboard in the meeting room. Lacking in-depth reports, the list was informed by NFL team executives' visits to local colleges and by newspaper clippings.

The lowly Eagles, awarded the first pick, chose University of Chicago halfback Jay Berwanger, the winner of the very first Heisman Memorial Trophy in 1935 (known that year as the DAC Trophy, for the New York City's Downtown Athletic Club). Unfortunately for Bell, Berwanger refused outright to play for Philadelphia, so his rights were traded to the Bears for much needed cash and players. But Halas had no luck signing the running back, either.

According to an Associated Press story in the *Youngstown Daily Vindicator*, Berwanger didn't sign with the Bears initially because he wanted to preserve his amateur status to try out for the 1936 US Olympic team in the decathlon. But after he failed to make the cut, the "one man football team," as he was known in college, couldn't come to terms with Halas. Berwanger went to work as a foam-rubber salesman in Chicago and never played a day in the pros. (Halas made out okay, though, as the Bears drafted two future Hall of Famers: Colgate University guard Dan Fortmann and West Virginia University tackle Joe Stydahar.)

Berwanger's decision to turn his back on professional football was not unusual, as only 24 of the 81 players selected opted to play in the NFL that year. One immediate consequence of the draft was that it lowered salaries, since a player could negotiate with only one team instead of essentially auctioning off his services to the highest bidder.

Changes to fine-tune the draft process were continual. The following year, the draft grew from nine rounds to 10. In 1939 it doubled to 20 rounds. With World War II raging in 1943, it was expanded to 30 rounds, based largely on the assumption that many of those drafted would also be drafted by the military (and guess which draft took precedence). During the war, the NFL voted to stop using the term *draft* and referred to players as being on the "preferred negotiations list."

In 1946 a new eight-team league emerged to challenge the NFL: the All-America Football Conference (AAFC). With so many former football players now discharged from the military and eager to play again, there was a surplus of talent. But for the first time in its history, the National Football League faced serious competition for

THE BEST TEAM DRAFTS OF ALL-TIME

1958 Green Bay Packers Draft

Key Selections: LB Dan Currie, Michigan State U. (round 1); RB Jim Taylor, Louisiana State U. (round 2); LB Ray Nitschke, U. of Illinois (round 3); G Jerry Kramer, University of Idaho (round 4).

Interestingly, the roots of Green Bay's dynasty came in a draft just before the arrival of new coach Vince Lombardi. Currie would be a mainstay of the '61 and '62 title teams, and Kramer would open many holes for Taylor, while on the other side of the ball, Nitschke would close a lot of holes to help the Packers win five NFL championships in seven years—including victories in the first two Super Bowls.

1961 San Diego Chargers Draft

Key Selections: DE Earl Faison, Indiana U. (round 1); RB Keith Lincoln, Washington State U. (round 2); DT Ernie Ladd, Grambling State U. (round 15).

These three formed the nucleus of one of the most explosive teams ever. They were at the heart of three straight American Football League title game appearances, winning the 1963 AFL championship, 51–10, over the Boston Patriots. Such was the Chargers' dominance and talent on both sides of the ball that there was talk of a "Super Bowl" against the NFL champion Chicago Bears.

1963 Kansas City Chiefs Draft

Key Selections: DT Buck Buchanan, Grambling State U. (round 1); G Ed Budde, Michigan State U. (round 1); LB Bobby Bell, U. of Minnesota (round 7); P/RB Jerrel Wilson, U. of Southern Mississippi (round 11); T Dave Hill, Auburn University (round 24).

In the draft of 1963, a year after winning the AFL title as the Dallas Texans, the relocated and renamed Kansas City Chiefs started building the foundation for what is still the franchise's only Super Bowl championship team. Hall of Famers Buck Buchanan and Bobby Bell were at the core of one of the most talented defenses of all time, one that boasted seven all-stars in their championship season of 1969, while Budde and Hill anchored the offensive line for more than a dozen years. Versatile punter Wilson, along with placekicker Jan Stenerud, the first Norwegian in the NFL and the first man at his position to land in the Hall of Fame, made up one of the best kicking duos in NFL history.

1964 Dallas Cowboys Draft

Key Selections: DB Mel Renfro, U. of Oregon (round 2); WR Bob Hayes, Florida A&M U. (round 7); QB Roger Staubach, US Naval Academy (round 10).

Through the decades, from the drafting duos of Tex Schramm and Gil Brandt to the Jerry Jones–Jimmy Johnson tandem, Dallas has executed some brilliant drafts in its history, but none has produced three Hall of Fame players, like this one in '64. The versatile Renfro was named to the Pro Bowl his first 10 years, six as a safety and four as a cornerback. He had tremendous speed and was a shifty kick returner. "Bullet Bob" Hayes, an Olympic gold medalist track star, had world-class speed and changed the way the game was played. Staubach, a four-time passing champion, was mobile, courageous, and a tremendous leader, as evidenced by his late-game heroics: during an 11-year career, the 1963 Heisman winner delivered 23 game-winning drives in the regular season and playoffs.

1965 Chicago Bears Draft

Key Selections: LB Dick Butkus, U. of Illinois (round 1); RB Gale Sayers, U. of Kansas (round 1).

Though they were not part of winning squads that went deep into the playoffs, no other team has come close to producing two players from the same draft whose unique, once-in-a generation talents changed professional football.

1968 Miami Dolphins Draft

Key Selections: RB Larry Csonka, Syracuse U. (round 1); S Dick Anderson, Colorado (round 3); RB Jim Kiick, U. of Wyoming (round 5).

Among the best-ever drafts for running backs by a team. This duo would be at the core of the Dolphins' perfect season in 1972 and back-to-back Super Bowl titles that year and next. Anderson would be the backbone of the stingy No-Name Defense.

1971 Pittsburgh Steelers Draft

Key Selections: WR Frank Lewis, Grambling State U. (round 1); LB Jack Ham, Penn State U. (round 2); G Gerry Mullins, U. of Southern California (round 4); T/TE Larry Brown, U. of Kansas (round 5); DT Ernie Holmes, Texas Southern U. (round 8); S Mike Wagner, Western Illinois U. (round 11).

Following a terrific 1969 draft that delivered Joe Greene and L. C. Greenwood, this '71 crop included a productive receiver, a pair of steady offensive linemen, and the addition of three starters to one of the greatest defenses of all time. It helped coach Chuck Noll turn around things for a long-suffering Pittsburgh franchise and establish a dynasty.

1974 Pittsburgh Steelers Draft

Key Selections: WR Lynn Swann, U. of Southern California (round 1); LB Jack Lambert, Kent State U. (round 2); WR John Stallworth, Alabama A&M U. (round 4); C Mike Webster, U. of Wisconsin (round 5).

How does it get any better than drafting four Hall of Fame players who helped your franchise dominate for a decade? A bonus included the signing of undrafted free agent Donnie Shell after the 17-round event. The hard-hitting four-time All-Pro safety would produce a career worthy of his Hall of Fame nomination.

1981 San Francisco 49ers Draft

Key Selections: DB Ronnie Lott, U. of Southern California (round 1); DB Eric Wright, U. of Missouri (round 2); DB Carlton Williamson, U. of Pittsburgh (round 3).

Defensive coaches George Seifert and Ray Rhodes molded this talented trio of draftees into a foundation that was central to the success of the 49ers' dynasty.

1983 NFL Draft—Year of the Quarterback

Key Selections: John Elway, Stanford U. (round 1); Todd Blackledge, Penn State U. (round 1); Jim Kelly, U. of Miami (round 1); Tony Eason, U. of Illinois (round 1); Ken O'Brien, U. of California, Davis (round 1); Dan Marino, U. of Pittsburgh (round 1).

While Eason, Blackledge, and O'Brien were steady contributors to their teams, the '83 draft yielded three Hall of Fame quarterbacks—Elway, Kelly, and Marino—who combined for 10 Super Bowl appearances.

1996 Baltimore Ravens Draft

Key selections: OT Jonathan Ogden, U. of California, UCLA (round 1); LB Ray Lewis, U. of Miami (round 1); DB DeRon Jenkins, U. of Tennessee (round 2); WR Jermaine Lewis, U. of Maryland (round 5).

Ozzie Newsome's first two picks as general manager of the brand-new Baltimore Ravens became twin franchise pillars who produced long and storied careers on their way to the Hall of Fame.

signing players, which caused salaries to escalate. The salary wars threatened professional football's existence. In late 1949, following the AAFC's fourth season, and four years after the war ended, peace came to the sport as well. A merger agreement was reached in which the 10-team NFL would adopt three of the upstart league's franchises (the Cleveland Browns, Baltimore Colts, and San Francisco 49ers) and combine a fourth, the Los Angeles Dons, with its own LA Rams. The three orphans left behind—the Buffalo Bills, New York Yankees, and Chicago Hornets—would be out of luck and, like the All-America Football Conference, out of business, although their players were free to try catching on with an NFL club for the 1950 season.

Between 1947 and 1958, the National Football League offered a "bonus selection," wherein one team, selected by random lottery, received an extra pick prior to the draft. Once a team won the bonus selection, it was not eligible again for future lotteries. That element certainly helped the Eagles and Packers, as their bonus picks brought each a Hall of Famer in Chuck Bednarik (Philadelphia, 1949) and Paul Hornung (Green Bay, 1957).

The 1950s and 1960s saw an explosion in scouting, as teams sought to improve their chances for success via the draft. The early pioneers were the Los Angeles Rams. Stemming from a philosophy developed by owner Dan Reeves, that success in football hinged on the ability to discover overlooked talent, they were the first to set up a scouting department.

But the template for how effective scouts operated in the ensuing decades can really be credited to Eddie Kotal, a compact running back for the 1929 champion Green Bay Packers, who became a college coach. In 1942 Kotal returned to the Packers organization as a backfield coach and scout for longtime head coach Curly Lambeau before he was hired as the Rams' chief scout in 1946.

The tireless Kotal was often on the road for more than two hundred days a year, traveling from campus to campus all over the country, typically logging hundreds of miles a week. At each school, he'd observe players, study game films, and interview coaches, then go back to his hotel room and write reports at night.

There would be other legendary scouts, including Sarge Mac-Kenzie and Dick Gallagher, who were key in helping Paul Brown build the Cleveland Browns into multiseason champions beginning in the late 1940s; and Jack Vainisi, whose talent scouting skills led directly to the Packers' 1960s dynasty under Vince Lombardi.

Art Rooney Jr., with the help of Bill Nunn Jr., were the key scouting talents behind the Pittsburgh Steelers' domination in the 1970s. Art was the team owner's son, while Bill was a former sportswriter who had developed contacts at many black colleges. Thanks largely to Nunn's efforts, many of the Steelers' future stars—Joe Greene, Mel Blount, John Stallworth, Ernie Holmes, Dwight White, Donnie Shell, and L. C. Greenwood—came from schools with largely black enrollments.

Tex Schramm, an avid disciple of Dan Reeves's philosophy when he worked for the Rams, took those views with him to Dallas in 1960 and, as general manager, built a winning Cowboys franchise with the help of relentless scout Gil Brandt.

With scouting on the rise throughout the league, there were a few coaches who believed in trading versus building through the draft. One was Schramm's 1970s rival George Allen of the Washington Redskins. Allen, who enjoyed success as a Rams coach from 1966 to 1970 despite a rocky relationship with owner Reeves, preferred dealing with veteran talent, so rookies rarely made his club. That can work sometimes on a short-term basis, but Schramm was of the opinion that, in the long run, it is preferable to field a good young team than a good old team. To that end, he looked to strengthening the roster each year by drafting quality young players.

It was during this period that scouting and the draft took on clandestine characteristics of the Cold War era.

When another new league, this one called the American Football League (AFL), was founded prior to the 1960 season, it and the NFL began drafting many of the same players. A huge battle for talent commenced. Larger universities and colleges were no longer the only ones on a scout's agenda as he toured the country. Small schools, particularly small black-oriented colleges, saw substantial growth in the number of their football players drafted into professional football. Nothing was left to chance, as no school was off-limits in the endless search for talent.

Pete Rozelle, commissioner of the NFL beginning with the 1960 season, had worked as a public relations man for Dan Reeves and the Rams. He hoped to squash the AFL after it scored a coup in 1964 by signing University of Alabama quarterback Joe Namath. The brash 21-year-old garnered great media coverage across the country as the New York Jets' $400,000 prize.

With so much at stake, Rozelle devised a plan called Operation Hand-Holding, also known behind the scenes as the NFL's babysitting program. Just as he had learned from Reeves that the key to draft success was to establish relationships early on in the process, the new commissioner felt the same principle applied when it came to *preventing* college prospects from signing with the AFL.

Rozelle drew on his personal experience trying to secure highly coveted Louisiana State University running back and Heisman winner Billy Cannon for the Rams in 1959. (For the record, Cannon wound up signing with the AFL's Houston Oilers.) In Operation Hand-Holding, team scouts and officials, and even local businessmen, basically attached themselves to top prospects in the two weeks leading up to the draft. They'd watch the young athletes like hawks and attempt to sell them on the merits of their league. Then on draft day, a call center was set up in New York, and teams were connected with players and their supervisors, who helped negotiate terms.

"The big war between the leagues was enjoyable in a lot of ways," said Gil Brandt, a personnel executive for the Dallas Cowboys from

1960 to 1988. "Guys hiding college players from guys in the other league. Flying kids all over the country. Guys on the phone trying to locate players. It was unreal."[20]

While each league had its share of victories in signing talent, both were losing millions of dollars in the process. In April 1966 Tex Schramm initiated a series of clandestine talks with AFL founder Lamar Hunt. On June 8, 1966, Rozelle announced at a press conference that the two leagues had agreed upon a landmark merger, one that would finally be consummated in 1970 with the NFL absorbing all AFL clubs.

Other parts of the agreement took effect far more quickly. The 1967 football draft would be a combined affair, shortened to 17 rounds. Ten years later, it was reduced further to 12 rounds.

In 1979 the draft was changed forever with the introduction of television coverage. Not surprisingly, the idea of essentially broadcasting a *very, very long* business conference that would be interrupted every 15 minutes for a general announcement was not received enthusiastically at first. Legend has it that when the brand-new cable TV outlet Entertainment and Sports Programming Network—soon to be known by its acronym, ESPN—proposed to Commissioner Rozelle that it carry live coverage of the draft, he seemed perplexed, asking, "Why would you want to do that?"

Actually, team owners had voted unanimously against it, but after an appeal by the network's new president, Chet Simmons, they reluctantly allowed it. ESPN, looking for any association with the National Football League, was overjoyed to take this chance. The broadcast became a success thanks to ESPN's bringing into the studio a young man by the name of Mel Kiper Jr. While he was in high school during the late 1970s, the teen was already dedicated to football talent evaluations and while attending Essex Community College in Baltimore in 1981, he formed Kiper Enterprises, producing reports year-round. From this genesis he would become the guru of millions of "draftniks" who composed their mock draft lists by using his book *Draft Report*, published annually from 1979 to 2013, as their bible. The publicity generated by Kiper cultivated public interest in the draft, to the point where in 1988 the NFL moved the draft from weekdays to the weekend; ESPN's ratings of the coverage improved dramatically.

In years to come, a lexicon of words and phrases came to define the draft: "pro days," "on the clock," "draft is a crap shoot," "an inexact science," "legwork," "preparation," "luck," "the great guessing game," "paralysis by overanalysis," "a can't-miss prospect," "a risky business," "it's an unscientific study," "prototype," "productivity," and, last but not least, "character." Nowadays, with so much money at stake, every team works through various scenarios, loaded with tracking metrics, ready for all alternatives.

You hear phrases such as "scheme fit," which evaluates how the measured skills and grades would translate from college to the NFL. Or "trait-based analysis," which focuses on quantifying into metrics a player's more subjective qualities, such as processing speed, field leadership, scheme recognition, and so on.

Still, whatever analysis systems the experts rely on, they have to take into consideration many factors because they have less than 10 minutes to generate selections that determine the future of their franchises. Even with all this data at a team's fingertips, all too often the analysis fails to improve on-field production, as one team's Carson Wentz (legitimate starting QB in the big time) is another team's Johnny Manziel (troublesome washout).

Adding to the drama is the misinformation that team executives deliberately plant in the media to try to divert attention from their real draft-day interests while they are hunkered down in their "war rooms."

"Here's what I think the best innovation to that draft was," said Fred Gaudelli, named producer of ESPN's NFL draft coverage in 1990. "Anytime you can take someone behind the curtain to see how things are done, that is what I think our ultimate mandate is:

take people to a place they've never been, or take people to a place they cannot get into. We think about that no matter what we're producing."

Making the annual NFL draft riveting television took some time to catch on with viewers. Gaudelli, currently the executive producer of NBC's *Sunday Night Football* and *Thursday Night Football*, understood that the key was getting access to powerful figures' war rooms. It turned into the ratings success that it is today only after a powerful team owner, Jerry Jones of the Dallas Cowboys, embraced the idea of bringing viewers the insider's perspective.

"We were fortunate," Gaudelli reflected. "Jerry was a different thinker; he was not bound by the traditions of old coaches and old owners. He was trying to sell his team, and when we approached him on it"—1990 draft TV coverage—"he got behind it. Then I think Tampa Bay was next. Rich McKay, the general manager, and the coach, Tony Dungy, allowed us in. Before you know it, we are getting into six or seven of these rooms. We could have done more but ran out of budget." To make ESPN's draft coverage more engaging and entertaining, both Gaudelli and his predecessor, John Wildhack, took a page from the old "Up Close and Personal" approach started by Roone Arledge at ABC Sports when it launched Olympic coverage in the 1960s.

"Wildhack started getting into players' homes," said Gaudelli. "He was getting some great scenes, like Andre Ware on the phone with Lee Corso, and while Paul Tagliabue is making the announcement, he started getting special moments that brought emotion into it, and I tried to expand on that."

Held every April, the draft now serves as a highly effective advertisement for the NFL halfway between the climax of one season with the Super Bowl and the beginning of the next with July's training camps. In a bit of symmetry, while the Super Bowl produces the current champion, the draft has a significant impact on the future champion, and oftentimes it is at those subsequent training camps where the chemistry between the veterans and prospective rookies develops in the quest to become the next winner.

From a stodgy, smoke-filled informal backroom gathering to a huddled, highly informed army of experts for each team in place today, the draft has become one of the NFL's marquee events. It attracts millions of viewers, inspires countless mock draft lists, and instigates endless barroom arguments, as many fans consider themselves experts; they passionately enjoy second-guessing the selections made (or not made) based on the innumerable hours of toil by their favorite team's trained observer-scouts, coaches, GMs, and owners.

Make no mistake, despite all the massive resources applied to it, the draft remains professional football's roulette. There has been plenty of gambling on player selections, with good and bad examples abounding. For instance, the Steelers franchise has enjoyed the fruits of some of the best drafts of all time, but it certainly let a few big fish get away, particularly at the quarterback position. Because of rumored drug problems, in 1983 Pittsburgh passed on Dan Marino, who went on to become one of the most prolific passers in NFL history. A quarter century earlier, management also failed to ring up Len Dawson, who would enjoy a Hall of Fame career in Kansas City, leading the Chiefs to victory in Super Bowl IV.

But perhaps the Steelers' most haunting mistake happened back in 1955. Pittsburgh spent its ninth-round pick on a crew-cut former walk-on who'd played at the University of Louisville, but cut the hometown kid without ever letting him play a down. The latter took his game over to Baltimore, where he became one of the best quarterbacks ever. That kid was John Unitas.

There are countless variables involved in a draft, but one persistent truth is that the quarterback position can really make or break a team. That is one reason why 49ers coach Bill Walsh never gambled and took a quarterback in the first round. He snatched Joe Montana in the third round and obtained Steve Young in a trade. Of course, the classic example was the University of Tennessee's Peyton Manning and Washington State University's Ryan Leaf, who went numbers one and two, respectively, in the 1998 draft. The former had a Hall of Fame–caliber career, while the latter was an expensive bust for the San Diego Chargers. Not to be forgotten in the overlooked department was Tom Brady, who did not find an NFL home until the sixth round as pick number 199 of the 2000 draft.

How important has Bert Bell's idea of the draft been to the success of the NFL? In the ensuing years, the man himself would often say, "On any given Sunday, any team in the NFL can beat any other team."[21] That is probably more true today than at any other time in NFL history. Bell's notion of "the Pick 'em Game," conceived more than 80 years ago, deserves a lot of credit for that.

CHAPTER EIGHT

THE CHESS MASTERS: FIRST QUARTER

Even though coaches use different approaches to get the most out of the talent on their roster, the common denominator is their ability to get a diverse group of individuals to build an esprit de corps, because teams become successful when players trust one another enough to surrender "me" for "we." The head coach is the driving force that molds the entire team into a single unit with a single purpose. The ability to get inside the heart and mind of each player and take him where he can't take himself is a very difficult task and requires a special person. Here are a few early pioneers who set the tone for what is required to have success coaching in the National Football League.

GEORGE HALAS

It was a time when the head coach did not have 15 assistant coaches, but, then again, for a man like George Halas, he was used to juggling many different roles. Not only was he a league builder, but also as a player, general manager, owner, and coach of the Chicago Staleys-Bears, Halas had a unique perspective of the game.

A shrewd businessman, Halas was known for being at once tightfisted and generous. Although he could be referred to derisively as someone "who tosses nickels around like manhole covers," Papa Bear also helped send one of his players to dental college. When running back Brian Piccolo was diagnosed with advanced cancer in 1969, Halas paid all his medical expenses.

Linebacker Ed O'Bradovich helped Chicago to its 1963 world championship win over the New York Giants with a key interception in the third quarter. The Bears, trailing 10–7, took possession at the Giants' 14 and promptly ran the ball in to take the lead for the first time all day. They never gave it back. The following year, O'Bradovich grew so exasperated while negotiating a new contract with Halas that he finally threw up his hands and said, in jest, "Okay, I'll write *you* a check for five hundred dollars!"

But perhaps Halas's best business maneuver came in 1925, when he signed college football legend Red Grange to the Bears and organized the subsequent promotional tour featuring the Galloping Ghost, which put the NFL on the road to becoming a major player in the world of sports.

As for his talents as a coach, Halas was a clever strategist. Along with University of Chicago coach Clark Shaughnessy, he reshaped the T-formation to produce such a complex array of options that it was later copied by many teams after the Bears' dominating 73–0 win over the Redskins in the 1940 championship game.

Halas was among the first to analyze game-day films of opponents and station assistant coaches up in the press box for a bird's-eye perspective during games. But it was his people skills that proved even more important to the success of a forty-year coaching career that included six championships, twice being named coach of the year, suffering only six losing seasons, and retiring as the winningest coach in football history.

He could be crusty, ornery, and tyrannical at times, but what made Halas so successful was that he spent more time learning about people than studying x's and o's. And it all began even before the very first year of the league, when he ran a company football team: the Decatur Staleys.

"I think Halas had to be one hell of a recruiter to surround himself with all these players and coaches from all over the country," said Don Pierson, a veteran Chicago sportswriter who covered the Bears for many years. "It helped that they got jobs with the Staley company and could practice football on company time."

GUY CHAMBERLIN

Though his coaching career would be quite brief when compared with that of George Halas (the list of NFL coaches with careers lasting 40 years is not very long; in fact, Papa Bear's is the only name on it), Guy Chamberlin, nevertheless, enjoyed tremendous success in just six seasons.

The Nebraska native was a powerful ball carrier about whom one opponent said: "Trying to tackle Chamberlin was like sticking your head and shoulders into a lawn mower."[22] An all-American running back in 1915, he all but single-handedly helped the University of Nebraska Cornhuskers edge Knute Rockne's Fighting Irish, 20–19. Chamberlin not only scored two touchdowns rushing, from 10 and 20 yards out, but also threw a 35-yard TD pass for the winning score as his school won the Missouri Valley Conference (forerunner to the Big Eight Conference and the second oldest collegiate athletic association after the Big Ten) championship. After serving in World War I, Chamberlin began his pro career in 1919, finding himself playing alongside a legend.

Alternating in the backfield with Jim Thorpe, Chamberlin, a slashing-type runner with a strong stiff-arm and knees pumping high, was part of a dynamic duo that led the Canton Bulldogs to the championship of the Ohio League.

Now in the newly formed APFA (soon to be the NFL), Chamberlin caught the eye of George Halas, who persuaded him to join his Decatur Staleys. "Chamberlin was the best two-way end I've ever seen," the talent sage would say later. "He was a tremendous tackler on defense and a triple-threat performer on offense."[23] The star two-way end would be a key figure in back-to-back championships for the Staleys in 1920 and 1921.

Chamberlin returned to Canton in 1922 as a player-coach. His Bulldogs won the NFL title that year and the next. The franchise's owner could no longer afford them, however, prompting a move to Cleveland, where the Chamberlin-coached squad won a third straight championship in 1924.

Then that team, too, folded.

It didn't matter. Titles seemed to follow the young coach wherever he went, for in 1926 he landed in Frankford, a section of Philadelphia, and led the Yellow Jackets to the NFL crown. "Over five years, Chamberlin won four championships with three different teams, a coaching record without parallel in National Football League history," Halas said in admiration of his former player and teammate.[24]

STEVE OWEN

Steve Owen would have a much longer, steadier coaching career than Guy Chamberlin. Going from being a vagabond wrestler to a right guard making $50 a game playing for the Kansas City Blues in 1924, in just three years, "Stout Steve" would become the captain of the 1927 New York Giants team that went 11-1-1 and earned its first NFL title.

And a mere three years later, he would launch a very successful career coaching just one team. From 1930 (his one season as co-coach with Benny Friedman) to 1953, Coach Owen guided the Giants to 10 division titles and two NFL championships. One of those championships came in 1934 and was captured in historic fashion. (See chapter 6, "Sneakers, Slaughters, and Going Inside.")

In an age of minimal substitutions, Owen devised the two-platoon system. But the New York coach's key strategic contribution to the game was a development called the "umbrella defense," involving stunts and blitzes, including a 6-1-4 formation in which ends dropped into coverage, placing the defensive emphasis on coverage rather than on the pass rush. A novel concept at the time, it would later become known as the 4-3, when a former Giants defensive back named Tom Landry incorporated elements of that system into his long and successful run as head coach of the Dallas Cowboys.

RAY FLAHERTY

One of Owen's players on the 1934 Giants championship squad, Ray Flaherty would also become an innovative coach. (It was Flaherty, you'll recall, who astutely suggested that the Giants change their footwear to sneakers to combat the wintry elements in their momentous comeback victory over the undefeated Chicago Bears in the championship contest.) Though his seven-year tenure would be a lot shorter than Owen's, the former receiver and defensive end never had a losing season helming the Boston/Washington Redskins, the New York Yankees, and the Chicago Hornets in the All-America Football Conference.

However, there can be no doubt that the low point in Flaherty's football career and in Redskins history was the horrendous 73–0 annihilation by the Bears at Griffith Stadium in the 1940 title game. (Just a few weeks before, on the same field, the Redskins had beaten the Bears by similar digits, 7–3.) However, in some measure of redemption, his Redskins would defeat Chicago two years later in the 1942 championship game.

Coach Flaherty is credited with a pair of innovations tied to offense: the screen pass, and a platoon system in which he had two offensive personnel groupings that excelled at both rushing and passing respectively.

JIMMY CONZELMAN

What he lacked, comparatively speaking, in advancing the strategic side involving x's and o's like colleagues Owen and Flaherty, Jimmy Conzelman made up for as one of the most charismatic coaches in the formative years of the NFL.

In addition to being a disciple of George Halas—having been his teammate on the Great Lakes Naval Training Station squad that won the 1919 Rose Bowl, and, the following year, his quarterback for the 1920 Decatur Staleys—how could someone with the middle name Good possibly go wrong?

Conzelman was a player-coach for the Rock Island Independents, Milwaukee Badgers, Detroit Panthers, and Providence Steam Roller, the latter of which won the championship in 1928. A talented writer and speaker, Conzelman was a natural-born leader, too: his commencement address at the University of Dayton in 1942 made quite an impact. Titled "The Young Man's Mental and Physical Approach to War," it became required reading at West Point. Although Conzelman would come and go from the NFL over a period of years, tackling other ventures, he did coach perennial cellar dwellers the Chicago Cardinals to the 1947 title, earning him coach of the year honors.

When looked at in the context of today's hypercommitted NFL coaches, 24/7, 365, it is fascinating that Conzelman pursued such a varied life professionally. He was not only a football player, coach, and team owner, but also a pro baseball player, major league baseball executive, playwright, author, orator, actor, and newspaper publisher.

POTSY CLARK

Potsy Clark, like Jimmy Conzelman, was a talented speaker and much sought after all across the country. In between those engagements, though, he found the time to display great talent in transforming inferior teams.

Growing up a farm boy, Clark would become the star quarterback for Bob Zuppke's University of Illinois teams. In his first year, 1914, they went undefeated, winning the Western Conference crown. He also showed talent at shortstop and had offers from Major League Baseball but knew his interest lay in coaching football.

After various coaching stints, Clark got his first NFL head coaching gig taking over the reins of the Portsmouth Spartans in 1931. His team was part of history in 1932: at the end of the season, the Spartans met Chicago in a specially arranged indoor play-off game because heavy snow in the Windy City made playing outdoors impossible. What the Bears-Spartans game helped bring about was convincing the eight-team league to drop one team, add three new franchises, in Philadelphia, Pittsburgh, and Cincinnati, and split into an East Division and a West Division for the 1933 season, which culminated in a championship game.

Clark had guided the Spartans to three straight winning seasons. In 1934, the heart of the Great Depression, they left small Portsmouth, Ohio, for Detroit. A year later, Clark's Lions won it all, defeating the New York Giants, 26–7, for the NFL crown.

After becoming coach of the football Brooklyn Dodgers, playing at Ebbets Field, Clark turned a rotten team into a competitive one.

By the time he retired after 10 years, only three coaches—Curly Lambeau, George Halas, and Steve Owen—had more wins than Clark.

CURLY LAMBEAU

Earl "Curly" Lambeau was a founder of the Green Bay Packers in 1919. He was the team's first star player and its coach for 31 years. Winner of 229 games, Coach Lambeau guided Green Bay to unprecedented success in the early days of the NFL. There were the three straight championships from 1929 through 1931. He also led the Packers to titles in 1936, 1939, and 1944.

More of a motivator than a tactician, Lambeau's biggest contribution to the game would have to include his embracing and furthering the air game. It wasn't quite Air Coryell named after head coach Don Coryell and his high-flying, stat-shattering, historic offenses of the San Diego Chargers in the late 1970s and early 1980s (see Chapter 35, "They Wore Out the Chain Gang")—but with quarterbacks such as Arnie Herber and Cecil Isbell throwing to game-changing receiver Don Hutson at a record-setting pace, the game would never be the same. Green Bay's quarterbacks dominated in their brief careers: Isbell played only five years yet led the league in passing twice, while Herber was the NFL's top passer three times.

CHAPTER NINE

THE EARLY DYNASTIES

The decades of the first quarter of the National Football League produced three significant dynasties: the 1920s Canton Bulldogs, the New York Giants of the 1930s, and the 1940s Chicago Bears.

The Bulldogs began their terrific run well before the league was conceived.

CANTON BULLDOGS

In a sports-mad city, where the Canton Athletic Club was organized in November 1904 to operate both baseball and football teams, some big names wielding gloves and bats, such as durable hurler Cy Young, played in the area.

Another athlete played for the baseball Cincinnati Reds (hitting just .247 in 1917), but his legacy was to be found on the gridiron, not the diamond. After owner Jack Cusack agreed to pay him a then-astronomical sum of $250 a game, the world's best athlete and football player, Jim Thorpe, would lead the Canton Bulldogs to four consecutive Ohio League championships from 1915 through

Pro football's first back-to-back champions: the 1922–23 Canton Bulldogs.

Courtesy Dr. James F. King

1919. (There was no season in 1918 due to World War I and a severe influenza outbreak.) The Ohio League was essentially the height of professional football before and after World War I.

On the football side, the Bulldogs drew large crowds and got the best of their neighboring rivals the Massillon Tigers, as a direct result of bringing in Thorpe as well as a couple other all-Americans. Canton was the class of the professional game—such as it was in those haphazard, disorganized days.

After assuming ownership of the Bulldogs in 1918 from Cusack, who went off to Oklahoma to work in the oil business, young local businessman Ralph Hay saw his team dominate in 1919. Canton (9-0-1) outscored its opponents 195–20; six of its victories were shutouts. Meanwhile, behind the scenes, Hay spearheaded a group looking to create a cohesive, enduring new professional football league.

On September 17, 1920, the engaging entrepreneur hosted a historic meeting with other team owners in his automobile show-room. Together they formed the American Professional Football Conference (APFC). Play began two weeks later. The name was soon amended to the American Professional Football Association, but not for long: in 1922 the APFA became the National Football League.

Surprisingly, the Canton team struggled during the maiden sea-son, finishing eighth; then it clawed its way up to only fourth place in 1921. But in the first year under the NFL banner, a new pack of Bulldogs, put together to reflect the style of freshman coach Guy Chamberlin, simply crushed opposition.

Retaining just a handful of players from the previous season, he added a mixture of rookies and veterans and his own immense tal-ents, and Canton rolled to a 10-0-2 record. The unquestioned star on offense was spry Texan tailback Lou Smyth. Operating behind the twin pillars of offensive tackles Link Lyman and Pete Henry, Smyth, a powerful runner and accurate passer, became the first player ever to lead the league in both passing touchdowns and rush-ing touchdowns in the same season. But Chamberlin prided himself on a team that had a stifling defense. The Bulldogs produced nine shutouts, holding opponents to just 15 points while they scored 184. In the season finale, Canton shut out the Toledo Maroons, 19–0.

The price of success was high, however. Though he was proud to proclaim his team "true world champs," the high cost of funding such a talented team forced Hay to bail out as owner. Despite that, the following season it would be more of the same, as the strong Bull-dogs outscored their opposition 246–19, recording eight shutouts.

With a heavy heart, Hay sold his team to Cleveland's Samuel Deutsch, who also owned the NFL's Cleveland Indians. Deutsch proceeded to take on several members of the Bulldogs, including Lyman and Coach Chamberlin, and in 1924 renamed his team the Cleveland Bulldogs. Finishing 7-1-1, they edged the 6-1-4 Bears for a third championship. Chamberlin became the first coach to three-peat as an NFL champ.

However, in 1925, Canton businessmen purchased the rights to the team from Cleveland and once again, now known as the Canton Bulldogs, played in Canton during the 1925 and 1926 seasons. At the end of the 1926 season, the team disbanded.

Before the 1927 season, the NFL underwent a major metamorphosis, shedding 10 of its 22 teams as part of its strategy to focus on big-city locales. Sadly, Canton, a dynasty that had gone 27-1-4 from 1922 through 1924, did not make the cut and was disbanded. However, the National Football League recognized the importance this Ohio city played in its history and, in 1961, selected Canton as the site for the Pro Football Hall of Fame, which opened two years later.

NEW YORK GIANTS

It was a former Bulldogs player who would propel the New York Giants to prominence in the 1930s. Future Hall of Fame tackle Steve Owen would bring that defensive focus that brought the Canton-Cleveland franchise so much success.

But first, any talk of the New York Giants dynasty of the 1930s would not be complete without a tip of the hat to one of the most underrated figures in football.

Dr. Harry March, who has been called "the father of professional football," was an interesting character: Broadway producer, war correspondent during the Spanish-American War, playwright, adventurer, *and* he'd earned his MD from George Washington University Medical School. Growing up in Canton, March devoured football, playing and attending many, many games. In the early 1900s, at the same time that he was busy running his own medical practice, he was one of the team doctors for the Canton

Bulldogs, then of the Ohio League. He became a promoter and historian of the sport, later writing a book, *Pro Football: Its Ups and Downs,* in 1934.

After serving as a lieutenant in the medical corps during World War I, March moved to New York City. There he met a businessman named Tim Mara, whom he convinced to purchase an NFL franchise for New York City in 1925. For the next eight years, the doctor worked in the New York Giants front office, first as team secretary, then as its president. It was his football savvy that essentially helped a fledgling league survive with a franchise in the most crucial of locations. March, who is credited with discovering coach Steve Owen, was central in helping the Giants win their first NFL championship in 1927.

The story goes that Harry March was so devoted to the sport and the success of the Giants that he called upon his adventurous spirit in an effort to secure talent. In the summer of 1931, the Giants executive bought a vintage World War I submarine chaser from the US government. After disarming its depth charge launcher, he picked up five players from the Saint Louis area, and then took nearly two weeks sailing down the Mississippi River, across the Gulf of Mexico, around Florida, and up the coast to New York, arriving in time for training camp.[25]

The football-crazy doctor would eventually break off from the NFL and, in 1936, launch the second American Football League, (the first, the aforementioned effort by Red Grange and his agent Charles "C. C." Pyle in 1926 lasted one season). March's eight-team league had a two-year run before folding, but it did have an impact. It introduced "major league" football to the West Coast with the Los Angeles Bulldogs. March's AFL was also home of the Cleveland Rams, which continue to exist as the Los Angeles Rams.

During that era, there was one team that wasn't even close to folding. Just the opposite.

CHICAGO BEARS

With their run, which actually began back in 1932 and stretched through 1946, the Chicago Bears defined the term dynasty. Dominant on both sides of the ball, during that stretch, the "Monsters of the Midway" played in nine championship games, winning six titles. Out of those teams, 13 players made the Hall of Fame. (In comparison, the Packers' dynasty of the 1960s produced 12 Hall of Famers.)

Naturally, much credit should go to the keen eye and football savvy of George Halas.

But his game plan was also applied to the league as a whole. Halas juggled striving for success for his own team and for the NFL in general.

"Halas did have some unique gifts," longtime Bears reporter Don Pierson observed. "To think that he was only twenty-five, sitting on that running board in Canton, speaks to his vision. He has been described as very optimistic, passionate, enthusiastic. He had many things go wrong, but he would dwell on what went right. . . . It was his vision to see what the possibilities of professional football were." Comparing him with Facebook cofounder Mark Zuckerberg, Pierson added, "They could see what could sell."

As with any sport, winning sells. And the Bears won. Again and again. They did it with offense. They did it with defense. They did it on the arm of Sid Luckman, the legs of Bronko Nagurski, and the shoulders of Danny Fortmann and Texan center Bulldog Turner. And through those years it was all accomplished under Halas—who even recruited players abroad while serving in the US Navy during World War II.

Perhaps nothing captured the Bears dynasty better than the 1940 NFL championship game versus the Washington Redskins, in which visiting Chicago absolutely stifled its opponent. Less than a minute into the game, Bears running back Bill Osmanski swept left and scored on a 68-yard touchdown, and Halas's club never let up for the next four quarters. The mighty Bears forced nine turnovers, including three interceptions run back for TDs, while six different members of the offense rushed for one or more touchdowns apiece.

The story goes that as the points piled up, officials had to beg Halas not to kick any more extra points, as they were running out of footballs. (Back then, there were no nets erected to prevent balls from sailing into the grandstand; thus, crowds screamed for more scoring in order to have a fighting chance for a memento.)

The final score was 73–0, the largest margin of defeat in NFL history.

Using his knowledge gathered from his playing days, working with strategy experts in refining the old T-formation, and simply demonstrating a knack for handling talent, George Halas produced one of the longest dynasties in NFL history.

"Halas was very steady in his way," said Mike Ditka, a Bears head coach from 1982 through 1992, during which time his clubs posted an extraordinary .631 winning percentage and the 1985 squad took home a Super Bowl Trophy. "He knew what he was going to do, and he did it. His way. He had to take from Peter to pay Paul to keep the Bears afloat, but he persevered. The NFL became what it became, and the Bears became one of the great franchises and were outstanding, winning all those titles in the forties under Coach Halas."

CHAPTER TEN

THURSDAY'S FEAST

The Thanksgiving tradition we enjoy today where football is consumed as much as turkey, stuffing, and pumpkin pie, can actually be traced back to President Abraham Lincoln.

Yes, the Pilgrims are credited with starting the tradition of Thanksgiving in America, but it was our 16th president who issued an 1863 proclamation calling on Americans to "set apart and observe the last Thursday of November next as a day of thanksgiving." Americans across the country readily embraced the concept of a day of gratitude and feasting.

And not long after Lincoln's declaration, college football would take the new national holiday and celebrate. In 1876, when the game was still evolving from a rugby hybrid into the sport we know today, the Intercollegiate Football Association (IFA) kicked off its first Thanksgiving championship game as Yale defeated Princeton, two goals to none, playing in New York City during the school break. Toward the end of the nineteenth century, it would become quite a gathering and one of the social events of the year, with nearly 40,000 fans attending the annual games.

The University of Michigan also began scheduling games on Thanksgiving Day starting in the late 1880s. Then the pilgrimage went west, and, from Texas to Oregon, local fans for both colleges and high schools planned their holiday around a game. Many high school teams would play on Thanksgiving usually to wrap up the regular season.

As for the pro game, in 1920 the brand-new American Professional Football Association wasted no time in scheduling a contest for Thanksgiving Day. The undefeated Akron Pros, on the shoulders of African American tailback Fritz Pollard, downed the Canton Bulldogs, led by Jim Thorpe, a Sac and Fox Indian, 7–0. A couple years later, legendary collegiate player Red Grange made his professional debut with the Chicago Bears before a record crowd at Cubs Park on Turkey Day.

But our modern tradition of Thanksgiving and NFL football going together like turkey and stuffing can be pinpointed to 1934 and the city of Detroit.

Radio executive George Richards had just bought the Portsmouth Spartans and moved them from Ohio to Detroit and renamed them the Lions. Determined to draw attention to his team, which toiled in the shadows of the city's long-established popular baseball team, the Tigers, Richards dreamed up a Thanksgiving Day matchup between the defending NFL champion Chicago Bears and his Lions.

With his business savvy and industry contacts from his time working in New York City, Richards was able to secure more than 90 radio stations to broadcast the game nationwide. The Lions boasted a 10-1 record, while the Bears were a perfect 11-0. The promise of a late-season chance to tie for first in the league, and the opportunity to see it happen on a day off from work, fueled ticket sales in the Motor City. The game drew more than 25,000 fans, 11,000 more than usual, to University of Detroit Stadium. Even though the Lions lost, 19–16, the clever marketing move was a success, as the Thanksgiving Day football game tradition has continued in Detroit ever since (with the exception of 1939 to 1944).

The next year, the Lions won the NFL championship with a lot of help from a 14–2 win over the Bears in the Thanksgiving game.

In the 1950s, as professional football began to surge past the college version in popularity the Lions were no longer the little-known team that started the NFL Turkey Day tradition. In fact, they were so talented that a *Time* magazine cover story on Thanksgiving week 1954 proclaimed them the best in the game:

> Of all the pro teams, the best (for the last three seasons) is the Detroit Lions. And the best of all the Lions, the best quarterback in the world, is Robert Lawrence Layne, a blond, bandy-legged Texan with a prairie squint in his narrow blue eyes and an unathletic paunch puffing out his ample six-foot-one, 195-pound frame. Layne, a T-formation specialist, led the Lions out of the National Football League's cellar, called the plays and fired the passes that won them the national championship in 1952 and 1953.

The year 1953 also saw another history-making event, as the DuMont Television Network became the first network to televise Thanksgiving games. CBS would take over in 1956, and then, in 1965, the first color television broadcast of an NFL game was the Thanksgiving matchup between the Lions and the Baltimore Colts.

The following year, with TV usage in America growing at an incredible rate, the NFL was looking to grab some of that enormous audience—especially Tex Schramm, general manager of the struggling Dallas Cowboys. He decided to make the Cowboys the second team to start a Thanksgiving Day tradition.

On November 24, 1966, before a national TV audience and a record crowd at the Cotton Bowl, the Cowboys beat the Cleveland Browns, 26–14. To that point, the six-year-old franchise had lost twice as many games as it had won, with a woeful 25-53 record. But the Thanksgiving 1966 game seemed to reverse the Cowboys fortunes: that year, in which they topped the NFL East, kicked off 20 straight winning seasons.

"Pro athletes know that performing on holidays is part of the business," said Cliff Harris, a four-time All-Pro Cowboys safety. "Because of a short week of preparation, it is mandatory that players focus on the task of winning and not extra festivities. However, playing on Thanksgiving is also a great opportunity, because all eyes are on you, and should you come out victorious, a ten-day break afterward makes the leftovers taste a lot better."

Harris, who also played on Thanksgiving during his college days, more often than not enjoyed those leftovers because the Cowboys have among the highest winning percentage of any NFL team playing on the holiday.

But for many of the players, playing on the holiday built a bond between teammates that extended beyond the locker room.

"I think that is one of the reasons the Cowboys were so close, because of the Thanksgiving Games," said Herschel Walker, a Dallas running back in the eighties and again in the nineties. "I tell people, you see players most every day of their lives, but it is different when you gather at a teammate's house with their family. So now you have this extended family of players, wives, and their kids. You all become one."

Fellow running back Barry Sanders of the Detroit Lions, concurred, recalling, "Yes, it was pretty common to go around to different teammates' families. I spent tons of time at Lomas Brown's house and Jerry Ball's house. Their wives put together a terrific Thanksgiving meal." The Hall of Famer revealed another tradition that was part of this annual holiday:

"We'd also have a tradition where rookies would be told where they could go to pick up their free turkey for the holiday. It'd be caught on tape showing their disappointment at receiving a paper turkey. Rookies fell for it year after year."

As a careerlong Detroit Lion, Sanders played in 10 Thanksgiving games and averaged more than 93 yards rushing. His most memorable performance came during his 2,000-yard season in 1997, when he ran for 167 yards and three touchdowns to lead the Lions to a 55–20 win over the Chicago Bears. Scoring on runs of 40, 25, and 15 yards, Sanders was a key to the Lions' win, as they rallied from a two-touchdown deficit.

Through the decades, millions of fans have enjoyed NFL games on Thanksgiving, and while there have been some real turkeys, many have gifted us with great performances and memorable moments. Here are a few highlights:

1929: CHICAGO CARDINALS 40, CHICAGO BEARS 6

The Cardinals defeated their crosstown-rival Bears largely on the strength of six rushing touchdowns by Ernie Nevers. And by converting four of six points-after-touchdown, Nevers accounted for all 40 of his team's points.

1951: DETROIT LIONS 52, GREEN BAY PACKERS 35

In what would mark the first of 13 consecutive Thanksgiving games against the Packers, Bobby Layne had one of his finest days, throwing for 296 yards and four TDs. The high-scoring affair included not one but two punt returns for touchdowns in the third quarter *by the same player*: Lions rookie safety and punt return specialist Jack Christiansen, who topped the league with four that season. His first return covered 71 yards; just minutes later, Christiansen cradled the ball at his own 11 and brought it all the way back, effectively putting the game out of Green Bay's reach.

1962: DETROIT LIONS 26, GREEN BAY PACKERS 14

Before 57,598 fans at Tiger Stadium and that national television audience, Detroit's stellar defense—which included five future Hall of

Fame inductees—mauled Packers quarterback Bart Starr for a staggering 10 sacks en route to handing Green Bay its only loss of the season.

1974: DALLAS COWBOYS 24, WASHINGTON REDSKINS 23

Perhaps the greatest game ever on Thanksgiving occurred on November 28, 1974. It matched up those same intense rivals—the Washington Redskins versus the Dallas Cowboys.

Washington defensive lineman Diron Talbert led the trash-talking during the weeklong buildup to the opening kickoff. "If you knock Staubach out," he said menacingly about the great Dallas quarterback, "you've got that rookie facing you. That's one of our goals. If we do that, it's great. He's all they have." The rookie in question was untested Clint Longley, who had not taken a snap all year.

Sure enough, down 16–3 with 9:57 left in the third, Staubach was knocked out of the game with a concussion. The Cowboys had traded disgruntled backup Craig Morton to the Giants in late October, leaving only Longley. Cowboys coach Tom Landry had no choice but to put the game into the young man's hands.

What the Redskins did not know was that the brash 22-year-old had the faith of his teammates. Leading his squad with a 35-yard touchdown pass followed by a long scoring drive, heading into the final quarter, Longley had America's Team on top, 17–16. However, thanks to former Cowboys running back Duane Thomas's 19-yard TD run, the Redskins wrested back the lead, 23–17. Now Longley and the Cowboys were on their own 40 with no timeouts and just 1:45 left in the game. Three plays later, facing a fourth-and-6 from the 44, Longley coolly connected with Bob Hayes on a 6-yard pass to keep the drive alive.

It all came down to this: 35 seconds left, ball at midfield. Fans old enough to remember sitting in an easy chair working on a turkey leg have the following play ingrained in their memories.

Coach Landry sent in the play, but wide receiver Drew Pearson called an audible in the huddle. Pretty brave thing to do, especially for a second-year player who'd turned the ball over just a bit earlier.

"I told Clint I was going to do a turn in, take off. I was hoping for a bracket-type double coverage, where the cornerback takes you outside and the safety on the inside for the post and in routes. I wanted that type of double coverage because it was the easiest to beat, especially if you are going deep," he explained.

Like all great receivers, Pearson felt everything slow down on that key play and just sort of "got in tune" with the ball falling from the sky heading his way. "Clint threw one of the prettiest deep passes of all the quarterbacks I worked with," remembered Pearson, who made the Pro Bowl that year and two more times in an 11-year career, all of it spent wearing number 88 for Dallas. "It was a perfect spiral, and I could count the revolutions as it fell into my arms. Everything was in slow motion, and I was surprised that I had gotten that wide open. Both defenders were badly beaten on the play. Mike Bass was never a factor. And, of course, once Kenny Stone bit on the fake, it was over for him. So, it felt really surreal as I trotted into the end zone for a touchdown."

Dallas scored an improbable 24–23 comeback win led by a quarterback who'd go on to play just eight more games in his career, but Clint Longley will forever be the star of one of the classic Thanksgiving games of all time.

1993: MIAMI DOLPHINS 16, DALLAS COWBOYS 14

The defending Super Bowl champion Cowboys, hosting on a rare ice-laden field at Texas Stadium, had Miami beaten until Dallas defensive tackle Leon Lett unnecessarily and unsuccessfully tried to recover a field goal his team had blocked. Had the ball stayed untouched, the play would have been whistled dead—game over. Instead, Miami recovered the ball at the Dallas 10 with three seconds left, enough time for Pete Stoyanovich to kick a game-winning 19-yard field goal.

2002: DALLAS COWBOYS 27, WASHINGTON REDSKINS 20

Down 20–10, the Cowboys came back to post their tenth straight victory over the archrival Redskins. Dallas running back Emmitt Smith ran for 144 yards, becoming the only player in history to pass 17,000 career yards rushing.

In 2006 the NFL added a third game on Thanksgiving night, with a rotating host team. Now a full day of football has become as much a part of Thanksgiving as feasting and family. Thanks, Abe.

CHAPTER ELEVEN

UNCLE SAM'S TEAM

Heading into the decade of the 1940s, the National Football League persisted through a flurry of unstable franchises, sparse crowds, competition from other upstart pro leagues, and even the Great Depression.

Its perseverance in the face of such adversity would serve it well with the demands of World War II on the nation. From 1941 to 1945, more than a thousand players interrupted or postponed their pro football careers, trading their cleats for combat boots to join Uncle Sam's team as part of the armed forces, and headed overseas. (Sadly, football, as well as many other potential careers, were ended before they began by death, injuries, and psychological trauma from service in World War II.) The NFL would be tested like never before, yet it would survive this too and go on to ultimately enjoy tremendous success.

It began on that date that will "live in infamy," Sunday, December 7, 1941. Several NFL games were under way when the Japanese attacked Pearl Harbor just before eight o'clock in the morning, Hawaii time, or about 2 p.m. on the East Coast.

In the middle of a game between the New York Giants and the Brooklyn Dodgers, the public address announcer at the Polo

Grounds told all servicemen to report to their units. The same thing happened at Chicago's Comiskey Park during the rival match between the city's Cardinals and Bears. And in our nation's capital, at Griffith Stadium, where the Redskins were hosting the Eagles, the speakers rang out for high-ranking government and military personnel who were in attendance to report in.

The next day America officially entered World War II.

Two weeks later, the Bears would be crowned champions for the second year in a row after their 37–9 thumping of the Giants in the title game. Only 13,341 hard-core fans came out to Wrigley Field to watch Chicago win its fifth championship. Already America was preoccupied with the ominous specter of having been abruptly catapulted into a major war, as Japan's Axis allies Nazi Germany and Italy declared war on the United States on December 11. There was serious concern that the league might be suspended during the global conflict.

By the end of 1941, nearly two million men had been conscripted for service, and two hundred thousand more volunteered. The 1942 baseball season began as scheduled, but team rosters were depleted, as even many star players, such as Hank Greenberg, Bob Feller, Joe DiMaggio, and Ted Williams, now belonged to Uncle Sam. Shortly after the attack on Pearl Harbor, baseball commissioner Kenesaw Mountain Landis wrote to President Franklin D. Roosevelt, inquiring whether or not America's pastime should be discontinued during World War II. In what has since become known as the "Green Light Letter," on January 15, 1942, the president responded by saying, "I honestly feel that it would be best for the country to keep baseball going."

So, the NFL's new commissioner, Elmer Layden, interpreted that as applying to the NFL as well.

Earlier in 1941, NFL leadership had gone through structural changes. Layden was named the first commissioner of the NFL. He replaced Carl Storck, who'd served as interim league president since the death of longtime president Joe Carr in 1939. With Layden's hiring, the office of president was abolished.

Layden had made college football history at Notre Dame in 1924, when he and fellow seniors Don Miller, Jim Crowley, and Harry Stuhldreher became known as the Four Horsemen manning the backfield for coach Knute Rockne. The Fighting Irish rolled to a perfect 10-0 season, which it capped on January 1, 1925, by disposing of Stanford University in the Rose Bowl. But Layden was by no means the only candidate for the formidable new position that the powers of the NFL had devised.

Though Carr had been a fine administrator, at this crucial juncture the NFL movers and shakers wanted a more visible and charismatic figure—someone along the lines of baseball's Landis, a former federal judge with an authoritarian, self-righteous air. They thought they'd found the proper person right there in Chicago with influential sportswriter and accomplished promoter Arch Ward, but he turned them down.

The NFL settled on Ward's recommendation, Layden, and, under difficult circumstances, he would perform the job admirably through 1946. After the momentum it had gained in the 1930s, the now depleted league was simply trying to survive. Layden had to take drastic measures. One team, the Cleveland Rams, was forced to suspend operations in 1943, while several other clubs had to merge to stay afloat. The Philadelphia Eagles and Pittsburgh Steelers teamed up for a season. In 1944 Pittsburgh merged again, this time with the Chicago Cardinals, and in 1945 the Brooklyn Tigers joined forces with the Boston Yanks. (Today's baseball fans in Beantown and the Big Apple would no doubt consider such a team name abhorrent.) For most of those teams, there was no advantage when it came to gaining talent. And for a few, it really added up to simply having twice as many lousy players.

By the time the 1943 season kicked off, the NFL was in trouble, facing third-and-long from its own 1, so to speak, as more than 600 players and coaches—more than half the entire league—had joined the war effort, 355 of them as commissioned officers. Rosters were filled with some of the most unfit players in league history, because healthy players would never survive the public scrutiny of why they weren't serving their country. "There were guys with bad backs, poor eyesight, punctured eardrums, and bum knees. Those conditions could keep you out of service, but not an NFL game," explained the Pro Football Hall of Fame's Joe Horrigan.

Those players were often riddled with guilt, though, *as* they did not want to appear unpatriotic and cowardly. Almost every one of them held down a second job in the defense industry, working in factories producing ammunition, tanks, weapons, and other materiels at night. The NFL itself did quite a lot in terms of aiding the war effort with charitable endeavors. For example, the league donated the proceeds from 15 different preseason games to service-related charities. Its 1942 preseason college all-star game alone raised more than $150,000 for the Army-Navy Relief Fund. In addition, war bond rallies were held at stadiums around the country.

The public, feeling the NFL was doing what it could on and off the field to help the war effort (aided by the fact that many top colleges suspended their football operations), supported the league like never before. According to Horrigan, "There was a little bit of an ironic twist because people during war thought colleges had a lot of spirit; but many, like Harvard, suspended football during the war. They made the decision with the right frame of mind, but it unintentionally helped the pro game, because in some places the only football available was at the professional level.

"But make no mistake," he said, "it was a tough time because of the manpower shortage."

Though filling team rosters was difficult for NFL teams, filling seats was not. President Roosevelt understood the value of spectator sports during this crisis. In 1942 the NFL drew a record 1,115,154 fans, which increased to 1,234,750 in 1944. Just like going to the movies, spending a couple hours hollering approval over a ferocious hit or screaming at an opposing player for interference provided welcome escape from the brutality of war being reported in the daily papers and broadcast on the radio.

While NFL games helped public morale across the country, in the killing fields across the oceans, many NFL players, and even some coaches and owners, saw action in a most deadly conflict, serving in all theaters of war as tank commanders, infantrymen, paratroopers, naval officers, and pilots. It would be George Halas's second stint in the navy, as he'd served in World War I. Dan Reeves and Fred Levy Jr., co-owners of the Cleveland Rams, joined the US Army Air Forces (one reason why the NFL gave that franchise permission to suspend operations); Brooklyn Dodgers owner Dan Topping enlisted in the US Marines, while to the army went Alexis Thompson, owner of the Philadelphia Eagles, and entering the navy was Wellington Mara, co-owner of the New York Giants.

Among the players to serve on Uncle Sam's team were stars such as Otto Graham, Ernie Nevers, Chuck Bednarik, Lou Groza, Norm Van Brocklin, and Elroy "Crazylegs" Hirsch. More than a few distinguished themselves at the highest levels. Sixty-six men with NFL experience were decorated.

On November 16, 1941, while playing receiver for the Detroit Lions, University of Arkansas grad Maurice Britt caught a 45-yard pass from Dick Booth for the game-winning touchdown in a come-from-behind victory over the Philadelphia Eagles. It would be the only catch of his pro career. Two years later, almost to the day, Captain Britt was in the thick of the Allied invasion of Italy. Pinned down with his infantry company during a firefight, he lost an arm but still managed to kill several enemy soldiers and capture more Germans, earning him a Medal of Honor.

Another receiver, Jack Lummus of the New York Giants, joined the marines. He was in the first wave of troops to land on the Japanese island of Iwo Jima on February 19, 1945. As commander of a rifle platoon during the final assault near Kitano Point, he knocked out three enemy strongholds despite sustaining multiple wounds from grenade shrapnel. Lummus, charging into the line of fire to take out the pillboxes, stepped on a land mine, which blew apart both his legs. He commanded his platoon to carry on the fight. After being carried to the aid station, Lummus famously told the doctor: "Well, doc, the New York Giants lost a mighty good end today." He died later that day at the age of twenty-nine. For his actions, Lummus was awarded the Medal of Honor.[26]

Just six weeks removed from playing offensive tackle for the Giants in the 1944 NFL championship game, Al Blozis would be killed by enemy fire in the snowy mountains of occupied France while out on patrol searching for missing comrades. All told, 23 NFL players would lose their lives during the war.

Tom Landry fought for the real "America's Team." Dropping out of college to enlist, the future legendary coach copiloted a B-17 bomber that flew 30 missions. He survived a crash in Belgium while returning from a bombing run.

Chuck Bednarik, the last of the great two-way players, also served in the air, as a gunner aboard B-24 bombers.

Meanwhile, back on the home front, servicemen were always welcome guests at NFL games. Even Gen. Dwight Eisenhower found time to attend a Redskins game at Washington's Griffith Stadium.

Perhaps it is the perspective of Buffalo Bills head coach Marv Levy, a man who served both in World War II and had reached the pinnacle of the NFL, coming up short in four Super Bowls, that can put to rest that "football-is-war" mantra and, in doing so, honor those who have served our nation in times of military conflict.

In January 1994, before Super Bowl XXVIII, after his Bills had suffered three straight title-game defeats, Levy was asked if the upcoming contest was a "must-win" game.

"This is not a must-win," he said evenly. "World War II was a must-win."

THE FIRST QUARTER ALL-TIME TEAM

ENDS	Don Hutson Green Bay Packers	Bill Hewitt Chicago Bears/ Philadelphia Eagles
TACKLES	Cal Hubbard New York Giants/ Green Bay Packers	Joe Stydahar Chicago Bears
GUARDS	Dan Fortmann Chicago Bears	George Musso Chicago Bears
CENTER	Mel Hein New York Giants	
RUNNING BACKS	Jim Thorpe Canton Bulldogs/ Oorang Indians	Bronko Nagurski Chicago Bears
QUARTERBACK	Sammy Baugh Washington Redskins	
PUNTER	Sammy Baugh Washington Redskins	
HEAD COACH	George Halas Chicago Bears	

(This was an era in which they played on both sides of the ball.)

Second Quarter

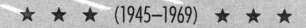 ★ ★ ★ (1945–1969) ★ ★ ★

CHAPTER TWELVE

A MORE COLORFUL GAME,
A BETTER GAME

The history of African Americans playing professional football preceded the launch of the National Football League. It began when running back Charles Follis took the field for the Shelby (Ohio) Athletic Club in 1904. A superb player on both offense and defense, local papers called him the Black Cyclone for his tremendous speed and breakaway power. In the 1904 opener, the six-foot-tall 200-pounder demonstrated his prowess with an 83-yard touchdown run.

Follis was also well respected by his white teammates, who helped him stand up to the racial taunts and physical threats of opposing teams and fans. One of them, a 23-year-old Ohioan named Branch Rickey, would spend his life in baseball, first as a player and then as a visionary baseball executive. In 1945, as president and general manager of the Brooklyn Dodgers, he all but single-handedly bucked the American pastime's longstanding segregationist policy by signing an African American standout named Jackie Robinson to a contract with a Dodgers minor league affiliate. Two years later, Robinson was promoted to the parent club, breaking the sport's shameful race barrier. To Rickey, Charles Follis was "a wonder," and a source of inspiration for his engineering such a momentous break-through.

A few other African American players from the pre-NFL of the early 1900s were Gideon Smith, Henry McDonald, and Charles "Doc" Baker. All faced the same issues that would affect pioneering black players in the National Football League in the ensuing decades, as they confronted and surmounted racial barriers that began in a less tolerant America more than a century ago.

McDonald, a halfback for the Rochester Jeffersons, recalled a game against Canton in which the Bulldogs' Greasy Neale, a native West Virginian, shoved him out of bounds, cocked his fists, and shouted, "Black is black, and white is white, and where I come from, they don't mix!"

Jim Thorpe jumped in between them, saying firmly, "We are here to play football." According to McDonald, "Thorpe's word on the field was law. And we never had any problem after that."[27]

But blacks in general did have problems long after that, and it is hard to imagine the perseverance it required to withstand not just verbal and physical abuse but also being prohibited from joining white teammates in hotels, restaurants, and on public transportation.

The numbers point out how hard it was to make progress. From 1920 until 1933, only 13 African Americans played on NFL teams. From 1933 until 1946, there was none.

One of the great pioneers of progress was Fritz Pollard.

Coming from an athletic family (his father had been a champion boxer during the Civil War), the lightning quick and tough African American played halfback in the Ivy League for Brown University. He became the first man of his race to be named to a backfield position on the All-America team named by Walter Camp. At the time, the former Yale coach called Pollard "one of the greatest runners these eyes have ever seen."

By 1920, he was the star player for the Akron Pros, one of the NFL's charter franchises. Pollard not only played in the NFL's first season, he led the undefeated Pros to their first championship, topping George Halas and his Decatur Staleys as well as defeating Jim Thorpe twice in head-to-head matchups with the Canton Bulldogs. The following season, he officially took over leadership of the team, becoming the NFL's first African American head coach (officially a co-coach with Eglie Tobin) while playing every down as the team's best player.

However, Pollard remained a marked man on and off the field, and the team's owners were concerned for him. To avoid potential trouble, Pollard had to dress at the owner's cigar store, then be driven to the park just before game time, sprinting onto the field just as teams were ready to kick off. On the field, he was a target of especially rough play. Pollard responded in a typically restrained yet direct manner. "I would pay them no mind, but I would know who the player was," he explained. "And at the first opportunity that presented itself, I'd kick them right in the guts or hit my knee up against their knee, knocking it out of joint. And then I let them know quietly why I did it."[28]

By the time he hung up his cleats, Pollard had achieved another significant milestone: being the first African American to play quarterback in the NFL. He earned a posthumous induction into the Pro Football Hall of Fame in 2005. Equally impressive was his ability to spot up-and-coming African American talent, which he did as co-coach of the Akron Pros in 1921 and then as player-coach manager with the Milwaukee Badgers the following year. One of those players was Paul Robeson.

Son of a slave who escaped at age 15, joined the Union army, and then, after the Civil War, attended Lincoln University, Robeson entered Rutgers University on an academic scholarship. At six foot two and 190 pounds, he stood three to four inches taller and weighed 20 to 30 pounds more than most other players at the time.

After the 1918 season, Walter Camp selected Robeson as a first-team all-American at end. He then went into professional football after graduating in 1919.[29]

As a tackle and end, Robeson's size made him particularly adept at breaking up plays coming his way. Though he did love the game, not to mention the comparatively lucrative compensation and the status it conferred in the African American community, Robeson was looking ahead to other things: during his two years in the NFL, as an Akron Pro in 1921 and a Milwaukee Badger in 1922, playing alongside Fritz Pollard in both cities, he spent the off-seasons studying at Columbia University Law School, in Manhattan. A true Renaissance man, Robeson was also a renowned stage and film actor, bass baritone singer, and, somewhat controversially, a political activist.

Despite the stifling conditions, a few other black players managed to achieve some success in the 1920s and early 1930s, including Duke Slater, Bobby Marshall, Joe Lillard, and Ray Kemp. But when the 1933 season drew to a close, Lillard, a tailback for the Chicago Cardinals, and Kemp, a Pittsburgh Pirates tackle, would be the last black players to wear NFL uniforms until 1946.

While there is no clear-cut evidence of a formalized racial barrier, reduced opportunities for African American players became evident in 1927. The year before, so many franchises endured such heavy financial losses that the NFL was reduced from 22 teams to a mere dozen, thus making it difficult for many players, regardless of color, to get a job playing football. It did not help that a rival league, the American Football League, led by Red Grange, disbanded after the 1926 season, leaving a large number of players scrambling to enter or reenter the NFL.

A combination of other factors was at play, too, all of which limited openings for black players. The college game dominated then, and as there was little media coverage in the black communities, potential African American players were not as aware of the pro league.

Also, the main recruiting grounds was the primarily white-oriented universities where few blacks played—two notable exceptions being Pollard and Robeson.

Because pro football was much less popular than both the college game and Major League Baseball at that time, the NFL suffered even more from the ravages of the Great Depression. In 1932 the league fielded an all-time low eight teams, extinguishing still more hopefuls' pigskin dreams.

After World War II, many football players returned home looking to launch or resume their pro careers. So many, in fact, that a new league was formed in 1946: the All-America Football Conference. But although the end of World War II spurred a new sense of social consciousness, segregation and discrimination remained prevalent throughout the United States. Nevertheless, also in 1946, one year before Jackie Robinson broke baseball's color barrier, the reintegration of professional football began. The NFL's Rams, having left Cleveland for Los Angeles, signed Kenny Washington and Woody Strode, while in the new AAFC, the Cleveland Browns signed Bill Willis and Marion Motley. (See chapter 13, "Otto-Matic.")

Paul Brown of the Cleveland Browns was among the first to reintegrate professional football when he signed fullback-linebacker Marion Motley in 1946.

Courtesy of Cleveland Browns

Some credit for the Rams' signing of Washington and Strode goes to Halley Harding, an outspoken African American columnist for the local black community's newspaper. In his *Los Angeles Tribune* column, So What, Harding continually pressed Rams executives, particularly general manager Chile Walsh, as to why the Rams would not employ black players. He also accused the NFL of lacking gratitude toward the African American athletes who'd helped establish the fledgling league during its touch-and-go early days, such as Pollard, Robeson, and Lillard.[30] Harding's impassioned words helped trigger the NFL's reintegration. Another factor may have had an impact, too: when the Rams were negotiating a lease to play in the Los Angeles Coliseum, the commission charged with operating the stadium expressed reservations over its prospective tenant's discriminatory policies before ultimately going ahead with the deal.

The Rams signed Washington, a six-foot-one halfback, and, a few months later, Strode, a 32-year-old end. They'd been football teammates on the 1939 UCLA Bruins, along with one Jackie Robinson. As Strode explains in his candid 1990 autobiography, *Goal Dust*, "When Kenny signed, they had to get him a roommate. He could've gotten along with the white boys on the team, Bob Waterfield and Jim Hardy, and all those boys from UCLA and USC. But I think he meant that he had to have a running mate; another black person to live with on the road. They asked him to select somebody. Kenny told them he wanted me. They spoke of my marriage to a Hawaiian. They try to use my marriage to keep me off the team. But Kenny had power at that point, and he said, 'I want my buddy.'[31]

"Traveling with the Rams made a big impact: we discovered how popular we were across the country. The black kids outside California used to tell Kenny and me how much they enjoyed listening to our games on the radio while we're still playing at UCLA. Until that time, we didn't realize what a unique thing we had done."[32]

That season, the Rams averaged more than 31,000 in attendance per game, the highest it had ever been.

But like Paul Robeson before him, Strode would find greater success in other forms of entertainment, especially film acting. From 1941 until his death in 1994, he appeared in some six dozen motion pictures, including the John Ford classic *The Man Who Shot Liberty Valance*, and had a famous turn in a gladiator duel against Kirk Douglas in *Spartacus*, directed by Stanley Kubrick.

Looking back, the footballer-turned-actor did not remember his NFL experience with much joy. "If I have to integrate heaven," Strode told a reporter in 1971, "I don't want to go."

Sadly, by the time Kenny Washington arrived in the NFL at the age of 28, he no longer possessed the skills that had made him an all-American in college, having already undergone three knee operations. Still, during his three seasons as a Ram, he averaged 6.1 yards per carry.

African Americans did set milestones for excellence through the years. These include safety Emlen Tunnell, who anchored the staunch New York Giant defense for 11 seasons and in a Hall of Fame career in 1952, he actually gained more yards on interceptions and kick returns (924) than Rams star running back Dan Towler who led the NFL in rushing (894) that year (1946). Running back Joe Perry of the San Francisco 49ers being the first to gain 1,000 yards rushing in back-to-back seasons (1953 and 1954) and the first African American to be named the NFL Most Valuable Player. Still, the NFL would not complete its reintegration until 1962.

For many years, longtime Redskins owner George Preston Marshall resisted employing African American players on his team. He owned the franchise from its inception as the Boston Braves in 1932 until his death in 1969. As a matter of fact, he once quipped: "We'll start signing Negroes when the Harlem Globetrotters start signing whites."[33] In 1937, the year he moved the renamed Redskins team to the nation's capital, Washington reeled off the first of two championships and six division titles over the next nine years largely on the arm strength of Hall of Fame quarterback Sammy Baugh. But beginning in 1946, the club never won another title under Marshall's ownership; in fact, it was barely competitive, posting only three winning seasons through 1961.

Without question, the owner's stubborn refusal to sign black athletes contributed to the team's poor record. "Thanks to the Marshall Plan," lamented one sportswriter, "the Redskins were the 'whitest and worst' team in professional football."[34] Even after his team finished in the basement in both 1960 and 1961 with a collective 2-21-3 record, and even with the civil rights movement gaining momentum, Marshall refused to budge. Black players he passed on would go on to star for competing teams—not exactly a winning strategy. At one point, the Pulitzer Prize–winning sports columnist Shirley Povich of the *Washington Post* took the owner to task. "The Redskins' colors," he wrote, "were burgundy, gold, and Caucasian."[35]

Then the administration of the new president, John F. Kennedy, stepped in. US Secretary of the Interior Stewart Udall told Marshall bluntly that if he did not integrate his team, the Redskins would lose their lease to play in the newly opened DC Stadium, which sat on federal land. In December 1961 Marshall complied, albeit reluctantly, drafting that year's Heisman Trophy winner, Ernie Davis. The star halfback from Syracuse University had other ideas, snapping, "I won't play for that SOB." And he didn't. Washington had no choice but to trade its draft pick to the Cleveland Browns in return for two African Americans: future Hall of Fame halfback-flanker Bobby Mitchell and running back Leroy Jackson. At any rate, when the Redskins assembled for their 1962 team photo, for the first time, you could pick out some black faces: Mitchell, Jackson, and an offensive guard they'd acquired from the Steelers, John Nisby. He and Mitchell both made the Pro Bowl that season, and Washington improved to 5-7-2. At long last, every team in the National Football League could claim to be integrated. Shortly after George Preston Marshall's death, under a new coach named George Allen, the Redskins turned into a perennial powerhouse and would finish at or near the top of the standings all the way into the 1990s.

Opportunities for minorities would become far more plentiful beginning in 1960, when the American Football League began play. It had more to do with pragmatic decision-making than anything else, because the AFL struggled as a business from the opening kickoff and could not afford to be prejudiced. In order to compete against the established NFL for fans, its eight teams, divided into two divisions, needed to hire the best players to put on a good show.

For the first time, there was a strong emphasis on finding talent from historically black schools such as Texas Southern, Prairie View A&M, Grambling State, Tennessee State, Florida A&M, North Carolina A&T, and Alcorn State. In December 1962 the AFL's Dallas Texans, about to metamorphose into the Kansas City Chiefs with the start of the 1963 season, became the first franchise to spend its number one draft pick on a black player from a historically black college: Junious "Buck" Buchanan of Grambling State College. A few days later, at the separate NFL draft in Chicago, the New York Giants, too, picked a six-foot-seven defensive tackle—but in the 19th round, making him the 265th pick overall—a fact that spoke volumes about the value the two leagues placed on minority players.

"The AFL was more in touch with recruiting from black colleges than the NFL was in those days," observed Tom Flores, a journeyman quarterback in the 1960s who would later win a pair of Super Bowls as head coach of the Oakland/Los Angeles Raiders. "You had black players coming out from smaller schools like Grambling, and with the success of Buck Buchanan, Ernie Ladd, and Willie Brown, it opened the eyes of the NFL."

In the early 1960s, San Diego Chargers head coach Sid Gillman did something unheard of for the times: assigning roommates based on position, not skin color. The Bears would gain more notoriety a couple years later when they paired up running backs Gale Sayers, a black man from Kansas, and a white teammate from Florida named Brian Piccolo. Their brotherly friendship resulted in an Emmy Award–winning TV movie, the 1971 tearjerker *Brian's Song*.

As the first overall selection in the 1963 AFL draft by the future Kansas City Chiefs, tackle Buck Buchanan was the first black number one draft choice in professional football history. Junious, a six-time all-star, helped his team win a Super Bowl on his way to the Pro Football Hall of Fame.

Courtesy Kansas City Chiefs

Gillman had experienced prejudice himself. He was rebuffed for head-coaching positions in college football, particularly among the Big Ten schools, because he was Jewish. One must imagine that had Ohio State University hired Gillman, an alumnus, known for his bombing orders (long downfield passes, that is), its style of football would have been *very* different from the "three yards and a cloud of dust" grind-it-out-on-the-ground approach of longtime OSU coach Woody Hayes.

Speaking of the Big Ten, linebacker Bobby Bell was an all-everything at the University of Minnesota, playing both offense and defense. Although the local NFL franchise, the Minnesota Vikings, expressed interest in him, he saw what was happening when it came time to play in the pros.

"There were racist problems in both leagues, but the bottom line was that the AFL knew good product is what sold, so they went after the best players available regardless of color," said Bell, the Texans/Chiefs' seventh-round draft pick for 1963. Kansas City would represent the American Football League in the first Super Bowl, in January 1967; win its division in 1968; and then return to Super Bowl IV in January 1970—the last one before the two leagues merged—and upset the NFL's best, the Vikings. Bell, a Hall of Famer, attributed a lot of the franchise's success to the progressive philosophy of its owner, saying: "I could have been white. Lamar Hunt simply wanted the best players. It didn't matter if you were green, red, or brown."

However, the quarterback position was seemingly off-limits to African Americans for decades. Even though they had made progress up and down the lineup, it was at the most prominent, "thinking man" position, QB, where progress was slowest.

There was never any overt rule against black athletes playing quarterback in the NFL. As early as 1953, the Chicago Bears' aptly named Willie Thrower became the first African American to take a snap behind center in the modern NFL era, but he was a backup. In 1968 a rookie for the Denver Broncos named Marlin Briscoe became the first African American starting quarterback. However, the following season, as a member of the Buffalo Bills, he was slotted as a wide receiver. Briscoe reluctantly played that position for five different teams over the next five years before retiring.

James Harris was a starter for the Buffalo Bills on and off from 1969 to 1972. In 1974, while playing for the Rams, the former Grambling star became the first quarterback to start a playoff game, defeating the Redskins, 19–10. He was also named MVP of that season's Pro Bowl.

In 1978 Doug Williams became the first black quarterback to be drafted in the first round since the 1970 AFL-NFL merger. As a member of the 1987 Washington Redskins, he went on to become the first black quarterback to win the Super Bowl, a 42–10 romp over the Denver Broncos, and was named the game's MVP. He had an excellent game—18 for 29 for 390 yards and four touchdowns— despite the media's trying to escalate the race issue throughout the whole buildup to the title tilt.

"No question that was being pushed by the media," he acknowl-

THE LATIN QUARTER

Like African Americans, Hispanic Americans established a presence early on in the NFL as well. In 1929 Spanish-born running back and punter Jess Rodriguez signed with the Buffalo Bisons, while his brother, Kelly, played for the Frankford Yellow Jackets the following season. Waldo Don Carlos became the first Latin player to be part of a championship team, playing both ways for the Green Bay Packers in 1931.

In the rough-and-tumble days of the NFL in the 1950s, nobody was tougher than young Latino running back Ricardo "Rick" Casares, who started his career with an 81-yard touchdown run and never looked back. In 1956, his sophomore year with the Chicago Bears, he led the NFL in rushing.

Tony Casillas, an NCAA champion at the University of Oklahoma, was a dominating defensive tackle who also earned two back-to-back Super Bowl titles with the Dallas Cowboys in the nineties.

Anthony Munoz, an 11-time Pro Bowl offensive tackle, played for the Cincinnati Bengals and is a member of the Hall of Fame.

Manny Fernandez was at the core of the No-Name defense of the Miami Dolphins, including their historic undefeated season of 1972.

Joe Kapp quarterbacked the Vikings to a Super Bowl appearance, and fellow Latino passer Jim Plunkett led the Oakland Raiders to two Super Bowl titles, including being named MVP of Super Bowl XV in 1981.

edged, "but you have to put stuff like that to rest to stay focused. That was easy for me because I knew who I was. I knew what color I was." Williams laughed at the memory. "They were not springing a surprise on me. It may have been a surprise to them, but I think at the end of the day, we concluded I was the quarterback of the Washington Redskins who just happened to be black."

Even though many first-rate black quarterbacks have since plied their talents in the NFL, including Steve McNair, Daunte Culpepper, Donovan McNabb, Michael Vick, Cam Newton, and Russell Wilson, among many others, it is a shame that we will never know the potentially record-shattering numbers Warren Moon might have put up had he been drafted into the NFL out of the University of Washington.

Moon entered the NFL as a 27-year old rookie in 1984 for the Houston Oilers after having dominated the Canadian Football League for six seasons. With Moon in the pocket, the Edmonton Eskimos won five straight championships, barely missing a sixth in 1983, while their quarterback was named league MVP.

The Los Angeles native drew inspiration in his youth from two minority quarterbacks. "As a kid growing up, I really idolized Roman Gabriel. He was a quarterback of the Rams. I related to him because me being black and he a minority as well, being of Filipino descent," Moon said. "Then when James Harris came along, he was someone I really focused on right there in my hometown. Watching him every week gave me hope."

Like some others, Moon had to fight a lot of prejudice and preconceived notions about black quarterbacks back in the 1970s, both in getting into a big-time college and then the NFL. But the young man had a mantra that drove him eventually to greatness: *"My ears heard all the negative things, but my heart didn't listen."*

Despite the late start, Moon was more than ready to enter the NFL. His stats there would include throwing for nearly 50,000 yards, playing in nine Pro Bowls, and being enshrined into the Hall of Fame. By the time he retired in 2000, at the age of 44, he had spent 17 years in an NFL uniform, all but the last two as a starting quarterback.

Today's locker room is evidence of how far the game has advanced regarding race.

"To go through the blood, sweat, and tears and get your head knocked around, the physical and mental part, the camaraderie, is just unlike anything else," said receiver Don Beebe, who appeared in four Super Bowls with the Buffalo Bills and won one later playing for Green Bay. Beebe, born in Aurora, Illinois, happens to be white.

"If people could learn from what an NFL locker room is like when it comes to racial discrimination, our world would be better for it," he said intently, "because there is none. I love those guys. Bruce Smith, Thurman Thomas. I love them. They love me. We don't look at the color of the skin, we're brothers. That is what an NFL locker room is like, and people can learn from that."

Progress has been made, but the next few decades offer a great opportunity to fully open up management positions to minorities—not just pacing the sidelines as head coach but also taking their places in the executive suite, as general manager, team president, majority franchise *owner*.

In his Hall of Fame acceptance speech in 2017, San Diego Chargers running back LaDainian Tomlinson perhaps captured it best when he said:

"Football is a microcosm of America. All races, religions, and creeds, living, playing, competing side by side. When you are part of a team, you understand your teammates—their strengths and weaknesses—and work together toward the same goal, to win a championship. Let's not choose to be against one another. Let's choose to be for one another. I pray we dedicate ourselves to being the best team we can be. . . . Leading the way for all nations to follow."

CHAPTER THIRTEEN

OTTO-MATIC

With World War II having depleted its personnel, and, in turn, the caliber of play, the National Football League was understandably cautious about expansion. However, that did not stop a plethora of offers from well-heeled potential owners wanting to finance new teams from coming in. Each one would be rebuffed by Commissioner Elmer Layden.

Enter Arch Ward, the well-respected and influential sportswriter of the *Chicago Tribune*. It had been his idea for Major League Baseball to hold an annual All-Star Game, beginning in 1933, and, of course, we all know how popular that turned out to be. Likewise, the following year, he organized a football extravaganza, Chicago Charities College All-Star Game, which pitted the reigning NFL championship team against a squad of all-stars from the college ranks. Later called the College All-Star Football Classic, it routinely lured immense crowds—eighty thousand, ninety thousand, a hundred thousand—to Chicago's Soldier Field year after year. You might recall that Ward was held in such high regard that in 1941 the NFL's owners asked him to become the league commissioner. Five years later, they were doubly sorry that he'd turned them down.

The newspaperman had decided to parlay his knack for developing new sports properties into creating a league of his own through his relationships with many of those same wealthy, influential entrepreneurs who'd been turned away by the NFL. Ward's new pro football league, set to unveil itself in September 1946, would be called the All-America Football Conference (AAFC).

Armed with an abundance of players in the marketplace, the new eight-team league aggressively went after experienced NFL players and college stars. A bonus was the fact that many of these athletes had kept their skills sharp by playing with military sports teams during the war.

The prescient Mr. Ward also saw opportunity on the West Coast. Bear in mind that pro football had yet to expand west of the Mississippi River. With the war over, and air transportation becoming increasingly available and affordable, more and more young men (and their families) were belatedly taking Horace Greeley's famous advice to "go west." The AAFC shrewdly established two franchises on the West Coast: the San Francisco 49ers and the Los Angeles Dons.

The Southern California squad had a little bit of showbiz behind it, as the Dons were under the ownership of actor Don Ameche, a good friend of Ward's. The debonair movie star had helped set things in motion a few years earlier by assembling a group of Hollywood celebrities to invest in a new NFL franchise. Wintry Buffalo was their target, but only temporarily: once the war was over, and national transportation restrictions lifted, they would relocate the team to sunny Los Angeles.

However, the NFL owners, led by the remarkably shortsighted George Preston Marshall, considered the venture not viable economically. Arch Ward, on the other hand, welcomed them to the AAFC. Ironically, the NFL's Cleveland Rams vacated Ohio to set up shop in (three guesses) LA just in time for the 1946 season, anyway. The two teams had to share the Los Angeles Coliseum, not to mention the affections of Southern California football fans.

The new league boasted promising rosters fairly deep in talent. It had two recent Heisman Trophy winners in Angelo Bertelli (Notre Dame, '43), who would QB the Dons, and University of Georgia Bulldog Frank Sinkwich ('42), signed by the New York Yankees. The Croatian-born running back had played for the Detroit Lions, winning the NFL Most Valuable Player award in 1944. But while serving in two branches of the US military the following year, he damaged his knee, and so when Sinkwich reported to training camp in 1946, he was a Heisman winner in name only. Nevertheless, it was a highly recognizable name. More than a hundred other athletes with NFL experience suited up for the All-America Football Conference's maiden season, as did 40 of the 66 latest college all-stars.

Up to this point, three different leagues—all called the American Football League (AFL)—had challenged the NFL for supremacy. The first one, built around young Red Grange, survived only one season, 1926. The next two lasted two seasons each: 1936–37 and 1940–41. Now the National Football League emerged from its foxhole to find itself yet again in a war over talent and the public's loyalty.

AAFC-1946	
WESTERN DIVISION	**EASTERN DIVISION**
Chicago Rockets	Brooklyn Dodgers
Cleveland Browns	Buffalo Bisons
Los Angeles Dons	Miami Seahawks
San Francisco 49ers	New York Yankees

Even though the AAFC succeeded in bringing pro football to the West Coast and was able to survive the initial years without benefit of network television coverage, the league's foremost legacy is its having seeded one of the great dynasties in pro football history. This team would include arguably the greatest coach of all time (Paul Brown), and the greatest quarterback of all time (Otto Graham), in addition to leading the reintegration of the sport by anchoring the franchise with a pair of African American players who would wind up in the Pro Football Hall of Fame (Bill Willis and Marion Motley).

Paul Brown (center) is considered by many the greatest coach in pro football history.

Courtesy Cleveland Browns

In the short history of the All-America Football Conference, the Cleveland Browns were so dominant—winning the championship all four seasons, losing only *four* games out of 54 during that entire span—that the competitive imbalance contributed to the league's folding after the 1949 season.

As one of three AAFC teams to be welcomed whole into the National Football League in 1950, the Browns kept right on rollin'. For the first 10 years of the franchise's existence, from 1946 through 1955, the team won an astounding 84 percent of its games and appeared in the league championship (AAFC and NFL) *every season*, winning seven times.

Coach Brown brought an impeccable resume to Cleveland: his Massillon High School team won six Ohio state championships in nine years; he led the OSU Buckeyes to the 1942 national championship; and he'd also coached successfully at the military's Great Lakes Naval Training Station, his time there highlighted by a brilliant upset of Notre Dame in his final game.

When launching the Browns, Brown wanted to use the T-formation. There were quarterbacks available skilled in that formation, such as Stanford's Frankie Albert and the aforementioned Angelo Bertelli. So it surprised more than a few observers when the coach went with a young man steeped in single-wing play.

Otto Graham was an all-American tailback at Northwestern University, where he was also a talented basketball player. "He beat my Ohio State teams two of the three games we played against Northwestern," Brown recalled. "He could throw as well as run to his right and run to his left. He had great peripheral vision from being a great basketball player. The more I thought about him, the more I considered him the ultimate."[36]

Even though in college Graham ran and blocked more than he threw, Coach Brown had also observed that the young man from Waukegan, Illinois, possessed poise, leadership, great ball-handling skills, and a fierce competitive streak.

For the type of running game that fit his philosophy, Brown chose Marion Motley.

"There's an old saying in football that the best play is straight ahead," he explained during an interview in 1953. "We had that man going straight ahead all the time: Marion Motley at fullback.

Motley had the speed of a halfback to go with his two hundred forty pounds."[37]

The burly yet cat-quick back, in playing for Coach Brown at the Great Lakes Naval Training Station during World War II, proved he could be a triple threat in his own way. He was not only a powerful runner and devastating blocker but also a fine pass receiver (and credited with inadvertently helping to develop the draw play).

During a game, a botched pass play caused quarterback Otto Graham to improvise a handoff to his fullback. A stunned Motley, who had been expecting to block on the play, instead ran for a big gain. Coach Brown made a mental note of the improvised play's success and began to work it in as a regular component of his play calling, quickly creating several different versions of it. Motley's move would become a staple for every team: the draw play. It was designed to look like a pass play, with the offensive linemen dropping back as if to pass block. But as the defenders rushed quarterback Otto Graham, he'd hand off to Motley, who would sprint toward the line. The offensive line would then block the overaggressive pass rushers to the sides, opening sizable holes for the fullback to run through. More often than not, he'd bowl over a few more opponents for a solid gain; in his nine-year career, Motley averaged an impressive 5.7 yards per carry. Standing six foot one, he also played strong-side linebacker on defense, where his heft came in especially handy on goal-line stands. In 1968 Marion Motley became the first black player to be inducted in the Hall of Fame.

The Cleveland coach was a fundamentalist, and perhaps no other player epitomized better what he demanded than two-way lineman Bill Willis, a featured player under Brown at Ohio State.

"Tactics doesn't mean a blooming thing," Brown once said, "if your men aren't blocking and tackling and knocking somebody down—if they aren't 'leathering' somebody, as we put it. This goes back to the mental state of your team. As a matter of desire and willingness to pay the price it takes to win. That means going out and running into people."[38]

From 1946 to 1953, Willis was a force in the pits. He not only made the tough tackles, "leathering" opponents with regularity, but was part of an offensive line that gave Graham time to throw to his swift and clever receivers, Dante "Gluefingers" Lavelli and Mac Speedie.

One of Willis's line mates was Lou Groza, a fellow Buckeye who would also become Brown's chief kicker. Both Groza and Lavelli saw rough action in World War II—in Okinawa and the Battle of the Bulge, respectively. Their military backgrounds were a good fit for Paul Brown's tough, disciplined approach.

Though Coach Brown had an innate ability for recognizing talent, some future stars, whether late bloomers or due to differing philosophies, did slip through his organization over the years, including Len Dawson, Jim Marshall, Doug Atkins, and Willie Davis, but things worked out for all parties.

The coming-out party for the Cleveland Browns in their 1950 NFL debut generated tremendous publicity. Bert Bell, who'd succeeded Elmer Layden as league commissioner, wanted to road test the Browns right away. To heighten the drama, he scheduled their season opener all by itself on the Saturday night before the first Sunday action.

It was the most talked-about game in NFL history to that point, pitting the four-time AAFC champs against the team that Bell used to own: the Philadelphia Eagles. Anticipation from fans and the press was so high that some dubbed the game "the World Series of Pro Football."

Of the 71,237 fans who filed into Philadelphia Municipal Stadium that mid-September evening—more than any previous NFL or AAFC championship game, and one of the largest pro football crowds to date—many if not most probably shared the prevailing skepticism that the Browns were not as good as their AAFC record suggested. Redskins owner George Preston Marshall, who would become known for being on the wrong side of history more than once, was quoted as saying dismissively of the AAFC, "Their best team could not beat our worst team."

Otto Graham recalled: "We kept reading derogatory remarks in the papers. Paul Brown, who I think was a genius, would never say a word. He just took those clippings and put them on the bulletin board. The NFL would say their worst team could beat our best team. We read that kind of stuff for four years."

The Browns had been hearing it season after season and were tired of it. "We had four years of constant ridicule to get us ready," said Brown. His team was focused.

In terms of a powerful champion playing an opponent from an "inferior" league, this tilt resembled Super Bowl III, which would take place nearly two decades later. As with the 1968 Baltimore Colts and New York Jets, the Eagles were widely considered one of the NFL's strongest-ever champions, with a stifling defense, while many discounted the Browns' success as being due to the weak competition in their now-defunct league.

It must be remembered that the Eagles had won three straight Eastern conference crowns and the last two National Football League titles. Defensive-minded head coach Greasy Neale had developed a 5-4 formation, led by Hall of Fame linebacker Chuck Bednarik, that was widely copied by other teams.

It would not matter. Like Jets coach Weeb Ewbank did against the Colts, Paul Brown exploited some previously unknown weaknesses in the Eagles' much-heralded defense. Philly could not double-team all three receivers, who were very efficient on timing patterns. The Browns swapped out running back positioning and sent them out into pass patterns, a tactic the Eagles had never seen before.

With Graham throwing for three touchdown passes and rushing for one, Motley knocking over defenders like bowling pins, the Browns won decisively, 35–10. It served as a wake-up call for the established league. That season, the Browns rolled to a division-best 10-2 record, then defeated the New York Giants in the playoffs to host the Los Angeles Rams, formerly of Cleveland, in the NFL championship game on Christmas Eve.

For football fans, as well as for the sport itself, Santa couldn't have dropped off a better present, as many consider the 1950 Browns-Rams postseason contest to be one of the most exciting in history, featuring five lead changes. Throughout the regular season, Los Angeles, with its quarterback duo of veteran Bob Waterfield and 24-year-old Norm Van Brocklin throwing to talented receivers Tom Fears and Crazylegs Hirsch, had presented one of the great aerial shows ever seen. In the championship duel, however, Cleveland's passing attack prevailed. Waterfield and Graham each amassed about 300 yards, but the Rams' field generals were picked off five times, while Graham connected for four touchdowns and only one interception. In addition, he rushed for nearly 100 yards—wearing sneakers. However, it was almost all for naught.

Down 28–27 late in the game, Graham fumbled away the ball. Thinking he had cost his team the title, the quarterback stood dejectedly on the sidelines, staring at the game clock. However, Cleveland's defense got the ball back, and Otto, like a man possessed, made the most of the opportunity, running and throwing his way to set up a game-winning 16-yard field goal by Lou Groza. Final score: 30–28.

The Cleveland Browns became NFL champions in their first season coming over from a supposedly inferior league. Graham's performance exemplified Coach Brown's cornerstone philosophy, of which he revealed, "I want men who play for the sheer joy of licking somebody. With the best ones, the money part is fine, but it is just something that comes along with the playing. The great pros are all like that. It's so hard for them to quit."

CHAPTER FOURTEEN

BECOMING MORE THAN A SIGNAL CALLER

It took some time for the passing game to develop, one reason being the ball itself. The shape of the "foot ball" in the early 1900s was rounder, more like a soccer ball, than the style we know today. How interesting it would be to see how far and how accurately the Atlanta Falcons' Matt Ryan could hurl one of those watermelons of yesteryear.

But even prior to the air game gaining impact, the quarterback was the chief game caller, as the backfield position terms were derived from their alignment.

Quarterback, halfback, fullback. From the center, the fullback was all the way back, the halfback crouched halfway back, and the quarterback stood a quarter of the way back. So, the QB got the ball first and decided where the other two would go.

"When referring to the signal caller, you could not coach from the sideline. So, the team captain was generally calling the plays. And often that made the quarterback the prime candidate as team captain, but not always," explained Joe Horrigan, executive director of the Pro Football Hall of Fame. "But it did evolve into that lead-

ership role for the quarterback position. From directing the teammates in the huddle to being the first to handle the ball and making
the play happen."

BENNY FRIEDMAN

The first player to make it happen on a consistent basis, demonstrating the exciting possibilities of an aerial attack, was Benny Friedman. It was still a fat ball during his playing days, but he was one
of the rare guys not afraid to throw it. Playing for the Cleveland
Bulldogs, New York Giants, and Brooklyn Dodgers from 1927 to
1934, Friedman revolutionized the forward pass at a time when the
league's rules discouraged passing.

It wasn't quite Kurt Warner's Greatest Show on Turf, with five
receiver options, seventy years in the future, but in 1929 Friedman
led the New York Giants to a 13-1-1 record, scoring a stunning 312
points for an average of nearly 21 per game, while the league average
was just over 8.

To put the Giants of 1929 in perspective, the 1950 Rams averaged an all-time record 38.8 points; however, their total of 466 represented only 13 percent of the league's scoring. When quarterback
Tom Brady and receiver Randy Moss propelled the 2007 Patriots
to an amazing all-time tally of 589 points, their total represented
merely 5.3 percent of the league's scoring.[39]

Red Grange called the five-foot-eight-inch, 172-pound Friedman the best quarterback he ever saw. Reflecting on Friedman in
the late 1960s, Grange said, "Anybody can throw today's football.
You go back to Benny Friedman playing with the Giants, he threw
that old balloon." For a little man to throw a giant ball for 20 touchdown passes in one season was a tremendous feat. In his first four
NFL seasons, Friedman tossed 54 touchdowns. No one else came
close.

As a result of others witnessing the success Benny had passing—and the subsequent jump in attendance—the league slimmed down the ball for the express purpose of making it easier to throw. As a matter of fact, the dimensions were modified twice to improve its aerodynamics to give us basically the same pigskin projectile that Jared Goff of the Los Angeles Rams and his fellow QBs throw today.

With the more conducive size and shape, it wasn't long before the next great passer—er, in this case, slinger—arrived on the scene.

SAMMY BAUGH

First-round draft choice Sammy Baugh came to the Washington Redskins in 1937 as a highly touted quarterback who'd just led the Texas Christian University Horned Frogs to a national championship. The first thing you noticed about the lean six-foottwo rookie was his unusual sidearm delivery, which he'd developed as a teenager. In his backyard, young Sammy used to take a rope and suspend an old tire from a tree limb, then practice passing for hours on end under the hot Texas sun. He'd try to throw the football through the swinging tire from every angle and distance, often while running, as if evading a stampede of opposing defenders. Eventually he could whip the ball sidearm out of a wide

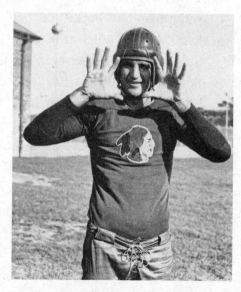

Punt, pick off, pass—Washington's Sammy Baugh could do it all.

Courtesy Washington Redskins

stance and thread the needle from any position. As the *New York Times* recounted in his obituary:

Baugh was taking the field for his first practice session with the Redskins when his coach, Ray Flaherty, handed him the football.

"They tell me you're quite a passer," Flaherty is said to have remarked.

"I reckon I can throw a little," Baugh replied.

"Show me," Flaherty said. "Hit that receiver in the eye."

To which Baugh supposedly responded, "Which eye?"[40]

In his first NFL season, Slingin' Sammy made All-Pro, racking up more than 1,000 yards in the air. He capped off 1937 by throwing three touchdown passes in the championship game, as Washington defeated the Bears, 28–21. In completing 18 of 33 passes for 335 yards, Baugh made a lot of believers on that cold, windy day in Chicago. And he had a style of play that was many years ahead of its time.

The Redskins operated out of a double wing formation, which was well suited to Baugh's passing skills, as it allowed four receivers—two backs and two ends—to get downfield quickly. Sammy had a quick arm, keen timing, and uncanny accuracy. He didn't wait for a receiver to get several yards open before risking a floating pass; instead, he threw to his spot just as his receiver made his turn. It was innovative because it meant that he could resort to passing for short yardage the way other teams relied almost exclusively on the off-tackle run. (Hmm, sounds like the early ancestor to Bill Walsh's West Coast offense!)

Like most tailbacks, Baugh could also run. Here was another interesting dimension he brought to the game because the defense never knew when he was going to abruptly apply the brakes and put the football in the air. In 1943 the multifaceted talent led the NFL not only in passing but also in interceptions—catching them, as a defensive back, not throwing them—and punting. As a matter of fact, he won four punting titles and retired in 1952 as the NFL's career punting leader (averaging 45.1 yards).

Slingin' Sammy was a winner. During his 16 years in a Redskins uniform, the club appeared in championship games five times, winning two. That alone caused attendance to swell, but Baugh was also a fan favorite who enjoyed signing autographs. At a time when most other teams were still struggling to fill seats, the Redskins enjoyed a string of 40 consecutive sellouts. The league, seeing how the aerial game excited the public, responded by enacting a new rule in 1938: a 15-yard penalty for roughing the precious passer.

SID LUCKMAN

One of Baugh's rival quarterbacks, Sid Luckman directed the Chicago Bears' attack from 1939 to 1950 as the point man behind a reimagined and lethal T-formation. With its man in motion, it bore more than a passing resemblance to today's basic set. However, Luckman came to the Bears from Columbia University, which used a single-wing formation. So it took a lot of extensive work and persuasion by George Halas to convince the 22-year-old Brooklynite that he was the right back to operate the T 2.0.

The concept behind the revised T-formation system, devised by Halas along with Clark Shaughnessy and Ralph Jones, was to spread the field and force the defense to cover more area. The coaching staff worked with Luckman for many, many hours, going over footwork, faking, spinning, setting up faster, and running one way and throwing another.

The training paid off handsomely. Luckman carved up NFL opponents, leading the Monsters of the Midway to four championships during the 1940s, including the historic mauling of Sammy Baugh and the Redskins, 73–0, in 1940. The United States entered World War II late the next year, but when players returned from the service, the next great quarterback emerged from the navy and would become synonymous with winning championships.

OTTO GRAHAM

From 1946 to 1955, Otto Graham piloted the Cleveland Browns to the championship game of their league (first the AAFC, then the NFL) *every year* during that 10-year period, winning seven of them. That will be a tough record to match, especially considering that most dynasties usually last only four or five years.

Graham led the NFL in passing yardage twice, was deadly accurate, and was the top-rated passer of his time as well as a smart runner.

Though quite capable, and although he did make some checkoffs, or audibles (seeing how the opposition is positioned then changing the play call at the line of scrimmage), Graham was not allowed to call his own plays. His coach, Paul Brown, felt he could gather more information from different sources while letting the quarterback focus on execution. Brown used a shuttling system of guards to bring plays into the huddle. However the plays were called, Cleveland's record from that era shows it worked, and worked great. (See chapter 13, "Otto-Matic.")

Speaking of huddles, ever wonder how this part of the game came about? Its origins were borne out of necessity when two distinctly physically challenged teams squared off against each other.

"You could pretty much trace it back to the Gallaudet school for the deaf in Washington, DC," Horrigan explained. "Football teams at deaf schools obviously did things by hand signals. But you couldn't be doing hand signals at the line of scrimmage against another deaf team, because they'd know what your play is. So, they'd go back, get in a circle, and communicate there."

In the huddle, all ears are tuned to the quarterback. What early pioneers such as Baugh, Luckman, and Graham (along with Norm Van Brocklin, Bobby Layne, and Bob Waterfield) share with today's great signal callers is an ability to perform a job that is really like no other. The physical requirements are rare enough: size, quickness, coordination, strength, and a special ability to throw the ball. Then there are the essential mental and emotional qualities such as intelligence, toughness, sound judgment, adaptability, courage, and, as the field general, the ability to lead other men. Out of the hundreds that have tried, some of the very best in recent years include Dan Marino, John Elway, Brett Favre, Jim Kelly, Troy Aikman, Dan Fouts, Drew Brees, Warren Moon, and Steve Young, to name only a few.

Two more names from the modern era should be acknowledged in depth for excelling in this most difficult of positions, where one must not only perform but also do so at a consistently high level, despite the constant threat of violence and guaranteed attrition that comes from facing continuous punishment from relentless marauders with each snap.

PEYTON MANNING

Son of a veteran NFL quarterback and brother of a two-time Super Bowl MVP, Peyton Manning produced one of the most prolific careers the position has ever seen. And he did it with a lot more than just QB genes. Yes, he was loaded with talent, and while overachievers work hard because they have to, Manning drove himself as if he lacked the natural skills.

Adam Vinatieri, entering his 25th season in the NFL in 2019, played against Manning during his 10 seasons kicking for the New England Patriots, then became the quarterback's teammate on the Indianapolis Colts in 2008. "I don't know if I have seen a player that has been more studious about the sport," he reflected of Peyton Manning, "I would put him up there in terms of wanting to know all aspects of the game with some of football's best coaches. He is a commander on the field," said the 46-year-old veteran, a surefire future Hall of Famer himself.

Manning, who retired on top in 2016 after having won his second Super Bowl, this one with the Denver Broncos, was one of the game's great strategists. He knew so much not only about his own players but also his opponents, his famous "Omaha" shout was simply a device that signaled as the play clock wound down he was going to Plan B and for subsequent protection adjustments by his teammates. Manning also excelled more than most signal callers about knowing where the blitz was likely to come from then being very precise with where he wanted to go with the ball. Those elements of his game made for a very successful combination.

After Manning set more than 30 school records at the University of Tennessee, the Indianapolis Colts made him the number one overall pick in the 1998 draft. A five-time NFL Most Valuable Player, number 18 set records that included 55 touchdown passes and 5,477 yards in a season—at the age of 37, in 2013—and accounting for nearly 72,000 yards and 539 TDs in his 17-year career.

Jim Sorgi, Peyton's backup with the Colts for five seasons, interacted with him closely in practice, on the sidelines, and in meetings.

"I remember studying film with Peyton," he said. "He was so intelligent and so observant because he would notice the smallest thing, and then, sure enough, come game time, it would be a difference maker. Could be a half-yard difference in where the safeties lined up. Could be a half yard inside or outside of where the linebacker positions himself, and he'd changed the play in the blink of an eye.

"Peyton had tremendous mental capacity," continued Sorgi. "He could pull something back from early spring training that had not been given any attention to since, and it would come into play in a key November game. If you tried to attack us one-on-one, Peyton would tear you apart with the type of personnel that we had. If the defense tried to sit back and play Cover 2 zone defense, he had the patience to just chip away. Peyton was a terrific chess player on the field because he could play any game you wanted to go with."

Basically, a Cover 2 splits the deep part of the field into two halves with the two safeties providing deep help for the outside corners. Underneath, the corners and linebackers split the fields into five short zones. It is up to the defensive line to generate pressure on the quarterback. To be most effective, linebackers have to be able to adjust to multiple threats in their assigned zone and corners have to be very physical and jam the receivers at the line.

With his highly competitive and zealous nature, teammates witnessed the little things Manning did that would often lead to victories. According to Adam Vinatieri, "Peyton was always intense all the time—not in a high-strung way, but he always knew what he was supposed to do and what everybody else was supposed to do. I think he elevated everybody's play.

"Whether we were on a team bus or on a plane," he recalled, "Peyton was constantly speaking with receivers and then the linemen about particular assignments, making sure they knew check downs etcetera."

(Check down is a term that refers primarily to a safety valve option for a quarterback on a pass play if his primary target is not open. Typically it is a running back that receives the throw.)

The way he ran his offense, with a no-huddle offense, with the checks at the line of scrimmage, it got to the point where if the defense tried to substitute, Manning would attempt to hurry up and run a play in order to get the 5-yard offside penalty. He didn't allow defenses to get too intricate. Watching Peyton, you could see how he processed information very quickly. In the no-huddle, he could sit at the line of scrimmage and toy with the defense for 15 seconds and get them to do something that he could take advantage of. And far more often than not, he did.

Adam Vinatieri has had the good fortune to play with both Manning and Tom Brady, but he pointed out how certain elements in Manning's style lent themselves to helping a team off the playing field if he wanted to.

"There are a lot of similarities and subtle differences between Tom and Peyton, which shows there are a lot of ways to win. I would say for Peyton, he was not only a coach on the field but also the general manager on the field, and, as a result, he even elevated the performances of coaches, ticket managers, and front office people. I think Peyton has a great potential to be a head coach or general manager with his micromanaging style—in a good way—tirelessly making sure everything is done in the proper way."

TOM BRADY

Ever since watching Joe Montana and the 49ers at Candlestick Park growing up in the San Francisco Bay Area, Tom Brady has used his own intensity and determination to propel a career guaranteed to find him in the Hall of Fame.

"Tom was a huge 49ers fan. A huge Joe Montana fan. He knew what success looked like," said Montana's longtime teammate Randy Cross, then an offensive guard, now a broadcaster. "Like young players on the pro golf tour today: they knew what Tiger Woods looked like and what it was going to take to be that good. And in a lot of the same ways, so did Brady. Now, was he that dominant in high school? No. Was he that dominant in college? No. But he knew what he wanted to be. And he made it happen. That is the most outstanding thing to me."

Brady's road hasn't always been smooth; as a matter of fact, his determination went to another level after scouts were not blown away by his performance at the NFL Combine in 2000. As a result, the University of Michigan grad was not picked until the sixth round, 199th overall, by the New England Patriots.

There are a lot of guys who come out of school as Heisman winners and all-Americans and other accolades who seem to backpedal when they get to the pros. Brady, in contrast, arrived without those honors, yet his diligence and continual improvement did not escape the knowing eye of head coach Bill Belichick. As he moved up the depth chart, the ever-determined young man was ready when destiny called.

In the second game of the 2001 season, nine-year veteran Patriots quarterback Drew Bledsoe was crushed in a tackle by New York Jets linebacker Mo Lewis. Suffering internal bleeding and a collapsed lung, he would be out for the rest of the season—and the following year, playing in a different city. The unproven Brady stepped in and never looked back. He carried New England to its first Super Bowl title that year, leading his team to five more NFL Championships since and has been league MVP three times. As the National Football League starts its one hundredth season, he is 42 years old and primed for more.

One of the reasons Tom Brady has enjoyed so much success is that he shares his coach's unrelenting intensity, work ethic, and ability to focus on the next opponent. Quarterback-turned-broadcaster Phil Simms, himself a two-time Super Bowl champion with the New York Giants in 1987 and 1991, offered this perspective:

"Tom is driven. Even Tom Brady, in all his greatness, knows the atmosphere in New England is such that you must *keep* delivering. There are no free passes. That keeps a person on edge—even one as decorated as Tom Brady, who could potentially go down as the greatest player in NFL history."

And it was in the eighties as well as the seventies and the sixties, some of the all-time great quarterbacks gave fits to many of even the best defensive units that were ever assembled. Most of those passers would certainly thrive in today's game as well.

FRAN TARKENTON

"Fran Tarkenton was such a competitor," praised Drew Pearson, a clutch receiver for the Dallas Cowboys from 1973 to 1983. Posing an intriguing question, he added, "Can you imagine Fran in today's spread offense?"

Most fans who saw him play, for almost all of the 1960s and 1970s, would likely agree. Not only did Tarkenton develop the art of scrambling to buy time (and, by the fourth quarter, wear out defensive linemen), but also he was a very good play caller and exhibited a strong arm for someone relatively small for the position, at six foot tall, 190 pounds.

With his quick feet and natural instincts, the impromptu magician might run . . . or might drop back 20 yards before deciding what to do. It all began following his very first pro game, in 1961, as a new member of the Minnesota Vikings. After getting really beat up by the Chicago Bears during an exhibition tilt in his rookie debut, the 21-year-old from the University of Georgia decided he needed to alter his approach and set out to change how the position was played—for his own survival.

His teammate Gary Larsen, a fearsome defensive tackle, recalled a classic example:

"Fran did not practice scrambling; it was all instinctive. He had an uncanny ability in sensing defenders in the area. I remember an exhibition game down in Dallas at the Cotton Bowl on a very, very hot August afternoon. Fran must've run sideline to sideline and ended up going out of bounds. Well, by the time he flipped the ball back to the ref, all four Dallas defensive linemen had their helmets off, gasping for breath. It was going to be a long day for them."

One of those chasing him, the great Cowboys tackle Bob Lilly, enjoyed the challenge. "Tarkenton was fun to play," he recalled, "because you never knew what he was going to do. He kept you on your toes."

Because he was so mobile on his own toes, the quarterback's arm was somewhat overlooked. Yet Tarkenton, in 13 seasons with the Vikings, interrupted by five years as a New York Giant, wearing number 10 in both cities, completed 342 touchdown passes and threw for more than 47,000 yards. Fran-tastic retired after the 1978 season as the NFL's all-time passing leader.

"I think he was underrated in that he also had a great ability for being accurate throwing on the run, and deep too," Larsen pointed out.

Vikings defensive end Jim Marshall agreed, saying, "He had a great arm and knew how to use it. A lot of quarterbacks after Fran tried to emulate his style of play because of his success."

Even other accomplished quarterbacks could not help but be impressed.

"I was a big fan of Fran Tarkenton," said Roger Staubach. "He was a playmaker who made things happen. Tarkenton was at the forefront of making big plays out of nothing."

But unlike the Cowboys' star passer, who won two Super Bowls, the Vince Lombardi Trophy eluded Tarkenton in three attempts, in 1974, 1975, and 1977. As all football fans know, fairly or unfairly, the quarterback position gets more glory and more blame than any other.

Tarkenton's counterpart in Super Bowl IX would know no such failure.

TERRY BRADSHAW

Terry Bradshaw's cannon of an arm guided the Pittsburgh Steelers to four Super Bowls, winning them all. Yet the early years of his career hardly offered any sense that the native Louisianan would go on to such greatness.

Linebacker Andy Russell played for the Steelers through the lean years and also played a part in a couple of their Super Bowl wins. He recounted his observations of the highly touted rookie from Louisiana Tech, the number one draft pick in the country in 1970.

"First, I thought Bradshaw was one of the most gifted quarterbacks of all-time. You put him on the forty-yard line, the fifty-yard line, and hang a tire through the goal post, and he could throw through it. He was so talented. It just took him awhile. I remember a couple times he'd throw a little swing pass to a running back like Franco Harris or Rocky Bleier, but he'd throw it nine hundred miles an hour.

"I asked him, 'It's a simple pass; why do you do that?' Terry said, 'I don't want Coach Noll to think I'm good at that pass. I want to go deep,'" Russell recalled with a laugh. "So that tells you how he was thinking as a young guy. But he had grown up significantly by the time we reached our first Super Bowl."

That kind of thinking would seem appropriate to someone with such impressive natural skills.

Steelers kicker Roy Gerela had watched Bradshaw for some time, having played against him in college as well.

"Terry was just a natural-born athlete," he said. "I don't think he ever lifted weights; he was gifted with strength. I still think he holds the state javelin throw record for Louisiana. He could throw a ball seventy-five yards without any effort at all."

And his views did not change when they became teammates.

"Punter Bobby Walden and I would go down to one end of the field while the defense was practicing on the other end; he'd wear us out with the velocity on his throws," Gerela recalled. "We'd get worn out running routes, so I'd tell Terry, 'Hey, we'll stand fifteen yards downfield.' So I'd extend my hand across the sideline, and he'd wear our hands out raw, so we'd say, 'Screw you, Terry,' and he'd just laugh. He had a good sense of humor, but Terry was a relentless worker. No one really talks about how much work Terry did on the side to improve." Another aspect of his game that tended to get overlooked was his ability to tally up yards on the ground. Not only was number 12 fast, but he was strong and tough to bring down.

Bradshaw struggled mightily his first two seasons, with a worrisomely lopsided ratio of just 19 touchdowns to 46 interceptions.

It did not help that local fans and the media questioned his intelligence and called him a country bumpkin. But as Terry matured, what emerged to complement his physical abilities were his leadership, courage, and a flair for rising to the occasion.

Vince Ferragamo, a third-year quarterback who started for the Los Angeles Rams in Super Bowl XIV against the Steelers in 1980, could not help but be impressed.

"What I loved about Bradshaw," he reflected, "was that he really had no fear. As a young quarterback observing him, that is a lesson I really learned that day. You take it to your opponent relentlessly without fear. He threw three interceptions that day, but he kept firing away and, guess what, he won. He just lit it up," said Ferragamo of Bradshaw's MVP performance. "I liked the way he carried himself. He was a gambler, but was never really fazed by anything and could throw the deep ball as well as anybody." The Steelers' 31–19 victory, coming on the heels of the previous year's electrifying seesaw battle against the Cowboys, which they held on to win, 35–31, was the last of Bradshaw's four Super Bowl titles. For the second year in a row, he was named the game's MVP.

It just seemed that under the brightest spotlight of football's biggest game Terry shined.

"The bigger the game, the bigger Terry got, and the more competitive he became," Gerela praised. "You could just see it in his eyes and facial expression. He was the kind of person who was not going to be denied. Terry got a bad rap from some writers early in his career questioning his intelligence. They put all that garbage in the papers, and, of course, fans believed all that. I think that tore his heart up a bit. But you have to admire him for overcoming all that and playing to the level he did. When you mention all-time great quarterbacks, well, Terry is four for four in Super Bowls. He has won it all each time. In my eyes, Terry Bradshaw is the best quarterback to ever play the game."

It was in two of those Super Bowls, among the best ever played, that Bradshaw outdueled another all-time great quarterback: Cowboy Roger Staubach.

ROGER STAUBACH

Like Bradshaw, Staubach was not lighting things on fire coming out of the gate as he entered the pros in 1969. For one thing, at age 27, he was an older rookie, having served four years in the US Navy, including a stint in Vietnam. Another factor, in Roger's eyes, was that he wasn't given a chance to succeed the Cowboys' charismatic quarterback, Don Meredith, who retired following the 1968 season, soon to materialize in the broadcasting booth on ABC-TV's *NFL Monday Night Football*.

For his first two seasons wearing the Cowboys white and blue, Staubach mostly watched highly capable Craig Morton. Though a year younger than the 1963 Heisman Trophy winner, Morton had racked up four years as Meredith's backup. Going into the 1971 season, head coach Tom Landry opted to platoon the two. The quarterback controversy only destabilized the team, which at the season's midpoint was a sluggish 4-3. In game number seven, a tough 23–19 loss against the Chicago Bears, Landry sometimes alternated quarterbacks on each play! The club's veterans, upset with the whole situation, blamed a lack of leadership on the field. In fairness to both quarterbacks, it's hard to take charge when you're commuting back and forth from the huddle to the bench.

"Patience isn't one of my overwhelming qualities," Staubach admitted, looking back. "Tom Landry, as good a coach as he was— and I think he's the best—didn't yet understand the importance of leadership at quarterback. We were losing a lot of continuity, as players were taking sides. I was frustrated. The team was floundering. Whether it was Craig or me, we needed to have one leader, and fast, as the season was slipping away."

Dallas Cowboys coach Tom Landry goes over strategy with his quarterback Roger Staubach.

Courtesy Dallas Cowboys

Landry chose Staubach, and the rest, as they say, is history. With number 12 at the helm, Dallas won its last seven regular season games, plus the division and conference championships, and then barreled over the Miami Dolphins, 24–3, in Super Bowl VI. Staubach, just a month shy of his 30th birthday, led the NFC in passing and helped the Cowboys to an NFL high 406 points. Combine that with a stingy defense that went 23 quarters without yielding a touchdown—the equivalent of almost six games—and it's easy to see how Dallas went from midseason mediocrity to an unbeatable juggernaut, avenging its heartbreaking 16–13 loss to the Baltimore Colts in Super Bowl V.

Perhaps patience wasn't his strong suit, but one trait that Roger possessed in spades was a capacity for instilling confidence in his teammates, as well as the coaching staff, that they were never out of a game. With his scrambling ability, arm, and leadership, he led by example time after time. Demonstrating uncommon grace under pressure, "Captain Comeback" engineered 23 game-winning drives (many in pivotal games) during his standout career.

One of his main targets over the years was receiver Drew Pearson, who joined the Cowboys in 1973 fresh from the University of Tulsa.

"We had a lot of confidence in Roger and never really felt out of any game," he said. "Respect is earned, and Roger earned it every day the way he carried himself. What made him great was his character. We knew he was somebody we could trust. He was somebody who was going to give everything to the game from his preparation, practice, and meetings. All we had to do was get in line and follow that example," Pearson explained.

"But most of all, it was his toughness. Roger was a tough son of a gun. And he was so competitive in everything that he did. We played pickup basketball. He couldn't stand to lose a little three-on-three hoop game. Those things are what made him. And my career was made by playing with Roger for eight years. There are a lot of great receivers in the NFL, but they don't have great quarterbacks, and, as a result, are not recognized as having had great careers."

Many of the great athletes have a tremendous competitive drive, but when you hear over and over from teammates, coaches, and opponents that Staubach's competitiveness was otherworldly, one has to wonder where it came from. After all, off the field Staubach is a mild-mannered, devout Christian who doesn't give off the impression he'd feed you to the lions whenever you stepped onto the playing surface.

By way of explanation, Staubach reflected on his childhood. "Well, when I was back in Cincinnati, my mother went back to work. My dad was a great guy, but neither of them finished college. I had terrific parents and some athletic skills. The drive came from those early days, wanting to make my parents proud in whatever I did. Sports seemed to be the avenue to pursue, as most kids in our community played several sports. Instead of becoming the best student in the class, I chose sports to excel at. But I did not slack off in my studies." Staubach chuckled. "I was very competitive in sports, but I was not a sore loser. Never was. If I lost, I had this fixation that I was going to make up for it the next time instead of sitting around and sulking."

BART STARR

Another quarterback with deep Christian beliefs and a strong competitive nature was Bart Starr. Despite his not possessing some of the higher skill levels shared by the best of the best, it is easy to forget that even though he had a deeply talented supporting cast composed of many Hall of Famers on both sides of the ball, and one of the best coaches of all time in Vince Lombardi, the Green Bay Packers quarterback was the key to their success. And some of his esteemed teammates are the first to acknowledge that.

"Bart's preparation was off the charts," said his longtime fullback and fellow Hall of Famer, Jim Taylor. "Knowing the defenses, his level of concentration and experience—it all went into Bart's performances because as quarterback you needed to maximize your production for your team to have the best chance at victory."

The other half of the great Packers running duo was halfback Paul Hornung, also a member of the Pro Football Hall of Fame and a Heisman Trophy winner. He was impressed not only by Starr's physical skills but also by his leadership.

"Bart is special. He is very smart. Plus, I think what Bart is not given enough credit for is his accuracy. More quarterbacks in the league had stronger arms, and it was Bart's precision that really was key to many of our wins. Bart was also a great leader. It was his huddle, leading by example, rarely making mistakes."

One of Starr's defining games was the appropriately labeled Ice

Bowl. The 1967 NFL championship game played on December 31 between Green Bay and Dallas took place, in the words of ESPN broadcaster Chris Berman imitating the voice of NFL Films' legendary narrator John Facenda, "on the frozen tundra of Lambeau Field," where the game-time temperature was 13 degrees below zero with a minus 48 windchill.

The entire season came down to one play, and it stands as a shining example of Starr's game intelligence on display. At first, it looked like the Packers might run away with the game, as two aerial touchdowns to receiver Boyd Dowler put Green Bay up quickly, 14–0. But in the second quarter Dallas took advantage of two Green Bay fumbles—even wearing gloves, the players could barely feel the football—to come within 4 points at halftime. At the beginning of the fourth quarter, the Cowboys stunned the Packers and the capacity crowd of nearly 51,000 by deftly executing a 50-yard halfback pass from Dan Reeves to a wide-open Lance Rentzel, the flanker.

With only five minutes remaining, Starr calmly and methodically drove the Packers down the field until they were faced with a third-and-goal at the Cowboys' 1-yard line. Only 13 seconds remained on the clock, and the Packers had used all their timeouts. Ordinarily, Coach Lombardi might have sent out Don Chandler to boot the easy field goal for a 17–17 tie and send the game into overtime. But with the field so hard and slippery, there was no such thing as a gimme. The plan was for Starr to give the ball to running back Chuck Mercein.

As Starr prepared to take the snap from the center, he decided otherwise. A handoff might be muffed; or Mercein could easily slip or stumble on the arctic surface and fall short of the goal line—and a third consecutive NFL title—as the clock ran out. Instead, number 15 tucked the ball in his breadbasket, put his head down, and plunged behind right guard Jerry Kramer into the end zone for a miraculous 21–17 win. Talk about guts! If his subordination had failed, how would *you* like to go back and face Coach Lombardi?

"I don't think there's any question that's why he is up there with the great ones, with his poise under pressure in the biggest games," said Dallas's Dan Reeves, who would become a longtime NFL coach. "The ones that can raise themselves when everything is on the line—that is hard; hard to find those kinds of players. He would definitely be one of the picks of all the ones you watched perform in clutch situations. And he was quite humble about all his successes."

JOHNNY UNITAS

In another of the NFL's defining games, a whole nation watching on television would bear witness to the talents of an emerging superstar, one who would go on to regularly produce in clutch situations.

The 1958 NFL championship game between the Baltimore Colts and New York Giants took place in historic Yankee Stadium on a dreary afternoon. Uneven, sloppy play and costly mistakes marked the contest for both teams. Still, the Giants, known for their great defense, held a 17–14 lead in the fourth quarter. It was then that young Colts quarterback Johnny Unitas took over. He basically invented the "two-minute drill" with his bold play calling and pinpoint passing. Baltimore tied the game on a 20-yard field goal. Then, in the league's first sudden-death overtime, Unitas carried his team to the New York 1 before letting running back Alan Ameche do the honors and lunge uncontested into the end zone.

In the opinions of some football historians, it was the greatest game in pro football history.

It had been a rough struggle for the young man to reach the pinnacle of the sport. But he would use this biggest of games as a showcase for what he could do. And he would go on to do it time after time.

Unitas, rejected by Notre Dame because of his frail build, had put up a fairly unspectacular collegiate career at the University of

Louisville. Nevertheless, in 1955 he was drafted in the ninth round by his hometown Pittsburgh Steelers.

He never made it past training camp. After the Steelers cut him, the 22-year-old worked construction. He also became the quarterback for the semipro Bloomfield Rams in western Pennsylvania, where he made a grand total of $6 a week while playing on an all-dirt field. Even at this low point, the stoop-shouldered, thin-legged passer never lost confidence in his abilities.

And when coach Weeb Ewbank of the Colts gave the young hurler one more chance to make it in the NFL, Unitas would make the most of it and go on to produce one of the great Cinderella stories in sports history. He quickly earned the respect of teammates and opponents alike for his perseverance, cool confidence, play calling, and, most of all, his toughness.

His favorite target, receiver Raymond Berry, recounted the kind of player Unitas was:

"He would have made a tremendous linebacker. He had that kind of mentality. He was physically and mentally tough. I remember one game against the Chicago Bears where a defensive end broke in and slammed John across his face. It broke his nose, and there is blood all over. We pleaded for him to call a time out. He just calmly shook his head no, picked some dirt up off the field, and rubbed it up his nose. Then he stepped in the huddle, called the play, and we scored a touchdown."

Center Bill Curry played both with and against Unitas. As a member of the Rams late in his career, he became good friends with 14-time Pro Bowl defensive tackle Merlin Olsen, part of Los Angeles's menacing defensive line of the 1960s known as "the Fearsome Foursome." One day after practice, Olsen came up to Curry and really wanted to know how the skinny QB could be so cool and tough.

"Is Unitas human?" he asked in all seriousness. "I would tackle him with my shoulder pad on his sternum as hard as I could, driving him to the ground, trying to break him in half. Just to see him flinch one time. And I looked down in his face at those cold, blue eyes, and they never changed expression, they never flinched. And I knew, dadgummit, he is going to get us again. All he would do is get up and throw a touchdown pass." That is the way he made opponents feel.

Curry had his own observation from the six years he spent snapping the ball to number 19, beginning in 1967. Although the game is emotional, and coaches and teammates can get a player all pumped up, this quarterback led his team in a different way.

"John Unitas was the offensive captain and Fred Miller was the defensive captain," he recalled. "In the locker room before each game, Fred would say something to fire us up and then turn to John and ask if he had anything to say. Unitas always said exactly the same thing. Standing by the door, feet crossed over each other, he would look around the room, stare everybody in the eye and calmly say, 'Talk is cheap. Let's go play.' Then he'd turn around and walk out to the field. We would run through the wall for him." Unitas led Baltimore to three NFL championships and one Vince Lombardi Trophy, while leading the league in passing four times.

Another great quarterback from Pennsylvania—born roughly a Unitas-to-Berry-bomb distance away from where Johnny U was raised—would take his own style of cool to the highest levels of the sport.

JOE MONTANA

Like Unitas, Joe Montana was comparatively slight of build. His teammates often kidded him about his "bird legs." And pro scouts had some hesitations about his arm strength. But, like the great ones, it was what was inside Joe that made him a winner.

"Instinct. His physical ability and his instinct," said 49ers owner Eddie DeBartolo. "He wasn't a massive quarterback like Ben Roethlisberger, but what he was is a winner. He didn't have the strongest arm, but it was as strong as it had to be. Joe had a heart that was three times the size of any other quarterback in the league. And he knew how to win."

After winning a national championship as the quarterback for Notre Dame, Montana's success continued right on into the NFL. He guided the San Francisco 49ers to four Super Bowls and came out on top each time. Joe Cool's reputation for being unflappable under pressure is exemplified by the fact that he was the first player to be named Super Bowl Most Valuable Player three times, in 1982, 1985, and 1990. The one time he didn't win MVP, in Super Bowl XXIII in 1989, the honor went to his favorite receiver. We think you know who that is, but if not: Jerry Rice.

Super Bowl XXIII is one of two defining Joe Montana performances. Playing at Joe Robbie Stadium in Miami, the 49ers found themselves trailing the Cincinnati Bengals, 16–13, with only 3:20 left in the hard-fought game and the ball on their own 8-yard line. Number 16 calmly drove them down the field, completing 8 of 9 passes for 92 yards and rifling the game-winning touchdown pass into the waiting arms of wide receiver John Taylor with only 34 seconds left.

Jerry: I think what made Joe so great was his coolness under pressure. Joe never got rattled. He came to work every day totally committed. He was all in, and he never pointed fingers. He was also that comeback kid. I knew if we had time on the clock, we'd win that football game. The textbook example is the final drive in Super Bowl XXIII. Him leading us all the way down the field to win it was something we were accustomed to seeing every day. He was a great motivator who made players around him better. His teammates were totally committed to him.

Montana completed 23 of 36 passes for a Super Bowl record 357 yards and two touchdowns.

But his numbers would be even more impressive the following

January at the Louisiana Superdome, in Super Bowl XXIV despite going up against one of the best defenses in the league. Coach Dan Reeves's Denver Broncos were the stingiest team in the NFL, allowing just 226 points all season. They also led the American Football Conference in forcing turnovers, with 43.

That did not faze Joe Cool. Montana destroyed the imposing defense, going 22 for 29, good for 297 yards and five touchdowns. Three of them went to Jerry Rice, including a 20-yard hookup to open the scoring in a game that ended 55–10. A lot of coaches on the opposite side of the field walked off in stunned bewilderment. Retired Dallas Cowboys safety Charlie Waters, a defensive coach on the Broncos, was one of them.

"Joe had a great feel to scramble around and salvage a play," he said appreciatively. "What separates an All-Pro player from an average player has to do with awareness and making decisions, and that guy could make some decisions. He could read what you were doing and could see into the future. He knew where the players would be going. We went in to Super Bowl XXIV with the best defensive team in the league. He was throwing on timing, and it was mind-boggling." At halftime, San Francisco was already way out in front, 27–3. "We went into the locker and just looked at each other and said, 'Oh my God, what the hell has happened here?!'"

Denver defensive coordinator Wade Phillips summed it up: "We tried rushing three men, four men, five men. We tried everything, and nothing worked. The way Montana was playing, we could've rushed eleven or dropped eleven, and it wouldn't make any difference. He was uncanny."

Montana was a perfect fit for head coach Bill Walsh's West Coast offense, a system in which the quarterback often moves around more than in a conventional offense with specially designed rollouts and bootlegs that are tied in with the patterns being run by the receivers (including running backs and tight ends) emphasizing more of a quick, horizontal passing attack as a form of ball control.

Quick, mobile, able to read defenses rapidly, tremendous balance and rhythm with decisive footwork, he also possessed a fine touch and an ability to put the ball where the receivers could do something with it after they caught it. And in Walsh's system, Montana knew there was always a place to go with the ball.

And the ball found the end zone more often than not when it counted the most.

"Some guys get tighter the bigger the game is, but Joe just seemed to get better," said guard Randy Cross, who helped protect the prized quarterback in the first three of those four Super Bowls. "If every game were a Super Bowl, Joe would have retired undefeated."

CHAPTER FIFTEEN

TAKING FLIGHT

The tall, skinny wide receiver paced nervously back and forth in the Green Bay locker room before playing his first game in the NFL. Rubbing his queasy stomach, the rookie admitted to a veteran sitting on the bench that he was scared to death about going out there and facing opponents who were much bigger and faster than he faced in college. The vet looked up from tying his cleats and with an easy grin assured him everything would work out fine.

With the first pass thrown his way, the rookie hauled in Arnie Herber's high-arching throw in full stride past midfield. He raced on toward the goal line, untouched. His first play as a professional was an 83-yard touchdown pass. It was the only touchdown of the day, as Green Bay knocked off its rivals, the Chicago Bears, 7–0.

As they walked off the field after the game, that same vet slapped the young man on the back, smiled, and said, "What was there to worry about, kid?"

DON HUTSON

With that debut on September 22, 1935, that nervous young man, Don Hutson, would change the game forever. The fleet-footed receiver, who'd led the University of Alabama to a national championship, harnessed a lethal repertoire of novel moves that defenders had never seen before—false steps, jiggling hips, shoulder feints, and all at different speeds—to leave them sprawled on the ground, wondering where he'd gone. In just 11 seasons, Hutson led the NFL in receptions eight times; set a league record by catching at least one pass in 95 consecutive games; and, in 1942, became the first receiver to top 1,000 yards in a single season, with 1,211. He and the football were so inseparable that as a defensive back, he intercepted 30 passes. Oh, yes: as a placekicker, he made 176 points after touchdown without a single miss and connected on seven of eight field goal attempts. Is it any wonder that the years he played, from 1935 to 1945, would become known as the Hutson era?

One of his most frequent victims over the years was division foe the Bears. Hutson was so good that Chicago coach George Halas quipped famously, "I just concede Hutson two touchdowns a game, and then I hope we can score more." Most coaches and opposing players came to feel the same way about the Alabama Antelope. As Greasy Neale stated, "Hutson is the only man I ever saw who could feint in three different directions at the same time."[41] A lean six foot one and 180 pounds, the two-time league Most Valuable Player led the Packers to championships in 1936, 1939, and 1944. When he retired at 32, he owned just about every NFL pass-receiving and scoring record. Hutson was so supreme that with every fifth pass he caught, he crossed the goal line. His 99 touchdowns was a record that stood for 44 years. He had 488 career receptions; over the same period, the second-best pass catcher in the league, Jim Benton of the Cleveland Rams, caught 288.

A sprinter in college, running a 9.7-second 100-yard dash, Hutson used a loping gait to lull defenders into making a split-second guess as to where he'd go on his move, and that was all the time he needed. In the blink of an eye, he'd be off, with nothing but chalk lines and open field before him. Almost single-handedly, Don Hutson revolutionized football and moved it toward today's emphasis on the pass as the crucial offensive weapon.

In the modern era, there was a receiver who reinvented the bomb, and he too used his tremendous speed to find his way into Canton.

RANDY MOSS

From the very first time Randy Moss put on an NFL uniform in 1998, he promised to "wreck the league" as a rookie for the Minnesota Vikings. Like Hutson before him, Moss made defenders spend most of their time looking at the back of his jersey. Part of Moss's confidence and drive came from the fact that he'd been passed up by a few teams in the draft. One of those teams was the Dallas Cowboys.

On Thanksgiving afternoon in 1998, before 64,366 fans in a sold-out Texas Stadium, Dallas fans witnessed what they could have had. Even though the rookie caught just three passes, each one was for a touchdown. Talk about being a deep threat: Moss averaged 54.3 yards per catch that day in leading his team to victory.

That was just the start.

Moss had caught two touchdowns in his first-ever NFL game, and a record 17 as a rookie. He led the league in touchdown catches five times.

The Freak, as he was lovingly called, proved to be one of those rare talents that the NFL has seen only a handful of times in its history. The six-foot-four receiver would enjoy a long and distinguished career serving as a focal point for two of the greatest offenses ever to play: the 1998 Minnesota Vikings (556 points scored) and the 2007 New England Patriots (589). (See chapter 35, "They Wore Out the Chain Gang.")

Moss's brilliant speed allowed his quarterbacks to place the ball on predesignated spots, confident that he would arrive there alone.

His teammate on that record-setting Patriots team, Wes Welker, saw firsthand what set Moss apart: "He is just a freak of nature. He'd tell Tom Brady, 'Don't throw where I'm at, because I'm not really running yet. So just launch it, and then I'll really start running.' And I was sitting there going, 'This is ridiculous. I'm using every ounce of my being just trying to get off the line of scrimmage.' He's talking about running and moving through lower gears running. He certainly made it easier for Tom to get him the ball."

What the great receivers all have in common is their ability to make it easy for their quarterback to get them the ball. Some relied on precise patterns and great hands, others used their size in traffic, a few had tremendous leaping ability, some were just plain tough and could endure the pounding over the hard routes across the middle. To name just a few, Antonio Brown, Julio Jones, James Lofton, Steve Largent, Cris Carter, Art Monk, Andre Reed, Terrell Owens, Charlie Taylor, and Tim Brown represent a cross section of those talents a receiver must have for success. In the late fifties and early sixties, the development of the tight end had a great impact on the game's development.

RAYMOND BERRY

Raymond Berry roamed the field as a split end and the main target of Johnny Unitas for the Baltimore Colts from 1955 to 1967. His Hall of Fame numbers include 631 receptions for 9,275 yards, averaging nearly 15 yards a catch, and 68 TDs. The six-time Pro Bowler led the NFL three times in both receptions and reception yardage, and two times in touchdowns. His team won the NFL crown twice.

However, the statistic that perhaps best captures his essence is that in 13 seasons, Raymond Berry fumbled only one time. This concentration, awareness, and deep mental tenacity helped the six-foot-two Texan overcome a number of physical challenges. A weak and deficient sacroiliac joint occasionally caused misalignment in his back, which, in turn, affected his legs, so that, for a time, one leg was slightly shorter than the other. To help secure his spine for all the twists and turns of being a pass receiver, Berry wore a back brace throughout his career. Furthermore, his vision was weakening to the point that he went to a specialist to be fitted for special contact lenses, which was quite rare for the times, as the technology was still experimental.

"It just so happens I was working with one of the pioneers in the contact lens field at the time," Berry recalled. "He fitted me with contact lenses specifically designed for use by a football player. A normal person does not go through the many different wild eye gyrations that a receiver goes through: looking over your shoulder, being hit about the head. So he designed a pair that would be slightly larger and more stable under such rigorous conditions. It worked perfectly."

On road trips to the West Coast, Berry would wear dark goggles to help him see the ball against the bright sun. It made him look like a World War I biplane pilot, but they were effective for him until his eye doctor came up with tinted contact lenses, which worked really well.

Berry's obsessions, such as with eyewear, translated to other areas of play. He squeezed Silly Putty, the malleable, taffy-like kids' toy found in any five-and-dime, to exercise his hands and wrists as a hedge against fumbling. (Apparently, it worked!) The eccentricities increased. For example, "The game pants that we had were of very high quality, and they gave you maximum flexibility and firmness, so I started wearing game pants for practices," he explained. "I probably drove equipment managers nuts too."

THE TIGHT ENDS

It began as a role with a tricky skill set. On one hand, tight ends have to be big yet mobile enough to help fellow offensive linemen lead the blocks at the point of attack for the running back to go through. Then, on the very next play, he might be the receiver asked to bring the precise skill of a pass catcher to immediate action, all while his concentration is being severely tested by an army of free-flying safeties and punishing linebackers bearing down on him with bad intentions. Should he manage to hang on to the pass, he's then supposed to get the short, hard yards to provide first downs for his team. Talk about demanding.

Mike Ditka was one of those early pioneers at tight end. Possessor of both the right size and demeanor, he blew away everyone with a tremendous rookie year in 1961 for the Chicago Bears. He caught 56 passes for more than 1,000 yards, averaging 19.2 yards a reception—unheard of for the position—and also scored 12 touchdowns. Ditka's 75 catches in 1964 would be a long-standing record for tight ends.

The former player, coach, and broadcaster talked about being part of that early group of tight ends that helped shape the position: "Bill Wade [the veteran quarterback of the Bears when the young Ditka arrived in Chicago] used to throw to me at a time when no one threw to tight ends. They started doing that when Baltimore's John Mackey and I came into the league. Green Bay had a fine tight end in Ron Kramer, but they did not throw to him a lot. He was perhaps the best blocking tight end the game has seen."

Mackey debuted in 1963 and immediately became another burly player with a bad disposition and good hands to make a name for himself at tight end. Coming out of Syracuse University, the native New Yorker was a human wrecking ball with an unyielding temperament. Not only could he provide jarring blocks like a guard, but also, at six foot two and 225 pounds, his massive thighs and a nasty straight-arm made him a veritable tank rolling downfield with the ball.

He blocked as well as the other tight ends did and yet had the power to toss aside defensive backs as well as the speed to outrun them to the end zone. Mackey simply became the most feared tight end in football. Opponents would watch game films week after week, just in awe as time and again they saw how Mackey would block, release, take a short pass, and then proceed to bounce off defenders or stiff-arm them into the ground and outrun the others for a touchdown.

But that position was also the seed for the more receiver-oriented role that tight ends play today after the revolutionary offensive guru Don Coryell, head coach of the San Diego Chargers, drafted Kellen Winslow in 1979.

The six-foot-five, 250-pound tight end from the University of Missouri was big enough to play anywhere along the offensive line. Yet he was fast enough and sure-handed enough to become a primary receiver in the high-powered San Diego offense, which featured Dan Fouts throwing to a bevy of talented receivers such as John Jefferson, Charlie Joiner, and Wes Chandler, along with James Brooks and Chuck Muncie coming out of the backfield. (See chapter 35, "They Wore Out the Chain Gang.")

Despite being only one of many weapons, Winslow was the most productive receiver in pro football between 1980 and 1983. His success gave rise to a multitude of tremendous tight ends who would shine in the NFL with their reception skills. Two, Tony Gonzalez and Antonio Gates, will likely end up in the Hall of Fame.

What the new wave of tight ends share is not only great hands but also awesome speed for their size. However, one of the all-time greatest wide receivers, one who would own several NFL records by the time he was through, probably would not come close to beating those larger tight ends in the 40-yard dash.

That wasn't all. Meticulous about his weight, Berry made a note of everything he ate, studied nutrition, and carried a weight scale on the road with him. At one point, he became fixated on eating liver as a dietary staple. "The single most important thing I learned was the power of liver, one of the most potent items on all the food charts," he said. "Though I didn't really enjoy it, I really began to eat liver several times a week during the season. I remember having some oral surgery done during the off-season, and the dentist said to come back in twenty-four to forty-eight hours, as he wanted to see how things progressed. When I returned and he examined me, he said he had never seen anybody heal this fast. He asked me what I thought my explanation for that was. I attributed it to eating liver. It is a very potent food."

A more orthodox part of his regimen entailed studying film, although that, too, he did compulsively. And when he wasn't doing that, the graduate of Southern Methodist University (SMU) would head to the stadium when no one was around to practice cross patterns or polish a multiple-moves system using all different kinds of fakes—inside, outside, double, triple—to fool defensive backs so that he had a balanced attack going short or going deep with different looks. They were key to his success because Berry never scared anyone with his 4.8 speed. "I came into football with a lot of limitations," he acknowledged candidly. "I wasn't fast, big, or strong. I knew I had to concentrate more, practice harder, give more of myself than most."

Another key was the fortuitous timing of the arrival of a struggling quarterback named John Unitas in 1956. "It was an interesting time," Berry recalled. "He had been cut by the Steelers, and I was due to be cut by the Colts coming back for my second year, having done very little in my rookie year. Thinking we were in the same situation, we started working together. It was fortunate that we had a head coach, Weeb Ewbank, who had learned from Paul Brown in Cleveland to leave the quarterbacks and receivers on their own on the field after practice so they could work on their timing and patterns together. So, we'd run route after route after route, developing our timing and an understanding between us."

Practice, practice, practice. All of it helped him develop the precision route running, great hands, and an assortment of moves to get enough separation that made Raymond Berry a top pass catcher of pro football. In the Colts' overtime win over the New York Giants in the 1958 NFL championship, Berry set a championship game record with 12 catches for 178 yards and a touchdown. In the final drive of regulation and the overtime session, he came up with five big catches.

When his brilliant playing days were over, ironically Berry's first job in coaching involved working directly with the fastest player ever to lace up cleats in the NFL: Bob Hayes of the Dallas Cowboys, who arrived in 1965 as a two-time Olympic gold medal sprinter at the 1964 Summer Olympics in Tokyo.

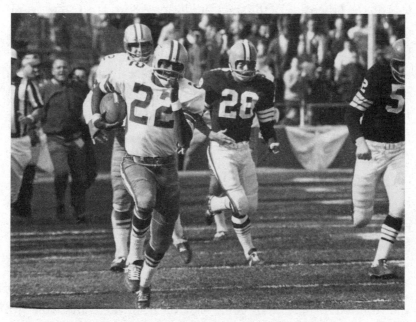

Bob Hayes's world-class speed changed the game forever.

Courtesy Dallas Cowboys

BOB HAYES

Many track athletes have sought success in pro football, but Bob Hayes was a football player who happened to be the world's fastest human. His fleet-footed approach to play forced defenses to devise zone coverages to corral the world-class sprinter. One of his quarterbacks on the Dallas Cowboys, Roger Staubach, vividly recalled that speed in action.

"One time, we were at our own fifteen-yard line, playing the New York Giants. I hit Bob about midfield, and Spider Lockhart was all over him. By the time Bob crossed the goal line, he was five yards ahead of Spider. I believe it was the longest pass play of my career. That is how fast Bob Hayes was," Staubach said. "So, teams had to get away from playing man-to-man. And Bob Hayes had a lot to do with teams converting to a zone defense."

Bullet Bob, who grew up in Jacksonville, Florida, went to college on the other side of the state, at Florida A&M. His Dallas teammate Dave Manders remembered the impression he made during his rookie season. "Don Meredith would get to the line of scrimmage and recognize the defense," said the center, "and if they were in a certain formation, I can still hear it today: 'Two! Five! Nine! Hut! Hut!' We went to the freeze protection. Everybody went to the inside. We pick off the blitz, and Hayes is wide open by ten to fifteen yards, and he's gone. It worked quite frequently."

Sprinters who tried football before and after him often failed because they lacked good hands or durability, and they were often lean and thin muscled. Hayes was five foot eleven and a muscular 185; he looked like a football player, not a sprinter. With the help of receivers coach Berry and Frank Clarke, the Cowboys' all-league split end (who would move to tight end), Hayes learned to improve his hands and run better routes. His game took off from there and won him posthumous induction in the Pro Football Hall of Fame in 2009.

Charlie Waters, the All-Pro defensive back who played his entire career for Dallas, had ample opportunity to assess Hayes every day in practice and observe him from the sidelines on game day. "When one person changes the way defenses have to play, he is worthy of Hall of Fame credits," he said. "Once he figured out a way to catch the ball, he took off. Everybody tried to coach him a certain way to catch it. But I said, 'Bob, do whatever way is comfortable for you. You're going to be wide open, and nobody's going to catch you.'"

In 1971 Hayes would be joined by another future Hall of Fame receiver, Lance Alworth, and together they'd help Dallas go all the way and defeat the Miami Dolphins in Super Bowl VI.

LANCE ALWORTH

Lance Alworth added an exclamation point to his 11-year career by scoring a touchdown in that Super Bowl, but it was his nine years with the San Diego Chargers that got him into the Hall of Fame, making him the first player from the American Football League to be so honored.

However, it almost didn't happen, because like the first great receiving superstar, Don Hutson, Alworth didn't feel he was talented enough to play pro ball. Though he was a productive tailback at the University of Arkansas and a skilled punt returner, at six feet and 180 pounds, he didn't think he could take the pounding in pro ball. Thus, as a rookie in 1962, he was pleased when Chargers head coach Sid Gillman converted him to flanker. Unfortunately, a torn muscle in his right thigh limited Alworth to just 10 catches in four games. It also cast doubt among fans and the media, who hinted that he was a bit gun-shy when it came to contact.

All that was put to rest in 1963. In his first full season, Alworth became an instant star, with 61 catches for 1,205 yards and 11 touchdowns, averaging nearly 20 yards a catch. The Chargers won 12 of 15, including the AFL championship. Lance was an all-star.

Not only did he make it a habit to play with assorted ailments—broken ribs, a bruised back, fractured wrist, and pulled muscles—but Alworth also displayed an acrobatic flair that brought crowds to their feet, especially when he was on the other end of a long bomb from quarterback John Hadl, grabbing the pass in traffic with a perfectly timed leap.

Willie Brown, a Hall of Fame defensive back for the Oakland Raiders, faced down some of the all-time great catchers in a pass-happy league filled with talent at that position, such as Otis Taylor, Don Maynard, and Lionel Taylor, to name a few. "The guy that gave me the biggest challenge was Lance Alworth," he said. "Had to play him twice a year. He had tremendous speed and jumping ability, and the thing about him was that when he came off the line, you really didn't know if he was going to run a pattern or block. There is no question he could block; he did some things that were unbelievable for a guy his size. I had to watch him all the time, and he'd go very hard on every single play."

Among his many achievements, Alworth, a seven-time All-Star, would break Hutson's record of catching at least one pass in 95 consecutive games and lead the AFL in receptions three times. Another accomplished receiver in the junior league, Charlie Hennigan, a two-time AFL champion with the Houston Oilers and a five-time AFL All-Star, once said, "A player comes along once in a lifetime who alone is worth the price of admission. That player is Lance Alworth."

PAUL WARFIELD

Paul Warfield never topped the league in receptions, but he had few peers when it came to gaining yards per catch and turning receptions into touchdowns. Despite playing for two of the greatest running teams of all time (the Cleveland Browns with Jim Brown and then

This is how most defenders
saw Miami wide receiver
Paul Warfield: from behind.

Courtesy Miami Dolphins

Leroy Kelly in the sixties and the Miami Dolphins' backfield trio of
Jim Kiick, Larry Csonka, and Mercury Morris in the seventies), the
Ohio State graduate's talents were well known in both leagues.

"The word to describe Paul Warfield was *smooth*," said his Miami teammate Larry Little, a Hall of Fame guard. "If he played
today, nobody could touch him. He played for us, a ground-game-
oriented team, yet he made All-Pro with limited catches simply because everybody knew how great he was. And he was a fierce blocker
who would knock your head off."

Along with Bob Hayes, at the time of his induction in 1983,
Warfield was the only receiver enshrined in Canton who averaged
more than 20 yards a catch. He led the NFL twice in touchdown
receptions (career total: 85), was an eight-time Pro Bowler, and in
1973 Warfield caught 11 touchdowns on just 29 catches in helping
Miami to its second straight world championship.

Dolphins quarterback Bob Griese had this to say about what
made Warfield such a special player: "Paul had tremendous speed

and hands, but, really, he was simply smart. We'd have two-a-day practices back in August. After the second practice, no one stayed out. But Paul used to ask me to work with him on routes, and it wasn't just simply a given pattern, but rather he'd devise the most complex coverage, and that is what we'd work through. It could be a DB jamming him and a safety coming over the top. We'd work out any number of scenarios, and it'd become shorthand during a game. He was always thinking ahead."

Oakland's Willie Brown remembered that, just like Lance Alworth, Warfield demanded his best efforts. "We had some really good battles over the years," he said fondly. "He was a very good route runner. I remember this one time, he came off the line about five yards and jumped in the air, changing directions! I couldn't believe it. I told myself, 'Okay, I'm going to have to stay on top of this cat because he's got too many moves!'"

JERRY RICE

Over the course of a record-filled 21-year career, Jerry Rice demonstrated many of the skills possessed by the greats such as Hutson, Moss, Hayes, Berry, Warfield, Alworth, and the rest. Number 80 was smooth, played through injuries, posed a deep threat, had terrific hands, was dedicated to practice, and exhibited a propensity for winding up in the end zone.

The decade of the 1990s was a record-breaking time for receivers. Just the year before, Seattle's Steve Largent had retired holding three NFL career records: catches (819), yards (13,089), and touchdowns (100). All three toppled in 1992, when Art Monk of the Washington Redskins surpassed his catch total, with 847; James Lofton of the Buffalo Bills reached 13,821 yards; and Jerry Rice caught 10 more touchdown passes to bring his eight-year total to 103. Rice would end up leading them all. After retiring in 2004, the

49ers receiver held the records for catches (1,549), yards (22,895), touchdowns (197), as well as all-purpose yards (23,546). Inducted into the Hall of Fame in 2010, Rice is considered by most to be the greatest receiver of all time.

It all started with his approach: you play like you practice.

"Jerry's motor never stopped," observed Joe Montana, the quarterback who launched so many of those air deliveries. "He believed in practicing all out. He'd take a catch and run it all the way for a touchdown. No wide receivers did that in practice.

"At speaking engagements, I tell the audience, 'Do you think it is a coincidence that Jerry is the all-time touchdown leader by far in the NFL?' No, because that is what he did every day. That is the way he was, and he was fun to be around."

Jerry: By always practicing at one hundred percent tempo, that prepared us for whatever we faced. Having the scout team in game situations, for example, was a real good tool for getting us ready. It was very important for me to work hard in practice to get that timing down. For when it came to the ball game, it was like I had a clock in my head; if I got held up for a second, I might have to cut my route off a bit shorter. Joe was the same way, so we were able to get into a rhythm, and that is when you deliver an offense at its best. It becomes second nature during the pressure situations of a game. It comes to a point where the preparation has been so ingrained in your mind and body that you don't even have to think about it. The everyday repetition pays off. Some players slack off during the week and then say, "Let's turn it on today." Well that doesn't work. You have to do it every day.

Like many of the very best, routine was very important for the veteran receiver to stay in that all-important rhythm. Even though he didn't take home his uniform to wash or bring a scale on the road like Raymond Berry, Jerry had a few quirks of his own tied into those components.

> Jerry: Weight was very important to me. If I wasn't at a certain weight—if I was, like, at a hundred ninety-two pounds, and my target weight was a hundred ninety—I'd go to the stadium early to work out. I'd ride the bike, do the StairMaster, run stadium steps, calisthenics, until I got where I wanted to be at. Then go run around during the game. And afterward, I'd be at one eighty-four!
>
> On game day, I could never eat. I was consumed by butterflies— always anxious to get out on the football field. If I ever had breakfast, it'd be fruit. If we had a pregame meal for a later kickoff, I could not eat anything. I wanted to be hungry. I wanted to be light. And it always worked in my favor. People couldn't believe I did not consume much food yet had so much energy. I could just run all day. I think it was just the way I trained my body, because I was not the type of person to eat a big breakfast. When I got up in the morning, I'd work out.
>
> Regarding my uniform, I was superstitious as to how my jersey had to fit just right and be tapered to where defenders couldn't easily latch on to it. I had to have brand-new pants. I had to have new shoes. Everything had to be spanking new. I completely drove our equipment manager and trainers crazy! They'd yell, "Uh-oh, here comes Jerry!" because I'd try on so many pairs of pants right before the game.

And it all started as an accident. Or perhaps fate. San Francisco head coach Bill Walsh told the story that he was out on the road for a scouting trip. After a long day, he came back to his hotel room, plopped down in a chair, and flipped on the TV. It just so happened that what appeared on-screen was a game between two NCAA Division II football teams.

As Coach was reviewing some notes from that day's work, he'd glance up at the game occasionally. Every time he did, it seemed that one player on the Mississippi Valley State University Delta Devils was making all the plays. By the time the young man called "World" scored his fifth touchdown of the game, Walsh was so certain that this Jerry Rice would make a terrific wide receiver in the NFL that he arranged a draft-day trade to move up in the first round. (The nickname, incidentally, was bestowed upon Jerry because of his ability to catch pretty much anything thrown in his general direction.)

Walsh's instincts were, of course, correct. Rice would become one of the all-time best, but he endured a rocky start to playing at the professional level. He is the first to admit that in his rookie season of 1985, he dropped some passes he should have caught. After one miserable half against the Rams, he burst into tears in the locker room at halftime. But this is a similar story shared by other greats such as baseball's Mickey Mantle and Willie Mays. Both were just nineteen when they graduated to the majors in 1951, the Mick with the New York Yankees and the Say Hey Kid across the Harlem River with the New York Giants. Their first weeks playing at the sport's highest level were full of struggles, tears, and self-doubt. By midseason, though, it was clear to all that the two young power-hitting, fleet outfielders were stars in the making.

That poor outing against the Rams may not have been the turning point for Jerry, but from that year on, it would be the defensive backs who'd need hankies, as number 80 became the most dominant touchdown scoring-receiver in the history of the game. "He came in the league as a shy person with a tremendous amount of talent," recalled the 49ers' owner, Eddie DeBartolo. "We had traded up to get him before New England, who really wanted him. Bill loved him. As the years went by, he got more and more confident with that great talent, and he worked hard at it.

"And now he is where he belongs: in the Hall of Fame. Without question, the greatest all-round football player who has ever played the game. His talent and total dedication to the game. I was surrounded by guys like this. If you had a list of the top twenty players that ever played this game, Ronnie Lott, Joe Montana, and Jerry Rice are probably in the top ten, with Jerry being number one."

"Win or lose, Bill always wanted more from me.
He was the greatest motivator and coach."

Copyright Michael Zagaris

CHAPTER SIXTEEN

LAMAR HUNT: A CORNERSTONE OF THE NFL'S MOUNT RUSHMORE

Arguably the three most influential people in the history of the National Football League—the ones whose faces would be etched in the NFL's version of Mount Rushmore—are George Halas, Pete Rozelle, and Lamar Hunt. Of his many contributions, it was Hunt's creation of the American Football League in 1959 that transformed professional football and helped turn a fairly regional sport into a national pastime.

Despite coming from one of the wealthiest families in the world—his father was Texas oil tycoon H. L. Hunt—it was sports that flowed through Lamar Hunt's veins. His passion was so consuming that, in his youth, friends nicknamed him "Games." And it was in games where the Texan found fulfillment, despite the fact that his athletic skills were limited. While studying geology at Southern Methodist University, he spent three years on the Mustangs football team as a reserve running back and wide receiver, playing behind a junior college transfer who would go on to enjoy great success in the NFL: Raymond Berry.

Lamar's talents lay in the business side of the spectacle of sport.

Because he had the heart and soul of a sports fan and saw football for its entertainment value, Hunt was a natural when it came to understanding the entertainment world and how it could promote the game. And he did not wait until he graduated to pursue endeavors in that world. His first sporting venture, while still in college, was operating a miniature golf course and a baseball batting cage.[42]

By the time he passed away in 2006, Lamar's vision and his passion shaped the sporting landscape of this country like few others have before him. His love of athletics extended beyond football, leading to his involvement in six different professional sports leagues and seven sports franchises. He was essential to the development of both the North American Soccer League and World Championship Tennis, and was also a founding investor in the six-time world champion Chicago Bulls of the National Basketball Association. But for the humble, reserved, and compassionate Dallas resident, who resembled an accountant in his dark-rimmed glasses, short-sleeve button-down shirts, and well-worn shoes, his greatest achievement was building a successful professional football league.

Despite his resources, Hunt had to overcome many obstacles to get the AFL up and running. In fact, the idea for a new league came to him only after his dream of owning an NFL franchise failed to bear fruit.

NFL team owners, having already weathered the Great Depression and World War II, as well as swatted down challenges from the All-America Football Conference and two other upstart leagues, were reluctant to consider expansion just when their business was reaching a new level of prosperity in the late fifties. Adding teams meant more fingers in the pie.

Early in 1959, Hunt, then just 26, spoke with George Halas, chairman of the NFL expansion committee (and about to enter his fifth decade as coach of the Chicago Bears) and Commissioner Bert Bell about the possibility of putting a new franchise in Dallas. Halas and Bell concurred that the league was not ready to expand.

Furthermore, the NFL had ventured into that city in 1952, with disastrous results. The ownership group of the Dallas Texans, unprepared for the financial losses it would incur, forfeited the franchise after an 0–7 start. So, the league took over the team and basically reverted to its old road club system, this one operating out of Hershey, Pennsylvania, for the last five games, all on the road. The Texans managed to win one game that season (their lone victory was a "home" game against the Bears, 27–23, in front of 3,000 fans at Akron, Ohio's Rubber Bowl) before quietly folding, seemingly drawing the curtain on professional football in Dallas for the foreseeable future.

With expansion out, Hunt set his sights on buying an existing team, then transplanting it to Dallas. He flew to Miami to meet with Walter Wolfner, the millionaire owner of the woeful Chicago Cardinals. The club was hemorrhaging money, having finished last in the East Division six of the last 10 years. Wolfner rebuffed him and, as Lamar was leaving his office, added haughtily that there were many other interested parties who wanted to own an NFL franchise. In other words, forget about it, son.

But the stubbornly optimistic young man would not be denied bringing pro football to his city. On the flight back to Dallas—sitting in coach as always, despite being the son of a billionaire—a lightbulb went on in Lamar's head. He proceeded to sketch out his concept of a brand-new football league, including everything from budgets to schedules to costs versus revenues to potential team locations. Lamar preserved that stationery, as he did so many other artifacts, in a limestone cave north of Kansas City, Missouri. These included notes he doodled on, snippets of phone conversations—anything he felt held some interest or jogged his memory or brought him a chuckle.[43]

As a baseball fan, Hunt was inspired partially by Major League Baseball's tremendously successful two-league structure in which teams shared television revenue. And from his studies and observations, shaped partly by the extraordinary impact of the nationally televised 1958 NFL sudden-death championship game between the Colts and the Giants, Hunt saw that the pro game was becoming very popular—and increasingly attractive to TV programming execs. He was convinced that plenty of cities would support a football team.

First, he sat down with Bud Adams, also the son of an oil magnate, in Houston. I'll join in, said the 36-year-old entrepreneur. Hunt then used his extensive contacts to crisscross the country and line up potential owners for his fledgling endeavor. A mid-August 1959 meeting of the Foolish Club (a self-coined term of endearment) nailed down commitments from owners in Denver, Los Angeles, New York, and Minneapolis. Buffalo and Boston were added a few months later, and when Minneapolis dropped out to join the NFL as the Vikings, Oakland came aboard. Later in the fall, Joe Foss, former governor of South Dakota and a charismatic World War II fighter ace, was named the new league's commissioner.

Earlier, Lamar had received some help from an unexpected fairy godfather: Bert Bell. The NFL commissioner had been in the hot seat lately, as the US Congress was pressing him to explain why the National Football League shouldn't be prosecuted for being a monopoly. When Bell learned of Hunt's plans, he asked the potential business rival if he could announce the emerging league at the Congressional hearings. By claiming to welcome and cooperate with the newcomer, Bell would be demonstrating to the US Justice Department's Antitrust Division that the NFL had no wish to preserve its virtual monopoly. Sure, Bell was using him for his own gain, but Hunt didn't care. The appearance before Congress would be great PR for the American Football League, set to kick off in September 1960.

Cooperation between the two parties did not last long. George Halas contacted both Hunt and Adams and offered them NFL franchises if they would scrap their plans for the new league. The two refused—after all, they had commitments from six other franchise owners. The senior league tried another underhanded tactic, announcing abruptly that it would field a team in Dallas after all come 1960—to be called the Cowboys—and possibly other expansion clubs in other cities where the AFL had already staked a claim.

The shootout between the NFL and AFL was on.

Taking a script from his beloved entertainment world, Lamar Hunt would lead his posse across the hostile frontier of a daunting new venture with the same quiet confidence and steely determination of Hollywood leading man Gary Cooper. Like Cooper in so many classic Westerns, Hunt would ultimately come out ahead in his showdown with the NFL.

Hunt's Texans fared only a little better than the previous Dallas team had. Struggling to secure a sustainable share of support in Dallas competing against the NFL's Cowboys, and despite winning the AFL Championship in 1962, Hunt moved his team to Kansas City before the beginning of the 1963 season. The Chiefs gradually built themselves into a reliable contender, becoming the first club to represent the junior circuit in the first Super Bowl, against Green Bay in January 1967. Always innovative, the founding father of the AFL christened the championship game between the two league champions (the first two events were called the AFL-NFL World Championship Game then became known retroactively as Super Bowls) in addition to proposing using Roman numerals for a majestic touch. And after Vince Lombardi died of colorectal cancer in 1970, it was Lamar who suggested naming the Super Bowl trophy after the coaching legend. He was also a driving force behind implementing the two-point conversion, team revenue sharing, and the momentous AFL-NFL merger.

Founder of the American Football League and owner of the Kansas City Chiefs, Lamar Hunt was one of the most influential people in the history of the sport.

Courtesy Kansas City Chiefs

CHAPTER SEVENTEEN

THE LONG SHOTS

From an idea he scribbled down on a piece of airline stationery, Lamar Hunt's vision of a new professional football circuit became a reality on September 9, 1960. The first game in American Football League history took place that Friday night, with the Denver Broncos defeating the home team Boston Patriots, 13–10.

Though the debut was full of turnovers, poor passing, and shoddy tackling, the AFL was in play. Some of the players were NFL castoffs, some were bartenders and warehouse workers, and many had some college experience, but, in general, there was more pro football experience in the front office and coaching positions than on the field. Six of the eight head coaches had NFL backgrounds. And the two who didn't—Hank Stram, coaching Hunt's Dallas Texans, and Boston's Lou Saban—were "rookies," but they would become two of the most successful coaches in the league.

What was not successful was the AFL's first season. Despite enthusiastic players and clever promotions, the league did not receive a lot of attention from the media. Most franchises lost money—a lot of it. Hunt's team, despite having to compete against the NFL's expansion Cowboys for fans, was one of the few to hold its own, largely due to the owner's clever promotions at the Cotton Bowl. There was a Huddle Club, where, for $1, a youngster received a membership card, a Texans T-shirt, and an end zone seat to all home games. Teenagers were admitted free to the end zone if they presented a ticket stub from a high school game. On Meet the Texans Night, the hoopla consisted of kicking 65 footballs into the crowd (Can you imagine that happening today?) and distributing free orchids to women patrons. On Friends of the Barber Day, free admission was granted to all barbers who wore their white coats to the stadium.[44]

Lamar also hired 30 attractive women, mostly teachers, to serve as Texans Hostesses. Their job was to drive around door-to-door in Renaults emblazoned with the team emblem to help push season ticket sales during the summer.[45] Later, following his divorce from his first wife, one of the pretty women behind the wheel, Norma Knobel, would become Mrs. Hunt.

With their owner's showbiz flair, the Texans averaged a solid 24,500 at home games, highest in the league in 1960.

Crucial to the AFL's survival was television. Rising star producer at ABC, Roone Arledge, had a flair for making fans connect with athletes using what would become known later as his "Up Close and Personal" approach. It helped take the upstart league to new heights after it signed a five-year contract with ABC worth $10 million in 1960.

Arledge was influential in convincing the league to place players' last names on the backs of their jerseys (the NFL traditionally had not) and for using innovative camera moves and graphics to help a pass-happy, high-scoring league forge deeper, more personal connections with its fans. Many games included covering the sidelines and interviews with players not wearing their helmets, to help increase awareness of the new league.

And so, on December 23, 1962, millions of football fans across the country got to watch the East Division's Houston Oilers host the Dallas Texans of the West in the third AFL championship game.

Dallas had a super backfield consisting of running backs Abner Haynes and rookie of the year Curtis McClinton Jr., along with new quarterback Len Dawson, voted the AFL player of the year after having bounced around the NFL for five seasons. The Texans won eight of their last 10, finishing 11-3, which netted Stram the coach of the year award. (The American Football League played a 14-game season; the NFL would break with tradition the following year and add two games to its 12-week schedule.)

The Oilers, also sporting an 11-3 record, were the AFL's version of the mighty baseball New York Yankees, seeking their third consecutive league championship. The first two postseason contests pitted them against the West Division's Chargers, who moved south to San Diego from Los Angeles in 1961 but got edged out by Houston's potent offense both times. The Oilers' quarterback since their inception was 35-year-old George Blanda, also an NFL hand-me-down. He'd played 11 seasons for the Bears, mostly as a second-string QB, but was valued more for his foot than his arm. He doubled as the placekicker for Houston, too.

Playing in Houston's Jeppesen Stadium, a glorified high school field, 37,981 boosters—about 1,000 above capacity—turned out, many of them having to sit on folding chairs set up around the running track that ringed the field. The visitors struck first. Following an interception by linebacker E. J. Holub, Dawson drove the Texans downfield but had to settle for a 16-yard field goal by Tom Brooker. (More about him in a moment.) Then Abner Haynes, lining up as a flanker, displayed some fancy footwork, corralling a perfectly placed pass and running it in for the score. Before the half was over, Blanda got picked off again. This time Haynes bulldozed his way into the end zone, making it 17–0.

But the second half was a mirror image of the first. Blanda, relying on experience, threw a touchdown pass, then booted a 31-yard field goal early in the fourth quarter to bring Houston to within 7 points. Now the Dallas defense, led by future Hall of Fame safety

Johnny Robinson, stepped up. The former Louisiana State University star tackled fellow LSU Tiger Billy Cannon at the goal line, forcing Blanda to kick a field goal; then he intercepted a Blanda pass at the goal line to prevent another score.

An incoming weather front had sent the temperature plummeting and churned up angry wind gusts. The conditions didn't seem to affect Blanda, who piloted the Oilers to a game-tying touchdown and then almost won it with his toe.[46] But as the 17–17 game entered its final minutes, the Dallas defense stiffened once again. Linebacker Sherrill Hedrick blocked Blanda's 42-yard field goal attempt, setting the stage for a sudden-death finish in what would become pro football's first six-quarter game.

The Texans appeared sluggish as overtime began, and Blanda marched the Oilers from his own 9-yard line to the Dallas 35. But he was picked off yet again, this time by Bill Hull, and the first overtime period wound down without a score. Len Dawson, looking back on this red-letter game for the AFL, explained the Texans' approach.

"We were not moving the ball that well, and they did have a strong offense," he said. "Main thing is, we did not want to give the ball away, so my play calling was pretty conservative." Dallas had a pretty fair kicker in rookie Tommy Brooker, who made 54.5 percent of his field goal attempts that year. "The idea was not to turn it over, so when we could get to that point, we'd have a good shot at it."

Sure enough, 2:54 into the second overtime, Brooker connected from 25 yards out to end pro football's longest day to that point. Consuming nearly 78 minutes, the exciting game was hailed as the AFL's finest hour to that point. Sportswriters and broadcasters universally declared it the league's coming-of-age moment.

Still, several franchises remained rickety financially, including the league champs. H. L. Hunt, when asked how long his son could afford to lose $1 million a year, replied famously, "About a hundred and fifty years." He probably could have, too. But Lamar was determined to climb out of the red and into the black. To that end, he relocated the team to Kansas City and renamed it the Chiefs. Barron Hilton, vice president of the Hilton Hotels chain, had already moved his Los Angeles Chargers to San Diego, while on the opposite coast, a business consortium headed by an entertainment mogul named David "Sonny" Werblin assumed ownership of the hapless New York Titans. He would make sweeping changes, starting with a name change to the New York Jets in time for the 1963 season.

Werblin, born and raised in Brooklyn, began his career as a talent agent during the big band era. You didn't need to be a talent professional though to see that the Titans had very little, and not a single marquee player. The new Jets president sought to rectify that. At the AFL draft in November 1963, the team outbid crosstown rivals the Giants for the services of highly coveted Ohio State star running back Matt Snell. And at the following year's draft, Werblin claimed and soon signed a quarterback from the University of Alabama. Joe Namath had just taken the Crimson Tide, coached by the legendary Paul "Bear" Bryant, to an NCAA Division I championship. Werblin saw more, though, than a prodigious football talent. The 21-year-old from Beaver Falls, Pennsylvania, possessed star quality and would no doubt thrive playing in the media capital of the world. The St. Louis Cardinals of the National Football League had also drafted Namath, but Werblin landed him by laying out the then-unimaginable sum of $427,000—equivalent to approximately $3.4 million in today's dollars. A string of injuries over the years would prevent Namath from reaching his enormous potential on a consistent basis, but as far as Jets fans from that era were concerned, the investment was well worth it.

The war for talent between the two leagues was intensifying to the point where it would threaten the very existence of professional football.

Pete Gogolak, a Hungarian immigrant, became pro football's first soccer-style kicker and helped lead the Buffalo Bills to back-to-back AFL championships in his first two years, 1964 and 1965.

However, following his rookie season, he was displeased with the contract offered him; so displeased that he deliberately took a pay cut, played out his option, and became a free agent in time for the '66 season. (See chapter 38, "The *Foot* in Football.") Before Gogolak, it was almost unheard of for a player to jump from one league to another. Willard Dewveall, a receiver with the Bears, switched to the Oilers in 1961, but he was going to quit Chicago regardless and was not nearly as well known as Gogolak.

Over the next five years, although the leagues competed for new collegiate talent, they adhered to an unwritten understanding not to sign each other's veteran players, as it helped depress wages. However, the New York Giants, playing in the NFL's largest market, found itself saddled with struggling rookie kicker Bob Timberlake, who made just one field goal in 15 attempts (a .067 percentage) in 1965. Seeking an upgrade—as well as constantly looking to steal the rising Jets' thunder—the late Tim Maras's son Wellington, now the Giants' co-owner and president, decided to ignore the owners' gentleman's agreement.

Gogolak explained what happened: "There was a clause that said when you signed with a team, you were obligated to play for them for two years. But one could play out their option. However, in order to do that, you had to take a ten percent pay cut in your second year. I took the cut and was playing for nine thousand, nine hundred bucks. Again I had a very good year." Indeed he did, accounting for 115 points, second best in the league, and leading all AFL kickers in field goals made.

"A week before my contract ran out on May 1, 1966, Buffalo offered me twenty K. I said, 'You guys were playing the game with me for two years. I am not going to sign.' Of course, being an established player, I was hoping that every other AFL team was going to call me bidding for my services. So, I became a free agent—but nobody called me. Clearly, the AFL owners talked to each other. It is the boys' club, and I understand. But over in the NFL, Giants owner

Wellington Mara said, 'I want this guy.' Wellington called, and I soon signed with the Giants for four years. Thirty-five thousand dollars per year, no bonus."

The Gogolak signing further accelerated the interleague war for talent.

Acquiring players became a cloak-and-dagger game. With its Operation Hand-Holding efforts, the NFL had each franchise provide a group of coaches and scouts to form a pool of babysitters and hand-holders. Often they would hide out a prospect until the draft was completed and the prized player had signed with the team that drafted him.

On November 28, 1964, the day of both the NFL and AFL drafts, Chiefs scout Lloyd Wells convinced Otis Taylor, a gifted receiver from Texas's Prairie View A&M, to evade his NFL handlers by slipping out the back window of his Dallas hotel in the wee hours. They raced to the scout's car and drove all the way to Kansas City, where Taylor would produce an exceptional career.

Prospective players were usually provided a fine luxury hotel room large enough for a bunch of friends, plus fine food and music. If an NFL coach or scout found that the young player wasn't interested in his club, he would try to steer him to another team in the league. The NFL's talent-signing system was developed to a point where young players would be offered open contracts, meaning they could choose the club they wanted to play for, as long it wasn't a team from the dreaded American Football League.

Veterans in both leagues were becoming disgruntled over the wages being doled out to unproven rookies. To them, the amounts were simply inconceivable: for instance, linebacker Tommy Nobis, the number one overall pick in the 1966 NFL draft, signed with the brand-new expansion team the Atlanta Falcons for a reported $600,000, while running back Donnie Anderson took down $711,000 from the league champion Packers. The owners grew concerned not only about the exorbitant salaries, which they feared would eventually price them out of business, but also by the deterioration of interest and morale they began to observe among the other players, which is to say most of them. If left unchecked, that would soon spill over to deterioration at the gate and in TV ratings.

By the spring of 1966, the battle for rookie talent as well as proven stars had reached such epidemic levels that it threatened to ruin professional football on the whole. In addition to hefty paydays for rookies, established talent were also looking for better deals. It was announced that Roman Gabriel, the Rams talented quarterback, had signed a three-year contract with the Oakland Raiders to become effective in 1967 or after Gabriel had played out his option in Los Angeles. Bears tight end Mike Ditka was talking contract with the Houston Oilers as was 49ers quarterback John Brodie. Green Bay star running back Paul Hornung was said to be in negotiations with the New York Jets. Things were spiraling out of control.

Lamar Hunt, as always the voice of reason, and looking to better the sport, met secretly with Dallas Cowboys general manager Tex Schramm regarding a possible merger between the two leagues. How secretly? The two of them convened in a car in a parking lot at Dallas Love Field Airport to hammer out the details.

On June 8, 1966, Commissioner Pete Rozelle of the National Football League officially announced that the NFL and the AFL had reached an agreement to merge into a single league by 1970. In the meantime, the two leagues' champions would meet each January in a new AFL-NFL World Championship Game. That game would later become known as the Super Bowl.

As for the structure of the new National Football League, it would have a National Football Conference (NFC) and an American Football Conference (AFC). The NFL brought 16 teams to the party, including the New Orleans Saints, who would begin play in 1967; the AFL, just the original eight, plus the Miami Dolphins, set to bow in 1966, and two years later, another expansion club, the

Cincinnati Bengals. Commissioner Rozelle insisted upon an equal number of teams in both conferences, or 13 apiece. Therefore, come 1970, three NFL teams would have to switch to the American Football Conference: Cleveland, Pittsburgh, and Baltimore. The move helped solidify the merger and led to some of the game's most exciting and hard-fought rivalries. Each conference was then divided into three divisions: Western, Midwestern, and Eastern. The first two had four franchises each, while both Eastern Divisions had five. Future expansion would no doubt take care of the imbalance.

| The NFL in 1970 ||
AFC	NFC
Western Division	**Western Division**
Denver Broncos	Atlanta Falcons
Kansas City Chiefs	Los Angeles Rams
Oakland Raiders	New Orleans Saints
San Diego Chargers	San Francisco 49ers
Midwestern Division	**Midwestern Division**
Cincinnati Bengals	Chicago Bears
Cleveland Browns	Detroit Lions
Houston Oilers	Green Bay Packers
Pittsburgh Steelers	Minnesota Vikings
Eastern Division	**Eastern Division**
Baltimore Colts	Dallas Cowboys
Boston Patriots	New York Giants
Buffalo Bills	Philadelphia Eagles
Miami Dolphins	St. Louis Cardinals
New York Jets	Washington Redskins

To settle the championship, a three-week round of playoffs was instituted. The first round was to include the six divisional winners, along with the second-place teams with the highest winning percentage. The four winners of the first weekend's games would fight for their respective conference championships on the second weekend, and the two survivors—the NFC champs and the AFC champs—would face off in the Super Bowl.

This system was still four years away. From 1966 through 1969, both leagues went through several permutations. The '66 season retained the same structure as before, with each league sending the best in its West, the AFL's Kansas City Chiefs and the NFL's Green Bay Packers, to the Los Angeles Memorial Coliseum for the first interleague championship game on January 15, 1967. Pro football now wrapped around into the new year.

The American Football League looked the same in 1967, too, but, oddly, the National Football League underwent a drastic renovation, even though it would be for only three seasons before the football world as fans knew it was to be upended. Now there were four divisions of four teams each: Capitol, Century, Central, Coastal. The AFL had its one championship match between East and West, which the Oakland Raiders won in a 40–7 rout of Houston. The NFL, however, added an extra game to its postseason: with four divisions, you had the Coastal and Central winners go at it (Rams versus Packers), and the next day, the teams that topped the Capitol and Century Divisions (Dallas and Cleveland). To get to the Orange Bowl, the site of that year's grand finale, Green Bay and Dallas treated fans to the classic Ice Bowl.

The NFL remained stable for the final two seasons before the merger, but in 1969—its tenth and final year—the AFL decided to squeeze another game into the postseason by adding the two second-place teams as wild cards. Certainly the 11-3 Chiefs were deserving; they happened to have the misfortune of sharing the West Division with 12-1-1 Oakland. But the 6-6-2 Oilers, who needed binoculars to see the 10-4 New York Jets *way* ahead of them? It could have been embarrassing if Houston had somehow knocked off the Raiders and been one game away from Super Bowl IV. Presumably, the AFL powers that be sighed with relief when Oakland rolled to a 56–7 laugher. The other wild card, Kansas City, squeezed past both the Jets and Raiders to reach Tulane Stadium in New Orleans, where the Minnesota Vikings would await them.

Super Bowls I and II were anticlimactic affairs, especially given the thrilling 1965 and 1966 NFL championship games between Green Bay and Dallas. (The AFL title games those years? Not so much—both runaways.) The Chiefs surprised everyone by keeping pace with the Packers through the first half, trailing just 14–10. But they never scored another point, while Vince Lombardi's team added three touchdowns to win, 35–10. The next year, against Oakland, it was more of the same. Bart Starr and company gunned the engine from the start and put the game out of reach by the third quarter. Thanks to a meaningless late touchdown by Oakland, the 33–14 final score made the contest appear more competitive than it really was.

Both times, the representatives of the American Football League had been outmatched and outclassed. Having had to fight for respect its entire existence, the losses hurt. But with the merger two years away, the junior circuit was to win back much of its pride by taking Super Bowls III and IV, shocking the sports world in the process.

First came cocky Joe Namath and the New York Jets' historic upset over the formidable Baltimore Colts in Super Bowl III. Then Len Dawson and Kansas City returned as 14-point underdogs to avenge their humiliation from three years earlier, this time against the Vikings. They took the field wearing a patch on their red and white jerseys reading "AFL-10," signifying the American Football League's 10-year existence. It was the last game to be played by an AFL team.

The night before Super Bowl IV, Lamar Hunt hosted a small dinner party in New Orleans. After telling the story of how the Minneapolis franchise double-crossed the AFL back in 1960, the mild-mannered, plain-speaking owner began pounding his fists on the table and started yelling "Kill! Kill! Kill!" to the mostly festive crowd.

His team would scalp the "Purple People Eaters" defensive line and quarterback Joe Kapp in a dominating 23–7 victory. But the real victory was for the man known as "Games," whose vision and determination more than a decade earlier had taken pro football to such levels of success and popularity that it is hard to quantify or express the extent to which pro football is indebted to Mr. Hunt.

The American Football League produced many Hall of Fame players and became a popular draw over the years with its exciting, distinctive brand of wide-open ball. It had some of the game's most potent offenses, such as the San Diego Chargers and Houston Oilers (see chapter 35, "They Wore Out the Chain Gang"), but it also had champions, like Lou Saban's '64–'65 Buffalo Bills, that won primarily with strong defense. It also saw a great rivalry develop between the Oakland Raiders and Kansas City Chiefs, one that still lives on (see chapter 23, "Bad Blood"). With stirring victories in Super Bowls III and IV, and having forced a merger with a long-established league that had been in play for nearly a half century, Lamar's long shots had made it.

★ ★ CHAPTER EIGHTEEN ★ ★

THE GREAT SPORTS MARRIAGE

NFL broadcasting on a national scale has come a long way since the DuMont Network televised the 1951 championship game between the Los Angeles Rams and the Cleveland Browns. It was a back-and-forth heavyweight battle that saw multiple lead changes and was tied at 17 until a pair of future Hall-of-Famers Norm Van Brocklin and Tom Fears connected for a game-clinching 73-yard pass play to give the Rams the crown. The live telecast of Super Bowl LI in 2017, the only Super Bowl game to be decided in overtime, currently holds the largest total viewership in US television history, peaking at 172 million viewers. That topped by tens of millions some of the greatest TV moments of all time, including the final episodes of *M*A*S*H* and *Cheers*, the farewell of American institution Johnny Carson from *The Tonight Show*, and the miniseries *Roots*.

You couldn't have scripted a more dramatic spectacle, as Tom Brady and the New England Patriots, facing a 25-point deficit in the third quarter, got up off the mat and suddenly poured on a relentless attack until they tied the dumbstruck Atlanta Falcons 28–28 with under a minute left in regulation. Then, after winning the overtime coin toss, the Patriots, acting like they had a plane to catch, stormed toward the end zone like Civil War general William Tecumseh Sherman on his march from Atlanta to the sea. Brady pitched the ball to running back James White, who burst through four Falcons tacklers to cross the goal line for a 34–28 come-from-behind victory. Talk about Must See TV.

More generally, the NFL's regular season accounts for the largest consistent annual nationwide viewership for any television event in US television history, representing almost 70 percent of US households, more than 80 percent of total US television viewers, and more than 60 percent of the 2019 US population of roughly 328 million individuals.

Now, if you ran a stopwatch during a typical three-hour NFL telecast, the cumulative action would total something like 12 minutes. So how can that translate into such a ratings winner year after year? What is it about the sport that lends itself to television, and what is it about the elements of a broadcast that make football such compelling programming?

"Football is not merely the sport best suited to the screen, judging by ratings and viewer responses, it simply is one of the most important aspects of American television culture," said Michael Weisman, former executive producer for NBC Sports. "Any good game has more excitement than most prime-time series. The action isn't faked or scripted. Football may be the most honest excitement available on television. This is real drama."

And it is that action, those violent moments in which oversize gladiators hurl themselves full speed at each other, that draws viewers faithfully week after week, season after season.

"It's brutality. It is three-dimensional chess. With twenty-two players on the field, there are eleven skirmishes going on," noted David Hill, former chairman of Fox Sports. "It's controlled violence. There's nothing better."

It is both the physical mayhem and the pace of the game that make it a near-perfect television property. Through the decades, technical innovations have added greatly to the visual appeal. Instant replay, slow motion, and isolated camera shots provide reviews of the spectacular action that in many respects created an art form. For example, the skills of cameramen (as well as the audio engineers' tweaking and placement of the microphones) using their telephoto lenses make it possible to pull in tight on the action so that the viewer all but feels the intensity as the behemoths at the line of scrimmage—in the pits—collide and claw for the man with the ball; or sees the laces on an arcing, rotating football thrown with a perfect spiral and about to sail into a receiver's waiting hands.

These innovations have widened the appeal of the game because they have allowed viewers to get more personally involved in the process, and to develop a better feel for the game and its contestants.

"A lot of it has to do with the way the game itself is played," said Fred Gaudelli, NBC's producer of *Sunday Night Football*. "Think about the end of a football game: you are not going to get nineteen time-outs like you would at the end of a basketball game, where it becomes a foul-a-thon and basically saps the drama out of the game. You might get a time-out in an NFL game, but it's only the last thirty seconds unless you take commercial, and that late in the game, we're pretty much out of commercial time."

Football's visual appeal on television eventually overtook baseball as America's national pastime. Chris Myers, a veteran network multisport play-by-play announcer, talked about the attraction of football over baseball in terms of scheduling. "There are only sixteen games a year, so each week is a happening," he said. "One of the problems with Major League Baseball is that the season is just too long, so the regular season doesn't mean as much. In the NFL, every game takes on major, major significance."

There was a time, however, that the NFL relied more on radio, film newsreels, and the live gate to build the sport. It would be nearly 20 years after the league kicked off before its first game was even televised. NBC aired the Brooklyn Dodgers–Philadelphia Eagles game from Ebbets Field on October 22, 1939, which was transmitted back to the studios in Manhattan and to the few sets that were available and in use mostly in the New York area.

Despite the struggling DuMont Network having only 18 primary affiliates in 1954, two years before it would cease operations, along with a number of stations with "secondary" affiliations (dwarfed by the number of stations available to NBC), it did broadcast Saturday-night NFL games during the 1953 and 1954 seasons. It was the first time that National Football League games were televised live, coast-to-coast, in prime time, for an entire season. This predated *Monday Night Football* on ABC by 17 years. In 1958 NBC televised the NFL championship game in which the Baltimore Colts defeated the New York Giants, 23–17, in overtime. This showing catapulted the NFL to new levels of popularity nationwide and opened up new possibilities to the league, to sponsors, to fans, and to network executives.

It would be young commissioner Pete Rozelle who saw the possibilities of how television could make the NFL achieve economic status as a major player on the pro sports scene. A former Rams PR man who became the team's general manager, Rozelle immediately grasped that the NFL's future would be intimately tied in with the rise of television as America's most important medium of popular culture. While more traditional owners were worried about how this new-fangled broadcast source might affect their ticket sales, the commissioner foresaw how television could not only grow the game by exposing the NFL to fans unable to attend in person, but also provide its own significant revenue stream by allowing the league to sell valuable broadcast rights and advertisements. Over the course of his nearly 30 years in that position, Rozelle's keen insights about the value of network television partnerships were a key factor in the NFL's ascent to the pinnacle of the American sports business world.

In 1961 Rozelle rolled up his sleeves and quickly moved the league's offices from the outskirts of Philadelphia to Rockefeller Plaza in New York to help the NFL establish better ties to the television and advertising industries. One of the first orders of business was convincing the league's owners (and Congress, which had to approve a special exemption to antitrust law) to agree to a new revenue-sharing plan that allowed the NFL to sell its leaguewide broadcast rights as a single package and then distribute the proceeds in equal shares to all teams.

The innovative plan made it possible for small-market teams such as the Green Bay Packers to remain financially competitive with teams located in larger, more lucrative media markets. The economic parity thus helped to maintain at least a semblance of on-field competitive balance. With the owners agreeing to that, Rozelle proceeded to negotiate the NFL's first leaguewide TV deal, with the CBS network consenting to pay $4.65 million a year for the right to broadcast NFL games through the 1962 and 1963 seasons. Under the revenue-sharing plan, that meant that each NFL team would begin the season with over $300,000 in its coffers. Rozelle's economic model quickly demonstrated its worth, since each franchise was essentially guaranteed profitability before even playing a single down or selling a single ticket.

The NFL's new competitors, the freshly formed American Football League, signed a five-year, $10.6 million contract with ABC in 1960. Then in 1964 NBC signed a deal with the AFL for more than $7 million annually over five years.[47] These TV contracts played a major role in helping to keep the AFL viable until its merger with the NFL later in the decade.

All those vast sums television networks pay out for rights makes their choice of on-air personnel all the more important. Even though the formula has been set for decades, pairing a seasoned play-by-play announcer with a game analyst (usually a former player or coach), having a superstar name in the booth is no guarantee of ratings success.

A few of the very best game announcers that set the standard

and enjoyed long careers include Ray Scott, Curt Gowdy, Pat Summerall, Jack Buck, Dick Enberg, and Al Michaels. Some of the analysts that enjoyed long, distinguished careers in the booth include
Al DeRogatis, Tom Brookshier, Merlin Olsen, Hank Stram, and
John Madden.

But just how important are announcers for a television broadcast of an NFL game? One of TV sport's brightest minds, Don Ohlmeyer, who had long felt that the folks in the booth talked too much,
wondered the same question. On Saturday, December 20, 1980, the
16-time Emmy Award-winner and the first producer of *Monday
Night Football*, took a meaningless season-ending game between
two mediocre teams—a 3-12 New York Jets squad against a Miami
Dolphins team floundering one game above .500—and turned it
into a historic happening, although the stunt ultimately stained the
producer's great career.

Viewers who tuned in to the tilt at the Orange Bowl probably
thought the broadcast was experiencing technical difficulties with
its audio. Instead of commentators delivering the play-by-play and
chatter, the only voice was that of the stadium PA announcer, in the
background, offering more information than he normally would.

"You would hear the PA announcer say throughout the game,
'They're measuring for the first down,'" recalled Michael Weisman,
the telecast's coproducer. "And: 'That last drive, totaling sixty-eight
yards, took five minutes and seventeen seconds.'"

Additional graphics and field microphones were added. Even
though the technology of the time would have allowed for a continuous score graphic and a running clock, both of which would
have eliminated the need for the stadium announcer to constantly
provide that information, it did not occur to the production unit to
utilize it.

In a sloppy game that included seven turnovers, the Jets eventually won, 24–17, but there really weren't any winners. Despite earning better ratings than it should have, due to sheer novelty value,

the game proved to be too much work for viewers—even armchair quarterbacks with a deeper knowledge of the game.

"Unless you have somebody there to say, 'All right, here's what's at stake,' it lacks a degree of drama," Weisman said.

The importance of presenters to describe the very action was validated. "All the stuff I've done in my career," Ohlmeyer once quipped on national TV, "and that's what I'm going to be remembered for. It serves me right."

Overall, television has served its NFL viewers very well. In particular, nothing has been more important for fans, players, coaches, officials, and announcers than the replay feature. "The early days of instant replay really allowed people to study the game, what worked and what didn't work," Weisman noted. "You could see defensive guys like Sam Huff"—number 70 at linebacker on the New York Giants—previously lost amid the crush of bodies in motion, "becoming famous because cameras isolated on him. Instant replay in the early years certainly brought the game closer to fans. Instant replays helped in star making because you could see the hand-to-hand combat."

Over the years, the replay has benefitted from advances in technology and one of the best tools in today's TV coverage of NFL games: the super-slo-mo replay. "That is tailor-made for football," said Drew Esocoff, NBC's director of *Sunday Night Football*. "You get the emotional impact of it when you see the person's eyes and face as they are being hit or delivering a hit. You see if a guy's feet were in-bounds or if his knees were down. Was the ball out of his hands? They used to call it a game of inches; now it is a game of frames. You have to have clear, unobstructed frames, and that's what all this high-def technology allows you to do."

The National Football League first adopted a limited instant replay system in 1986. The current system, implemented in 1999, brought the opportunity to challenge referees' on-field calls. Today the NFL uses it automatically for every turnover, every scoring play,

Monday Night Football has long been at the forefront of television technology.

Photo by Joe Faraoni/ESPN Images

as a tool for the officials. Its expanded usage illustrates its importance in ultimately serving the viewer.

In the never-ending game of improving service for the viewer, the competition between television networks is a constant battle in the coverage of all sports. There are three innovations where football has led the way. The first is the aforementioned replay. Another would be the superimposed first-and-10 line, as it is hard to watch a football game now without it. Making its debut during the 1997 football season, this graphic enhancement using sophisticated modeling based on precise measurements and ingenious real-time image processing provides the viewer at home with an immediate visual appreciation of where the offense has to take the ball to make another first down. And the third? Fox Sports's debut of the continual clock and score on-screen.

NBC, ABC, CBS, and ESPN were the well-established presenters of NFL broadcasts, but in the early 1990s, a new player entered

Television has played a major role in the popularity of the NFL.

Photo by Phil Ellsworth/ESPN Images

the field. Fox would take the sport's television coverage to new heights and force its veteran competitors to step up their game.

It is one thing when an established network tests out its latest gadget during a game, but it is quite another when one commits to the idea of building an entire network around not fumbling the football, a very expensive one. Well, it was certainly perceived by critics as a dicey and pricey proposition in 1993 when a fledgling fourth network, Fox, owned by Rupert Murdoch, bid $1.58 billion to win the broadcast rights to the NFC (known as the NFL until 1970), which had been owned by CBS since 1956.

The Australian-born media mogul further raised eyebrows when he hired a fellow Aussie to build the network's sports division from scratch. But Fox management, having seen the critical role that soccer programming had played in the growth of UK satellite service British Sky Broadcasting, or BSkyB, believed that sports—and specifically professional football—would be the engine that would turn Fox into a major US network the quickest.

That Aussie, David Hill, in charge of getting Fox's NFL presentation in place by the 1994 season, recalled his first days in office. "Fox had nothing," he said. "When I arrived, I was given a yellow legal pad and an IBM Selectric typewriter. I had to create a sports division from nothing. With no engineering and no infrastructure— not even a logo—no theme music, and no talent, in eight months."

But Hill had the experience of having started a sports division from nothing at the Nine Network (also called Channel Nine) in Australia and then doing the same at what became BSkyB. "The reason I believe I was selected was in having set up two major sports divisions," he reflected. "I knew what *not* to do. I see people starting in media and falling into the same mistakes. Looking back on the huge success of building two sports divisions, I suppose that is why Mr. Murdoch took the huge gamble on an Australian out of London to create a broadcast system of American football." To him, Murdoch's "huge risk" with the football deal was nothing of the sort.

"It was absolutely vital for Fox," he insisted. "In fact, it is the reason why Mr. Murdoch and Chase Carey [Rupert's chief lieutenant] were so gung-ho on getting it. Fox had only just begun broadcasting seven days a week and was in maybe sixty percent of the country. Now all of a sudden Fox is in one hundred percent of the country. NFL football was the must-have property. And despite the critics, look what happened! It was the cheapest deal anyone has ever done in the history of sports."

Hill would take his sports and documentary experience gained abroad to establish improved graphics, including an embedded scoring bug and audio enhancements. He also scored credibility points by signing top announcers John Madden and Pat Summerall. The always effusive Madden brought expert insight into strategy, having coached the Oakland Raiders for 10 years, during which time they won three-quarters of their regular-season games, eight divi-

sion titles, and got fitted for one Super Bowl ring. Summerall, solid and
steady, had been describing games
on the air ever since 1962, following
a nine-year NFL career mainly as a
kicker.

"Still, I think the most important thing that Fox Sports did was
putting on a one-hour pregame
show," Hill continued. "When we
announced that, the roars of laughter and contempt were risible, and
that came from the other networks.
But when you are putting out a big
bet on a sports contract, you have
to try and leverage as much revenue
as you can. And that comes from
creating a stand-alone, bulletproof
show that people want to watch and

Through his innovations, Fox Sports
chairman David Hill helped bring the
NFL into twenty-first-century television.

Frank Micelotta/Picturegroup

advertisers want their products to be associated with. And from the
very beginning, our show outrated the others. And it has been that
way for twenty-four years."

Since the midsixties, when the broadcasters of NFL games really began to present various forms of pregame shows on a regular
basis, programs such as CBS's *The NFL Today*, hosted over the years
by, among others, telegenic former New York Giants star Frank
Gifford, were staid, cut-and-dry affairs full of *x*'s and *o*'s. But as networks competed for ratings throughout the ensuing years, the pregame format expanded to include colorful personalities who weren't
necessarily former players. Phyllis George, the 1971 Miss America,
came aboard in 1975, along with new anchor Brent Musburger and
analyst Irv Cross, a onetime NFL cornerback who'd made history as
the first African American color commentator on network football

broadcasts. Seven years later, legendary sports handicapper Jimmy "the Greek" Snyder added another dimension to the proceedings with his game picks. One aspect of the pregame show never changed, however: its 30-minute length. That is, until 1994, when the new kid arrived in town with a different mind-set.

Hill's experience informed him that the more the football television audience understands about the game, the deeper their involvement and their appreciation of the spectacle and the human dramas being played out on-screen. "What I did was fundamental," he said. "Most people are desperate to learn about sports. And what they're looking for are nuggets of information that they can make their own. So us moving to a one-hour pregame—which meant that CBS then moved to a one-hour pregame, which meant that ESPN then moved to a *two*-hour pregame—became a catalyst for this massive football education for the American public."

Each Sunday, the lessons begin.

The NFL's Super Bowl is the greatest ratings draw on television. Here broadcaster Chris Myers interviews Patriots receiver Julian Edelman after New England's 34–28 overtime victory over the Atlanta Falcons in Super Bowl LI, seen by 172 million viewers.

By permission of
Chris Myers

★ ★   ★ ★

CHAPTER NINETEEN

THE CHESS MASTERS:
SECOND QUARTER

Returning from World War II, most players were used to tough discipline from their military commanders, and this was reflected in the strict, authoritarian approach of the new generation of NFL coaches—George Allen, Bud Grant, Sid Gillman, Hank Stram, to name a few—who demanded that their teams follow their strategies to the letter.

EARLE "GREASY" NEALE

Greasy Neale was one of the original crossover athletes: starring at offensive end alongside Jim Thorpe on the Canton Bulldogs in 1917, while at the same time patrolling right field for the baseball Cincinnati Reds. He batted .357 in the 1919 World Series, leading the Reds with 10 hits in their eight-game win over the scandalous White Sox who became infamously known as the "Black Sox." Eight members of that Chicago team were accused of intentionally losing to the Reds.

Despite acquittals in a public trial in 1921, one result from the scandal was the appointment of Judge Kenesaw Mountain Landis as the first Commissioner of Baseball. Having been granted absolute control over the sport in order to restore its integrity, Landis permanently banned all eight men from professional baseball.

After coaching football at various colleges, including Yale, Neale, then 49, graduated to the NFL in 1941 as head coach of the Philadelphia Eagles. It was a slow start the first few years, but as the flood of servicemen returned from the war, and the talent pool increased exponentially, Neale's squad was in playoff contention on a regular basis. Loaded with an offense that featured quarterback Tommy Thompson, and a pair of future Hall of Famers in receiver Pete Pihos and running back Steve Van Buren, from 1944 through 1949, Neale's Eagles finished second three times and in first place three times.

But Neale's defensive talent was at the core of the team's success. He constructed a 5-2 formation that essentially took one of the defensive linemen from the 6-2-2-1 and converted him into a linebacker. In this way, swing passes and patterns into the flat could be covered with the same success as deeper routes. Neale's so-called Eagles defense eventually evolved into the 4–3 setup that NFL teams use today. Performing especially well in foul weather, Philly won the NFL championship in 1948 and again in 1949. It was the only team to win back-to-back titles via shutouts: 7–0 in the snow-ridden 1948 NFL championship game against the Chicago Cardinals, and, the following December, a 14–0 defeat of the Los Angeles Rams amid a driving rainstorm. The franchise would not win it all again until 1960, 10 years after Neale retired.

Though the Eagles soared on defense, in Detroit the emphasis was on the other side of the ball. Coach Ray "Buddy" Parker and dynamic quarterback Bobby Layne popularized what became known as the two-minute offense, which allowed a team to regroup quickly between snaps in order to squeeze out a few more scoring opportunities as time ticked down at the end of a half. The Lions succeeded Philadelphia as consecutive titleholders in 1952 and 1953.

CLARK SHAUGHNESSY

While Greasy excelled in defense and Buddy on offense, one of the great overall strategists in the history of the game was Clark Shaughnessy. He is credited not only with vastly improving the T-formation and the forward pass but also with innovating defensive schemes and developing the nickel defense (use of five defensive backs).

In the mid-1930s, Shaughnessy, a brilliant x's and o's man, modernized offenses and forever altered the sport by opening up the ground game with quick hitters, devising the counterplay (where the blocking scheme largely sets up in one direction and a shifty runner exploits a gap going the other way), the man in motion, misdirection, and the three-wide-receiver formation. The beneficiaries of his innovations were the Chicago Bears, although Shaughnessy was in no way affiliated with the club. At the time, he was in his third year as head coach at the University of Chicago Maroons. One night he ran into George Halas and mentioned that he had some ideas on how the Bears' coach could utilize the T-formation more effectively. He'd have utilized his so-called modernized T with his own college team, but the mediocre Maroons didn't have the talent to pull it off.

While continuing to coach at the university, Shaughnessy consulted part-time with Halas for $2,000 a month. He also worked closely with Chicago's rookie phenom, QB Sid Luckman. The Shaughnessy system emphasized ballhandling and intelligent decision-making by the quarterback. No longer would he merely be a glorified blocker in the single wing but, rather, the point man for every play. Beginning in 1940, the year that Shaughnessy left the University of Chicago to assume the coaching duties at Stanford

University, his pupil Luckman would pilot the Bears to four NFL titles over the next seven seasons.

Shaughnessy would also be the key strategist for *combatting* the modern-T offense. With offenses becoming increasingly aerial, he devised defensive schemes that stressed man-to-man coverages. In his first season at Stanford, Shaughnessy led the undefeated Indians to a Rose Bowl victory.

The Minnesota native coached only two years in the NFL, in 1948 and 1949 with the Rams. In Los Angeles, he developed the pro set (which has varied over time, but tried to prevent defenses from overloading to one side of the ball by having running backs split evenly behind the quarterback. In more recent times it expanded by replacing the strongside tight end with a slot receiver, in order to spread out opposing defenses even more and providing more options.) that used a three-wide-receiver system. Shaughnessy made this change primarily to capitalize on the open-field speed skills of running back Elroy Hirsch. On one play, he'd position Crazy Legs at halfback, then move him to flanker—all to confuse the defense. They further perplexed opponents by inserting a tackle-eligible pass play that scored a couple times for them. Los Angeles captured the Western Division crown before losing the NFL title game to the Eagles in 1949.

LOU SABAN

Lou Saban and Weeb Ewbank, both disciples of Paul Brown, enjoyed success as NFL coaches, though with differing personalities. Saban, two-time coach of the year, won back-to-back titles in Buffalo with an emphasis on defense at a time when the league was dominated by high-scoring offenses.

He later coached Denver, from 1967 through 1971, before returning to the Bills for another five seasons. The Broncos' Hall of

Fame running back Floyd Little offered a glimpse of Saban's coaching style: "He would not put up with much crap. Lou would often say, 'You're horrible! You're the worst football player I have ever seen! My grandmother can play better than you!' And that is how he'd build you up."

One afternoon, though, Saban almost went too far. It was just an exhibition contest in Utah, but the coach was so fired up, you'd have thought it was a playoff game. Storming into the locker room at halftime, he flipped over the refreshment table and launched into a tirade. Little recalled him yelling, "You guys are a bunch of wimps! I am tougher than anyone in this room! I can kick anyone's ass here! Stand up, anybody—I will kick your ass. Who wants me?" Saban was in his late forties at the time. Little explained what happened next:

"So, Rex Mirich, one of our defensive linemen gets up. Coach looks at him. Mirich is, like, six foot six, two hundred seventy-five pounds. Quite big in those days. Coach quickly gets a worried look on his face. There's a tense pause, then Mirich says: 'I just got to go to the bathroom, Coach.' You see a sigh of relief on Coach's face."

WEEB EWBANK

If Saban was a notorious hothead, Ewbank was the opposite. Hired as the Baltimore Colts' head coach in 1954, he led them to four winning seasons, which included championships in 1958 and 1959. Then, as head coach of the New York Jets for 11 seasons, beginning in 1963, his squad became the first AFL team to win a Super Bowl, in January 1969, thus making him the first coach to win championships in both leagues. And he did it with two exceptional quarterbacks: Johnny Unitas and Joe Namath.

Hall of Fame receiver Raymond Berry, himself an NFL coach with New England in the 1980s, revealed what he believes to be the secret of the diminutive coach's success. "Weeb was a coach well-grounded in fundamentals," he said. "Simplicity was his great strength. He gave us four bullets in a six-shooter, and we knew how to shoot them. We were never confused by what we were trying to do, and Weeb tapped into each player's total abilities. His simplicity became clearer and clearer to me over the years."

Ewbank was hired in a dual capacity as both head coach and general manager. He was generally well liked by his men, but his business tactics when negotiating players' contracts struck many as cheap and offensive. As a coach, you spend all season building up a player; then, over the winter, as GM, you tell him why he's not worth the salary he's seeking. One year, when it came time for Ewbank to negotiate with star wide receiver Don Maynard, he slid a piece of paper with a dollar figure written on it across the table. Maynard shook his head in disgust, pushed the paper back, and snarled, "Taxi drivers make more than that."

Kicker Jim Turner, who accounted for 10 of the Jets' 16 points in their Super Bowl III victory, left town a year later after clashing with the GM side of Ewbank. "He was the best coach I ever had, but he should never have been put in charge of negotiating contracts. The cheapest son of a bitch in the world," Turner said, laughing at the memory. "You kick clutch field goals in the championship games, you kick the crucial field goals in the league title and Super Bowl games, make six for six in the Pro Bowl, and he offers you just a five-hundred-dollar raise? I told myself, 'I have to get out of here.'" Turner did and performed quite well with the Denver Broncos for nine more seasons.

But at his core, Ewbank was a master strategist whose mantra, "Poise and execute," helped his players deliver the greatest upset in football history. This was appreciated by none other than his star quarterback, Joe Namath. "Weeb was a very smart man," Broadway Joe stated. "I have said this in semijest over the years, but it is really true: I played for five more head coaches, I believe, and Coach Ewbank kept getting smarter and smarter with each new coach I was around. In other words, I did not give Weeb, at the time I was playing for him, maybe I did not give him the kind of respect that I really grew to have for him later on."

BUD GRANT

Though he did not win the big games like Ewbank, Minnesota Vikings coach Bud Grant earned the respect of everyone who knew anything about the game. From 1967 through 1985 (he retired in 1984 but came back for one more campaign the following season), Grant took Minnesota to 12 division titles in 18 years, with four Super Bowl appearances.

What his players remembered most was his style of coaching. Not unlike Ewbank, it was steady and uncomplicated. A comparatively quiet leader, Grant showed no emotion on the sidelines, leading his team by example. Bud was a strong leader. But he never raised his voice, unlike his predecessor, Norm Van Brocklin, who was "more fire and brimstone," said defensive tackle Gary Larsen.

Grant was known for instilling discipline. For example, he required his players to stand in a straight line during the national anthem—toes on the white line, no scratching or spitting, look directly at the flag, helmets tucked under their arms. He did not allow heaters on the snowy, frozen sidelines of Metropolitan Stadium, the Vikings' home from 1961 through 1982.

Born in Wisconsin, Grant was an accomplished two-sport player. He averaged 2.6 points per game in his two seasons as a reserve with the Minneapolis Lakers of the National Basketball Association, including the 1950–51 championship squad led by George Mikan. That fall, he moved on to professional football as a defensive end with the Philadelphia Eagles and merely led the team in sacks (an unofficial statistic at the time). Switching position to wide re-

ceiver for 1952, the 25-year-old topped the club in receiving yardage, hauling in 56 passes for 997 yards and seven touchdowns.

"He was a legitimate former pro player, so he had the respect of
the players," said quarterback Joe Kapp. After 10 years coaching the
Winnipeg Blue Bombers of the Canadian Football League to four
championships, Grant replaced Van Brocklin as Vikings head coach
in 1967. For his quarterback, he tapped Kapp, also an American
who'd been working north of the border in the CFL since the 1950s.
Two years later, coach and QB made it to Super Bowl IV, only to lose
to the AFL's Kansas City Chiefs. There would be three more championship appearances in the next six years—Super Bowls VIII, IX,
and XI—all ending with Grant having to watch the opposing team
from the AFC celebrate.

Despite not being able to win the biggest game, the coach's philosophical approach helped him deal with that shortcoming. "Not a
good feeling, but my life would not be any different had we won four
Super Bowls," Grant explained. "You replay it, agonize over what
you did or didn't do, then you put it aside. It is hard, but you have to
get over the losing. You cannot let it eat you up. I have never looked
back at those Super Bowl games. That is not my legacy."

GEORGE ALLEN

Nor is it the legacy of George Allen. The fellow Hall of Fame head
coach also fell short, reaching Super Bowl VII but falling to the Miami Dolphins, 14–7.

Allen's coaching career got a boost after he helped George Halas
and Clark Shaughnessy build a dominating defense in Chicago that
led the Bears to the NFL Title in 1963. He began his head coaching
career in 1966 by taking over the hapless Los Angeles Rams, who'd
endured seven losing campaigns in a row. Through an improved
defense built around the vaunted Fearsome Foursome front line—

President Richard Nixon, a passionate football fan, poses with head coach George Allen and the Washington Redskins.

US National Archives

tackles Merlin Olsen and Rosey Grier and ends Deacon Jones and Lamar Lundy—Allen took his team to a couple playoff appearances over his five-year tenure.

Arriving in Washington, where the Redskins had only one winning season in 15 years, the fiery coach reached the playoffs in his very first season, and in five of seven subsequent campaigns. What's more, in his 12 years as a head coach, Allen never had a losing season. The keys to his success were attention to detail, the aforementioned accent on defense, a preference for seasoned veterans (he routinely had the oldest team in the NFL), and a groundbreaking emphasis on special-teams play. Allen, believing that rookies made too many mistakes—and turnovers drove him *crazy*—he often traded his draft picks for seasoned players. The Washington defensive unit had so many veterans it was nicknamed the "Over the Hill Gang." Hardly. That gang of geezers got the Redskins to the Super Bowl.

A tireless worker, George Allen was one of the greatest motivators in the league. "Every time you lose, you die a little," he said once, and by fueling the Redskins-Cowboys rivalry, he helped the NFL gain popularity.

SPECIAL TEAMS

In demonstrating his pioneering view about the importance of special teams, in April 1969, three seasons into his Rams tenure, Allen hired a little-known Stanford Indians assistant, Dick Vermeil, to become the NFL's first special-teams coach. The impact of this move on the return game in particular was dramatic. "He said he wanted to hire a full-time coach for the kicking game because he had lost a game due to a kickoff return for a touchdown, which cost him advancement in the playoffs," Vermeil explained. "So when the season was over, he took the entire staff and graded every single kickoff coverage throughout the season." It turned out that the pair of defenders that missed the tackles had not made any all season.

When Allen left for the Redskins, and Vermeil took over as head coach of UCLA, Allen's hire in Washington, Marv Levy, became the league's only special-teams coach. He was very impressed with Allen's commitment to this previously underemphasized part of the game. "We were teaching techniques people had not employed yet," Levy said. "And they still don't. There's a technique for blocking kicks, and you have to drill it over and over, and Coach has to keep guys on the roster that are good at it," Levy said. "The year we went to the Super Bowl, we blocked seventeen kicks: field goals, points after touchdown, and punts combined. We allowed a total of just forty-eight yards all year for punt returns.

"George Allen was way ahead of the game in a number of ways," he added. "He was the first to implement the nickel defense. He invented the term *sack*. I remember George said one time when we

Hank Stram and Len Dawson of the Kansas City Chiefs formed one of the winningest coach-QB combinations in NFL history.

Courtesy Kansas City Chiefs

were preparing for the Cowboys, 'We're gonna take that Craig Morton and pour him in a sack.'"

HANK STRAM

Like Allen, one of Hank Stram's strengths was an attention to detail. "He was as thorough and obsessed a coach as has ever lived," said his Hall of Fame outside linebacker Bobby Bell. "He never had a defensive coordinator, an offensive coordinator, or special-teams coach with the Chiefs. Never needed them."

A tremendous judge of talent and a leading innovator, Stram parlayed those skills into enduring success. "He was the first coach in professional football to run both the I-formation and the two-tight-end offense, still used in professional football today," noted Fred Arbanas, one of those tight ends.

In 1959 Lamar Hunt recruited Stram to coach his Dallas Texans of the new AFL, which commenced play in 1960. Hunt, a shrewd judge of talent, remembered Stram from the time he'd spent as a bench player at SMU when Stram coached there. In just their second season, the Texans won the AFL championship.

One of Stram's innovations on defense—a triple-stack formation that hid the three linebackers behind defensive linemen—was evidence of his skill at identifying and developing talent. Stram was a terrific teacher, several of his defenders became Hall of Famers: Bell, Buck Buchanan, Curley Culp, Willie Lanier, and Emmitt Thomas.

Oh, yes: with dozens of tailor-made suits, monogrammed shirts, and snazzy vests, Stram was quite the fastidious clotheshorse. Such was his attention to detail, both on and off the field, that he insisted his players get all dressed up when representing the team on the road. "We had custom blazers and slacks," linebacker Bell recalled. "I remember going into his office to complain about my ill-fitting uniform. I said, 'Coach, you are always preaching about looking good, but take a look at this uniform! Come on, Coach! If I look good, I play good.'"

Now, most NFL coaches probably would have dismissed the concern as utterly absurd. Not Hank Stram. "Sure enough, my uniform was reconstructed from top to bottom, and it all worked out. So, after one game, I told Coach, 'Look sharp, play sharp.' Coach Stram said, 'You're right.' He really liked that."

SID GILLMAN

Another dapper coach, often associated with wearing an iconic bow tie, was the Chargers' Sid Gillman.

Beginning his pro coaching career in 1955 with the NFL Los

San Diego Chargers head coach Sid Gillman has often been referred to as the father of modern offensive football.

Courtesy Los Angeles Chargers

Angeles Rams, Gillman orchestrated a diverse attack. You had quarterback Norm Van Brocklin throwing to Elroy Hirsch and Tom Fears, plus the aptly named Tank Younger and Ron Waller powering a strong running game. In his very first season, the new coach took them all the way to the championship game, although they lost to Paul Brown's Cleveland Browns, 38–14, in front of 85,693 fans at the LA Memorial Coliseum.

In 1960 Gillman left the Rams as well as the NFL, but not the City of Angels: the Los Angeles Chargers of the shiny and new American Football League named him their first head coach. The following season, the franchise headed south to San Diego, and that is where the 50-year-old Minnesotan wasted no time in establishing himself as one of the best coaches of all-time.

Gillman guided San Diego to the AFL championship game in five of its first six seasons, winning it all in 1963.

A mercurial personality with an endless desire for success, Gillman rode his contrarian theory—"If I can establish the pass, I will be able to run"—to great success. Generally considered the father of modern offensive football, he said often, "The field is a hundred yards long and fifty-three and a-third yards wide, and we are going to force the defense to cover every inch—and they won't be able to." He accomplished this by spreading out the field and bringing the running backs more into the passing game. Thanks to the success of Gillman's offense, the AFL soon became known as the passing league.

But don't let the bow tie fool you: behind that professorial image was "a mighty force of nature," said Chargers wide receiver Phil Tuckett, who, incidentally, went on to become a filmmaker after his football days ended. "On the one hand, you'd look at him and say, 'Why should I be fearful of this kind of short, chubby, balding man in a bowtie who looks like a high school biology teacher? Why should I be quaking in my boots every time he is around?' But he had a passion for coaching football. He was aware of what his legacy was for the development of the passing game."

Quarterback John Hadl came to the Chargers in 1962 from the University of Kansas, where he'd also been a running back. In making the conversion to an AFL gunslinger, Hadl quickly came to appreciate Gillman's dedication and expectations. "Sid was a very professional guy," he said. "From my first day, it was easy to see that he was very serious about what he was doing. Football was on his mind all the time. He'd leave the office at two or three in the morning and then be back there before anybody else arrived the next day. I was scared to death of him as a rookie, but as my career evolved, and I was calling the plays, we really developed a good rapport. There'd be some stormy times, but it was a good give-and-take overall. I learned so much from him."

Everybody did. One of the pioneering components to Gillman's success was his utilizing game film as a coaching tool. His father owned a movie theater, and as a kid, Sid worked there as an usher. Unbeknownst to Mr. Gillman, his young son used to illegally remove football segments of the newsreels, take them home, and study the clips on a projector his father had bought. Besides becoming one of the first football coaches to study game footage, Gillman divided film reels into offensive and defensive highlights, further to isolate specific plays and situations. Soon other coaches, as well as scouts, would do the same.

"When he would talk about the game plan, it was like a demented scientist in the basement, with his test tubes bubbling and everything," said Tuckett, laughing at the memory. "The way he coached football, you realized you were with somebody who was a zealot. But at the same time, it was always so intense. And you felt that if you said the wrong thing or ran the wrong pattern or missed a downfield block, that could be the end of it. He did not tolerate imperfection, especially in the passing game, and I was a wide receiver."

VINCE LOMBARDI

If there is one coach most associated with demanding perfection, it was Vince Lombardi, who philosophized, "If we chase perfection, we can catch excellence." The players in pursuit of their coach's vision knew that he expected maximum effort all the time and that he played no favorites. As Hall of Fame defensive lineman Henry Jordan quipped famously, "He treats us all the same—like dogs."

Lombardi's results in Green Bay say a lot about the effectiveness of his method.

The Packers' power sweep is a perfect example: a simple play in which the running back (usually Paul Hornung or Jim Taylor), with his blockers aligned seamlessly in front of him, swept around the end. Lombardi believed that if everyone carried out his job properly, no defense could stop it. He felt there could never be enough emphasis on repetition. He wanted his players to be able to run every play in their sleep (and in their nightmares at training camp, they undoubtedly did, over and over). If he called a play a dozen times, he expected it to work 12 times. Not 10. Not even 11.

"It was about knowing your assignment, exploding into it, and doing the best job you could possibly do play in and play out," said Taylor. "How bad do you want it? How hard are you willing to work for it? He instilled in us—all eleven players on offense, all eleven players on defense, and special teams, that the opponent was out to get you, so you'd better be ready to play mentally and physically."

Lombardi arrived in Green Bay in 1959 after having spent five years as the offensive coordinator for the New York Giants. On his first day, the new head coach lined up his squad—which had not had a winning season in 11 years—and hammered home in no uncertain terms how things were going to be. And if any players didn't like it? "Well," he said, "there are busses leaving Green Bay every half hour."

Hall of Famer Paul Hornung remembered that first meeting. "He set the tone for all of us with the omnipresent thought that we were going to win. And you have to be believable as a coach because if you start saying a lot of things and it doesn't happen, it won't take long for players to lose faith in your leadership. But we knew right away that Vince was a special coach and he was going to be the boss, because we did not have anything like that before he arrived. He was the epitome of discipline, diligence, and determination."

With a minimum of plays and maximum execution, as well as sensing who he had to push and who needed a pat on the back, Lombardi took Green Bay to the pinnacle of football: a .738 winning percentage, among the highest of all time; five NFL titles; two Super Bowl victories; and the establishment of one of the great dynasties in professional football history.

PAUL BROWN

Preceding the Packers' dynasty was that of the Cleveland Browns, who were led by a coach many consider to be the greatest of all time, Paul Brown. (See chapter 13, "Otto-Matic.")

The first coach of the Cleveland Browns and founder/head coach of the Cincinnati Bengals, and, as his coaching tree would show, one of the game's greatest teachers (among the branches, Don Shula, Weeb Ewbank, and Bill Walsh), Brown coached for 21 seasons in the NFL and had 16 winning seasons, with 11 playoff appearances and three league championships in all. Before that, from 1946 through 1949, he dominated the All-America Football Conference, winning the AAFC championship in all four years of its existence.

Brown was essential to reintegrating professional football, signing two African American players, Marion Motley and Bill Willis, in 1946.

His coaching philosophy included a strong organizational center whereby his system would flourish without any deliberate emphasis on one star player, but rather on a group of individuals committed to winning. Brown was about winning as a team, and he didn't care who got credit. Clearly, his players responded.

Let's review his achievements: helped create two of the 32 current NFL teams; advanced countless innovations, including playbooks, face masks, film study, sophisticated scouting systems, having offensive guards carry plays from the coach to the huddle, and helmet radio communications. When combined with his winning record, it is easy to say without reservation that no other coach has impacted the game more than Paul Brown.

CHAPTER TWENTY

WORKING OUT THE KINKS

E ven though new National Football League Players Association (NFLPA) rules, player salaries, and vast increases in specialists and resources are in play today, modern training camps still share many things with those of yesteryear. Veterans and rookies alike battle heat, humidity, and fatigue, in addition to coaches, isolation, boredom—and sometimes each other—in this annual summer survival session.

For the marginal veterans (as well as free agents and late-round draft picks), training camp is fraught with terror and anxiety. Players never know when that dreaded knock on the door in the early morning before breakfast will come, and "the turk" (the messenger associated with cuts) greets you with: "Coach wants to see you, and bring your playbook."

"I don't care how old you are, whether you're a rookie or a fifteen-year veteran," said defensive lineman Ron McDole, a survivor of 17 pro camps on four different teams throughout the sixties and seventies. "You are always looking over your shoulder. There's always someone behind you to take your place."[48]

Not a lot has changed through the decades of training camps, but perhaps the most noticeable is a lighthearted camaraderie that came with a larger number of players who were teammates for longer periods. Today, pranksters and mischief makers have largely gone the way of straight-on kickers in a more corporate NFL locker room environment. Long gone are the days of making rookies sing for their supper or put on a skit at the end of camp. Camp clowns are from a bygone era. With serious money comes serious business.

Back in the day, Lions quarterback Bobby Layne used to send rookies out to get him a six-pack of beer five minutes before curfew in Detroit, knowing full well that the favor would cost the gofer a fine. What could the rookie do? He couldn't refuse the best, most influential player on the team. Layne claimed he got fined so often by Buddy Parker that he finally started slipping a blank check in the coach's door on his way out of Lions camp.

One of the reasons for the pranks was the boredom that arose due to the teams' training camp locations, which were often remote by design. Management wanted all attention to be focused on getting into football shape and learning the plays. Campuses of small colleges located in small towns in secluded settings have been preferred by most. However, the great San Diego Chargers coach Sid Gillman, after his team had lost the AFL championship game in the league's first two seasons and then put up a poor 4-10 record in 1962, took the notion of remote camps to a new level in 1963.

Gillman searched for a place where there'd be no distractions. He found it: a failed dude ranch called Rough Acres. Isolating his squad in a secluded area approximately 70 miles east of San Diego, in the middle of nowhere, he began training camp in a most spartan of environments.

"We thought it was a joke and said Coach had to be crazy," recalled Paul Maguire, the team's punter and a linebacker. "Basically, it was a bunch of shacks. We ate, slept, and practiced there. He wanted to keep us isolated, and he did. You think anybody broke eleven o'clock curfew? Where are you gonna go? They had one little dive bar up the road with a lot of women with no teeth. Unless somebody was into the sheep, the wives of the roving players had nothing to worry about."

While there were no spectators lining up to watch practice, there were some "locals" who had to be monitored.

"Generally speaking," said quarterback John Hadl, "it was a real boot camp atmosphere. We were isolated up in the mountains. It had some unexpected dangers as well, because each day before we began, the practice field had to be cleared of poisonous snakes and tarantulas. A few teammates told me they got spooked from finding snakes in their rooms. That made it a little uneasy getting your proper rest after a long day toiling in the sun."

All-Pro running back Paul Lowe refused to go out at night. He had to be escorted to team meetings after the sun went down. But snakes sometimes found their way indoors. Often with a little help.

"One thing that freaks me out are snakes. Sure enough," Maguire remembered, "I came in one night half loaded, and a few of my teammates had put a snake in my bed. I ran right through my screen door. So, I'm sitting out there buck-ass naked in the middle of nowhere trying to find somebody to kill. It was not funny."

Despite the distractions, the players somehow managed to focus on football while bats hung from ceilings above their cots, snakes slithered through their toilets, rats scurried to and fro in the dining area, and even tarantulas crawled across their dirt-and-weeds playing field. "You know," Maguire reflected, "It was probably the best thing that ever happened to us because it brought our team together. It really did. That was Sid."

Coach Gillman and his creepy crawly friends helped produce one of the greatest seasons by any professional football team ever. The '63 Chargers finished 11-3, boasted the league's top offense and defense, and crushed the Boston Patriots, 51–10, in the AFL championship game.

Isn't that the desired result from any training camp? Perhaps more coaches should look to bringing in less food and more poisonous animals to their camps.

SURVIVAL OF THE FITTEST

Professional football players in 2019 have come a long way since the sixties, seventies, and eighties, when many of them would arrive at training camp from off-season jobs behind a desk working for a savings and loan or an insurance company. They'd have to be weaned off six months' worth of BBQ pork sandwiches, potato salad, beer, peach pie, and ice cream as they sweated back into shape under the hot sun with two-a-day drills in full uniform.

For those who made the effort back then to stay in reasonable shape during the off-season, it was an era of much more self-reliance and simply finding a facility to keep fit. Some of those players merely improvised yet enjoyed long, excellent careers.

According to Hall of Fame tight end Kellen Winslow, "In my day, there was no place to go to train. Today each team has a crew of strength and conditioning specialists, not some guy who was a high school gym teacher who joined us on the weekends. I mean, if I wanted a workout, I had to go to a twenty-four-hour fitness outlet."

During the 1960s and 1970s, Jim Marshall played 20 seasons as a defensive end. All but one were spent in Minnesota, where he made up one-quarter of the Vikings' ferocious Purple People Eaters. When he retired following the 1979 season, Marshall owned the career records for most consecutive starts (270) and games played (282). Very impressive for a life in the pits. And while he was known for taking on strenuous wintertime activities such as mountain climbing, snowshoeing, and sledding, the six-foot-four, 250-pounder attributed his longevity to basic weightlifting and running.

Self-reliance was what got Bears running back Walter Payton through the punishing seasons. It was his drive running up tortuous hills with a tire or a parachute roped behind him that produced powerful leg muscles that carried him to the Hall of Fame.

Winslow, Payton, Marshall all had an exceptional drive.

Jerry: Football is about willpower. I was known for training on an infamous hill in Edgewood County Park and Natural Preserve that was about two and a half miles up. The last eight hundred meters would be a real gut check. It could make you throw up. It could make you quit. And plenty of my workout guests did both!

Football is also about being able to play at a high level for four quarters. I wanted to be able to finish the fourth quarter at the same level I started in the first. Running that hill certainly helped shape me into this real durable player, providing my body with the ability to tolerate the pain—for twenty NFL campaigns.

My regimen also included a lot of time spent running patterns out in the field. Being explosive coming out of my cuts, catching the ball, not getting tired, and being able to finish. That includes a lot of dedication and sacrifice, like the times when you've got to roll out of bed, even though you don't *feel like* rolling out of bed. But still you get out there and commit to your craft. And give it one hundred percent no matter what. If I'm running that hill by myself, it might be easy to quit when nobody is looking, but I wasn't going to quit—because once you quit, it's easier to do that again and again.

That translation could be seen on the field, as Jerry's 303 games are by far the most ever played by an NFL wide receiver.

Today's ballplayers, who earn such magnificent wages that just a few productive years can set them up for life, don't have to worry about keeping a roof over their heads with an off-season job. Instead, with the accelerated competition for a lucrative roster spot, they leave no stone unturned in striving to always remain in shape. It is a time of fitness for 365. And it all starts with diet.

"Definitely the number one thing to extend your career is diet. You can get away with most anything when you're young, but as you get older, you have to monitor your diet much better if you want to continue to play," said linebacker Terrell Suggs, a former NFL defensive player of the year. After playing his entire career with the Baltimore Ravens, in 2019 the 36-year-old signed a contract to begin his 17th season as an Arizona Cardinal. "The metabolism slows down," he explained. "To continue to maximize your speed, strength, and flexibility, it's best to learn at a young age that your body is your business."

"Your body is your business." You hear that a lot today, especially among veteran ballplayers.

"Your body is an investment," running back Danny Woodhead said as he prepared for his ninth and ultimately final season in 2017. "A player can't be afraid to spend some extra money to keep their body right because it is an investment that can add two, three, possibly four years to your career. When you are younger, that is something you don't even think about. You don't care because you don't know.

"I think it's a process. When I was younger, I would just take a week or two off, but you learn as you get older that you need to have greater recovery time. Nowadays I take at least a month off. So, especially regarding the off-season, I have learned that less is more. As I've gotten older, I've also learned that specialists such as massage therapists and nutritionists can really help keep you right. If you do figure it out early, you are so far ahead of the game."

And the game behind the NFL game in the twenty-first century includes a lot more than weights, core fitness workouts, and running hills. All of those are certainly important. However, specialty performance training companies are a cottage industry now, with facilities popping up across the nation breaking down a client's biomechanics. And in addition to hiring personal nutritionists to prepare all their meals, all the physical exertion and gastronomic analysis are part of a total body-and-mind personalized conditioning system geared toward gaining an edge and producing throughout the long season.

Beyond the team's regimens, players also push themselves pretty hard, which has brought a new wave of specialists on to the scene. In addition to hiring a personal trainer to help them extend their careers through a punishing assortment of Romanian deadlifts, sprinting drills, sled work, hill sprints, squats, and tire flipping, they also turn to experts on the recovery side, which may cover meditation, yoga, hydration, psychological conditioning, and various massage therapies to reduce inflammation. It is all part of today's game plan for a ballplayer to maximize the cooperation of his body.

How far have pro football players come in their commitment to fitness? Well, arguably, in the last decade the fittest player in the NFL was . . . a punter! For many years, kickers were the butt of jokes stereotyping them as frail, paunchy, devoid of muscle, chain-smokers, and on and on.

Enter Steve Weatherford.

From 2006 through 2015, Weatherford was literally the sport's poster boy for fitness. *Nobody* was going to rough up this kicker: six foot three, 230 pounds, with 18-inch arms, V-shaped lats, striated delts, and washboard abs to go with massive pecs and thighs. Did we mention he could squat almost 500 pounds? In his 10 years as a pro, Weatherford never missed a game. He took a lot of pride in helping change the popular perception of the kicker as a part-time nonathlete.

"When I arrived in the NFL, nobody said, 'Oh my gosh, he is the epitome of physical fitness,'" said the University of Illinois grad, who studied the science of kinesiology. "But around my sixth or seventh year, people started to take notice." Weatherford was written about in *Men's Fitness* magazine, the website Bodybuilding.com, and *Muscle & Fitness* magazine, which named him the fittest athlete in professional sports. "To be honest," he said, "I am actually more proud of that accomplishment than being a Super Bowl champion." Weatherford punted four times in the New York Giants' thrilling 21–17 come-from-behind upset of the New England Patriots in Super Bowl XLVI.

Weatherford explained why.

"As a Super Bowl champion, I was one of fifty-three guys. I'm very thankful for that. But being labeled the fittest guy in the NFL had everything to do with my ability to remain disciplined and structured. Giving everything I had every single day. And that is just not all in the weight room, on the track, or on the football field," he emphasized. "It has a lot to do with the amount of sleep that you're getting and the food choices you make, which all ties back into attitude and effort. If you bring a positive attitude into every opportunity you have, you might not be successful the first, second, or third time, but, over time, your attitude and effort will surpass anybody in ability.

"To be honest, that is the only reason I made it into the National Football League."

Pride, drive, positive attitude, two-a-days, sled driving, nutcracker drills—these long-established terms have been joined by cryotherapy, hot yoga, muscle memory, bromelain, complex carbs, skill-specific training, and dynamic flexibility as part of today's NFL fitness lexicon.

It's a long season. You've got four preseason games and 16 regular-season games, and if you get into the postseason, you could be playing 24 football games in five months. Tough on the mind and body. On top of that, the National Football League is perhaps the most competitive professional sports league in the world. And with players getting bigger, faster, and more athletic, they're all learning at a younger age that "your body is your business."

There's a lot at steak—er, stake.

CROSSOVER

While most players have to work extremely hard during the off-season and at training camp just to have a chance at success in the National Football League, there are a rare few whose unique gifts have allowed them to excel at the highest level not only in football but also in other sports.

Ever since Jim Thorpe ran, jumped, threw, and hurdled his way to dominance in the 1912 Summer Olympics—then, later, did the same in football—athletes who excel in multiple sports have long fascinated fans. The examples are many and varied.

In 1946 future Pro Football Hall of Fame quarterback Otto Graham played guard and forward for the Rochester Royals in the National Basketball League, the forerunner of the NBA. He had already signed with the Cleveland Browns, but their inaugural AAFC season had not begun yet. Graham had the hoop talent, as he had originally gone to Northwestern University on a basketball scholarship. As a Royal, he played alongside two notables: Red Holzman, the future Hall of Fame coach for the New York Knicks; and Chuck Connors, also a major-league first baseman but best remembered for his post-sports career as a busy actor in film and TV, including starring in the popular Western series *The Rifleman*. The Royals beat the Sheboygan Red Skins for the NBL title. All told, Graham was on 11 pro teams, and all of them reached the championship game in their respective sports.

In 1954 former Ohio State star running back Vic Janowicz became the first Heisman Trophy winner to appear in both Major League Baseball and the NFL. Janowicz, who stood only five foot nine and weighed 185 pounds, played catcher and third base for the Pittsburgh Pirates in 1953 and 1954, then swapped his ballcap for a Washington Redskins helmet in 1954 and 1955.

San Francisco 49ers quarterback John Brodie threw for more than 30,000 yards and 214 touchdowns and was the NFL MVP in 1970. The Stanford all-American also became a professional in a rare avenue for crossover stars: golf. He played on the PGA circuit during the NFL off-season for several years; then, after retiring from football, Brodie played on the PGA Champions Tour from 1985 through 1998, earning a dozen top-10 finishes and winning the 1991 Security Pacific Senior Classic by defeating George Archer and Chi-Chi Rodriguez in a playoff.

More recently, Brian Jordan played from 1989 through 1991 as a safety and kick returner for the Atlanta Falcons, ending his abbreviated NFL career with five interceptions and four sacks. The next year, at the age of 25, he switched to baseball, which is where he distinguished himself as a reliable run-producing outfielder mostly for the St. Louis Cardinals and Atlanta Braves. In 15 seasons, Jordan posted a career batting average of .282 with 1,454 hits and 184 home runs. In 1999, his first year back in Atlanta, he hit 23 round-trippers, knocked in 115 runs, and scored 100, helping the Braves to the World Series and earning himself an appearance in that year's All-Star Game.

When it comes to crossover athletes, certainly Herschel Walker deserves a tip of the hat. Make that *hats*. Throughout the 1980s and 1990s, not only did he dominate football in both college and the pros as a powerful record-setting running back, but also the Heisman Trophy winner was a world-class sprinter and an Olympic bobsledder. Among multi-sportsmen, Walker might hold the record for longevity: in his late forties, he continued to compete by fighting in mixed martial arts tournaments.

But perhaps the two athletes to achieve the greatest sustained success in the NFL and another sport—in both cases, baseball—are Deion Sanders and Bo Jackson.

Deion Sanders

Deion Sanders appeared in a record 641 MLB games and 189 NFL games. In his best season, 1992, the speedy outfielder for the Atlanta Braves hit .304, led the National League in triples, and swiped 26 bases. Living up to his nickname Prime Time, Neon Deion (his other nickname) starred in that October's World Series, batting .533, with four runs, eight hits, two doubles, and one RBI in four games—while playing with a broken foot.

Beginning in 1989, playing most of his career in Atlanta and Dallas, Sanders would be an eight-time Pro Bowl defensive back who showed his athleticism by catching 60 passes as a receiver. The native Floridian was a dangerous kick returner, too, taking nine all the way back for touchdowns.

"Deion Sanders was so rare in his skill set that in football he could play multiple positions," marveled New York Giants All-Star linebacker Carl Banks, now a broadcaster. "And he showed in baseball the value of speed. In the NFL, he was no novelty. You can put him back to return punts, you can put him in the wide receiver position, because he was good at those skills. Versatility is one thing, but to excel at the various skill sets is quite another. And that is what Deion had that made him special."

What separated Sanders was not only speed but also intimidation as a cover back. There's no doubt he carried himself with an undeniable swagger, but Sanders was appreciated by teammates because he worked as hard as anyone despite the obvious natural talents. He studied endlessly the nuances of the game and his opponents. And by neutralizing the opposing teams' best receivers, he freed his own linebackers and safeties to help in other areas. Unlike many DBs, more often than not, Deion could stand alone as an island.

"Listen," said his counterpart Bo Jackson, "there will never be another Prime Time. Just like he said when he was a freshman at Florida State, he was 'as quick as ex-lax.' He was very different from the ordinary defensive back. Even in the pros, quarterbacks were afraid to throw in his direction. He dared the quarterback to throw the ball to the receiver that he was covering because he was going to intercept it."

One of those quarterbacks he victimized for a pick-six or two was Hall of Famer Brett Favre, who said with a laugh, "I had the honor of playing against Deion Sanders in college and the pros. I can honestly say I threw several touchdowns to Deion." The three-time NFL MVP also reflected on being Sanders's Falcons teammate briefly in 1991, when Favre was a 22-year-old bench warmer.

"I have fond memories of my short stint in Atlanta because I got to practice and play every day with Deion, and he practiced as hard as anybody I've ever seen. Talentwise, he was head over heels better than anybody," said the quarterback, who landed in Green Bay the following year and promptly forged a golden career that lasted two decades. "I remember as soon as practice was over, a helicopter would land on the football complex, pick him up, and by the time I got home, he'd be stealing second base in the World Series. I thought to myself, 'I'm a pretty good two-sport athlete, having also played baseball, but, wow, this guy is incredible.'"

Bo Jackson

Bo Jackson was incredible in his own distinct way in that, not unlike Herschel Walker, he blended tremendous power with great speed.

A shake-your-head, transcendent athlete. There are very few human beings you can say that about. The famously funny Nike sneakers ad campaign "Bo Knows" showed him cloned and trying his hand at all sorts of sports: from cricket, to racecar driving, to surfing, to golf. In the real world, if he'd had the time to concentrate on a given endeavor, odds are he'd have mastered that too.

It all started not on the playgrounds (Jackson did not get into organized sports until later) but out in the woods of rural Alabama. Jackson attributes the development of his athletic skills to a Huck Finn–type existence in the countryside, running, jumping, throwing, fishing, and hunting, something he loves doing to this day.

"Yeah, been throwing rocks and making spears and bow and arrows and slingshots from scratch since I was about seven, eight years old," he explained. "It is one of my favorite pastimes. That is how I get away from being Bo Jackson and go do some things that I like doing.

"We did it with our own homemade equipment. It was the same for Jerry Rice where he grew up in Mississippi—we had to make our own toys; we had to make our own fun. I had an uncle who had chickens and other things like that. We would make slingshots and homemade bows and arrows, and we used to go out in the field to find the proper twigs as well as old caps from Coca-Cola bottles, and we hammered it around the twig. Then we would go get a chicken feather, stick it on the back end of the arrow, and then we would pretend we were hunting. As a matter of fact, just two weeks ago, I took some time off and went to a buddy's ranch in Billings, Montana, to hunt. I know there are some people that don't like that word, but I was raised that way. First time I went hunting, I was five years old."

Like the original crossover king, Jim Thorpe, Jackson turned that rural running around to success in organized track. He set state school records for the indoor high jump (six feet, nine inches) and the triple jump (48 feet, eight inches), but, interestingly, when it came to running, his coaches had to apply extra motivation for the Natural.

Bo was a two-time state champion in the decathlon, but both times he had built up such a commanding points lead before the 1,500 meter run that he never competed in that event. "Distance is the only thing I hate about track," he often said.

"Yes, I built up enough points between myself and second place, and so I would not have to run the mile. My legs were not built to go over two hundred yards," he contended. In order to do that, the young athlete made a deal with his high school track coach.

"He threw in the stipulation that I had to build up, I think, at least a fifteen-hundred-point lead over second place. I said, 'Well, if I do that, you have to buy me a Whopper with cheese and a large orange soda.' He laughed, but we came to terms and shook hands on it. In both my junior and senior years, when that last event came around, the mile, I was sitting in the stands, enjoying my Whopper and soda."

There'd be many defensive backs and pitchers wishing that Bo stayed on the bench enjoying a burger and pop during his brief but intensely successful NFL and MLB careers. After winning the 1985 Heisman Trophy as a running back at Alabama's Auburn University, Jackson opted to play baseball. Signing with the Kansas City Royals, the muscular six-foot-one outfielder and designated hitter learned how to hit the curveball and began swatting prodigious home runs starting in 1986. Jackson began to show his true potential in 1989, when he was voted to start for the American League All-Star team and was named the game's MVP for both his offense and defense. In the top of the first inning, he snared Pedro Guerrero's two-out line drive to left-center field to save two runs. Then, leading off the bottom half, in his first All-Star plate appearance, Bo blasted a monstrous 448-foot home run off Rick Reuschel of the San Francisco Giants.

Jackson was just getting started. In the second inning, he beat out the throw on a potential double play to drive in the eventual winning run. He then stole second base, making him only the second player in All-Star Game history to hit a home run and steal a base in the same game. The first? Willie Mays. Jackson finished the game with two hits in four at-bats, one run scored, and two RBIs. For the season, he smacked 32 home runs and drove in 105 runs, fourth best in the league.

Al Davis, owner of the Los Angeles Raiders, was a fan of Jackson the college gridiron star, having seen him play at Auburn, and was receptive to the idea of him pursuing both baseball and football. Soon a contract was negotiated where Jackson would be permitted to play the entire baseball season with the Royals and then would report to the Raiders once the season was finished.

Los Angeles's head coach, Tom Flores, remembered being initially puzzled by the whole thing.

"First of all, 1987 was a strike-shortened season," explained Flores, whose struggling team was "in a bit of a rebuilding mode. We signed Bo. To be honest, I was not thrilled. I was wearing down and also just getting tired of it all. I just wanted to get the team together and play as a unit after the strike. The strike had divided some of our veterans. Bo shows up, and I'm thinking, 'We already have Marcus Allen. What am I going to do with both of these guys?'" Allen, just 27, and one of the game's best running backs, was on his way to his fifth Pro Bowl in his first six years in the NFL.

"That all changed the first time I saw Jackson on the practice field," Flores recalled. "I said, 'Whoa! I think we will find something for Bo.' If we had Bo from day one, it would have been an entirely different season for us. He was just awesome. He was very powerful and incredibly fast for a guy that size. Coming over when the baseball season was done, he adjusted pretty quick. He was smart. Whatever we gave him, he took it and ran with it."

And ran and ran.

In his rookie season, he averaged nearly 7 yards a carry, the best among the league's leading rushers. But during his brief four-year NFL career, it was the way Bo ran that captured fans. He'd bull over defenders on one play, then outsprint everybody for a 90-yard touchdown on the next.

That was all on display on a Monday-night game against the Seattle Seahawks on November 30, 1987, which also happened to be the rookie running back's 25th birthday. Bo celebrated in style. His 14-yard touchdown catch put Los Angeles up, 14–7, in the second. And just before the half, Bo demonstrated how he could fly. Jackson, who ran the 40-yard dash in 4.125 seconds, beat everyone to the sidelines and then simply outran the entire Seattle defense for a 91-yard score. But he didn't stop after crossing the goal line, he just kept going through the end zone and into the locker room.

In the second half, he paid back Seattle linebacker Brian Bosworth, who had made disparaging remarks about the Raiders' rookie in the lead-up to the game. Jackson made him eat his words.

From the Seahawks' 2, Jackson took the handoff and ran straight at Bosworth. Lowering his shoulder, he drove the defender backward into the end zone and onto the ground. Touchdown, Raiders. By the end of Los Angeles's 37–14 rout, Jackson had gained 221 yards on just 18 carries. All of America now knew the former all-American knew football. (See chapter 24, "Prime Time.")

After making his first Pro Bowl in 1990, Jackson suffered an NFL-career-ending hip injury from a seemingly routine tackle at the end of a 34-yard run in a playoff game on January 13, 1991, against the Bengals. Football fans were left to wonder what might have been. Still, Vincent Edward "Bo" Jackson, the only man to be an All-Star in baseball and an All-Pro in football, is arguably the world's greatest living athlete in team sports.

Since Bo and Deion captivated America, being part of that rare breed of an athlete to shine in two sports, it has not been done to any real extent since. Not that the talent isn't out there, but there are several reasons for that absence.

One is that we live in an age of specialization. And it starts in high school sports, where competition for college scholarships have forced many young athletes to pick a single sport and focus on specific skill sets. Naturally, there are also the obvious physical and mental limitations. The fact of the matter is that only a handful of athletes at any time have the talent to play pro baseball and pro football at such high levels as to justify their participation in both simultaneously.

Finally, there is the compensation factor. Consider that in 1992, Sanders was making more than $2 million a year as the best cornerback in the NFL. These days, the highest-paid cornerback in the NFL earns $15 million a season.

"Are there more athletes out there capable of being professional in two sports today?" asked quarterback-turned-broadcaster Phil Simms. "Not a lot, but yes. However, today there are a lot of demands that each sport requires. Baseball is grueling. It is every day. I have talked to many professional baseball players, and every one of them has said there are times they have arrived at the ballpark and asked themselves, 'How can I do this again tonight?' You combine that with the physicality of football, and it is just too hard on the body. And you can make more than enough money in just one sport."

But even if a team owner making a big investment in someone who's not full-time might hesitate, sports is entertainment. Crossover stars are held in such high regard that there's got to be an athlete down the line who surely would love the challenge of joining the elite club headed by the likes of Thorpe, Bo, and Deion, and would insist on a contract to allow him the opportunity.

CHAPTER TWENTY-ONE

OVERTIME, ICE, AND *HEIDI*

Of the many games and plays during this era that have stood the test of time, three in particular loom large for demonstrating not only the inherent drama of the sport but also the different ways that television captures and enhances that drama, as well as its importance in reaching the vast majority of fans who prefer viewing the game from their living rooms than at the stadium.

OVERTIME

The 1958 NFL championship game between the Baltimore Colts and New York Giants was not close to being "the greatest game"—sloppy play led to seven turnovers—but it was one of the most impactful. Thanks to the first sudden death conclusion to a title game, with the Colts winning, 23–17, and a national television audience to witness it, the NFL was catapulted into an unprecedented level of public awareness.

At that time, the big sports were baseball, boxing, and college football. Pro football was more like a winter diversion, and, unlike college football, many of its teams did not play in decent stadiums able to hold 70,000 to 80,000 spectators. But just like Baltimore quarterback Johnny Unitas, the man who turned the two-minute drill into his own artistic stamp on the sport, pro football had risen from the sandlot days to marquee Sunday-afternoon status. With this game, it was on its way to becoming a core element of American mass popular culture.

"I think most of the drama came from the championship setting rather than the game itself. We came down to tie it in the final seconds. Then it became the first playoff game ever to go into sudden death. You can't have much more drama than that," said Unitas after the thrilling conclusion.

Certainly, the setting was right. Historic Yankee Stadium, center of the world's media capital. It was New York's stoppers—Andy Robustelli, Emlen Tunnell, Roosevelt Grier, and Sam Huff—who were key in getting the Giants to that title shot. New York won its final four games in a row, the last against the rival Cleveland Browns, on December 14. In the closing seconds of a 10–10 tie, kicker Pat Summerall crushed the frozen ball between the posts in a snowstorm so blinding that nobody knows if the distance was really only 49 yards. The very next Sunday, the two teams reassembled at Yankee Stadium for the divisional playoff. This time the Giants shut out the Browns in another low-scoring affair, 10–0. Meanwhile, Baltimore's Unitas showed his legendary toughness by overcoming two broken ribs and a punctured lung—sitting out only one week—then coming back in Week 9 to uncork a 58-yard touchdown bomb to Lenny Moore on the first play of the game against the Rams.

Unfazed by the magnitude of the December 28 championship game, the 25-year-old Unitas was on fire in Yankee Stadium as well. Standing tall in the pocket in the face of the vaunted Giants pressure, he teamed up with his go-to receiver, Raymond Berry, for 12 big receptions and also connected early on with a laser to Moore in traffic. Throughout, he demonstrated uncommon leadership, swagger, and, most of all, astute play calling.

By the fourth quarter, the Giants had a heroic goal-line stand and scored a touchdown of their own, followed by another, to take the lead, 17–14.

However, one of the crucial plays of the game has gone largely underreported. Colts defensive end Gino Marchetti stopped the Giants on a third-down run, preventing them from extending the drive and likely winning in regulation. To accomplish that, the All-Pro defender broke his ankle on the play and was forced to watch the remainder of the game from the bench.

Such was the respect he garnered from his intense study of opponents that Raymond Berry was the only one Unitas allowed to speak up in the huddle. "We had an understanding," the receiver explained, "because I had done so much film study of defensive backs and man-to-man coverage that I knew what plays I could get open on and ones that I probably could not. John relied on me to relay the information so we did not waste any plays at all. When we attacked the defensive back, it was a sure thing. What I think threw the Giants off was that this was a two-minute drive with the clock moving, and all these passes we were completing were inside routes: slants, square ins, hooks, post patterns. So, we did not attack the outside, where you might think it would be a logical place to go in that situation."(A standard practice of offenses, usually late in the first half or at the end of the game, trying to stop the clock by the use of outside patterns.)

Unitas had taken advantage of the clutch Marchetti play and after connecting with Berry three times for 62 yards, Baltimore tied the game with a field goal, and the first 60 minutes ended at 17–17.

Sudden-death overtime was all Baltimore. Unitas was in a zone, fooling the Giants with runs in pass situations and vice versa all the way down the field until fullback Alan Ameche went through a huge hole from the 1-yard line for the victory. And as jubilant Colts fans raced onto the field and tore down the goal post, a nation rose to its feet before small screens all across America.

In a clutch performance (12 catches, 178 yards, one TD) that would help propel him to the Pro Football Hall of Fame, Berry reflected on how the marriage of television and the NFL really came together on that cold Sunday afternoon in 1958.

"It was one of the first nationally televised NFL games. It was broadcast coast-to-coast. I think the exposure of that particular game, combined with the drama of it—and the overtime concept, which had never been seen by anybody before—the combination of those factors launched the game into history and had a huge effect that provided the NFL a level of acceptance by the American public that it had never experienced before."

The nearly 50 million Americans who watched on 11 million TV sets helped pave the way for the NFL to become "America's Game." It would be a springboard in replacing minuscule local television deals with national TV contracts worth billions of dollars and a network all their own. (Ironically, since the game was not a sellout, NFL Commissioner Bert Bell refused to lift the blackout in a 75-mile radius of New York, keeping to his philosophy that people should not get for free what they can pay to see at the stadium.)

THE ICE BOWL

Nine years later, fans who braved sitting in the stands where the temperature at game time registered a frigid 13 degrees below zero witnessed history as the Green Bay Packers edged the Dallas Cowboys, 21–17 in the 1967 NFL championship game at Lambeau Field.

But again, it was a national television audience that helped carry the Ice Bowl to legendary status. Viewers from sunny Florida to cool Oregon were riveted by how players could even show up in such conditions. Hall of Fame defensive back Mel Renfro recalled that things didn't look so bleak when the Cowboys stepped off the plane in Green Bay:

"We flew in on a Saturday, and it was a 'balmy' twenty degrees and sunshine. The field was excellent. We had a brief practice there, and we were licking our chops because our team was all about speed, and that was a definite advantage for us. We were very confident that we were going to win that game. But the next morning, we wake up to hear reports that it is seventeen below. We didn't think much about it until we got to the stadium."

Renfro's defensive teammate Bob Lilly learned of the weather change after his roommate, defensive end George Andrie, returned from early-morning church services. "George had gone to early Mass. When I woke up," Lilly said, "I looked out the window, and I couldn't believe how sunny and clear it was. Then George came in the room. He didn't say anything about the temperature outside. He simply got a glass of water, pulled back the curtain, and threw the water on the window. The water froze before it ran down to the window sill. And it was seventy degrees in that room. I said, 'My goodness, George, how cold is it out there?' He said, 'About nine below, and it's supposed to get to about twenty-five below with thirty-five-mile-per-hour winds.'"

Then, recognizing the rare, heroic opportunity that such weather offered, George told Lilly, "Most of our teammates have never played in conditions like this, so you and I are going to have to show them how it is by going out there with no warmup jacket on."

"By the time we get out there, it is twelve to fifteen degrees below zero," Lilly said. "We've got icicles hanging out of our noses. One of the trainers from the Packers comes over and says, 'You guys need to go in and let your icicles thaw out, because if you try to pull them out, you'll also tug off the membranes inside your nose. Also, keep Vaseline handy on the bench and apply it to your nose.' Back in the locker room, we bundled up with everything we could. An extra T-shirt, some had long johns, Saran Wrap on our feet. But Ernie Stautner said, 'No gloves! That's for sissies!'" The rugged Stautner, a

Cowboys assistant coach, had been a Hall of Fame defensive tackle for the Pittsburgh Steelers.

"So, we run out onto the field," Lilly continued, "and here come the Packers. They are wearing turtleneck sweaters, they've got on gloves, something warm around their heads, and here we are freezing our tails off."

A special heating system that coach Vince Lombardi had installed beneath the grass at Lambeau Field had worked fine during Saturday practice when the temperature dipped into the twenties, but the system broke down in Sunday's arctic conditions. The metal whistles stuck to game officials' lips; they had to yell "You're down!" to ball carriers.

Green Bay jumped out to a 14–0 lead, and it seemed like experience in the cold weather favored them. But Dallas scored a touchdown as Andrie rumbled in for a TD on a Starr fumble. And with a field goal and a second touchdown in the fourth quarter on a Dan Reeves HB option 50-yard TD pass to receiver Lance Rentzel, suddenly, with just 4:50 left in the game, the Packers trailed, 17–14. They had 68 yards of ice to go. Starr mixed handoffs and short passes, mostly to his running backs, to bring the team to the Cowboys' 3 with 1:11 left. It took two plays and most of the remaining time to get to the 1. There was time left for just one more play.

With just over a dozen ticks of the clock remaining and the temperature down to 18 degrees below zero, the Packers found themselves about two feet away from victory. Starr called time-out. The two previous running plays had gone nowhere. With no time-outs left, a running play seemed totally out of the question. A completed pass likely would win it. Even an incomplete pass might at least stop the clock and give the Packers a chance to tie the game with a field goal on fourth down and send it into overtime. After consulting with Packers coach Vince Lombardi, Starr returned to the huddle.

Lilly explained what was going on in the Cowboys' huddle as

his defensive unit stood near frozen on the goal line. "Well, we knew they were going for it," he said. "And we knew they were coming up the middle. I told Lee Roy Jordan, the captain, 'We need to call a time-out. Get a screwdriver and cut through some of this ice to create some footing here in the middle so we can hold our own. Otherwise we are just standing here on ice.' It was really slick. We did not do it. I don't even know if we had a time-out, but I thought it was a good idea.

"So, they come up the middle running a QB sneak, double-teaming Jethro Pugh. I think Chuck Mercein, who was ideally built for that game, hit Bart in the rear and gave him a little push. They always say they didn't, but I always see it on the film. Don't know if that mattered anyway, because there are no excuses. We got beat."

It was a smart call by Starr to keep the ball himself instead of handing it off to the running back, who could have slipped, stumbled, or muffed the handoff. At the same time, it was pretty bold, because if he failed, he'd have to face the wrath of Lombardi. Starr's dive gave Green Bay the championship, 21–17.

"I don't think there was much said," Renfro recalled of the mood in the Dallas clubhouse. "There were some teammates suffering from frostbite, and the concern was that there might be some permanent damage. So that's what our focus was. There was talk later that the game should never have been played under those conditions, and, looking back, I agree with that."

Dallas would have its day, but just enduring this one was the priority.

"It was a game of survival more than anything else," said Lilly. "We were pretty depressed. The only good thing I could think of was, during takeoff, as the sun set in the west, I said, 'Lord, thank you for getting us out of here alive.'"

To this day, the Ice Bowl is talked about as an all-time classic, and no doubt its national television audience created new Packers and Cowboys fans all across America. Less than a year later, stunned broadcast executives would learn just how passionate fans were about rooting for their favorite team on television.

THE *HEIDI* GAME

On Sunday, November 17, 1968, the New York Jets traveled to Oakland to play the Raiders. Two very good teams, both 7-2, both play-off bound, and both with a strong dislike for each other. The Raiders' gritty, blue-collar defensive players reserved special disdain for Jets quarterback Joe Namath, the AFL's glamour boy—which they expressed by pummeling Broadway Joe relentlessly with cheap shots and late hits, shoving his face in the mud until he gagged, punching him in the groin, elbowing his kidneys, and, one time, delivering a blow that fractured a cheekbone. But Namath never let on that it got to him. He stood tall in the pocket, and when he fired a 50-yard touchdown to Don Maynard, the Jets took the lead, 26–22, in the fourth quarter. Jim Turner added a field goal to put New York up by 7.

Oakland knotted things up at 29 after nimble-fingered receiver Fred Biletnikoff grabbed a 22-yard touchdown pass from quarterback Daryle Lamonica. However, with just over one minute left, New York's Jim Turner kicked a field goal to give the Jets a 32–29 lead.

Back in New York, Dick Cline, NBC's supervisor of broadcast operation control, was nervously looking at the clock, as the game was running long. It was almost seven o'clock eastern time, and the network was scheduled to air a made-for-TV movie, *Heidi*, starring Michael Redgrave, Jean Simmons, and Maximilian Schell, based on a nineteenth-century children's novel about a sweet orphan girl who lives in the Swiss Alps. The Timex watch company had paid $700,000, a substantial amount in 1968, to sponsor the heartwarming tale, and it never dawned on anyone at NBC that the game could possibly run over. Following a commercial break, at the stroke of seven, Cline dutifully replaced the game with *Heidi*. Suddenly viewers on the East Coast were being treated to the sight of a little girl in a dirndl instead of Joe Namath wearing dirt and shoulder pads.

Fans in the other time zones saw the game to its conclusion. Jets fans, probably reasonably confident that their team had put the victory on ice, missed an amazing—and devastating—finish by the Raiders. First, with 42 seconds left, Lamonica fired a 43-yard touchdown to halfback Charlie Smith to regain the lead, 36–32. Then, on the ensuing kickoff, Jets return specialist Earl Christy bobbled the ball. An unknown named Preston Ridlehuber grabbed it on the 2-yard line and rumbled in for the score. The Raiders had tallied 14 points in 9 seconds to win decisively, 43–32, in one of football's wildest endings.

"The *Heidi* game was so bizarre at the end, it was, like, looney tunes!" said Oakland running back Pete Banaszak. "It was a game of so much action. Things were happening so fast. There were probably sixty minutes of action in the last two minutes," he added with a chuckle. "But I do remember, we were very businesslike; just doing what we are supposed to be doing. Preston Ridlehuber—and I'll never forget that name for the rest of my life!—made the play of the game by recovering that fumble. It was one of those games that made the American Football League: close, high scoring, dramatic to the end.

"And yet, ironically, missed at the crucial moment by the largest TV market in America and home of the Jets."

Unfortunately for NBC, its troubles were just beginning. Overwhelmed by thousands upon thousands of angry Jets fans calling in to voice their displeasure, the network's switchboard crashed. NBC president Julian Goodman was forced to apologize publicly. However, Dick Cline had no regrets, because he surely would have lost his job had he not done what the network was contractually obligated to do.

Delbert Mann, the director of *Heidi,* said that the opening scenes contained key plot points, so if audiences joined the film even just a few minutes late, they would be lost. During a key dramatic scene in the TV movie, NBC ran a crawl providing viewers with the final score. This served only to incite more negative reaction, as fans realized they'd missed an improbable finish. While Jets fans fumed, Mann benefitted from what he called "priceless publicity."

On the losing side, Jets kicker Jim Turner, despite having contributed four field goals and two PATs, was philosophical about ultimately coming up short. "I remember arriving back home at the airport, and there were a lot of pissed-off people," he recalled. "It was a damn fine game; it was a real contest. The Raiders were a very talented team, and we went nose to nose with them."

Six weeks later, Turner and company would avenge the shocking defeat by turning the tables in the AFL championship game, this time with the Raiders on the Jets' home turf at Shea Stadium. After a Namath interception in the fourth quarter led to an Oakland touchdown and its first lead of the game, 23–20, number 12 quickly brought the deflated crowd back to life by connecting with Don Maynard on two consecutive pass plays of 52 yards and 6 more for the touchdown. New York held Oakland at bay for the final eight minutes to claim its first AFL flag, 27–23.

As for the so-called *Heidi* game, it altered forever the relationship between football and television. From then on, the game would become top priority. All other programming would just have to wait on the sidelines.

CHAPTER TWENTY-TWO

THE PIVOTAL GAME

Even though the AFL-NFL merger would be completed with the start of the 1970 season, there was great concern among owners of both leagues about the caliber of play in its year-ending championship. In the first two Super Bowls, then called the AFL-NFL Championship Game, the National Football League's representative from Green Bay trounced the American Football League's Kansas City Chiefs and Oakland Raiders, respectively, by a combined score of 68–24.

Two days before Super Bowl III, to be held in Miami's Orange Bowl, NFL Commissioner Pete Rozelle held a press conference announcing that the league would consider altering the structure of postseason play to allow two superior (meaning NFL, soon to become the NFC) teams to meet in the final game. Based on the owners' views, that was not so shocking.

But what shocked was this headline from the next day's *New York Times*:

ROZELLE INDICATES TOMORROW'S SUPER BOWL CONTEST COULD BE NEXT TO LAST.

For its entire existence, the AFL had been the underdog. It would be no different in January 1969. The Jets were overwhelming underdogs in Super Bowl III: 18 points, by most oddsmakers. This time the AFL champion faced a Baltimore Colts squad that had rolled to a 13-1 regular-season record on the strength of the league's top defense, which allowed a miserly 10.3 points per game. The Colts had three regular-season shutouts and with a prominent display of their defensive prowess blanked the Browns, 34–0, in the NFL championship game in Cleveland.

Enter Joe Namath. Tough, brash, poised, confident, and possessor of a tremendously quick release.

The two teams could not have been more different. The Jets were pro football's rebels with a cause. Defying league orders to cut their mustaches and long hair—with their leader, swaggering Broadway Joe, sporting white shoes and fur coats, and riding motorcycles, it was a sort of philosophical clash with the old-school, crew-cut, high-top-cleated, conservative Colts led by legendary quarterback Johnny Unitas and his backup, 34-four-year-old journeyman Earl Morrall.

Baltimore was the fifth stop in 13 years for Morrall, who spent much of his career warming the bench as a number two. That was the plan for 1968. But then Unitas went down in the final exhibition game, pressing Morrall into service. All he did was coolly guide the Colts to the best record in football and win the NFL MVP Award.

At a pre–Super Bowl party at the Doral Hotel in Miami Beach, retired standout NFL quarterback Norm Van Brocklin, then head coach of the Atlanta Falcons, had this to say about the Jets' leader: "I'll tell you what I think of Joe Namath on Sunday night—after he plays his first pro game," he said dismissively.

This was what the AFL's player of the year was facing, and he was tired of it.

On the Thursday before the game, Namath was accepting his award at the Miami Touchdown Club when an enthusiastic Colts fan interrupted. He boasted that his team would conquer the Jets—prompting sport's most publicized declaration.

As Namath recalled:

There was a fella in the audience that yelled out at me, "We're gonna kick your a––––s!" So I said, "Wait a minute, we've been listening to this kind of talk for ten days or so, and I've got news for you. We're gonna win the game. I guarantee it." I gotta admit, I was fed up. Tired of being told we have no chance. Comparing the AFL and NFL, and we're not getting enough respect. I understood we had lost the first two Super Bowls, but the AFL did not get respect from the other league, from the media, from football fans in general, other than the AFL towns. And even they were wondering about us. They wanted us to bring home a championship, but until you do it, it's hard for anybody to have that sincere respect.[49]

Naturally, Jets head coach Weeb Ewbank was not too pleased with his quarterback's proclamation. "I talked to him at our meeting the next day," Ewbank said. "I said, 'Dadgummit, why did you say that? We had them right where we wanted them.'"

But Broadway Joe's teammates had his back.

"Weeb basically said we didn't need to give the Colts any extra motivation," defensive end Gerry Philbin recalled. "Namath turned it around on Weeb, saying it was his fault for giving us all this confidence. But you know what? Namath believed in his team, and his conviction was contagious. When Namath guaranteed it, he really meant it, and that meant a lot to me as a player. If you have a quarterback this tough, and Joe was, you knew he could back up what he says. So, both the offense and defense took it to heart."[50]

One of Baltimore's strengths was its terrorizing blitz schemes. The defense manhandled offensive lines and was on top of the quarterback in the blink of an eye. However, with Namath's quick release, ability to read defenses, and call audibles, New York coaches put together a game plan based on the premise that the Colts would not change their ways. With all the tremendous success they enjoyed, why would they?

According to Jets tight end Pete Lammons, their confidence stemmed from knowing they could handle Baltimore's swarming meet-at-the-quarterback attack. "We'd love having any team blitz us," he insisted. "That played right into our strength. We had great blocking running backs in Matt Snell, Emerson Boozer, Bill Mathis, etcetera, and they were not afraid to take on linebackers right between the numbers. At the same time, they could all catch, and their quick little flares worked quite well in our favor."[51]

They certainly did. Namath would fire short passes to his backs to offset the blitz, but one of the game's key plays did not even result in any yardage at all. He threw an early long ball to Don Maynard. Though it fell incomplete, he knew the Colts were worried about the deep threat the stellar wide receiver presented. Unbeknownst to the NFL champs, Maynard was trying his best to hide an ailing hamstring muscle and would serve as an effective decoy all day. He didn't catch a single pass—but split end George Sauer Jr. grabbed eight for 133 yards.

As the game progressed under cloudy skies in Miami, what the 75,377 fans who paid $12 a ticket were observing—along with 55 million more watching on television—was a pattern of ball control by the Jets and the Colts squandering multiple scoring opportunities. After a scoreless first quarter, New York got on the board first. Snell's 35 yards on six carries and Namath's four completions for 43 yards accounted for most of an 80-yard drive that culminated in the running back's 4-yard plunge for a touchdown. The 7–0 lead stood up to halftime. Baltimore had five legitimate scoring opportunities, but a pair of missed field goals by Lou Michaels and three interceptions thrown by Morrall helped keep them off the scoreboard.

That third pick was de-Morrallizing. It was a trick play and the intended receiver, Jimmy Orr, was all alone in the end zone ready to tie the game, but the ball never arrived. From the Jets' 41, Baltimore tried a flea flicker play. Tom Matte ran off right tackle after taking a handoff, then pitched the ball back to Morrall. The play completely fooled the Jets defense, but the Colts' QB failed to see Orr and instead threw a pass intended for running back Jerry Hill that was intercepted by safety Jim Hudson as time expired in the first half.

Even though they were down by only a touchdown, the mighty Colts were in a bit of a stupor from which they never recovered.

"It almost seemed like our team was sitting on the sideline enjoying a Diet Coke, saying, 'We'll catch up no matter who we are playing against.' We were too casual," Colts linebacker Mike Curtis recalled. "That lackadaisical attitude ran through the entire game. I was fairly new—just a pup—but felt we were lacking focus. I was so pissed that I spent halftime banging my head against the toilet stall and beating up a urinal in the locker room. Turns out another teammate was doing the same thing in the shower, so I guess we were only beating the Orange Bowl plumbing."[52]

As he did in the first half, throughout the third and fourth quarters, Namath succeeded in breaking the rhythm of the Colts' defense, something no other team had managed to do all season. At the same time, the Jets' defense was forcing Morrall into having one of the worst games of his career. For the day, he completed a mere 6 of 17 passes for 71 yards, with those three interceptions. By the third quarter, he was replaced by Johnny Unitas, who had missed most of the regular season with an elbow injury.

The Jets never scored another TD. But their time-consuming drives brought them close enough for Jim Turner to kick field goals of 32, 30, and 9 yards, to make it 16–0 in the fourth quarter. It proved to be more than enough.

Baltimore finally scored with 3:19 left, as Jerry Hill ran the ball in from the 1-yard line to complete an 80-yard drive engineered by Unitas, whose tender right arm restricted him mostly to short passes. A successful onside kick gave the ball back to the Colts at the New York 44, but they could not capitalize. The New York Jets were pro football champions in one of the greatest upsets in sports history. As the final seconds ticked off the clock, Joe Namath jogged off the field, head down, his index finger pointing skyward—a gesture that said it all.

For members of that Colts team, it is a loss that lingers.

"Other than personal tragedy and death, honestly, it was the worst day of my life," admitted Bill Curry, the Colts' center. "And it remains so because we had invested so much of ourselves in building a great football team, and when we left that field, we knew we had thrown it away. We lost only two games in two years. We would be remembered as one of the greatest teams of all time, but the only thing we're remembered for is losing in the end."[53]

The Jets' win unified professional football. The victory by the underdogs brought respect to the entire AFL. Once the two leagues merged, the AFL-turned-AFC would go on to win nine of the next 11 Super Bowls. Super Bowl III was the game that made the Super Bowl *the Super Bowl.*

"I've broadcast sports for fifty years," said Curt Gowdy, one of television's legendary sportscasters. "I've done eight Super Bowls, a lot of Rose Bowls and Orange Bowls, World Series, eighteen or twenty NCAA tournaments, and eight Olympics. As I look back, my most memorable game was Super Bowl III because of its historical importance as one of the biggest upsets of all time in sports."

Jets defensive end Gerry Philbin reflected, "I've always said winning that game went beyond Jets over Colts. The Super Bowl was bigger than life. It was the AFL versus the NFL, and we represented the AFL. I was really happy for our league, which had taken a beating for years that we were not good enough. We proved we were as good as any team in the NFL. It was a victory for respect."

When appreciative teammates awarded the game ball to Namath, the quarterback flashed a grin of gratitude, then announced that he was going to present this ball to the league office as a symbol of the AFL coming of age in pro football. A rousing cheer followed.

THE SECOND QUARTER ALL-TIME TEAM

OFFENSE

WRs	Lance Alworth	San Diego Chargers
	Paul Warfield	Miami Dolphins
TE	John Mackey	Baltimore Colts
G	Jerry Kramer	Green Bay Packers
	Tom Mack	Los Angeles Rams
T	Ron Mix	Los Angeles/San Diego Chargers
	Jim Parker	Baltimore Colts
C	Jim Otto	Oakland Raiders
RBs	Jim Brown	Cleveland Browns
	Gale Sayers	Chicago Bears
QB	John Unitas	Baltimore Colts

DEFENSE

DE	Doug Atkins	Chicago Bears
	Deacon Jones	Los Angeles Rams
DT	Merlin Olsen	Los Angeles Rams
	Bob Lilly	Dallas Cowboys
LB	Bobby Bell	Kansas City Chiefs
	Dick Butkus	Chicago Bears
	Chuck Howley	Dallas Cowboys
DB	Willie Brown	Oakland Raiders
	Mel Renfro	Dallas Cowboys
S	Larry Wilson	St. Louis Cardinals
	Willie Wood	Green Bay Packers
P	Jerrel Wilson	Kansas City Chiefs
K	Jan Stenerud	Kansas City Chiefs
HC	Paul Brown	Cleveland Browns

PART THREE

Third Quarter

★ ★ ★ (1970–1994) ★ ★ ★

CHAPTER TWENTY-THREE

BAD BLOOD

In the week leading up to game day, then throughout the 60-minute battle itself, fans get to feel the full range of emotions—anxiety, excitement, anticipation, joy, anger, disappointment—euphoria, but that is all taken up several notches when the contest is being played against a rival.

Packers fans would take guns and fireworks into the streets in the wee hours of the night and shoot them into the sky just outside the Bears' Green Bay hotel to keep them awake. Raiders management was accused of sending in a nonessential player for the express purpose of starting a fight with a Chiefs star, hoping to get them both kicked out of the game.

What follows are some of the leading examples of the rivalries that make up some of the most intense matchups in the National Football League.

BEARS-PACKERS

Lombardi versus Halas; Hornung versus Butkus; Sayers versus Nitschke; in later years, linebacker Brian Urlacher versus quarterback Aaron Rodgers; big city versus small town—the Green Bay Packers–Chicago Bears rivalry, one of the oldest, bleeds history.

But for one Hall of Famer, what comes to mind when he thinks of the rivalry are the elements: "When you think of Bears-Packers, you think of bad weather," said Green Bay quarterback Brett Favre, singling out a clash from the 1994 season. "I always remember this one game because it represented what seems like the atmosphere between the two teams. It was in Chicago on Halloween night, and the rain was pouring down. And on this night, they were honoring Dick Butkus and Gale Sayers at halftime. We wore throwbacks and those were ugly, ugly uniforms. As part of our pregame, we always ran a play where I threw a ball between two linebackers to tight end Ed West. To say the rain was blinding and sideways was an understatement, but I threw a pass to him. I never threw a curveball so well in my life," Favre said, chuckling. "It him right between the eight and the six. His nickname was 'the Toolbox,' and you can hardly understand what he was saying. But he comes up to me and says, 'Whatever you do, don't throw the damn ball to me tonight.' The weather was that bad."

Green Bay overcame the 60-mile-an-hour winds to win, 33–6. Favre relied less on his "curveball"—throwing just 15 passes—that night than he did on his legs. He rushed for a career-high 58 yards—including a 36-yard touchdown run in the second quarter when he leaped over a Bears defender.

It was a rivalry borne of geography, but, for many years, you had two teams that were vying for the title most of the time. It is amazing looking at the records how few times they actually played for the title, but it seems like many of them were important games impacting the playoffs. The first meeting back in 1921 saw the Chicago Staleys shut out the Packers, 20–0. The following year, Chicago became the Bears, and the feud has existed ever since between these two teams that have won a combined 22 NFL titles and have appeared in seven Super Bowls and 55 playoffs.

"Vince Lombardi truly respected Halas," said center Bill Curry, who spent his first two NFL seasons in Green Bay before being traded to Baltimore in 1967. "He would lecture us, telling us, 'This man started the league. We love him, and we're gonna beat him to death.' But he really respected the old man and would enjoy talking with him pregame much more so than any other opposing coach."

Then there were two former exceptional players-turned-coaches who genuinely disliked each other: Mike Ditka and Forrest Gregg.

"I can remember one game when Forrest Gregg was the head coach of the Packers," said former Bears defensive back Leslie Frazier. "I believe it was the first play of the game. The Packers' defense ran Walter Payton out-of-bounds, but then also ran him up over the bench. That was ten or fifteen yards past the sidelines, so it is that kind of stuff—like a defenseman turning quarterback Jim McMahon on his shoulder—that intensifies the rivalry. It went beyond a ballgame. It was more like an alley fight."

Don Pierson, a longtime reporter on the Bears beat, recalled: "Back in '85, a Green Bay radio station took a bag of manure in the Bears locker room. Coach Ditka says, 'This is what they think of us,' so the Bears went out and kicked their ass. William Perry scored on offense." The 335-pound rookie, nicknamed "Refrigerator," who looked about as wide as he was tall, was known as an immovable defensive lineman, but Chicago let him carry the ball from the Green Bay 1-yard line that day. "They had a refrigerator out in the parking lot," said Pierson, "and Packers fans paid a dollar each to whack it with a sledgehammer. You go to a game in Green Bay today, regardless of who the opponent is that day, you can see fans chanting, 'The Bears still suck!'"

COLTS-PATRIOTS

Despite being AFC East division rivals from 1970 through 2001 (dating back to the Colts' time in Baltimore from 1953 through

1983), their intensified enmity wasn't prevalent until Indianapolis was moved into the newly formed AFC South following the 2001 season as part of an NFL realignment.

It was a rivalry based on the marquee appeal of two of the best quarterbacks the game has ever seen: New England's Tom Brady and Indianapolis's Peyton Manning.

Brady received his first start against the Colts—and the first of his glorious career—in the third week of the 2001 season, on account of an injury to then-first-string quarterback Drew Bledsoe. New England, 0-2, had scored just 20 points in its first two games, played two weeks apart because of the September 11 terrorist attacks on the United States. Both the NFL and Major League Baseball canceled all games until the following week. In front of 60,000 spectators at Foxboro Stadium, the Patriots manhandled the visiting Colts, 44–13. Brady, twenty-four, wasn't dominant, connecting on 13 of 23 passing attempts for 168 yards, and not one touchdown by air. But he didn't throw any interceptions, either—unlike the 25-year-old Manning, then in his fourth season as Indianapolis's starting QB, who was victimized three times, with two of them being returned for Patriots touchdowns. New England, behind the rookie, was to win 11 of its remaining 14 games, including a 38–17 pasting of the Colts in Week 6, and reel off three more victories in the postseason to win the franchise its first Super Bowl in three tries.

Beating Indianapolis became a habit for Brady. He prevailed the first six times he opposed Manning, including the 2003 AFC championship game and a 2004 AFC divisional playoff. It wasn't until the following year that Indianapolis forced a different outcome. In 2005, Manning notched a regular-season victory and a big win in the 2006 AFC championship game on the Colts' way to winning Super Bowl XLI. The 2007 Patriots' perfect 16-0 season included a comeback 24–20 victory in Week 9, their final visit to the RCA Dome.

And back and forth it went. In 2010 Indy's first trip to Gillette

Stadium since 2006 ended with a last-minute Manning interception, as New England held on to a 31–28 win. That would be the
last time the Patriots faced the Colts with Peyton taking the snap
from center; a severe neck injury sidelined him for all of 2011. Indianapolis, thinking the 35-year-old was finished, let him sign with the
Denver Broncos. Finished? Not quite. All he did was take Denver
to the postseason four years in a row. It wasn't until 2016, after winning the 50th Super Bowl, that Manning was ready to announce his
retirement.

Jim Sorgi, Manning's backup in Indianapolis, still revels in having been a part of what he called "one of the greatest rivalries in NFL
history: Colts-Patriots. Those Brady-Manning matchups. Those
Bill Belichick–Tony Dungy matchups. You had great teams with
excellent quarterbacks and coaches. But behind it all were terrific
fans who deeply supported their team and despised the opposing
team. The intensity was amazing for a regular-season game—just
unbelievably amped up, as if it were a playoff game. The tension surrounding those games is what made the sport so awesome. Not that
you don't have that week in and week out in the NFL, but a Colts-
Patriots game had a championship atmosphere."

STEELERS-RAIDERS

In what had to be one of the better "period rivalries," the heated
clashes pitting Oakland against Pittsburgh from 1972 through
1976 involved vast amounts of talent and often took place in a
playoff game. During those five seasons, the two teams split four
regular-season games and met in the postseason every year, with
the Immaculate Reception launching the annual late-December or
early-January battle.

On December 23, 1972, Franco Harris's miraculous 60-yard
catch-and-run on a deflected Terry Bradshaw pass beat the Raiders,

13–7, in an AFC divisional playoff game. The Raiders contended that the Steelers' John "Frenchy" Fuqua had batted the ball to Harris, in violation of a rule prohibiting two offensive players from touching a pass in succession. But officials ruled that the ball had, in fact, deflected off Raiders safety Jack Tatum, who collided with Fuqua and the pass at the same time. The final-minute touchdown gave the Steelers franchise its first playoff victory. (See chapter 31, "The Immaculate Reception, Hailing Mary, and the Epic.")

The following December, the Raiders came out on top, winning the 1973 divisional playoff, 33–14. Pittsburgh used the AFC championship game victories over Oakland (24–13 at Oakland in 1974 and 16–10 at Pittsburgh in 1975) as springboards to victories in Super Bowl IX and Super Bowl X, before the Raiders scored a 24–7 victory at home in 1976 on their way to winning Super Bowl XI.

"Those were some of the hardest-hitting games of all time," Raiders running back Pete Banaszak remembered fondly. "There always seemed like there was a lot at stake when we played each other. And you knew when you beat them, you beat someone good." While both teams were known for very physical play, there was also some funny gamesmanship involved as well.

It started with Raiders practices. Oakland equipment man Dick Romanski was tired of players stealing footballs, so he wrote "F--k You" on a dozen or so new balls for practice. That way, the players could not take them and give them away to kids. However, one found its way into the game. Steelers center Mike Webster broke from the huddle and settled himself over the ball. Just as he was set to snap it, he looked down, saw the four-letter word, and demanded a new ball.

"I remember that incident with the ball. After Webster gets into position and is hunched over the ball, all of a sudden he stands straight up. I think that should have been a penalty, but he shows the ball to the referee and says, 'Look! They wrote "F—k You" on it!' That is a true story, actually in the game, and I'll never forget it," said Banaszak with a chuckle.

On another occasion, Raiders offensive lineman George Buehler smeared Vaseline all over his shoulders and the upper sleeves of his jersey, to foil the viselike grip of the Steel Curtain's Joe Greene.

The rise of the Steelers' 1970s dynasty could not have come at a worse time for the Raiders and their die-hard fans. Because Joe Greene and company's controlling grip on the Lombardi Trophy really began in the Oakland-Alameda County Coliseum on December 29, 1974. It was the 1974 AFC championship game, and Pittsburgh dominated Oakland with a suffocating 24–13 victory. The Steel Curtain came of age that day, holding Raiders runners to just 29 yards on 21 carries, and would go on to defeat the Vikings to earn the franchise its first of four Super Bowl wins over the next six years.

"Yes, I think you saw the maturity of the defensive line show that day," stated Pittsburgh safety Mike Wagner. "The Raiders liked to run to their left side, which was the right side of our defensive line. You really saw Ernie Holmes and Dwight White develop as stars, not just living in the shadows of Joe Greene. And our offense had the firepower. So, both the offense and defense had terrific performances. Jack Ham made an amazing interception. J. T. Thomas also had a very good interception, but it went down to the end, for sure. I will tell you for all my teammates on defense, it was the key memory that really set the tone for all those championships. Winning that game said basically, 'Hey, we're good enough.'"

CHIEFS-RAIDERS

These two teams were good enough so often that it seemed each season came down to one of them advancing to the playoffs, if the one could beat the other. The Chiefs-Raiders rivalry is considered one of the NFL's most bitter. Since the AFL was established in 1960, the Chiefs and Raiders have shared the same division: first, the AFL

Western Division, and since the 1970 AFL-NFL merger, the American Football Conference West.

The rivalry started at the top. While AFL founder and Kansas City Chiefs owner Lamar Hunt worked behind the scenes with Dallas Cowboys GM Tex Schramm on the AFL-NFL merger, Raiders partner Al Davis had become the AFL commissioner in 1966. However, Hunt and Schramm agreed that the NFL's Pete Rozelle, not Davis, would become the commissioner of the merged league. Davis returned to Oakland, and the bitter feelings between him and the Raiders and Hunt and the Chiefs had begun.

"We hated each other," stated Pete Banaszak, Oakland Raiders running back during that era. "The word *love* was certainly lost in the vocabulary during that week. Things would happen soon as you landed in Kansas City. The bus from the airport would break down. Alarms would go off in your hotel at three o'clock in the morning. You'd receive crank calls to mess up your sleep in the wee hours. Many things happened to get you out of your rhythm. At the same time, there was a sort of mutual respect."

With three Super Bowl appearances between them, the Chiefs and Raiders were the top teams over the final four years of the AFL. But perhaps it would be a game in Kansas City, early in the 1970 season, the first under the NFL umbrella, that essentially captured their rivalry—one that featured not just hard hitting but also plenty of extracurricular play.

The defending Super Bowl champion Chiefs were just 3-3-1 when they prepared to host the Raiders. A victory over their rivals would be just the tonic to perk up their so-so-so-far season. Leading 17–14 late in the contest, Kansas City quarterback Len Dawson ran a bootleg for a first down that would have let them run out the clock. But Oakland's ferocious Ben Davidson, who stood six foot eight and weighed 275 pounds, only some of it his trademark sinister-looking handlebar mustache, speared Dawson while he was on the ground. Otis Taylor went after Davidson, and the benches emptied.

"I was in the safest place on the field," Davidson joked later. "I was buried under a pile of Chiefs."

According to KC's veteran linebacker Bobby Bell, "We hardly played a game against the Raiders when there wasn't a fight. I think Al Davis would pick out one of his rookies and put him in the game and tell him to start a fight. Al Davis was a good friend of mine. He loved his players. He loved the sport. But my gosh, he loved to win. Just like Coach Stram. And for Al, it was 'Whatever it takes.'"

Unnecessary roughness penalties were called against both Davidson and Taylor, and, under the rules of the day, the down was replayed. Kansas City wound up having to punt. In a series reminiscent of the *Heidi* game two years earlier, Daryle Lamonica took just 38 seconds to bring the Raiders from their 20-yard-line all the way to the Kansas City 41. With three seconds remaining, out trotted George Blanda to attempt an improbable 48-yard field goal. For the season, the 43-year-old kicker made only two of 10 attempts between 40 and 49 yards. But despite the effort of the Chiefs' leaping six-foot-nine Morris Stroud, who almost got a raised hand on the ball, the kick cleared the goal post, ending the contest in a 17–17 tie. The draw ultimately doomed KC in the race for the division title. The Chiefs finished 7-5-2, while the Raiders went 8-4-2 to win the AFC West.

But just a year earlier, the Chiefs had the upper hand.

The Raiders went 12-1-1 in the regular season, which included two hard-fought wins over the Chiefs by a combined 7 points. However, the AFL added wild card teams to the 1969 playoffs, which meant Oakland had to play its 11-3 rival a third time.

"Game three was full of gamesmanship," recalled Bobby Bell. "For example, it had not rained in Oakland for six months, yet the day we get out there for the game, the field was soaked in water. They'd purposely left sprinklers on. Our equipment guy would search the visitors' locker room for listening devices in Oakland.

Everybody wanted to win. It was like going back to the Roman days." He laughed. "You're always looking for an edge."

That third time, however, would not be a charm for the Raiders, despite their swagger. The Oakland players were so confident they were going to win, they had packed their suitcases and stored them at the stadium. The way they figured it, they'd put away Kansas City, break out the bubbly, then take the team bus to the airport for a flight to New Orleans, site of Super Bowl IV.

The Chiefs upset those plans by winning, 17–7. It was a defensive slugfest, with both teams combining for eight turnovers and just 440 total yards. Kansas City overcame an early 7–0 deficit to get revenge on the Raiders for the previous year's humiliating 41–6 playoff loss. The victory was doubly sweet for Kansas City quarterback Len Dawson, who would become MVP of the Super Bowl.

"It was," he said, "one of the most enjoyable things I ever saw: the Raiders' players having to put their suitcases back in their car trunks and unpack them at home, where they would have to watch us play the Super Bowl on TV."

Sometimes a head coach inflames a rivalry, as in the case of Marty Schottenheimer, Kansas City's coach from 1989 through 1998. Nose tackle Bill Maas, in the thick of it all for nine seasons, explained Schottenheimer's exceptional devotion to defeating the Raiders, who decamped to Los Angeles for the 1982 season, only to return home to Oakland in 1995.

"Marty made it a special rivalry," he recalled. "We'd come in Monday to review film from the prior game, but the locker room would be filled with signage: 'Raider Week,' followed by some expletives—they were everywhere. Coach drilled it in our minds: 'Raider Week.' It was definitely different from any other game.

"Now, there's a long history there, of course, but Marty made sure we understood that the Raiders' game was different from any other game, for whatever reason. During Marty's tenure, we were nineteen and two against them. He would say, 'Play our game, and they will implode' and they always did." Schottenheimer regarded the Raiders organization as arrogant thugs—a cheap-shot team that violated the game's spirit and was disrespectful to the NFL. He wasn't the only person in pro football to feel this way, but he took considerable satisfaction in beating them, again and again.

Still, no amount of victories could erase the memory of the physical mayhem. "There were fights all the time," Maas said. "I can't remember a single game when there wasn't a brawl. I remember one of their ends, Greg Townsend, beat up two of our guys pretty bad, and a tremendous bench-clearing brawl ensued. There were always, always fights. I remember meeting on the field one pregame with Howie Long, their defensive tackle. We got along well, had known each other for years, played in the Pro Bowl together. And he goes, 'Hey, man, I'm just tellin' ya, you'd better wear your knee braces today. These f————s hate you!'"

COWBOYS-REDSKINS

Hate. That is not a strong enough word to describe the fiercest rivalry in the NFL. If you were a player on either the Dallas Cowboys or the Washington Redskins, the mere thought of an upcoming contest between the two made you want to stuff your mouthpiece in on Monday, as your motor was already racing.

In their Thanksgiving clash in 1974, despite their star quarterback Roger Staubach getting knocked out and forced to leave the game, it was far from doomsday for Dallas. Unheralded young gunslinger Clint Longley came in and threw deep several times, including the game winner to receiver Drew Pearson, to give Dallas a come-from-behind 24–23 victory.

But while Staubach would take more shots from the Redskins through the years, he'd also get in his share of payback.

For example, in the last regular-season game of his career, on

December 16, 1979, Staubach brought Dallas back from 13- and 10-point deficits. His game-winning touchdown pass to Tony Hill as time expired snatched the division title from their archrivals. The two teams were tied for first, with 10-5 records.

"After they had the first-quarter lead, the game went back and forth," Staubach remembered. "We went ahead, 21–17. And then they got ahead, 34–21. We made two big scores at the end, helped by Larry Cole's big stop on John Riggins. It was a heckuva game because of the constant fighting back and forth throughout. I remember when it was 34–21, they thought it was over; the Redskins were over there on the sidelines, celebrating. We managed to come out ahead, 35–34. That really felt good," said Staubach, laughing at the memory.

But it is a rivalry because with all the close games, both teams have suffered their share of disappointments.

On October 8, 1973, at RFK Stadium, the first *Monday Night Football* meeting between the longtime rivals was a classic. In a mesmerizing reversal of their fortunes from the previous 56 minutes, the Redskins scored two touchdowns in the final four minutes. Then a brilliant goal-line tackle by strong safety Ken Houston preserved their 14–7 victory. Houston brought down running back Walt Garrison inches shy of a touchdown with just 24 seconds left. "That's the biggest tackle I've made in my life," he said.

"That goal-line stand was one of the great memories of our rivalry," said defensive tackle Bill Brundige. "Walt Garrison was a tough running back. He was very good at short yardage. Dallas had an excellent offensive line. Most players will never forget that play."

The modern battle of the Old West between these oversize Cowboys and Redskins kicked off with a song in 1959. The NFL was planning on expanding into Dallas (partly to seize the territory before Lamar Hunt's AFL team could claim the city), but ran into problems with one of their own.

Redskins owner George Preston Marshall owned a vast TV network across the South and did not want a competing franchise anywhere along the Sunbelt. So, other NFL owners banded together and bought the rights to the song "Hail to the Redskins," ("Hail to the Redskins/Hail Victory!/Braves on the Warpath/Fight for old D.C./Run or Pass and Score/We need a lot more/Beat 'em Swamp 'em Touchdown/Let the Points Soar/Fight On, Fight On 'til you have won/Sons of Washington") which was vital for the Washington owner's halftime performances and other entertainment elements, which were very important to him. Understanding he'd been outmaneuvered, Marshall had no choice but to approve the Dallas expansion in order to use his song.

But Marshall was still not singing a happy tune, because the upstart Cowboys stunningly defeated Washington more often than not throughout the sixties. In 1971 the owner brought in a new head coach: George Allen. If anyone loathed the Dallas organization more than Marshall, it was Allen, a proven winner in five seasons with the Los Angeles Rams.

"George Allen was the one that made the Redskins-Cowboys rivalry," Washington quarterback Joe Theismann said bluntly. "He'd tell us, 'The Cowboys think they are better than everybody. They don't play hard-nosed football like we do. I want to turn this into a fistfight. It is going to be a blood-and-guts brawl.'"

Dallas had more talent, so Allen looked to use any psychological edge he could find. Espionage, paranoia, and personal attacks all became part of the playbook.

"Many things you've heard about Coach Landry being spooked by George Allen's spy tactics are accurate," Cowboys defensive tackle Bob Lilly said. "We had our practice field on Forest Lane, off the I-635 Loop. When the Texans moved out of town, we got their old field, off Mockingbird. There was a hotel no more than fifty yards from the end of our field. Every year, there seemed to be a big telephoto lens peering from an open door down at our practice field, so every year the week we played the Redskins, Coach Landry would bus us over to practice at the Cotton Bowl.

"We almost lost every one of those where we worried about them," he added, laughing. "Cowboys security was looking under the bleachers, on the rooftops—everywhere. It went on and on."

But not everything Allen tried worked. "George would do something different and special every time we faced the Cowboys," recalled Washington's star running back Larry Brown. "One day he brought in a martial arts expert, Jhoon Goo Rhee, who had a commercial saying, 'Nobody bothers me.' George brought out some two-by-fours, then Jhoon proceeds to show us how we should beat the Cowboys, by making a karate chop, clearly cutting them in half. Then Coach Allen steps up, and he says, 'This represents the Dallas Cowboys!'

"As he tried to cut the boards in half," Brown continued, "his hand recoiled, and his thumb hit his eye. They had to take him down into the training room. Then big lineman Diron Talbert whispered in George Allen's ear, 'Those Cowboys are darn tough, aren't they Coach?'"

For the man most responsible for building what many believe to be the greatest rivalry in the history of the NFL, Allen's biggest win over Dallas could not have come at a better time. At RFK Stadium on New Year's Eve 1972, the Redskins dominated the Cowboys, 26–3, in the NFC championship.

"The reason that game was not more competitive was because *that* game was our Super Bowl," Brundige explained. "They were defending champs, and we just crushed them. The locker room was pure elation and one of the happiest moments of my career. George was leading the clapping, and everybody was celebrating." Washington advanced to Super Bowl VII at the Los Angeles Memorial Coliseum, but fell to the NFL's newest dynasty, the Miami Dolphins, who had a perfect '72 season, then tacked on three more wins in the postseason to close 17-0.

Stadiums also came into play. Dallas's Texas Stadium did not hold many fond memories for Theismann. "I hated that stadium," the quarterback said. "It was the stupidest thing in the world to have a hole in the middle of the stadium like that. There was a band of sunshine that you'd throw from shade into the sun. Fans weren't that great. Turf wasn't that great. I was never comfortable there."

One night, which happened to be his 35th birthday, he'd be especially uncomfortable.

On Opening Day, September 9, 1985, before a sold-out crowd and a national audience on *Monday Night Football*, Theismann tossed five interceptions as Washington got creamed by Dallas and its Doomsday Defense II, 44–14. However, the ridicule did not stop there, as those caring Cowboys fans wanted to "honor" Joe.

"Yes, it was my thirty-fifth birthday. I did throw five picks in that game. Toward the end, Coach Joe Gibbs tells me, 'I want to take you out and put Jay in.'" That would be 24-year-old rookie Jay Schroeder, out of UCLA. "I told Coach that I am not leaving. There's five minutes to go, and I am not walking out on my teammates. It is a mess, but I am going to finish it. We managed to score a touchdown. So, I told Coach Gibbs with about two minutes left. 'If you want me to sit, I will sit.'

"The second I sat on the bench in Texas Stadium, all the fans started singing 'Happy Birthday' to me. There was nowhere to hide, and you don't want to turn around and look at them. Let me tell you something: anytime you hear a player say that when they're sitting on the bench and they don't hear the fans, they are lying. That was sort of a low point in my career. I saw a sign at that game that read 'Happy Doomsday to you, Joe.'"

It would be no different for the Cowboys when they were the visiting team at Washington's RFK Stadium. "Playing against the Redskins in the nation's capital was always a special feeling," said Dallas running back Herschel Walker. "There was an extra intensity you could feel taking the field in Washington, and I'm sure the fact that we were called America's Team helped fuel that rivalry."

Dallas All-Pro defensive lineman Randy White experienced two instances at RFK that got personal with the fans.

"In one game at RFK, a Redskins fan pours a beer on my sister's head," he recounted. "My brother smacks the guy, who goes down. I didn't see this, but they told me my mom was hitting the guy with her pocketbook when security arrives. They kicked the Redskins guy out of the stadium, and even Redskins fans were cheering her. It was a rivalry on and off the field."

According to teammate Charlie Waters, he and White ended up in the stands one time.

"After Randy crashes into Joe Theismann, there was a big melee with the Redskins' linemen as the game ended. Then we proceed to untangle and head to the locker room through the dugouts, which had cement steps. We were wearing steel-tipped cleats. Since I'd slipped and got hurt there before, I had my head down and was walking very carefully.

"All of a sudden, some fan jumps on the top of the dugout, leans over, and cracks me over the head with a full bottle of beer.

"I look up, and he has the jagged part of the bottle in his hand and, with a menacing look, shouts down to me, 'Yeah, that was me, big boy, come and get it!'

"I look around, and there's Randy White standing next to me, and he says, 'Let's go get him!' We climbed to the top of the dugout and laid out about fifteen Redskins fans. It was a brawl, and it was one of the best times I ever had in uniform! I'm glad there was no film record of it, though; otherwise I'd have been kicked out of the league. Where were the cops when you needed them?" joked Waters.

CHAPTER TWENTY-FOUR

PRIME TIME

In a career filled with many accomplishments, perhaps the biggest of NFL Commissioner Pete Rozelle's 30-year career, from 1960 through 1989, was seeing his vision of prime-time football being played during the week. His dream became reality on September 21, 1970, when the New York Jets squared off against the Cleveland Browns in Week 1. The Browns prevailed, 31–21, and *Monday Night Football* was officially born.

The objective was finding an interested broadcast partner that shared his view of broadening football's appeal beyond the hardcore fan to the casual observer. It took an innovative sports producer named Roone Arledge, working at a struggling third network, ABC, to create a prime-time spectacle that was an instant hit and is still playing nearly a half century later.

"In 1970 ABC was number three of three networks," explained Michael Weisman, a former executive producer for NBC Sports. "NBC and CBS had more successful prime-time programming, so they were not interested in this new football broadcast plan, especially since women were the key demographic in that time slot. But like it said in the old Avis commercials, ABC tried harder.

"Roone Arledge, in his genius, knew he had to make it an

event. He had to have personalities, so he started with movie-star-handsome Frank Gifford, the reporting and sensationalizing of the game of Howard Cosell, and Keith Jackson, who was very capable and solid. Roone recognized he needed to have more sex appeal in the booth, and I'll say flat out that even though Frank was not as skilled a broadcaster as Keith Jackson, he was a very good-looking man."

To make the games more of a spectacle, Arledge used nine cameras, including one sideline and two handheld cameras, at a time when rival networks used only four or five for their Sunday broadcasts. This concept of using more cameras, more replays, more analysis, and more features than any previous professional football telecast was immediately embraced by viewers (and players), making *Monday Night Football* an instant, overwhelming success. The three-person broadcast team provided more colorful commentary and expert analysis, fitting perfectly with the entertainment-themed broadcast.

As a kid, veteran NFL play-by-play announcer Chris Myers watched it religiously. "It became more of a show rather than simply televising a sport," he explained. "Yes, they did justice to the game, but they certainly added some entertainment and flair. You know the weekend is over, and you're back into the grind of the week, with school or work, but I remember, in my youth, I'd say, 'Sunday is over, but, wow, we have another game tomorrow night!'"

Monday Night Football also benefitted the player, offering them a chance to showcase their talents to their fellow athletes who had the night off. "Back then, it was really a special deal," recalled Dolphins quarterback Bob Griese. "All your peers are watching you. When we were not playing, we were watching *MNF*."

Well, some of them were playing. Denver's Pro Bowl running back Floyd Little remembered a time where he almost did not get a chance to suit up for a *Monday Night Football* game.

"I was going to law school during the season as well. There were no excuses for missing classes, but I had a Monday-night game one time, and the teacher said he could not excuse me. It was a night class with serious students. So, I ask, 'What if I get tickets for everybody to go to the game?' the Broncos captain said. "I was able to get some teammates to let me have their comp tickets for my classmates as well as my teacher and his wife. So, we did not have any class that night. I remember later being told that Howard Cosell said, 'There's Floyd Little's law classmates over there.'"

But as four-time Super Bowl champion Pittsburgh Steelers safety Mike Wagner explains, there was a flip side to "showcasing your talents" on a Monday night game.

"Yes, you are very, very aware on Monday night you're out there with national exposure. You definitely want to win, and you'd certainly like to play well because if you don't, that will be glaring among the rest of the league watching you. I still have film from a Monday night game in which Earl Campbell ran over me a couple of times. It keeps me humble. *Monday Night Football* was the showcase. Back then, if you made the Pro Bowl, you were voted by your peers, not fans. So, while they could study you on film, back then *MNF* was one of only just a few ways peers could see you in action."

Over *MNF*'s long span, there have been many memorable moments and games. Here is a look at a few that represent why Monday continues to be prime-time television.

BO VERSUS BOZ

In his brief but glorious NFL career, Bo Jackson will be forever a part of *Monday Night Football* lore with a superb performance in his rookie season in 1987.

It was the Raiders versus the Seahawks, but the media had built it up as a battle between Bo and Boz.

Brian Bosworth was a superstar college linebacker out of Oklahoma who drew just as much attention with his flashy style and antics as he did with his fine play. The all-American linebacker had signed the largest contract ever awarded a National Football League rookie—10 years for $11 million—with the Seattle Seahawks two months after pledging he would never play for them.

This showdown between two promising rookies had tons of anticipation, mostly due to the Boz running his mouth the week before claiming he'd shut down Bo Jackson. (That didn't happen: Jackson ran for 221 yards and scored three touchdowns.)

Jackson remembers the anticipation for the game, but for a host of other reasons.

It was a special night for Bo. Not only was he celebrating his 25th birthday, but he just found out his wife was pregnant with their second child.

In a 37–14 Raiders win, the most memorable play came in a red zone play when Bo received a handoff and took it to the end zone, mowing down the Boz in the process.

Jackson credits his teammates for getting him into the end zone on this classic play, a 2-yard power drive through Boz.

"They had a lot of blitzes and other schemes to try to stop us. And it wasn't just me. It was also Marcus Allen, so I could not have done one-eighth of what I did on that Monday night game if I did not have my line blocking, Marcus blocking for me and so forth. Plus, we capitalized on everything that night," Jackson said.

"The goal-line play was late in the game and we knew they were sort of sucking wind. I believe it was a trap play. Marcus blocked the guy out, I cut up in the hole and then it was just Bosworth and me. I had just one thing on my mind and that was putting the baby in the crib. We met and it was a rule of thumb. My rule is that, and I learned this in college, if I can get my shoulder pads lower than yours, I am going to dominate you all day."

Bo knows history too as he gives a nod to emulating the great running backs that allowed him to score on that play.

"I go back and look at running backs like Earl Campbell, Larry Csonka, Walter Payton, when you see those guys run over players. They always get their shoulder pads under the defenders' pads. At that point, you have all the leverage. And you never stop churning your legs."

Bo knows . . . that it took two to make it a prime-time showdown.

"Listen, Bosworth has to be one of the brightest marketing minds in all of sports. I'm not mad at him. Hey, he did it the way he chose to. He marketed himself very, very well. As a matter of fact, Bosworth and I are very close friends now. Bosworth did what he had to, to keep his name in the limelight and to keep his fan base. At the time, Bosworth did not have the big Nike contract like I had," Jackson noted. "So Boz made his own social media—his own Twitter!—back then. It certainly helped, because it sold out that stadium. Come and see the Bo and Boz Show. Come and watch Boz bowl over Bo. It worked, as it had the nation watching that game."

THE MONDAY NIGHT MIRACLE

In what became known as the "Monday Night Miracle," the Miami Dolphins faced the New York Jets in a divisional showdown on October 23, 2000.

Having lost to the Jets in their last four previous encounters, the run-oriented Dolphins went away from their strength, capturing the Jets off-guard, and quickly built a 17–0 first quarter lead.

It did not help matters that Jets quarterback Vinny Testaverde was playing horrifically, fumbling and throwing interceptions. Accordingly, New York failed to get even a first down until the middle of the second quarter. Miami led at halftime, 23–7.

In the second half, Testaverde repeated his abhorrent play,

throwing his third pick of the evening, which was getting longer by the moment for the home crowd of 78,389.

Entering the final period, Miami enjoyed a 30–7 lead. Such was the lack of faith that thousands of Jets fans streamed through the exits.

But New York got a break when what looked like a sure interception instead became a Jets touchdown as rookie wide receiver Laveranues Coles scored his first NFL touchdown by ripping the ball out of the hands of Miami defensive back Sam Madison in the end zone for a score.

On their next possession, the Jets switched to a hurry-up and empty backfield formation. That combination proved deadly for Miami as Vinny and the Jets got their groove on. Testaverde spread the ball around to different receivers short and far. Now, with under 10 minutes left, the Jets cut the Miami lead to 10, 30–20. New York's defense held, and it became just a touchdown game after John Hall nailed a field goal with under six minutes to go. Wayne Chrebet's touchdown catch tied the ballgame at 30 with under four minutes left.

While it only took 11 minutes for the Dolphins to blow a 23-point lead, they got it back on one play. Jay Fiedler shot down the Jets as he connected with Leslie Shepherd for a 46-yard scoring play, and Miami was back on top, 37–30, with 3:33 left.

With two minutes to go, the Jets faced fourth-and-1. With a tough catch over the middle, New York earned a first-and-goal. Then tackle-eligible Jumbo Elliott juggled the ball on a 3-yard pass play from Testaverde but hung on for a game-tying touchdown reception.

Testaverde, who played so poorly for three quarters, had now joined Ken Stabler and Joe Montana as the only quarterbacks to throw four touchdowns in the fourth quarter.

But overtime started out bleak for New York. Even though Marcus Coleman picked off a Feidler pass, it was fumbled right back to Miami. Still, Coleman redeemed himself with another interception.

It was now 1:22 a.m. local time, and Jets kicker Hall's foot did not fall asleep as he booted a game-winning 40-yard field goal to win, 40–37, in the longest *Monday Night Football* game ever: four hours and 10 minutes. It was also the greatest comeback in Jets' franchise history. Testaverde would finish the night 36 for 59, with 378 yards and five TDs.

JERRY RICE ON *MNF*

"I never think about records. The most important thing is to win," 49ers receiver Jerry Rice said. But on this Monday night, September 5, 1994, the Hall of Fame receiver would get both.

In front of the home crowd at Candlestick Park, Jerry Rice passed Jim Brown's record of 126 career touchdowns in a 44–14 win over the Los Angeles Raiders.

> Jerry: I remember that play vividly. We break the huddle, and I go on motion, where I see Tim Brown, the Raiders' wide receiver, standing almost halfway on the field. I hear him say, "Jerry, you better not break this record against us on *Monday Night Football*!" I run straight down the field trying to stretch the defense, and I look back to see the ball that Steve Young had thrown was really high.
>
> Everything slowed down. I could see the rotation on the ball. I could not hear the crowd. You hear athletes all the time talk about being "in the zone." Coach Walsh always talked to his receivers about going up and attacking the ball. Don't give the defender any extra time or opportunities. I remember reaching for the ball with two Raiders going for it as well. I was able to hold on to it. Jim Brown, the greatest football player ever. To break his record on *Monday Night Football* is something I will never forget.

By the time his career was over, number 127 had become 208.

Late the next season, JR submitted one of the greatest performances by a wideout in the history of *Monday Night Football*. On December 18, 1995, Rice caught 14 passes for 289 yards (both MNF records) and two touchdowns, leading the 49ers to a 37–30 win over the Vikings.

The 49ers receiver explained how being on that platform inspired him:

> *Monday Night Football*, everybody is watching. *Monday Night Football*, you can make a statement. Let opponents know if you were going up against the 49ers or against me, it was going to be a battle for four quarters. I loved performing on that stage. If you go back and look at my football games, on *Monday Night Football*, Sunday night football, the playoffs and the Super Bowl, I felt I had to be at my very best and excel at those times. I felt I could play my best football on those stages and not a lot of players can do that. Focus in that way. They don't want that pressure. I loved the pressure. It brought out the best in me. And that is when I think I played my best football.

PRIME TIME THURSDAY

Not all of the best prime-time football has occurred on Monday night. On a special Thursday night version of MNF on September 20, 1985, there was an exceptional performance turned in by Chicago Bears quarterback Jim McMahon against the Minnesota Vikings.

McMahon had been released from Lake Forest Hospital only two days earlier after spending two nights in and out of traction for muscle spasms in his upper back. The day before the Bears' Thursday night game in Minneapolis in Week 3 of that 1985 season, an infection took hold in his right leg.

"I kinda had a rule many other coaches at that time had, and that was, 'If you don't practice, you can't play,'" Bears coach Mike Ditka said. "But he was driving me crazy: 'Put me in, put me in.' I said, 'You didn't practice all week, you're hurt, it's a short week. I think we can win the game with the team we have out there.' But we were not going anywhere without him, so I put him in, and he ends up working his magic, and we end up winning the football game. And the rest is history."

That "history" was the amazing third-quarter performance of McMahon, who, coming onto the field for the first time with less than 7:30 remaining in the third quarter, proceeded to throw for three touchdowns—two of them with his first two passes of the game.

On the first, McMahon threw a first-down pass to wide receiver Willie Gault for a 70-yard touchdown play. The next time he had the ball, following an interception by Chicago, McMahon threw a first-down strike to wide receiver Dennis McKinnon for 25 yards and a touchdown. Five minutes later, McMahon's seventh pass of the game, and fifth completion, went to McKinnon for a 43-yard touchdown and a 30–17 lead.

The Vikings kept it interesting, however, with Tommy Kramer connecting on a 57-yard touchdown pass to Anthony Carter to close the gap to 30–24, 5:30 into the fourth quarter. But the Bears answered again on the next series, as McMahon hit McKinnon down the right sideline for a 46-yard completion, and he scrambled for 18 yards to set up a 31-yard field goal from Kevin Butler for a 33–24 win.

McMahon checked back into the hospital the next afternoon and stayed for two more days of rest and observation of his infected leg. Tough guy Ditka could not help but be impressed by his quarterback.

"Well if you told him he couldn't do it, he'd do it. That is just the way Jim was. He was a tough guy," said the Bears coach. "We didn't always see eye-to-eye, but that is not important. What is important is what you can do to help the team win."

Chicago would go on to win 15 of 16 to claim the world title; teammates cite how McMahon's leadership on display that night really set the tone that carried the team through the long season.

"That performance demonstrated the kind of person Jim McMahon was," Bears defensive back Leslie Frazier said. "A tremendous competitor. If he could've stayed healthy, who knows how many championships we could've won? That night, his desire to play, even though he had been injured, we needed a spark. He comes off the bench and takes us to a whole other level not only for that game but for the rest of the season as well. I think McMahon had as much to do with the success of our team as anybody. We had defensive guys that would stand up and voice their opinions, but it helped to have one on offense as well and Jim was that guy."

THE TOUGHEST PASSING FOR BRETT FAVRE

Another Black-and-Blue Division quarterback who overcame personal adversity to inspire his team to victory was Green Bay's Brett Favre.

On December 22, 2003, just a day after his father, Irvin, died, Favre suited up to face the Oakland Raiders on *Monday Night Football*. Favre threw for 399 yards, completing 22 of 30, including four touchdowns for a 154.9 rating in a 41–7 shellacking of the Raiders.

"I know my dad would've wanted me to play," Favre said afterward. "I love him so much, and I love this game. It meant a great deal to me, to my dad, to my family. I did not expect this kind of performance, but I know he was watching tonight."

One of the reasons Favre flew to Oakland to play was that *MNF* held a special place for him and his father. "First and foremost, I lived for *Monday Night Football* growing up as a kid. I love Howard Cosell, when he would do the highlights: 'And now from Jack Murphy Stadium. . . .' My dad and I were absolutely glued to the television every Monday. This was an era when you didn't have instant access to scores and Red Zone TV. The chance to play on *Monday Night Football* was always an honor."

Favre was pleasantly surprised by the reaction of the normally notorious Raiders fans of the infamous Black Hole in the Oakland Coliseum.

"I played at the highest level I've ever played before or since. And while football fans can be pretty harsh, even for the home team, but to get a standing ovation when my name was called out [in Oakland on that Monday Night Game], what an honor. That is what I remember more than anything else on that night."

THE INJURY

It was another quarterback who was in the spotlight in one of the most iconic moments in televised sports history. On a *Monday Night Football* game on November 18, 1985, NFC East rivals the New York Giants faced off against the Washington Redskins.

Giants linebacker Lawrence Taylor pounced on Joe Theismann from behind during the second quarter of that game at RFK Stadium and the quarterback was trapped between Taylor and fellow linebacker Harry Carson. But it wasn't clear until the reverse angle of the play was shown why the tough Redskins quarterback wasn't getting up after the sack and why Taylor was frantically signaling to the sideline for medical help. The blow caused a gruesome break of Theismann's right leg between the knee and ankle. Viewers couldn't escape seeing the horror, and broadcasters told viewers to look away if they didn't want to relive it in the replay. It was a gruesome play that would be forever burned into NFL fans' memories.

Few remember that the Redskins won, 23–21, because what they witnessed from their armchairs across the nation in this prime-time contest would later be appropriately dubbed "The hit that no one who saw it can ever forget" by the *Washington Post*.[54]

Taylor and Theismann revisited the infamous play.

"We call stack 2 double hard, a formation designed to put the maximum pressure on the quarterback. We executed well, and Joe tries to slip through a little hole. The only problem was, I saw the hole before he did. And he broke his leg," said Taylor.

"Facing the Giants at home, I remember the intensity being like a playoff game," Theismann said. "We had the Hogs, won the Super Bowl in '82, record-setting offense, but the entire front seven of the New York Giants were awesome. The night never really was very comfortable for me, we should have been up 21–0 in the first quarter. I missed more than a few throws. We should have been ahead by a lot. So, Joe Gibbs called a flea flicker that I took the snap, turn around, hand the ball to John Riggins, he turns around tosses it back to me. I was feeling pressure but did not know who it was. It was Lawrence who grabbed my shoulder, and as he came around, it felt like his right leg caught my right leg between the knee and the ankle, and I hear what sounded like two muzzled gunshots: *'pow-pow!'*

"My reaction was that I just wanted people to get off of him," Taylor said. "He was really hurt. And I have been hurt before on the bottom of a pile. And it seems like forever for people to get off of you. Until that play, I never thought about my longevity in the NFL. I never worried about getting hurt or anything like that. But seeing that, it made me realize one's career can be all over in one play. It changed my outlook on football somewhat." To this day, Taylor refuses to watch any replays of the incident.

Theismann remembers a few details. Though LT would rather not see it ever again, there are certain things that remain vivid to this day in Theismann's mind's eye.

"Coach Gibbs comes over and says, 'Joe, we've been together for six years; you've meant so much to this team. This is a heck of a mess you've put me in."

"So, I'm going, 'Great, I got a broken leg, and I'm apologizing to this guy.'"

Being the competitor he was, Theismann insisted on watching the game to the end.

"When I got to the hospital, they had set up a TV with a coat hanger antenna on an old black-and-white set. It was outside the surgery room, and I would not let the doctor work on me until the game was over."

The compound fracture of the tibia led to insufficient bone growth during Theismann's recovery, leaving his right leg shorter than his left. As a result, the injury forced Theismann into retirement at the age of 36, but he would enjoy a long second career in the NFL as a broadcaster, including a stint on—you guessed it—*Monday Night Football*.

★ Two of the most influential figures in the history of the NFL: Pete Rozelle and George Halas. *(Photo by Jim Summaria)*

★ Jim Brown led the NFL in rushing for 8 of the 9 seasons he played. *(Courtesy Cleveland Browns)*

★ A member of the NFL's 75th Anniversary All-Time Team, fleet-footed San Diego Chargers wide receiver Lance Alworth ran straight into the Pro Football Hall of Fame. *(Courtesy Los Angeles Chargers)*

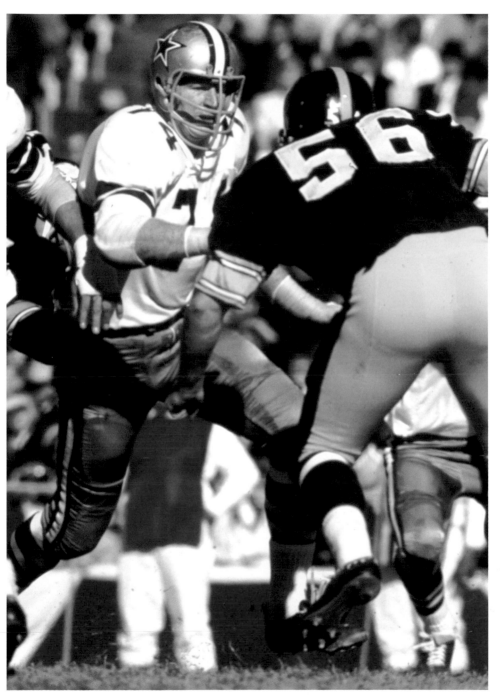

★ A seven-time All-Pro, Bob Lilly was the anchor of the Doomsday Defense. *(Courtesy Dallas Cowboys)*

★ Larry Csonka—The personification of a power runner. *(Courtesy Miami Dolphins)*

★ Don Shula stands alone as the winningest coach in the history of the National Football League with 347 victories (328 regular season, 19 playoff wins). *(Courtesy Miami Dolphins)*

★ Southpaw quarterback Ken Stabler (l) with the co-author, was an NFL MVP, Super Bowl Champion, and reached the Hall of Fame doing it his own way. By "studying the playbook by the light of a jukebox," The Snake helped forge the Raiders' aura. *(Courtesy of the author)*

★ A common sight, Detroit Lion running back Barry Sanders leaving defenders empty-handed. *(Courtesy Detroit Lions)*

★ Former Oklahoma quarterback Baker Mayfield, drafted No. 1 overall in the 2018 NFL draft, has Cleveland fans optimistic about the team's future. *(Courtesy Cleveland Browns)*

★ Houston Texans' defensive end J.J. Watt has received the AP NFL Defensive Player of the Year Award three times in his first five seasons. *(Courtesy Houston Texans)*

CHAPTER TWENTY-FIVE

DYNASTY

Beginning with the Canton Bulldogs of the 1920s, the New York Giants in the 1930s, the Chicago Bears throughout the 1940s, and the Cleveland Browns of the 1950s, each decade of the NFL's long tenure would be representative of an individual team's prowess, proof of domination across many areas of the game.

The key traits that most dynasties share:

- organizational stability;
- a head coach with time to settle in and implement his program;
- consistently successful drafts filling a roster with talented veterans and;
- having a brilliant quarterback and a controlling defensive unit that, together, produces a distinctly favorable gap in points scored versus points given up on a per-game basis.

In addition to the aforementioned, here is a look at subsequent decades' dynasties, in which bands of players achieved the highest form of success, winning it all on a repeat basis.

1960S PACKERS

The Packers of the 1960s took the torch from Paul Brown's Cleveland Browns and further defined the word dynasty. Led by future Hall of Fame coach Vince Lombardi and a dozen future Hall of Fame players, Green Bay won 73 percent of its games, tallying 96 victories, five NFL titles, and two Super Bowl victories.

The keys to Lombardi's success were based on simplicity, execution, and of course having that depth of talent to execute. The Packers had a sizeable contingent named to the All-Pro roster every year.

Somewhat underreported was the fact that he was aided by a young scout and personnel director by the name of Jack Vainisi, who was responsible for some key draft picks that would form the foundation of the Packers empire. Jim Taylor, Ray Nitschke, and Jerry Kramer were selected in rounds one through four of the 1958 NFL draft.

"Being a student of the Green Bay team, one thing I noticed with Lombardi was he used no trickery. He simply beat you with well-conditioned talent and execution," noted Mike Garrett, a running back who was part of the Kansas City Chiefs team that lost to Green Bay in Super Bowl I. "The Green Bay sweep, you knew it was coming, but try stopping it anyway. You had Taylor and Hornung running the ball at you behind guys like Gregg and Kramer, then they'd run short posts to their receivers. There were no surprises. They just out executed you. And their defense was stacked with future Hall of Famers like David Robinson, Willie Davis, Ray Nitschke, and Herb Adderley."

On the other side of the ball, quarterback Bart Starr was surrounded (and perhaps buried) by such talent that even the offensive linemen were quite well known. Do you know how rare that was back in the day? Despite being in the highest-profile position, the Packers field general, in his own low-key way, was the clutch player that made all that team's success possible.

Starr did not own a strong arm. He was similar to an off-speed pitcher, and he rarely threw deep other than as an element of surprise in short-yardage situations. But he could place the ball where defenders could not get to it. He wasn't a scrambler but could run, keeping the defenses honest.

Starr was Lombardi's kind of quarterback because he kept within the game plan, rarely made turnovers and proved to be exceptionally tough and accurate in an era where defenses got away with a lot of rough play. When he retired after the 1971 season, his career passer rating of 80.5 was second only to Otto Graham's 86.6.

"Bart wasn't really fast or elusive, but he had a fabulous mind," explained Dallas Cowboys defensive tackle Bob Lilly. "Like all the great quarterbacks, Bart had a sixth sense. His was an ability to feel where the weaknesses lie in the defense and attack that point whenever he was in a crucial situation. It could be a pass or a run but he, like Joe Montana later, could sense the pressure but never lose sight of the receivers. His timing was impeccable."

Starr may not have been the face of the Packers dynasty, but he certainly was its leader.

Chicago Bears defender Ed O'Bradovich played against Starr for years and went on to a long broadcasting career where he has seen many quarterbacks since.

"In today's game, with thirty-two teams, you are lucky to find ten good quarterbacks. Bart Starr was so steady, he rarely made mistakes. It was very rare that you saw a receiver having to leap very high in the air or turn back to grab a ball, as Starr's placement was superb. There is a reason he has among the highest postseason quarterback ratings in NFL history."

He had the team to back it up, too, starting with the power running game of Paul Hornung and Jim Taylor running the famed sweep behind Forrest Gregg and Jerry Kramer.

Hornung scored an NFL-record 176 points on 15 touchdowns, 15 field goals, and 41 extra points in the final 12-game NFL season.

Taylor ground out over 1,100 yards on 230 punishing carries—the first of seven successive seasons he would lead the team.

Lombardi instilled in his players a will to win plus an emphasis on fundamentals, and nothing better represented his philosophy in action than the Packers' power sweep, a play that one coach quipped "was merely execution—and the defenses were the ones to get executed."

Even though each player had a role to perform, the key to its success fell to the efforts of the center, the pulling guards, and the halfback. The play could blow up from the start if the center could not cut off the defensive tackle or middle linebacker to prevent the defender from breaking up the play behind the line of scrimmage. Another crucial component fell to the left guard who, based on how the defense reacted, had to decide whether to push the play to the inside or outside of the tight end. Behind the blocks of the fullback, tight end, and left tackle, the ballcarrier then decided whether to go inside or outside.

The sweep was the foundation on which the rest of the offensive plan was built, so the coach drilled them on it so often it became second nature. Its success would allow the Packers to control the game clock, slowly moving the ball down the field while wearing down the defense. Even when defenses made adjustments to try to stop it, Lombardi would either attack other weaknesses or would run variations of the sweep. At its core, the Packers' sweep was a simple play that depended on all members of the unit executing their responsibilities precisely. It was very successful.

Of course, it has often been said that defenses win championships and there was no shortage of talent on that side of the ball in Green Bay as well.

Meanwhile, six future Hall of Famers—defensive linemen Willie Davis and Henry Jordan, linebackers Ray Nitschke and Dave Robinson, and a defensive backfield starring Herb Adderley and Willie Wood—composed a unit that was among the very best in an era that produced tremendous defensive units.

With missing front teeth, menacing stare, and steady delivery of hard hits, middle linebacker Nitschke was the emotional leader who personified this side of Packers play. A seven-time All-Pro and the most valuable player in the 1962 NFL championship game, when Green Bay defeated the New York Giants, 16–7, he was elected to the Pro Football Hall of Fame in 1978 and was named to the NFL's All-50 Year and 75th Anniversary teams.

Still, teammates looked up to Starr to make it all work. Bill Curry, an offensive lineman, recalled a time in which their quarterback stood up to the big guy. "In a meeting Vince Lombardi is going through one of his tirades, saying 'you guys don't take responsibility! Blaming your mistakes on others!' All of a sudden a voice comes from the back. Everybody knew who it was. He goes in a strong voice. 'Wait a minute, Mister. If you're gonna rip us, get it right.' Lombardi was stunned. Bart stood right up in the middle of the meeting and said, 'I took responsibility. It's right there in the middle of that article. Read it carefully before you come in here and tell us we don't take responsibility.' Lombardi had no choice but to back off in a small way. He said, 'Okay, that's one guy, but the rest of you . . .'"

Lombardi could not abide defeat and would always push his players to redouble their efforts in their quest for a title. "If you accept losing" he famously once said, "you can't win."

And during the 1960s, nobody won like the Green Bay Packers.

"It is not rocket science," Jim Taylor chuckled. "Lombardi would drill us over and over to where there was no mistaking your assignment and responsibilities. You got to be the better man when they snap that ball."

1970S STEELERS

Winning four Super Bowls in six years, the Steelers proved they were the better men on a consistent basis during the 1970s. But where Green Bay had at least enjoyed some previous success during the days of Coach Lambeau and receiver Don Hutson during the 1930s and 1940s, for 40 years the Steelers didn't even win a division championship. The 1970s marked their emergence as a successful franchise on a regular basis.

Founded in 1933 as the Pirates (they became the Steelers in 1941), they finished above .500 only seven times in their first 37 seasons. However, the 40-year drought ended with a bang as the dynasty in Pittsburgh provided fans with a decade of dominance. From 1972 through 1979, the Steelers posted a combined record of 88-27-1 for a winning percentage of .759. In those eight years, they made the playoffs all eight times, played for the NFL championship four times, and won all four of them.

The personnel skills of its new head coach, Chuck Noll, got the ball tumbling in Pittsburgh's favor.

"The quality of players Chuck drafted were talented and just got better," said Rocky Bleier, a starting running back on that team. "Chuck had them playing as a team. You have to have an ego to play this game, and our team had egos, but egos that supported one another. And you have the leadership of Coach Noll and owner Art Rooney. People need to understand that when you are multidefending champions, opponents are gunning for you every week, raising their game, so the challenge becomes greater, the hurdles become higher, and knowing that anything can happen on any given Sunday, you have to play at a Super Bowl level every game."

Their beginnings weren't as fortuitous. "I'll never forget the first time Coach Noll addressed the entire team," recalled Andy Russell, already a veteran. "He says, 'You know, I have been watching game films since I have taken the job, and I can tell you why you have been losing. The reason you're not any good is because you're not any good.' You could hear a pin drop."

The times, they were a-changin'. The atmosphere in Pittsburgh had long been a lackadaisical one. Coach Noll was a serious man, but nothing was more serious than his desire to win.

"Before Noll arrived, players would go jogging, then, when out of sight behind some trees, snatching cigarettes from their shorts and smoking them before returning to the field out of breath," Russell said.

Russell agreed that the changes for the better came with the draft. Noll had his eyes set on defensive tackle Joe Greene. The driven young man who played his college ball at North Texas was an instant sensation at the pro level and became the foundation for the vaunted Steel Curtain defense.

In 1970 Noll took quarterback Terry Bradshaw from Louisiana Tech. While the Blonde Bomber would eventually become the focal point in leading Pittsburgh's offense to all their glory, his road was a lot rockier and took longer than Greene's. Even though he called his own plays and had a rocket arm, it would be several seasons before he really blossomed into a star.

The problem with the head coach and his quarterback stemmed from Terry's being the kind of person who needed a pat on the back; that simply wasn't Noll's style. He was not a rah-rah guy.

Though he struggled his first few seasons under Noll's tough love, Bradshaw overcame his erratic play with a self-discipline that brought out his natural leadership skills. He realized he didn't need to win every game on the strength of his rocket of a right arm. His interceptions went down, and smart play calling helped guide his team to the playoffs. In the 1974 AFC championship game against the Oakland Raiders, his fourth-quarter touchdown pass to Lynn Swann proved to be the winning score in a 24–13 victory. In the Steelers' 16–6 Super Bowl IX victory over the Minnesota Vikings that followed, Bradshaw completed nine of 14 passes, and his fourth-quarter touchdown pass put the game out of reach and helped take the Steelers to their first Super Bowl victory. He eventually led Pittsburgh to eight AFC Central championships and four Super Bowl titles.

With Bradshaw fulfilling his potential and the Steelers adding two wide receivers who could help stretch the field in John Stallworth and Lynn Swann, Pittsburgh's offense (with Bleier and Franco Harris carrying the ball) took more pressure off their great defense, including defeating the Dallas Cowboys, a team also dynasty-worthy, in two titanic 1970s Super Bowl games. (See chapter 41, "Now, That Was Super.")

"Chuck was always so mission-oriented," said safety Mike Wagner. "So, there we are down in New Orleans. We had just won our first championship, first in franchise history taking Super Bowl IX. All of us really admiring the trophy but the basic message from Coach Noll was, 'Well, this is great. Enjoy it for a moment, but I want you to start thinking very soon about next year.' He was always on a mission to make you better. One of his favorite expressions was: 'If you think you have arrived, you haven't.'"

Pittsburgh won its fourth and final Super Bowl of that dynasty by defeating the Los Angeles Rams in Super Bowl XIV.

Despite a valiant effort, Vince Ferragamo, the quarterback who came up short on the losing team, nevertheless came away quite impressed with the Pittsburgh squad as a whole.

"Everybody knew how to play with each other. Great teams play as a team and Pittsburgh personified that. Pittsburgh was one of the greatest teams of all time, and the proof is that you could plug them into any era, and they could adapt to the environment and win. You put those players up in their prime against any other players in their prime and they'd take care of them. They could run, throw deep, blitz, shut down the run . . . whatever it took."

1980S 49ERS

With a dominance that spanned multiple decades, during the 1980s and 1990s, the 49ers were considered the class act of the NFL. They had a remarkable string of 16 straight seasons with 10 or more victories.

But it is that word *class* that has multiple applications here.

The 49ers' owner, Eddie DeBartolo, believed that providing his coaches and players first class travel, accommodations, and practice facilities would go a long way in creating a winning mind-set. It paid off handsomely from the start including an NFL record for consecutive road wins. Astonishingly, from 1981 to 1989, the 49ers had a better regular-season road record than any other NFL team had at home.

"I used what I learned from my dad growing up with our company in Youngstown, Ohio, where we treated each and every employee like they were part of our family," DeBartolo said. "That was the foundation of what I wanted to create in San Francisco."

Still, the players knew nothing was going to be handed to them, simply because they looked good on paper and flying first class. There were expectations, from the owner, from the coaches, from the fans, and from the players themselves. Just like Pittsburgh's Coach Noll stressed to his team about not being satisfied with one title, 49ers receiver Jerry Rice explained how that mentality worked in San Francisco:

> There is a commitment you have to make to become a dynasty. A lot of work, sweat, and tears in an environment where you never feel that you have arrived. You hear people say all the time, "Just sit back and relish the moment," but you can't. You're constantly pushing yourself. Winning becomes one of the things we are possessed by. That is how you become a dynasty.

The chief architect behind the 49ers run was head coach Bill Walsh, with a big assist from defensive coordinator George Seifert who, along with Ray Rhodes, really built the defense, and would extend their success as head coaches. Having been on the staff of legendary coach Paul Brown among others, Walsh's main game plan was built around something called the West Coast offense, which relied more on short, precisely timed passes. It depended on a quarterback who was nimble of foot and mind.

Though he had worked out Phil Simms, who'd have fine success as a New York Giant, Walsh found his quarterback in Notre Dame's Joe Montana.

Coach Seifert, who observed Montana every day in practice and watched him in pressure-packed game situations, talked about what made him such a special player.

"Yes, there were obvious physical attributes, but certainly a key trait was Joe's coolness under pressure," praised Seifert. "You have to have good footwork, and I think he was well tutored by Sam Wyche and certainly by Bill Walsh, Mike Holmgren, and Paul Hackett; they all contributed to Joe's mechanics. Naturally, he fit well within the system. Joe was also extremely competitive. He was almost merciless in his desire to win."

In what is perhaps his finest hour (in a career filled with many fine hours), number 16 put on a superb display in Super Bowl XXIII. With his team down, 16–13, and just 3:20 left, Montana began a 92-yard game-winning march. It included several clutch catches by Rice, who would win the Super Bowl MVP, with a record 215 yards receiving. With 1:15 on the clock and a second-and-20 situation, Montana threw over the middle to Rice, who was finally hauled down at the Bengals' 18. Montana then connected with John Taylor for the 10-yard winning score.

"What people don't often see was when we broke out of the huddle, you could see in their faces, with Montana at the helm, they knew they were in trouble," 49ers offensive lineman Randy Cross said. "Halfway through that drive, Bengals coach Sam Wyche, who was wired for sound, is shaking his head looking at a playlist and talking to no one in particular, saying, 'How many times have I seen this?'"

Coming from behind or front-running, what the opponents saw would be déjà vu all over again because in the very next Super Bowl, Montana and Rice teamed up to crush the "Orange Crush" defense of the Denver Broncos.

In each of the first three quarters, Montana and Rice connected on TD passes. San Francisco was up, 27–3, at the half and cruised from there. The 49ers set 18 SB records in crushing Denver, 55–10, including most points in a game and margin of victory. At one point, Joe Cool had 13 straight completions, a Super Bowl record.

"Joe gets this sneaky little grin on his face when he's on. It is like he's saying, 'Everything's under control.' He had that smile right from the first series," said Rice, beaming at the memory.

Very few players get to play let alone win a Super Bowl. Even rarer are the athletes who had the good fortune to be part of something even more elusive: a dynasty. Safety Ronnie Lott talked about how it feels to be linked with the Browns of the fifties, the Packers of the sixties, and the Steelers of the seventies:

"Anytime you are mentioned among the greatest of the greats, especially to go back to the Browns in the great run that they had as well as the Packers and Steelers, all you have to do is read Vince Lombardi's quote about winning and what it takes to win. That sums it up in that we were not meant to be second. We were not meant to have moments of not believing that you can't be the best. Because of that, I've always felt that meet-

Cornerstone of a 49ers dynasty: quarterback Joe Montana and coach Bill Walsh.

Copyright Michael Zagaris

ing some of the all-time greats like Paul Brown you realize we've earned the right to be mentioned, our entire organization, secretaries, you name it earned the right to be called champions. What that exemplifies is that we think about those organizations [dynasties] were built by people who truly cared for one another."

> Jerry: Personal accolades are great, but the team concept, to be able to be part of a dynasty, that is the best reward. It is something you share with others for the rest of your life. My teammates helped me break a lot of records, but being a part of that winning tradition as a member of the San Francisco 49ers, that will be something I'll never forget.

1990S COWBOYS

One thing Dallas fans will never forget is how the largest trade to date in NFL history ended up being the key to creating their team's dynasty.

On October 13, 1989, the Dallas Cowboys sent their only Pro Bowl player, running back Herschel Walker, to the Minnesota Vikings in a deal that eventually involved a combination of 18 players and draft picks.

Earlier that year, on February 25, Arkansas oilman Jerry Jones bought the team and hired his former college roommate Jimmy Johnson to coach. Though Johnson had won a national title at the University of Miami, there was a rough patch due to the way they let go of Dallas coaching legend Tom Landry. Many fans were angered by Jones's maneuvers, and it didn't help when the team finished with a 1-15 season.

But Jones, a man of action, was determined to restore pride in one of the NFL's most-storied franchises. The owner's attitude perhaps was best captured by a sign in his office.

"It is two buzzards sitting on a limb, when one looks over to the other and says, 'Patience my ass! I'm gonna go kill something,'" Jones laughed.

That trade began returning big-time dividends when in the 1990 draft Dallas nabbed future Hall of Fame running back Emmitt Smith. And as receiver Michael Irvin and quarterback Troy Aikman began to regularly produce standout performances, the Cowboys quickly turned around. In 1989 they won just one game. In 1992 they won 13.

In 1991 Irvin and Smith became the first players on the same team to lead the NFL in receiving and rushing yards, respectively, in the same season.

In another key trade, the Cowboys traded quarterback Steve Walsh to New Orleans for an additional handful of draft choices. Players drafted or acquired as a result of the two deals—including defensive tackle Russell Maryland, offensive tackle Erik Williams, and cornerback Kevin Smith—would go on to play pivotal roles in the Dallas titles in '92 and '93.

Jimmy Johnson coached Dallas to back-to-back Super Bowl wins, but then resigned, and former University of Oklahoma coach Barry Switzer took over.

In 1994 Dallas reached the NFC title game but lost to San Francisco, 38–28.

The next year, with the addition of defensive greats Charles Haley and Deion Sanders, Dallas, in a battle to become the first team to win five Super Bowls, defeated the Steelers 27–17 in Super Bowl XXX and became the undisputed king of the 1990s.

2000S+ PATRIOTS

The undisputed kings of the NFL in the twenty-first century have been the New England Patriots. And the amazing thing is that they've done it in a variety of ways, with all kinds of different personnel, but all centered around two core components: quarterback Tom Brady and coach Bill Belichick.

In between championship game heroes like linebacker Tedy Bruschi, wide receiver Deion Branch, and kicker Adam Vinatieri, the fact is just one player—quarterback Tom Brady—is the only one left over from that original Super Bowl season in 2001.

The New England Patriots have dominated in an era with constant roster changes. Their dominance from 2001 through 2018 resulted in six Vince Lombardi Trophies, 10 Super Bowl appearances, and a record-breaking 16-0 regular season in which Tom Brady threw 50 TDs.

With narrow winning margins in their Super Bowl triumphs, New England did not dominate their opponents like the 1990s Cowboys did, nor did they have the depth of talent of prior dynasties: for example, the '75 Steelers and '93 Cowboys each had 11 Pro Bowlers, compared with three for the '03 Patriots.

There was also a group of players, led by Tom Brady, who weren't first-round picks but had big chips on their shoulders and always wanted more. (Brady was a sixth-round pick, essentially a draft afterthought, who made scouts cringe with his lack of athleticism and arm strength at the NFL Combine.) Even after winning their first Super Bowl, many of those Patriots carried the attitude of daring people to doubt them again.

One thing that has not been in doubt throughout New England's reign are the skill sets of the Patriots head coach.

Bill Belichick is a master at tactics and getting the right personnel to fill the gaps, getting the most out of their limited talent.

When combining that with Belichick taking a page from Chuck Noll's coaching book of not resting on one's laurels and to be a "tomorrow person," and imbuing his team with an unquenchable thirst for winning, New England has not looked back for more than a decade.

Belichick is unparalleled in his ability to break down teams, with no detail too small. He has also honed a personnel skill to find players with an ability to adapt from play to play and season to season despite the limitations wrought by the salary cap and free agency.

Randy Cross, a member of the 49ers' dynasty and a broadcaster of many Patriots games, sees some parallels with the great teams of the past.

"The one thing the teams like those Steelers and Cowboys and Packers and 49ers and Browns share, the one thing they excel at, is something I think people assume who are outside of football that everybody does, and even those inside of football almost scoff at, as a cliché, but Bill [Belichick] excels at getting people that can do a specific job or skill. He is signing players specifically for maybe twenty to twenty-five plays a game. Those that can function within the offense or defense and that is why they are there. They are not there to be the star. And there is not a whole lot of gray area as to your responsibility."

We've heard the mantra associated with Belichick: "Do your job!"

Former Tampa Bay safety John Lynch has developed a better appreciation for what Belichick has accomplished now that he is the 49ers' general manager. "What made him special is that in an era that has implemented a salary cap to create parity, it works but the fact that the Patriots have been to twelve AFC championships as an organization in sixteen years, or whatever, it blows my mind the way they have outdistanced the competition. It just isn't that the talent is interchangeable. It is that everyone buys into Belichick's 'Do anything for the team' ethos. Even with the sustained excellence when you have a great quarterback like Brady at its core, it is more than that, because as the names change on the roster, the success still continues."

In a steady stream of changing faces, Brady and Belichick (with credit to owner Robert Kraft) carry on the winning Patriots tradition established at the start of the twenty-first century. It has been a monumental achievement.

And because the game has changed so much, to compare dynasties through the different eras, well, it is best to simply state that achieving that status, in any era, is a rare distinction indeed.

CHAPTER TWENTY-SIX

THE ONE AND ONLY

How impressive an achievement was the undefeated season by the Miami Dolphins of 1972? In the 100-year history of the National Football League, no one had done it before, and no one has done it since.

Naturally, it all started with a devastating loss the year earlier.

On January 16, 1972, before 81,023 fans in New Orleans, the Dolphins were dominated by the Cowboys, 24–3 in Super Bowl VI.

"You can't find a more dismal place in all of sports than the loser's locker room after the Super Bowl," Miami running back Larry Csonka said. "And I will never forget, Coach Shula comes in and closes the doors, then turns to the players and says, 'I have been here before'"—a reference to his Baltimore Colts' painful Super Bowl III defeat at the hands of Joe Namath's New York Jets. "'I can tell you what is going to happen from here. We can point fingers, blame each other, and fall apart. Or we can stand and weather the storm together to come back and fight another day. The choice is up to you. A house divided won't stand.' I think that gave us what we needed. The first seed of the undefeated season was planted right there."

From the first day the players reported in, training camp was even more focused than usual under disciplinarian coach Don

Shula. Teammates policed themselves. They made sure there was no tardiness for meetings or late-night carousing breaking curfew.

That committed attitude served them well as they opened the season with four victories over the Chiefs, Oilers, Vikings, and Jets. However, in their Week 5 game against the Chargers, quarterback Bob Griese broke his ankle. But Shula's genius for preparation was never better demonstrated than in an off-season move he made (though his boss was reluctant to make the deal).

Shula had wanted Earl Morrall as his backup quarterback. He played for the head coach in Baltimore, but Miami owner Joe Robbie was not so sure he was worth the price tag.

"I told Joe I want to pick him up and he said, 'what is he making?' I said '90 thousand.' Joe says, '90 thousand for a backup QB, are you out of your mind?!'" Shula recalled with a grin. "I said I have a lot of confidence in him and he's won some games. Then Joe finally got back to me and said, 'Well if you really want him, go ahead, I'll try to figure out how to come up with the money.'"

Robbie would be glad he did.

But as Griese was being taken away on a stretcher, teammates were wondering what was left in Old Man Morrall, who compared himself to a veteran relief pitcher still capable of getting the job done.

"Well when Bob went down, I walked over to Earl and said, 'Hey old man, turn up that hearin' aid, buy ya' a bottle of Geritol and let's get goin'. He sure did," recalled Miami defensive end Bill Stanfill with a chuckle at the memory.

Morrall took control from the first snap and never looked back. He guided Miami to 10 straight regular-season wins.

Csonka and Mercury Morris played pivotal roles as they became the first backfield tandem to each rush for 1,000 yards in the same season. Running back Jim Kiick and receiver Paul Warfield hauled in clutch passes from Old Man Morrall. All were helped by a tremendous offensive line that included center Jim Langer and guards Bob Kuechenberg and Larry Little.

Of course, the Dolphins' defense was very instrumental in the run, dominating by making very few mental errors. Led by tackle Manny Fernandez, middle linebacker Nick Buoniconti and safeties Jake Scott and Dick Anderson, the unit topped the NFL in fewest points and fewest yards and was second in forcing turnovers. Kicker Garo Yepremian had made some clutch field goals throughout the season.

Finishing the regular season undefeated after wins over the Cardinals, Patriots, Giants, and Colts, Miami's first real struggle came in a narrow 20–14 victory at home over the Cleveland Browns in the divisional playoffs on Christmas Eve.

With so much at stake, after Morrall struggled in the first half of the AFC championship game against the Steelers in Pittsburgh, Shula made one of the toughest decisions of his career when he benched Morrall in favor of Griese.

"The offense was kind of slowing down, a bit sluggish, so Coach Shula came to me right before halftime and asked, 'Are you ready to go?' I said, 'Yes,' and he said, 'All right, you are in,'" Griese recalled. "Earl, being the consummate teammate and classy guy he was, said, 'Hey, I don't like it, but I will go along with anything you want to do.'"

With Griese at the helm, the Dolphins tied the game after punter Larry Seiple's 37-yard run on a fake punt set up a Miami touchdown. Miami won, 21–17, and was right where it wanted to be: in the Super Bowl, with a shot at redemption.

No one was more focused than Shula.

"When you're oh-and-two in Super Bowls, they don't say good things about you," the coach recalled. "And one of those things you never want said about you is that you can't win the big one. And that was what was being said, and the only way to eliminate that is to win."

Miami would face the Redskins, a veteran team under veteran-loving head coach George Allen. Washington was led by 33-year-old quarterback Billy Kilmer, who completed 120 out of 225 passes for

1,648 yards and a league-leading 19 touchdowns during the regular season, with only 11 interceptions, giving him an NFL best 84.8 passer rating. Kilmer had started the first three games of the season, was replaced in game four by 38-year-old Sonny Jurgensen, who he replaced when Jurgensen was lost for the season with an Achilles tendon injury.

Their powerful rushing attack featured Larry Brown, who gained 1,216 yards (first in the NFC and second in the NFL) in 285 carries during the regular season, caught 32 passes for 473 yards, and scored 12 touchdowns, earning him the NFL Most Valuable Player Award.

Kilmer also had fine targets to throw his wobbly passes to in future Hall of Fame receiver Charley Taylor and Roy Jefferson, who provided the team with two solid deep threats, combining for 84 receptions, 1,223 receiving yards, and 10 touchdowns.

A cagey, old Washington defense was led by linebackers Chris Hanburger and Jack Pardee behind a front line that included Verlon Biggs and Diron Talbert. Savvy cornerbacks Pat Fischer and Mike Bass roamed the back.

In the pregame locker room, Coach Shula did not have to say much about the Redskins and their personnel, he knew his players were self-motivated and ready because they were upset about being underdogs. The Miami players could not believe they were not the favorite, especially since they had not only defeated all three teams that beat Washington that season, but they were undefeated as well. However, Shula did remind them about the feeling they had coming up on the losing end of last year's Super Bowl and that their great 16-0 season would mean nothing if they came up short here.

The Dolphins played essentially flawless football in the first half. Late in the first quarter Bob Griese directed Miami on a 63-yard drive capped off by a 28-yard pass to Howard Twilley. Then, just before the half, Jim Kiick went over from the 1-yard line to give Miami a 14–0 lead.

Miami was thoroughly dominating the game, not only with a very effective ball control running game, but also a stellar performance by their No-Name Defense that suffocated Washington's offense in every facet. Still, an all-time bonehead play by the Dolphin kicker, Garo Yepremian, gave Redskins fans some hope late in the contest.

Leading 14-0 with just over two minutes remaining in the fourth quarter, in an effort to put the game out of reach (and create a bit of symmetry for Miami by ending a perfect season at 17-0 with a Super Bowl final score of 17-0), Yepremian attempted a field goal.

It was blocked by Bill Brundige, however, Yepremian was able to get to the ball before any other player did. But instead of falling on the ball (as he was constantly drilled by Shula to do in such situations) he picked it up and frantically attempted to throw a pass. The ball slipped from his hands and went straight up in the air. Yepremian then attempted to bat the ball out of bounds but instead batted it back up in the air, and it went right into the arms of his former Lions teammate, Redskins cornerback Mike Bass, who returned it for a touchdown. Luckily for Garo, his team managed to hold on to win, 14–7, thus completing the Dolphins' undefeated season. Yepremian later joked to reporters after the game, "This is the first time the goat of the game is in the winner's locker room."

"Our whole thought process was not just to get there, but to get there and win," said Shula. "So, if we had been fifteen and two and won the Super Bowl, that would have been a successful year. The fact that we kept winning and running the table, that only entered our mind late that we could do something that no one had ever done. So that became important, but never close to winning the last game."

Although it was the Dolphins' first Super Bowl title, what will always be remembered is the fact they went undefeated. In winning that last game, the 1972 Miami team became the One and Only.

Miami, led by Csonka, would enjoy that feeling again the very next year, as they dominated the Vikings in Super Bowl VIII.

In a brilliant Hall of Fame career that includes being the all-time winningest coach, Shula summed up what the '72 Dolphins achievement meant to him: "Well, doing something no other team, no other coach, has ever done makes it very special. It's got to be what it is all about."

Chasing Perfection

YEAR	TEAM	RECORD
1920	Akron Pros	8-0-3
1922	Canton Bulldogs	10-0-2
1923	Canton Bulldogs	11-0-1
1929	Green Bay Packers	12-0-1
1934	Chicago Bears	13-0-0[a]
1942	Chicago Bears	11-0-0[b]
1948	Cleveland Browns	14-0-0[c]
1972	**Miami Dolphins**	**14-0-0**
2007	New England Patriots	16-0-0[d]

[a] Chicago lost the championship game.

[b] Chicago lost the championship game.

[c] Cleveland was the undefeated champion of the 1948 All-American Football Conference, but the team would not join the NFL until 1950.

[d] New England won 16 consecutive regular-season games plus two playoff games before losing in the Super Bowl to the New York Giants.

CHAPTER TWENTY-SEVEN

THE WORKHORSE

Ever since the opening kickoff 100 years ago when Jim Thorpe could choose to drive an opponent back with a powerful shoulder dip or simply sprint past any opponent or later Cleveland's massive Marion Motley would take on all-comers crashing through the line plowing over would-be tacklers like bowling pins and in Detroit where a Barry Sanders juke would leave a defender clutching only air, it has been the running back that has been the steady core of the game since the National Football League's earliest days.

Sharing instincts, balance, and vision, some of the greatest athletes in the game have shined as running backs—the list can run pages, but to name a very few: Eric Dickerson, Steve Van Buren, Lenny Moore, O. J. Simpson, Joe Perry, Adrian Peterson, Curtis Martin, Marion Motley, Jamaal Charles, Bo Jackson, Franco Harris, John Riggins, Paul Lowe, Hugh McElhenny, Thurman Thomas, Ollie Matson, Terrell Davis, Le'Veon Bell, and, of course, Emmitt Smith, the NFL career leader in rushing yards (18,355) and rushing touchdowns (164).

All of them share, to varying degrees, the core skills: power, speed, and the abilities to block and catch the football.

SMALL BUT RESILIENT

From his first handoff fresh out of tiny North Texas State, small running back Abner Haynes was a bona fide breakout. This son of a preacher man proved he could do it all and was not only rookie of the year in 1960 but also the league's player of the year, leading the AFL in rushing.

"He was a franchise player before they talked about franchise players," said Texans/Chiefs wide receiver Chris Buford of his teammate. "Abner did it all: rushing, receiving, kickoff returns, punt returns. He gave us the dimension we needed to be a good team."

With Haynes leading the way, the Texans would win the 1962 AFL crown in an exciting overtime victory over the Houston Oilers.

For great running backs like Barry Sanders and Gale Sayers (and for many years Walter Payton), championships were a pipe dream. The teams they played for struggled, while large expectations were put upon their running games. An example of this was Floyd Little who, after a brilliant career at Syracuse University as a rare three-time all-American, toiled from 1967 to 1975 for the hapless Denver Broncos franchise where he was the team's captain all nine seasons, including his rookie year.

During his rookie campaign, Little led the NFL in punt returns with a 16.9-yard average. He led the NFL in combined yards in 1967 and 1968. In 1975 Little retired as the NFL's seventh all-time leading rusher with 6,323 yards rushing and 54 total touchdowns (rushing, receiving, and returns) but never reached the playoffs.

The compact, slightly bow-legged rusher whose number 44 is retired by the Broncos and who is a member of both the College and Pro Football Halls of Fame can relate to some of those great running backs who shouldered the load largely by themselves. "Barry Sanders always impressed me, because he did not have any help. When you have a running back surrounded by All-Pro linemen, quarterback, and wide receivers, it makes a big difference. Barry, Gale Sayers, Walter [Payton], myself, we had no help."

Another running back who played much larger than his size was Larry Brown, who rushed for the Washington Redskins from 1969 to 1976. Noted for his courageous running style despite his relatively small frame, he attributed it to having been raised on the tough streets of Pittsburgh's Hill District, where he "played tackle football in those streets."

Brown's relentless style, exemplified in his abilities to break tackles and gain yardage after contact, earned him an NFL MVP Award in 1972.

Teammate Bill Brundige admired Brown's lack of fear going up against much bigger opponents.

"Larry just kept churning. He never backed away from a hit. He was Lombardi's type of player."

TANKS IN CLEATS

Then there were the big guys who took on, well, other big guys.

For Pittsburgh Steelers defensive lineman John Banaszak, an unenviable assignment twice a year was trying to tackle running back Earl Campbell.

"Earl Campbell was the most powerful running back I ever played against," Banaszak explained. "And he messed up my big toe. And every time I talk about Earl Campbell, my toe starts to hurt. It was a goal-line situation, and he was coming through, and our technique was to get as low as we could go. Get down and drive through under the offensive lineman, and come up on the other side of the ball. And as I came up, I saw this huge thigh in front of me. It is amazing what can go through your mind in a split second. And in that split second, I'm thinking, 'Oh my God, that is Earl Campbell! Oh my God, that's his huge thigh! And I have to hit him!'

"And I hit him with my shoulder, and I could feel the searing pain, going from my shoulder all the way down the left side of my body into my planted left foot in the turf. I am waiting for the crowd reaction, because I knew I tackled him. But the quarterback, Dan Pastorini, had run a bootleg. Earl didn't even have the ball!"

When the Heisman Trophy winner from the University of Texas did have the ball, defenders usually scurried. Banaszak added an example.

On a Monday night game, Campbell had already run over the Steelers for more than 100 yards, but the final whistle was a ways away. And after his teammate, safety Mike Wagner, who was tired of getting his bell rung by trying to bring down the big guy by himself, implored his linemen up front to make some tackles, Banaszak retorted, "Mike, isn't that a bit beneath you to beg on the football field?"

Many safeties begged for help during Campbell's reign, during which the three-time All-Pro was the NFL MVP in 1979, a three-time offensive player of the year that led the league in rushing yards three times and rushing touchdowns twice. In addition to rushing for 1,450 yards in 1978, the first season to feature a schedule of 16 games, his performance helped the Oilers to a 10-6 record and play-off victories over Miami and New England.

Campbell shared a similar style to Larry Csonka, the Miami Dolphins' fullback.

There was a famous quote that many felt captured Zonk, as he was known. When Dolphins offensive line coach Monte Clark was asked about Larry's bruising running style, he responded, "When Csonka goes on safari, the lions roll up their windows."

It wasn't only the collision that got defenders, it was also what happened as they tried to bring him down. His legs were just so strong that he kept moving. He simply carried the attacker. Rarely did he fumble or drop a pass; Csonka was also an excellent blocker.

"He was just so tough," said his quarterback Bob Griese, who recalled a defining incident during a regular season game in 1970 against Buffalo. "I think the play that captured him was running over the left side then heading down the sideline. He puts a stiff arm on a DB and the ref throws a flag calling Larry for unnecessary roughness. Shula is excited, thinking he has fifteen more yards for the penalty, but Coach turns irate when he learns it is against Larry."

Csonka, a three-time All-Pro, had his best day when it counted most.

Miami rode the powerful legs of Csonka, who had a record-setting day (he rushed 33 times for two touchdowns and a then-record 145 yards) in running over, through, and around the tough Minnesota Vikings defense to give the Dolphins a 24–7 win in Super Bowl VIII.

If there was a predecessor to these AFC titans Campbell and Csonka, it would be a behemoth that went by a rather benign nickname, Carlton "Cookie" Gilchrist.

At six foot two and 243 pounds, Gilchrist was also a devastating

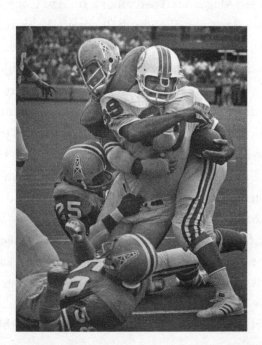

Miami's Larry Csonka was always difficult to bring down, but defenders knew they'd especially have their hands full near the goal line.

Courtesy Miami Dolphins

runner and splendid blocker, but at age 27, when he joined the Buffalo Bills, he was virtually unknown to American football fans. He
never played college ball, and he'd had a tryout with the Browns, but
it didn't stick.

Rumors and legends about Cookie trickled from Canada, where
he eventually landed on a team. It was said that when he carried the
ball, he carried an army of would-be tacklers like a brewery truck. It
was claimed he could boot 45-yard field goals and when he kicked
off, the ball was invariably put in the end zone. Not one for modesty,
Cookie proclaimed, "There is nothing in football I can't do."[55]

Who would argue with him? Certainly not his teammate at Buffalo, Paul Maguire.

Going into the season finale in 1964, the Bills were on the road
in Boston.

"We both had very good records and fighting for the division
crown and normally many players are playing pinochle and smoking and chatting before a game, but I remember our locker room was
unusually quiet," explained Maguire. "Then all of a sudden Cookie
jumps up and says, 'If we don't win this football game, I'm gonna
kick everybody's ass in this room!'

"I slipped quietly back into my locker because I knew he could
kick my ass. Then all of a sudden, Lou Saban and his coaches come
out of the room and want to know what the hell's going on," continued Maguire. "Then Cookie turns to Coach Saban and says, glaring, 'And when I'm done kicking their ass, I'm gonna kick *your* ass!'
Without saying a word, Coach Saban and his assistants turn around
and go right back into their room. They weren't coming out.

"Cookie takes the ball off tackle on the very first play from
scrimmage, and Chuck Shonta, the Patriots' safety, tries to meet
him but gets run over and knocked out. So, our quarterback, Jack
Kemp, rushes over to the sidelines and tells Saban, 'We got to get
this guy out of here because he's going to kill somebody!'

"And Lou says, 'Well, *you* tell him!'" Maguire laughed at the memory. "We were all afraid of Cookie. We tore up the Patriots that day."

Gilchrist was the first 1,000-yard American Football League rusher, with 1,096 yards in a 14-game schedule in 1962. That year, he set the all-time AFL record for touchdowns with 13, and he earned AFL MVP honors. Though he was with the Bills for only three seasons, he led the league in scoring in each of his three years as a Bill.

In his second year there, Gilchrist rushed for a professional football record 243 yards and five touchdowns in a single game against the New York Jets in 1963.

"If you look at some of the film in that game we played against the Jets in New York, he was so fired up he ran over six people on his way to a score. He was that kind of runner. He was the kind of guy that brought it all . . . every game. And not only was he a big guy, but he was also very fast. Scary," Maguire said.

Though Gilchrist did not lack confidence and stories of his exploits grew while he was winning Grey Cup championships up in the CFL, there is no doubt, for a big man, the Pittsburgh native had a lot of physical talent.

"First of all, let me say Cookie Gilchrist was the best *football* player I ever played with. I am not saying athlete. I am saying football player. And there is a distinct difference," explained Billy Shaw, a Hall of Fame guard and teammate of Cookie's at Buffalo.

"You really have to have played the game at a high level to understand what I mean. Cookie was one of those guys that could play multiple positions. He could have been a Hall of Fame tackle or guard. He could have been a Hall of Fame linebacker. He could have been a phenomenal tight end. He had excellent hands. He was as big as we were, yet at the same time he could run a 4.5 40. Cookie was just an amazing football player. One year he even did our kicking, field goals, extra points, and our kickoffs."

LIGHTNING QUICK

While backs like Campbell, Csonka, and Gilchrist usually ran over people, others like Barry Sanders and Tony Dorsett preferred to rely on their quickness, which often led to defenders lunging at air.

The numbers for Barry Sanders speak volumes. As a junior in 1988 playing for Oklahoma State he won the Heisman, rushing for 2,850 yards and 42 touchdowns in 12 games. Then he made an immediate impact in Detroit, winning the NFL's rookie of the year by rushing for more than a 5-yard average, tallying 1,470 yards. Through 10 seasons in Detroit, he averaged over 1,500 rushing yards per season and just under 100 rushing yards per game. In 1997 he became the third player to rush for more than 2,000 yards in a season and was named the Most Valuable Player.

"If you're playing Barry you are going to play a lot of eight up-front," said John Lynch, a nine-time Pro Bowl safety. "And I was the unblocked guy. But that also meant that your job was that you had Barry one on one. I never played scared, but I gotta admit when I played Barry I was shaking in my boots."

"I remember his eyes. He would scan the field then lock on to you. He would have no expression, but it is almost as if he was smiling at you as if to say, 'all right here we go.' His ability to stop, start, shift directions in full gear were out of this world. Somebody once explained that Barry Sanders would be tough to tag in a two-hand touch game in a phone booth."

Bill Maas, a two-time All-Pro and a former NFL defensive rookie of the year, saw experienced veterans come up empty against Sanders, so he adjusted his play accordingly against the elusive running back. "I missed him twice on one play," he said. "He could make anyone on defense look like a complete fool. And it didn't embarrass you because he did it to everybody. He made the best defenders look ridiculous."

While Sanders did not have enough talent surrounding him for

Detroit to be a regular contender, he did have the freedom to maximize the style that worked for him. However, for Dallas Cowboys running back Tony Dorsett, at least early on, the situation was the opposite. He was surrounded by plenty of talent, but he was severely restricted in implementing a running style that came natural to him. For a while, it appeared the best defense opponents had against him was his own coach. Dorsett was aggressive, but everything for Coach Landry was based on precision. It was like the clashing of an improv musician with a pragmatic, by-the-book engineer.

"I will never forget him saying on one particular play, 'On this down and distance, you got to do exactly this; I will put my coaching career on this,'" recalled Dorsett.

"I said, 'I'm not a robot you all. I am an instinctive runner. I run to what I see. I run to daylight. I start at the point of attack, and if it isn't there, I got to do what I do that got me here.'"

The Heisman winner out of Pitt had what was referred to as pace. It was deceptive speed that kept people off balance. Instinctively knowing when to slow down or speed up, he glided. It is a natural gift that few have, and though it took awhile for coach to understand it, once he did, the Cowboys' fortunes improved.

"I'll never forget one day before practice. We're gathered in a team meeting and Coach Landry addresses us," said Dorsett. "'Guys, Tony is a different type of runner. He is going to run to what he sees. You put your head on your opponent and then Tony is going to run to what he sees.' The whole room goes silent. Everybody is scratching their head like 'what?' Then during a break, a bunch of veterans come up and tell me, 'I can't believe it?! He changes his whole offensive philosophy around you?' I said, 'Hey man, I'm just trying to do what I do best.'"

Proving to be elusive, powerful, quick, and a terrific in-line runner, Dorsett would go on to earn the 1977 rookie of the year award, rushing for more than 1,000 yards, a big factor in their drive to winning the Super Bowl that season.

"Tony can run inside very well," quarterback Roger Staubach said. "When you have a speed that Tony had. You can try and shut him down running outside, but if he broke through the line of scrimmage on the inside, you'd have a very difficult time catching him. Tony made a lot of big plays just right up the middle. He was quick, smart, and strong. Getting Tony in '77 made a huge difference for us."

Dorsett himself, a Hall of Famer who rushed for more than 12,000 yards in a 12-year career, attributed it all to an ability to make it up as he goes along, riffing off the play called: "It is all instinctive, it is creative, it is impromptu, things are happening very quickly and my vision really helped me."

These are the same traits that would propel Chicago Bears running back Gale Sayers to greatness. Instinctive art that produced the capability to score on any play and from any place on the field.

It was a comparatively brief career (1965 to 1971) due to injury, but for his peers, teammates and opponents alike, the Kansas Comet had no equal when it came to elusiveness.

Those moves were never on display better than on a muddy field during his rookie season of 1965 in a record-setting performance against the 49ers, where he tied an NFL record by scoring six touchdowns via running, receiving, and an 85-yard punt return in a 61–20 rout of San Francisco.

"All I can tell you is that I have never seen a greater running back doing what he did. It was a pretty muddy field that day he scored six touchdowns. He was the only guy playing on it," said his teammate, tight end Mike Ditka. "I made a catch in the end zone slid through all the way into the dugout by third base. Gale returned a punt for a touchdown, he caught a pass for a touchdown, he did it all. He didn't have a long career and that is probably the only reason he is probably not the greatest football player I have ever seen, but he is darn near the top for what he did achieve."

Like Sanders, Sayers had an uncanny ability to change direction.

They could both run sideways about as fast as they could forward, with incredible abilities to change direction at tremendous speed.

Though Sayers won the NFL rushing title in 1966 and 1969, unfortunately the Bears struggled without a dependable quarterback, never made the playoffs, and basically were a .500 team during the career of number 40.

Nevertheless, at the time of his retirement, he was the NFL's all-time leading kickoff returner with a 30.56-yard career average. He also had a very impressive average of 5.0 yards per carry from the line of scrimmage.

Personal stats and playoff victories are only a pair of metrics. Football, at its core, is entertainment, and no one was more exciting to watch than Gale Sayers.

This was exemplified in one of his many electrifying punt returns.

"I was in the second wave and Sayers had already bolted through the first wave," recalled veteran Bill Curry about a particular play. "And I have a good angle, and Sayers was about two, three feet from the sideline, so he had to cut back where pursuit would get him or I was going to knock him out-of-bounds. There was no other place he could go. He didn't do either one of those things. Instead it was one of those *Star Trek* warp-speed moments. Sayers zips past me and moves on down the sideline like he was shot out of a cannon. I will never forget that empty feeling. He had that amazing acceleration."

DURABLE

Besides dependability in not turning the ball over with fumbles, one of the traits coaches hold most dear about their running backs is durability. Players that have produced year after year and do so while rarely missing a game. It is one area where many runners throughout the history of the NFL have proven their worth.

RECEIVING BACKS

Be it screen passes or patterns off check downs, NFL-level running backs are expected to handle such short passes, which are relatively uncontested in open space. However, backs like Keith Byars, Larry Centers, Tiki Barber, and Roger Craig ran receiver-type routes and used their after-catch running skills to propel their teams.

A perfect fit for Bill Walsh's West Coast offense, 49ers running back Roger Craig was superb as both runner and receiver. As a matter of fact, he was the first player ever to post 1,000 rushing and 1,000 receiving yards in the same season (1985). It was no fluke and in 1988 for his numbers of rushing for 1,502 yards and catching 76 passes for 534 yards, he was named AP offensive player of the year.

Across the Bay (at least for most of his career), Raiders running back Marcus Allen enjoyed a long career excelling in both rushing and receiving (and was a terrific blocker to boot).

Allen was the first player to gain more than 10,000 rushing yards and 5,000 receiving yards in his NFL career.

Down the coast in San Diego, the Chargers' LaDainian Tomlinson excelled as a rusher and receiver. He averaged 1,470 rushing yards in his first eight seasons, but also caught passes as well as any running back ever. His 624 receptions are second-most ever for a running back, and he once hauled in 100 in a season. (L.T. could also find the end zone with his arm, accounting for seven TD passes.)

But perhaps the best receiving running back of all time was the Rams' Marshall Faulk, who was bolstered by one of the great offenses in NFL history under Dick Vermeil and Mike Martz.

An AP offensive player of the year three straight seasons (1999–2001), Faulk caught 80 receptions in five straight seasons. A lot of receivers would take that number. The Rams' running back did that at the same time he was averaging nearly 5 yards a carry and 1,200 yards rushing. He was the MVP of the Greatest Show on Turf *and* was the MVP of the National Football League in 2000 after setting a new single-season record with 26 rushing touchdowns, doing it in just 14 games and without fumbling once.

However, there were a few who were so tough and so fit, that they produced year-in and year-out with an ability to dish out punishment, not something you'd associate with a long career.

Among those with such an aggressive mentality were Jim Taylor, Herschel Walker, and Walter Payton.

Epitomizing Lombardi's hard-nosed, fundamental way, Green Bay running back Jim Taylor boiled the game down to "defeating your man." A strong believer that the shortest path between two points was a straight line, the LSU grad was a relentless tank who rumbled for five 1,000+ yard seasons and in 1962 led the league in rushing (the only time Jim Brown did not) and was the NFL MVP.

Not above trash-talking, Taylor developed several personal rivalries throughout his career, most notably with New York Giants linebacker Sam Huff. Besides his ability to both withstand and deliver blows, which earned him a reputation as one of the league's toughest players, what the game boiled down to for the Hall of Fame running back was the mental side of the contest.

"It is a six-inch game, played between the ears," he once said.

Herschel Walker was another star hailing from the South who, like Taylor, could take and deliver blows.

The former Heisman Trophy winner and three-time all-American at the University of Georgia prided himself on both his speed and power. "I was not one to dance very much," he said. "There weren't too many people that were going to catch me after I got loose."

After setting pro football records with the NJ Generals of the United States Football League (Walker won the USFL rushing title in 1983 and 1985. He established a new pro mark for single-season rushing yards with 2,411 yards in 1985, averaging 5.5 yards per attempt in 18 games), he established himself as a premier NFL running back in 1988, becoming a one-man offense, reaching his NFL career highs of 1,514 rushing yards and 505 receiving yards, while playing seven positions: halfback, fullback, tight end, H-back, and wide receiver, both in the slot and as a flanker. He became just the tenth player in NFL history to amass more than 2,000 combined rushing and receiving yards in a season.

Still a tremendous physical specimen, it's unfortunate his NFL career is best remembered for the trade that sent him from Dallas to Minnesota, which propelled the Cowboys to three Super Bowl championships.

Though he was not as big or fast as Walker, Walter Payton did enjoy a long career which, like Jim Taylor, was partly due to a well-developed mental approach to the game. It was a mano-a-mano, beat-the-man-in-front-of-you stance.

"I think the thing that made Walter was his attitude. He had a 'I-can't-be-beat' attitude, that is what drove him," observed his coach in Chicago, Mike Ditka. "Yes, there were faster guys and there were bigger and stronger guys, but when you put together a whole package, there's nothing you'd rather see than giving the ball to Walter Payton running off tackle, running over a safety, and getting to the end zone.

"With Walter there was no challenge he would not take. If he wasn't going to run around you, he'd just as easily run over you. And we are talking about a guy that was not that big. He wasn't a regular weight lifter but he'd see some teammates struggling on a barbell, go over lift it 10 times then just walk away."

Compact and relentless, number 34 would bang into the line of scrimmage and bounce off people. He was also a shifty runner like the limp leg move he had, but he was basically a power runner. His legs were like pistons. They just would not stop. You practically had to gang tackle him to bring Walter down.

Durable? In his 13-year career, Sweetness missed only one game (despite taking a pounding in his first eight seasons, when Chicago did not have much talent around him). By the time he retired, Payton owned the all-time NFL records for carries (3,838 attempts) and yardage for more than 16,700 yards, running the ball 842 times more than Eric Dickerson, who was in second place at one point.

To this day, Jim Brown remains the standard by which all running backs are evaluated. His career rushing record (12,312 yards—in just nine seasons) has been surpassed, held for a long time by Walter Payton and now Emmitt Smith.

From 1957 to 1965, at six foot two, 232 pounds, the former Syracuse fullback with breakaway speed and tremendous power dominated the NFL. But really it was a combination of additional factors that enabled him to lead the league in rushing eight of his nine seasons and be named a three-time NFL MVP. In making nine Pro Bowls and eight First-Team All-Pro selections in his career, it was his mental toughness and tremendous balance that is somewhat underreported in crediting the success Brown enjoyed.

The numbers speak loudly. Brown averaged a touchdown per game over his 118-game career. He is also number one all-time with a 125.52 yards from scrimmage per game average. He led the league in rushing attempts, rushing yards, yards per game, and rushing touchdowns a combined 26 times.

His victims on any given Sunday included some of the game's greatest players.

"Jim Brown was the best overall running back I ever played against," said Hall of Fame defensive tackle Bob Lilly. "My first time facing him was up in Cleveland. We played home and home as they were in our division. Well, Coach Landry was always talking about Brown because he played against him for several years.

"So, I am playing left defensive end and Jim comes around to my side and I pursue him to the sideline, and I have him nailed. I was crouched, poised and saying, 'we're going to have a crash here.' But he jumps right over me, and I look back, and he's running straight down the field," said the big Cowboy, laughing at the memory.

"I said to myself, 'What just happened? I may be looking for a

new job.' He could do that, or he could run over you. One time he
bent my face mask clear around my head, but at least I prevented
him from scoring for one more play. He also had what we called a
limp leg, where you'd grab at it, and he'd pull it back and take off. We
played him one time in the Cotton Bowl where he ran right down
the sideline, and he ran fifty yards and scored after five Cowboys had
hit him as hard as they could but were unable to knock him out-of-
bounds. He was just fantastic."

One of Brown's peers was Green Bay star Paul Hornung. He recalled a special time he got to play on the same team with the Cleveland running back, yet was puzzled by how their coach handled it.

"Nobody can touch Jim. He was so big and strong and fast. I was
in an all-star game with Jim. I played quarterback. We did not start,
and Curly Lambeau was the coach. When we did go in, I handed the
ball off to Jim Brown about twelve straight times. Coach calls me
over and asks, 'What are you doing?' I said, 'What do you mean what
am I doing? I am giving the ball to the goddamn best player on the
field. That is what I am doing.' Coach was quiet after that. Jim was
special. His records stand alone. Clearly one of the greatest football
players of all time."

Speed, strength, grace, balance, and a determined mind-set, the
NFL had never seen anything quite like Jim Brown. Before or since.

THEY FOUND A LOT OF DAYLIGHT

YARDS PER RUSHING ATTEMPT (CAREER)

5.7	Marion Motley	1946–1955	Browns, Steelers
5.4	Jamaal Charles	2008–2018	Chiefs, Broncos, Jaguars
5.2	Jim Brown	1957–1965	Browns

AVG. RUSHING YARDS PER GAME (CAREER)

104.3	Jim Brown	1957–1965	Browns
101.2	Ezekiel Elliott	2016–2018	Cowboys
99.8	Barry Sanders	1989–1998	Lions

RUSHING TOUCHDOWNS (CAREER)

164	Emmitt Smith	1990–2004	Cowboys, Cardinals
145	LaDainian Tomlinson	2001–2011	Chargers, Jets
123	Marcus Allen	1982–1997	Raiders, Chiefs

MOST RUSHING YARDS (SINGLE GAME)

296	Adrian Peterson	2007	Vikings
295	Jamal Lewis	2003	Ravens
286	Jerome Harrison	2009	Browns

MOST RUSHING YARDS (SINGLE SEASON)

2,105	Eric Dickerson	1984	Rams
2,097	Adrian Peterson	2012	Vikings
2,066	Jamal Lewis	2003	Ravens

RUSHING ATTEMPTS (CAREER)

4,409	Emmitt Smith	1990–2004	Cowboys, Cardinals
3,838	Walter Payton	1975–1987	Bears
3,518	Curtis Martin	1995–2005	Patriots/Jets

MOST RUSHING YARDS (CAREER)

18,355	Emmitt Smith	1990–2004	Cowboys, Cardinals
16,726	Walter Payton	1975–1987	Bears
15,269	Barry Sanders	1989–1998	Lions

CHAPTER TWENTY-EIGHT

D!

"*ee-fense!*" has been the bottom-line rallying cry for fans since the sport's earliest days. One franchise synonymous with defense is the Chicago Bears. Currently led by one of the NFL's biggest game-changers, linebacker Khalil Mack, the 2018 version of the Bears harkens all the way back to the early 1930s and 1940s, when Chicago dominated the league on D.

With such a rich tradition, it is no surprise that they have produced two of the greatest units of all time.

'63 BEARS

The 1963 Chicago Bears flat out won the championship based on defense. Operating in tandem with a mediocre offense (ranked 10th of 14 teams), the Bears smothered the defending champion Green Bay Packers twice, took the divisional title, then won the NFL championship over the New York Giants thanks to the Bears intercepting Hall of Famer Y. A. Tittle five times, turning two of them into scores and winning 14–10.

With a defense that featured four Hall of Famers and five Pro

Bowlers, they allowed only 144 points all year while forcing 54 turnovers. All of the starting defensive backs intercepted at least six passes.

Tough Green Bay running back Jim Taylor had a lot of respect for them.

"That Bears defense was tremendously talented and you knew there'd be no quit in them like middle linebacker Bill George. They also had a couple very tough ends that can really hit in Ed O'Bradovich and Doug Atkins. They would beat the man in front of them then make the tackle. You had to be at your best because that whole unit only had an A game."

George Halas primarily coached the offense, so it was a young man by the name of George Allen who was instrumental in shaping up that D. Allen felt the key was increasing pressure. Before it was popular, the Bears blitzed (a strategy used by a defensive unit in which a player not on the defensive line attempts to pressure the quarterback. Typically, this will result in a linebacker or defensive back attempting to find a gap in the offensive line and tackle the quarterback). It was made easier because Chicago also excelled in single coverage against the pass. On top of that, lineman Atkins was such a dominant player that he required two blockers on just about every play.

O'Bradovich explained the reason for their success.

"Two words why we were so great: George Allen. In '62 Clark Shaughnessy got into it with Halas, so they moved George Allen up and in '63 he was the defensive coordinator. We were constantly shifting the defensive line. Sometimes we used six defensive backs. There were constant audibles thrown around. We would also blitz from every angle. Cornerbacks and safeties," explained the defensive end. "And running backs whether they tried to slip around the outside or through the middle as receiving options, we destroyed them. We called it hanging or grounding. Either way, they were no longer receiving options for that given play. It was the same physical approach with the wide receivers."

Allen's success did not go unnoticed by other NFL owners and he'd get his first head coaching job beginning with the Los Angeles Rams in 1966.

Beginning in the 1960s, defensive lines and units as a whole began earning nicknames that endured even through personnel changes. But whether they had a nickname or not, what they shared was the fact that in that era, players often stayed together for years, learned each other's moves, worked together as a unit, and blended individual talents as one.

THE FEARSOME FOURSOME

George Allen's Fearsome Foursome was one of those. Comprised of Rosey Grier, Merlin Olsen, Deacon Jones, and Lamar Lundy (and later Roger Brown), the famed defensive line would be the center at which Allen restored some glory to the franchise that had not had a winning season since 1958.

Drawing more than a million fans in the glory years of '67 and '68 riding his defensive line to the playoffs, Allen would enjoy five straight winning seasons. Though Los Angeles came up short in those playoffs (losing in '67 to Green Bay, 28–7, and in '69, 23–20, to Minnesota), the sold-out Coliseum was humming every Sunday with the chant of "dee-fense!"

Rosey Grier, traded from the Giants in 1963, was an intimidating tackle. However his career ended in '67 due to a torn Achilles tendon.

Tall and angular Lamar Lundy, drafted by both the NFL and NBA, was occasionally used as a receiver, grabbing 35 passes for 584 yards and six TDs during his career. On defense, the big guy had three pick-sixes.

Drafted in the 14th round in 1961, David "Deacon" Jones, an

All-Pro five straight years, would dominate with his head slaps and with Coach Allen is also credited with popularizing the word *sack*.

Defensive tackle Merlin Olsen, the 1961 Outland trophy winner, was selected to the Pro Bowl 14 straight times. They were big for their day, averaging 20 pounds more than their DL peers. They were all at least six foot five AND fast.

Perhaps tough guy quarterback Joe Kapp summed up the Rush Men aka the Fearsome Foursome best:

"Merlin Olsen, FTD flower salesman and Father Murphy on *Little House on the Prairie*. Lamar Lundy, eighteen pounds at birth . . . an eighteen-pound baby named Lamar? Rosey Grier was famous for his needlepoint. Deacon Jones has never been to a church in his life and sold tombstones in the off-season. Their names and images may have sounded gentle, but all they cared about was destroying quarterbacks!"

Kapp, who led the Minnesota Vikings in that '69 playoff win over Los Angeles, also had one of the all-time best defensive units as part of his team.

THE PURPLE PEOPLE EATERS

Like the Fearsome Foursome, the Purple People Eaters referred to Minnesota's front line of Carl Eller, Alan Page, Gary Larsen, and Jim Marshall. They were opportunistic and summed up their play with expressions like "Nothing Cheap and Nothing Deep," and labeled themselves "athletic, persistent, and weather resistant." And "weather resistant" meant a real home field advantage for the People Eaters and company. Playing in Minnesota after Halloween, opponents feared the wind and snow that howled through open Metropolitan Stadium (the Vikings' home from 1961 to 1981). Head coach Bud Grant's psychological ploys included no heaters on the sidelines and guys like running back Bill Brown and Kapp banging around in shirt sleeves.

"Yes, we couldn't let weather be a factor in the way we played," said Jim Marshall. "We had the attitude that we weren't going to let outside factors affect us and most of the time in that era it was good enough to win. For example, when the sun set over the back of Metropolitan Stadium, the temperature dropped fifteen to twenty degrees, and the icy, penetrating wind started whipping through. We'd start chanting 'Odin! . . . Odin!' the Viking god of war. It was a psychological advantage for us," the defensive end who played 20 years without missing a game said with a wink.

Also impressive was Marshall's line mate, Alan Page. He was voted to nine Pro Bowls, and was a six-time First Team All-Pro and three-time Second Team All-Pro. He was voted to the NFL 1970s All-Decade Team. And in a rarity for a defensive tackle, in 1971 he became the first winner of the AP Most Valuable Defensive Player as well as the AP Most Valuable Player of the NFL.

"I faced Alan Page. It was a war," recalled Kansas City Chiefs guard Ed Budde. "He wasn't really large, but he was super quick. Very fast off the ball like Bob Lilly and, like Bob, a true Hall of Famer."

Tony Dorsett, the Cowboys' star running back, who faced a lot of tough defenses, was impressed by the Vikings, a frequent opponent. That said a lot because Dallas produced not one but two great defenses: Doomsday I and Doomsday II.

DOOMSDAY I AND II

While Staubach and Dorsett rightfully grabbed a lot of headlines, these Dallas defenders grabbed the attention of their opponents in playing a central part of one of the winningest runs in NFL history. Cowboys head coach Tom Landry, a former New York Giants defensive coordinator, would establish schemes and groom talent that led to an amazing 20 consecutive winning seasons.

Version I reigned from 1966 to 1974 and included Bob Lilly and Jethro Pugh on the line, Lee Roy Jordan and Chuck Howley backing them, and a supremely athletic backfield in Mel Renfro, Herb Adderley, Charlie Waters, Cliff Harris, and Cornell Green.

Teammates and opponents alike had the utmost respect for the skills of defensive tackle Bob Lilly in particular.

"Bob Lilly was very quick and deceptively strong. And when he moves, then hits you, well, he really shook up offenses. Practicing against him was an exercise in futility," said Cowboys center Dave Manders. "When you think you had an angle on him, you didn't, and he could figure you out instantly. He was the best football player I ever played against."

Miami Dolphins running back Larry Csonka enjoyed a very successful career. But one of his most disappointing games was a loss to Dallas in Super Bowl VI.

"You could see Lilly just loved the game," he observed. "Some players play with rage. But Lilly had no need for all that jumping around and trash talking. He was strong, silent, and deadly. Bob Lilly and Joe Greene are twins, as far as how they approached the game, how they played it, how they treat people. They are class individuals. They are as apt to help you up as knock you down, but when the ball is snapped, they have no friends, and they take no prisoners."

Even among themselves, Dallas defenders took no prisoners, as some of the most physical play took place on the practice field.

"We had intrasquad games every year, and the winners got steaks and the losers got hot dogs," said veteran running back Dan Reeves. "Lee Roy Jordan and I lived about fifty yards from each other. We were really good friends and would often drive to work together. We run a trap play up the middle, and Lee Roy hit me so hard he busted my face mask, busted my lip, I got blood all over the place, and I said, 'Dang, Lee Roy what are you doing? It's just a scrimmage!'

"He said, 'If my grandmama put on a helmet, I'd knock the hell out of her too.'"

Defensive backs Harris and Waters managed to survive those intrasquad games and would extend their careers to anchor the backfield for Doomsday II that terrorized offenses from approximately 1975 to 1982. That version was led by a tremendous front line that featured Randy White and Ed "Too Tall" Jones, as well as the 1977 NFL defensive player of the year and member of the 1970s All-Decade Team, Harvey Martin.

Martin was simply a consistent talent who could make big plays from either the tackle or end position. At six foot nine, 270 pounds, Jones was a hulking force at the end position. And as good as those two were, the player who often gave blockers the greatest fits was Randy White. Incredibly strong and super quick for a man who stood six foot five and weighed 260 pounds, the hardest part of his transition to the pros was where to line him up.

Though he would go on to a Hall of Fame career, it took a while for Coach Landry to figure out the optimum position to take advantage of White's enormous talents. One of the challenges is that the flex often goes against instincts.

"I think it was my third season," White recalled, "and at training camp, I went from middle linebacker to playing outside linebacker to playing weak side linebacker. I am covering Tony Dorsett one-on-one coming out of the backfield, and I'm going, 'This ain't gonna work.' So, one afternoon, Coach Landry called me into his office, and he doesn't tell me but asks me, 'Randy, what do you think about us moving you into the defensive line?'

"At that time, I was getting a little frustrated because we had Ed Jones at one end and Harvey Martin at the other end, so I am thinking, 'Well, if I don't make it at defensive tackle, where am I going to play on this team?'

"So, I told Coach, 'Listen, I will play anywhere you think I can help this team win football games.' So, he says, 'Okay, we're going to move you into the defensive line.' And that was it."

From 1977 to 1985 White worked and worked, including his quickness and agility through a form of Thai boxing, and was named first-team All-Pro every single year.

"The Manster!" screamed Dorsett. (That was White's nickname of half man, half monster.) "Come on! The Manster was going a hundred miles an hour at all times! Randy White was just unfrikkin' believable. You've heard the expression 'You practice like you play?' Well, that was Randy White. He was a beast."

"The Manster": Hall of Fame tackle Randy White of the Dallas Cowboys zeroes in on Dan Marino.

Courtesy Dallas Cowboys

Coach Landry was the rare individual who was equally adept at devising schemes on offense and defense, but there have been a few special coaches that were simply brilliant on defense. One of those was the architect of the Miami Dolphins's No-Name Defense of the early 1970s.

THE NO-NAME DEFENSE

"Our biggest secret weapon was Bill Arnsparger," said Dick Anderson, Miami's safety and the 1973 NFL defensive player of the year. "Bill was brilliant. The key to our defense

Tom Landry was that rare head coach who was equally adept in developing offensive and defensive strategies.

Courtesy Dallas Cowboys

for those years was we progressively improved and had fewer points scored against us. One of the prime examples of how good Bill Arnsparger was we had just 165 points scored against us in 1972. In 1973 we only allowed 150 and just five touchdown passes against us. After he left to the Giants in '74, we made the playoffs, but we gave up more than 120 points than the previous season."

The No-Name Defense may have had a low Q rating, but the players had a high IQ when it came to producing as a unit, as they rarely committed mental errors.

An example of the brilliance of Arnsparger was the creation of the 53 defense.

Starting in 1970, he began building an innovative defense where he essentially invented the dual-purpose edge-rusher that would become the foundation of every hybrid playbook in the league. It started after one of the linemen got hurt and Bill Matheson was the biggest linebacker, so he lined up at defensive end. It was named after his number, 53.

What Miami did was basically a 3-4. But when the ball was snapped, it was a 4-3. With any one of the four linebackers being the fourth guy to rush, it created chaos for the opponent's blocking assignments.

Add in Bill Stanfill, who was probably the most underrecognized player on the team. Both ends, Stanfill and Vern Den Herder were both very fast, quick and good athletes for big men. And Manny Fernandez was a stopper in the middle. The key was the coordination of the calls by Arnsparger that they just did not make mental errors. His players had total confidence that every call he would make would be the right call. Nick Buoniconti was a comparatively small middle linebacker but very savvy and aggressive.

The undefeated 1972 Dolphins still get all the attention, but the fact is the 1973 Dolphins played better defense, allowing 21 fewer points against a tougher schedule of opponents. The 150 points allowed in a 14-game season (which included back-to-back shutouts) set a record at the time.

"Looking back through time people want to talk about the Steelers, 49ers, Patriots yet no one really realizes we had the best one-year, two-year, three-year, four-year, and five-year record of all time," stated Anderson. "Nobody in the history of the NFL has surpassed the record Miami had from the period of 1970 to 1974. Strangely, because we were so effective as a team not many want to recognize the value of that team. Our success was based on togetherness. The unselfishness and those things you are supposed to do in sports."

THE STEEL CURTAIN

As a teenager, future Hall of Fame safety Ronnie Lott idolized Pittsburgh's Steel Curtain. And much like fellow safety Dick Anderson, he feels the Steelers' defensive success "came from not necessarily how they played together, but really how they believed in each other. That they cared about each other."

It all started when new coach Chuck Noll selected for his first pick defensive tackle Joe Greene. Subsequent drafts yielded linebackers Jack Ham and Jack Lambert, linemen L. C. Greenwood and Ernie Holmes, defensive backs Mel Blount and Mike Wagner among others. Between 1972 and 1979, the Steel Curtain never fell out of the top 10 in total defense, ranking in the top three six times.

In a matchup in Super Bowl IX, the Steel Curtain rose to new heights with such a dominating performance that it basically knocked down the more well-known Purple People Eaters a few pegs. The Vikings offense was limited to an all-time low 119 yards and nine first downs, a record for futility. The Vikings only score came on a blocked punt. And adding insult to injury, Pittsburgh forced Minnesota into a safety for a final 16–6 score.

While Greene was the unit's soul, the fire came from Lambert, who was so hostile that Greene once quipped, "Jack's so mean, he doesn't even like himself."

Pittsburgh would go on to win three more Super Bowls. The main thing was there was no offensive counterpart to the type of players the Steelers put on the field. You had defensive ends such as L. C. Greenwood and Dwight White who could run 40 yards in the 4.7, 4.8 range and massive, cat-quick tackles such as Joe Greene and Ernie Holmes. There was no one on offense to handle the linebackers with 4.5, 4.6 speed who were seemingly everywhere at once. Then you add in linebacker-sized cornerbacks. There was no easy route.

"When I think of the Steel Curtain, it was not only strong but also it had a mind-set of attacking you. It was bent on destruction," Lott said. "They had a unified mission of being the toughest group to the point that it became the mantra of the steel curtain. It was designed to have a belief that the curtain was not just of steel, but of destruction."

It helped that Coach Noll was aided by some brilliant defensive minds like Bud Carson and George Perles.

"Our core defense was Carson's Cover 2, though that does not mean we played that all the time. What you have to have in Cover 2 was big cornerbacks, because they have containment responsibilities on running plays," explained Pittsburgh safety Mike Wagner. "They are the outside support, not the linebackers, not the ends, not the safeties. So, you have to have corners who are not only able to cover but also are willing and able to tackle. You don't always see that in corners, but if you have been around Mel Blount and J. T. Thomas, you could see that they were both big for their position."

For example, while Dallas was shifting their offense, Pittsburgh might be shifting their defense two or three times before the ball was snapped.

"We always tried to put ourselves in the best position based on tendencies to give us the best chance of stopping anybody on offense," explained Wagner. "We had talent. We had effort. We had schemes that we believed in, so that together I think really helped us."

'85 BEARS

Though it would not last as long as that in Pittsburgh, talent, effort, great schemes, and brilliant coaching came together to really help produce another of the great defenses of all time in the 1985 Chicago Bears.

Defensive coordinator Buddy Ryan had earned his stripes helping build top defenses with the Jets (part of the Super Bowl III staff) and the Purple People Eaters in Minnesota.

In 1978 Ryan was hired by George Halas as the Chicago Bears defensive coordinator.

Over the next several years Ryan's philosophy evolved and with the arrival of linebacker Mike Singletary, who had a great ability to control the middle of the field, the seeds of the 4-6 defense took form, which, at its core, involved putting pressure on the quarterback.

Ryan's work-in-progress included the 4-6 starting out as a nickel defense with extra run support, but it turned into a blitzing defense that sometimes left only three players in coverage. So, while receivers ran fairly free, the problem was that passers essentially didn't have any time to find them because, in essence, all eight men close to the line were potential pass rushers, thus offenses had trouble accounting for them all. Again, the 4-6 was predicated on pressuring the quarterback, employed with a combination of talent and confusion.

"If you have to commit blockers to our linebackers then invariably you are going to have some people singled up inside. And Buddy thought Steve McMichael, Richard Dent, and I were not blockable with just one person," Dan Hampton, a member of the NFL's 1980s All-Decade Team, pointed out. "So, for example, if I was drawing a double-team, someone would be a free runner for us. And if that is the case, we like our chances. That meant the quarterback has to make a real quick decision. And the receiver has to be really good at getting open in a hurry. Otherwise it is going to be a sack, a pick, or something else bad."

Something bad almost happened to the budding Bears defense before it could really come together, because after Halas fired head coach Neill Armstrong, the owner was looking to clean house and get rid of Ryan as well. However, the players wrote an impassioned letter to the owner on Ryan's behalf. It worked. Buddy remained the team's defensive coordinator.

However, he and new head coach Mike Ditka "didn't exchange Christmas cards." One of the many things they did not see eye to eye on was the role of William Perry.

Coach Ditka had studied film of William Perry, a rotund defensive lineman at Clemson, and wanted to draft him, but it would be a while before he found his way on the defensive line because Ryan did not like rookies and especially "fat ones." Buddy called him a "wasted draft choice," but William was a happy-go-lucky young man and never let that bother him. So, Ditka used him on offense, as a blocker, runner, receiver, and even passer.

"You have to understand, Fridge was actually an incredible athlete. During Week 1 of practice for the Super Bowl, we were at Notre Dame before heading to New Orleans. Some of the players were goofing off before practice, and some started challenging each other as to how far they could throw the football," said Hampton. "[DT-Steve] McMichael threw it 48 yards, [DE-Richard] Dent 60 then [QB-Jim] McMahon 65, Walter Payton threw it 70, Fridge grabs the ball and throws it 82 yards. We were all stunned and amazed. With his big hands, it was more like throwing a baseball. One example of William's underappreciated athleticism."

To Fridge's credit, he went on a diet. About halfway through the season, when William was getting some notoriety for his offensive plays, he had dropped weight and Buddy began starting him and Hampton was moved over to end. Ryan thought it made them a better defense overall. Certainly a key upfront was the tremendous skills and instincts of defensive end Richard Dent, who had such an outstanding first step that it also served as a distinctive stride on his way to the Hall of Fame.

"Richard had a nose for the ball that few do," said Hampton. "Such were his instincts, that he was very rarely fooled or out of position. It is something you can't teach. Like Lawrence Taylor, Richard was a natural that just dominated that outside edge like few ever have."

During the 1985 regular season, Dent led the NFL with 17 sacks and also had 11 forced fumbles.

Of course, the backfield and front line were supported by one of the great linebacking units in NFL history—Wilber Marshall, Mike Singletary, and Otis Wilson.

One of the lesser known reasons for the Bears great dominance that season was the internal competition that took place every week.

"I think one valuable key to our defense was that we competed with one another. When we went in on Monday morning to look at film, everyone wanted bragging rights. That meant proving yourself on Sunday," stated Dent. "You had to be the best you could be in that week's game to be king of the hill on Monday. The linemen, line-backers, defensive backs—we all strove to be perfect. We pushed each other to higher levels."

After going 15-1 during the regular season (the lone loss came at Miami on a Monday Night Game), the Bears would push each other to levels unseen before in a historic playoff run.

Led by the defense that continued their dominating ways, Chicago became the first team in league history to deliver shut outs to both their playoff opponents as they defeated the Giants 21–0 and then the LA Rams 24–0.

Against New York they sacked Phil Simms six times. Against Los Angeles, they held superstar running back Eric Dickerson to just 46 yards (he had run for 246 yards the prior week against Dallas) and quarterback Dieter Brock to a mere 66 yards passing while completing less than a third of his attempts.

In Super Bowl XX, that defense was on tremendous display as by the end of the first half they had essentially moved the Patriots backward (−5 rushing and −14 on pass plays for a net halftime yardage of −19). Their first four possessions lost 22 yards and two fumbles. They didn't even get a first down until just over four minutes to go.

In finishing things off with a 46–10 dismantling of New England (123 total yards allowed, seven sacks, six takeaways), the 1985 Bears showed again that truth behind the notion that defense wins championships.

In three pressure-packed, one-and-done games, in both stats (16 sacks, 10 turnovers while allowing a mere 10 points) and in intimidation, with untold psychological harm on opposing quarterbacks as well as offensive coordinators, the 4-6 Bears defense was simply exceptional in the playoffs.

"I doubt if any defense will ever play as well as that defense did for those three games," Ditka said.

CHAPTER TWENTY-NINE

A JOB FAIR LIKE NO OTHER

Before the NFL draft, over 300 prospective young men seeking employment in the lucrative world of professional football will undergo a series of medical and psychological exams, interviews, and physical tests where just a half-inch in the vertical leap, a .10 of a second in the 40-yard sprint, and just a few pounds in the bench press can be worth hundreds of thousands of dollars.

The NFL Combine (officially the National Invitational Camp) is a key step in a player's journey to the NFL. It is the first chance for coaches and general managers, the key decision-makers, to put a face to the scouting report.

With memories of expensive busts still fresh, teams don't leave anything to chance with players in which they are about to invest, in many cases, millions of dollars. As a result, players are examined to their core physically and mentally by their potential employers.

"Do we have a problem with that? Yes," said DeMaurice Smith, the executive director of the NFL Players Association. "I mean, can you imagine: after you've applied for this great job, they say to you, 'Hey, your résumé looks great. Tomorrow you have to go through a full day of medical screening before we offer you a job.' It would make everybody's head explode.

"To the public, they make it look like it is a measurement of their physical ability. What happens outside the view of the public is that they are taking evaluations of players medically and psychologically that very few professionals in any other business would put up with."[56]

Still, that doesn't stop prospects from wanting to participate. All but about a couple dozen players who are drafted each year attend the combine. Their expenses are paid by a nonprofit corporation, to which all 32 NFL teams contribute the estimated $2 million it takes to put on the combine. "If a team makes a mistake on one kid, it will cost them more than to put this on," said Jeff Foster, president of National Football Scouting. "We can save them millions of dollars."

And it was the idea of saving that launched the event in the first place.

Due to the high costs of examining a prospective player, NFL teams in the '60s began sharing resources and information in order to reduce individual team's costs and allow for more standardized testing and measurement.

The NFL's first scouting organization, LESTO (Lions, Eagles, and Steelers Talent Organization), was started in 1963, with headquarters in Pittsburgh. The next year it became BLESTO, when the Bears joined. Then it was known as BLESTO-V, when the Vikings came on board. And by 1971, with the addition of the Bills, Colts, and Dolphins, the group was known as BLESTO-VIII.

About the same time as LESTO kicked off, there was CEPO (Central Eastern Personnel Organization), which began as a joint venture of the Colts, Browns, Packers, and Cardinals. Its name was changed to United Scouting after the Falcons, Giants, and Redskins joined, and then to National Football Scouting in 1983 to avoid confusion with the United States Football League, which began operations that year. Confused yet?

Still another group, called TROIKA, also launched in 1964, teaming the Cowboys, Rams, and 49ers. It was renamed Quadra when the Saints joined in 1967. In 1982 National Blesto and Quadra Scouting Organization combined and centralized the evaluation and testing process. That year, the first National Invitational Camp was held. Then in 1985 this event was renamed the NFL Combine. After holding the event in Phoenix (1985) and New Orleans (1986), the NFL moved the combine to its home city of Indianapolis, where it remains today.

Centralizing the camps allowed teams to conduct more thorough evaluations of draft prospects. In addition to considering a player's medical history, clubs were able to spend more time on physical and psychological testing, giving the personnel departments a more thorough impression of the player before the draft.

Today a committee of professional NFL talent evaluators coordinates the process for selecting which prospects will be extended an invitation to attend the National Combine. The NIC, led by Jeff Foster, who has been president of NFS since 2005, coordinates the registration process and player logistics.

Individual clubs are free to evaluate any draft-eligible prospects they wish to, including those who have demonstrated personal conduct that restricted their invitation to the National Combine (draft-eligible prospects will not be permitted to participate in any aspect of the combine if a background check reveals a conviction of a felony or misdemeanor that involves violence or use of a weapon, domestic violence, sexual offense, and/or sexual assault. The NFL also reserves the right to deny participation to any prospect dismissed by either their college or the NCAA.). These evaluations may take place at any location permitted under league rules.

For example, each university has a Pro Day, during which the NCAA allows NFL scouts to visit the school and watch players participate in NFL Combine–type events together. These Pro Days are held under the belief that players feel more comfortable at their own campus than they do at the combine, which, in turn, leads to better performances. College teams that produce a large quantity of NFL prospects—USC, Alabama, and Ohio State among others—usually generate huge interest from scouts and coaches at their Pro Days.

Foster, a former scout for the Kansas City Chiefs, said what the talent evaluators are looking for most at the four day job fair is emphasized on four core components—medical and psychological testing, player interviews, and physical skill tests. What every team values most coming away from Indianapolis is medical, number one, and interviews, number two.

After getting checked in, they're ushered to a hospital for lab work, X-rays, an electrocardiogram (EKG) and, for many players, MRIs. These tests are designed not simply to test their fitness in the NFL, but to make sure they're healthy enough to participate in the combine's on-field workout.

"That first evening, the interview process begins," said Foster "Each team is allowed to conduct private fifteen-minute interviews with up to sixty players during the combine. The league and each team have conducted their own training for what's appropriate and what's legal to ask in a job interview-type setting."

The next morning, players first undergo drug testing and base-line neurological testing, then closer examination by each team. At Lucas Oil Stadium, seven rooms are set aside for medical exams. Five or six teams share a room, and the players are looked at by each doctor in each room. At that point, a player may be asked to undergo additional MRIs either at the stadium or at a hospital. The entire process could take two or more hours (there were 400 MRIs and 2,000 X-rays in four days in one recent combine).

After the physical exams, players proceed to mental exams, which can include measuring of intelligence and cognitive ability to creating a personality profile.

"While every prospect undergoes a pair of tests—the Wonderlic

Cognitive Ability Test and one the league created called a 'player assessment test' —about two dozen teams conduct some form of additional psychological testing," Foster explained.

After more than two days of interviews and exams, players take on what attracts the most attention from fans: the on-field drills. Players tackle such tests as the 40-yard dash, bench press, vertical jump, broad jump, 20-yard shuttle, three-cone drill, 60-yard shuttle, and various position-specific drills, among other physical evaluations.

And though changes have been amended, and further changes will evolve as expert committees examine all the parameters that the combine presents, still, some players have gone on to very successful NFL careers despite perceptions made from their results at the combine.

Six-time Super Bowl champion Tom Brady did not shine at the combine and fell to the 199th pick of the 2000 draft.

Anquan Boldin, a three-time All-Pro receiver, after registering a relatively slow time in the 40-yard dash, fell to the 54th pick of the 2003 draft.

Terrell Suggs was coming off an NCAA-record 24-sack season at Arizona State and was considered a lock to be a top-5 pick. Then he struggled at the combine, dropping him down in the draft; yet he has gone on to six Pro Bowl appearances and was AP defensive player of the year in 2011.

"I am not sure how I would change it," Suggs said of the combine. "I would probably make it smaller, for sure, so that more players would get a fair shake. I did not really get to enjoy the combine. It was so nerve-racking. I wanted to run fast. Wanted to do heavy lifting. I didn't enjoy it and didn't perform well. But Ozzie Newsome [the Ravens' GM] didn't really care about those numbers. He knew I could play. Also, teams put too much emphasis on the results of the combine."

Brett Favre realizes the system is not perfect and suggests that experienced scouts and coaches should lean back more on their instincts and experiences as part of a mix with the results of the combine. "Ron Wolfe [Packers veteran personnel executive] said it best one time when he goes. 'The thing that gets lost in the shuffle is this: 'Can the guy play? Is he a football player?' He may not score high at the combine. We see that all the time. We see guys not invited to the combine and have great careers. We see guys that were not drafted and have great careers. We've seen guys score high on the Wonderlic and do forty reps at two hundred fifty pounds but never amount to anything."

Perhaps the most infamous example of "never amounting to anything" and how much it can set back a franchise was the saga of quarterback Ryan Leaf, the San Diego Chargers' first pick in the 1998 draft. Arguably, Leaf became the biggest bust in NFL draft history.

The combine has become one of the biggest NFL events after the Super Bowl, one that leads into the yearly draft and simply helps keep the league in the news that time of year.

"We are going through a bit of a transition right now with the league and honestly I do not know what is going to happen in terms of moving forward in management of the combine," said Foster.

Hard to tell what those changes will entail, though opening up more of it to the fans a la "the NFL Experience" seems to be one route. With so much at stake, new processes that can help better predict future performance such as more position-specific tests are likely to be introduced.

The NFL Combine has come a long way in having successfully centralized, standardized, and cost-effectively managed the evaluation of human potential. However, they are continually looking for more accurate tools for measuring human physicality and mental aptitude because every executive knows once a draftee is selected, millions of dollars are committed with the hopes of a large economic return (via greater ticket and merchandise sales), but that commitment can also have expensive consequences if it does not pan out.

As we begin to see some of these measurables change, what is not likely to change is the growing interest in the Job Fair Like No Other.

CHAPTER THIRTY

HE'S GOT CHARACTER

The locker room is the most unpolitically correct place you could ever imagine being in. The longer you're there, the more damage it does to you when you go out into the real world. Nothing is off limits," said 10-year veteran defensive end Bill Maas.

Just about every team, has a practical joker to help keep things light. But when it comes to outright characters, here's a look at a pair of excellent quarterbacks, a mammoth Hall of Fame defensive end, and a running back with the absolute perfect name for this subject. These legends had a talent for the sport and a whole lot of charisma, playing the game (on and off the field) with comedic style.

BOBBY LAYNE

An all-American quarterback at the University of Texas, Bobby Layne was a three-time NFL champion and six-time Pro Bowl quarterback during the 1950s.

A member of both the College and Pro Football Hall of Fames, whose number 22 was retired by the Detroit Lions as well as the

Lions teammate: "How can you see through those bloodshot eyes?"

Courtesy Detroit Lions

Longhorns, Layne got there because he was a demanding field general who got the best his players could offer. Week-in and week-out.

Layne was well aware of the "what-have-you-done-for-me-lately?" aspect of pro ball. He famously quipped, "You're either in the penthouse or the outhouse depending on your performance last Sunday."

Teammates loved hanging around with him. "Bobby was not only a terrific QB, he was a joy to go out with as there were always women around him, and I needed all the help I can get," said one teammate who preferred to go nameless.

His reputation for playing just as hard on the field as he did off it was on display when he completed seven of nine and ran for 48 yards, including a touchdown, leading Detroit to its first title in 17 years with a 17–7 victory at Cleveland in 1952.

And his game came with a brashness that bordered on arrogance. Confident in his ability to lead a football team, Layne once supposedly said, "I never lost a game. Sometimes, I just ran out of time."

The very next year, Layne took advantage of the limited time he did have and took Detroit to a second straight championship. Down to the Browns 16–10 with 4:10 left to play, in front of the home crowd at Detroit's Briggs Stadium, Layne, loved by the fans for his free-wheelin' attitude, showed his mettle.

As he entered the huddle, legend has it that Layne told his teammates, "Now if you'll just block a little bit, fellas, ol' Bobby will pass you right to the championship."

With the 54, 577 fans roaring with excitement, ol' Bobby delivered.

A pair of completions to Jim Doran for 17 and 18 yards helped get Detroit to the Cleveland 36. Facing a third-and-1, Layne took it himself to get a new set of downs. Moments later, Doran again would be on the receiving end of Layne's pass. This time it resulted in a 33-yard touchdown. Layne's buddy Doak Walker made the conversion, which provided the margin of victory, 17–16.

After Walker retired, Layne took over the kicking duties in 1956 and 1957, and in 1956 led the league in field goal accuracy. In 1956 the Lions finished second in the conference, missing the championship game by only 1 point. In 1957, the season of the Lions' most recent NFL championship, Layne broke his leg in three places in a pileup during the 11th game of the 12-game season, against the Cleveland Browns. His replacement, Tobin Rote, finished the season and led the Lions to victory in the championship game in Detroit, a 59–14 rout of those same Browns.

Layne played the last few seasons of his career with the lowly Pittsburgh Steelers.

In his popular book *Fatso*, Baltimore Colts Hall of Fame lineman Art Donovan recalled this exchange with Layne:

"I remember playing the Steelers in an exhibition game in the

Orange Bowl in Miami. Layne was dropping back to pass when three of us fell on him. I looked at him and said, 'You all right, Bob?' He said, 'Yeah, Fatso, I'm all right. But don't do it again, because I'm going to meet you afterward. I'm having a big party, and you're all invited.'"[57]

For the Steelers' season finale against the Cardinals in 1958, team owner Art Rooney said Layne was hungover from a night of partying with Bob Drum, the *Pittsburgh Press* sportswriter. But Bobby had his greatest game in a Steelers uniform that snowy day, throwing for 409 yards and two touchdowns in a 38–21 win so nobody minded that he wasn't exactly fit.[58]

Performing in an era when Americans were becoming increasingly paranoid due to Sen. Joseph McCarthy's televised hearings implying that Communists were lurking in many closets, fans took comfort in the fact that on Sunday afternoons everybody's all-American took their minds off the growing hysteria with a patented performance in which a huddle would often include the following exchange.

Lions teammate: "How can you see out there through those bloodshot eyes?"

QB Layne: "Block your man, and I will show you."

JOE DON LOONEY

The strange journey of running back Joe Don Looney (isn't that the greatest name for a "character" in this chapter?) was a bizarre odyssey on a certifiably twisted road. That one-man Crazy Train had stops in Oklahoma, New York, Baltimore, Detroit, Washington, Vietnam, and New Orleans.

The son of a football player, Joe Don showed his own promise as a high school senior, but his behavior failed him first at his dad's alma mater, TCU (his father, Don, was an end on the 1937–39 TCU

Joe Don Looney, a true character.

Courtesy Washington Redskins

Horned Frogs squads, teaming with legendary quarterback Davey O'Brien. Both would later sign with the Philadelphia Eagles following college), then Texas. However, in giving it the ol' college try at Cameron Junior College in Oklahoma, Looney was the star of the team that won the Junior Rose Bowl championship.

With a Mr. America build, a chiseled six foot two, 210 pounds, to go with reportedly 9.8 speed in the 100, Looney's breakaway speed and power as well as punting abilities, lured some of the all-time greats to take a chance on him. Each one thinking they'd be the ones to corral him, but this hell-raisin', broncin' buck tore through every fence they put up. Oklahoma coach Bud Wilkinson was the first legend convinced he could tame the Loon.

As a junior, Looney was the third-string fullback until the fourth quarter of the first game of the season. With Oklahoma losing to Syracuse and only two minutes remaining, Looney made what was called an "impossible" 60-yard run for a touchdown to win, 7–3. The

Oklahoma quarterback, Monte Deere, couldn't believe what had happened. "I knew what play I was going to call as I walked to the huddle," Deere said later in the locker room, "but Looney said, 'Just give me the ball, and I'll score a touchdown.' So, I just gave him the ball." Looney finished the season fifth in the country in rushing and first in punting.[59]

A terrific storybook beginning, but it would not end well. The promising back's senior year was marked by missed practices and his complaints that he was being used as a halfback instead of as a fullback and that the best players were not actually starting because there was too much politics.

He nonetheless played a key role in the Sooners' Big Eight championship, earning a trip to the Orange Bowl. Looney averaged more than 6 yards a carry in leading his team in rushing yards (852). He also led the Sooners in scoring (62 points) and the entire nation in punting average (almost 44 yards a punt). Pro scouts were mesmerized with his combination of power and breakaway speed. What they didn't see was what took place away from the field.

The man the *Saturday Evening Post* would later label "the marvelous misfit" also found ways to distinguish himself at the University of Oklahoma. He frequently roamed the halls of his dorm naked. He consumed the writings of William Goldman (author of *Soldier in the Rain* and *The Temple of Gold*) and enjoyed repeat performances of a recording of French composer Maurice Ravel's *Boléro*. He also took an index finger from a cadaver body in his human anatomy class, stuck it in a matchbox, and proudly displayed it to coeds. Joe Don introduced football recruits to prostitutes, stole puppies from a dog pound, and participated in the muggings of pizza delivery boys.[60]

In his second year with the Sooners, Looney purposely smacked a coach in the throat with his elbow during a practice drill. One questionable individual performance and a humiliating loss to the University of Texas later, Wilkinson suspended Looney from the team.[61]

Though Looney was selected by the New York Giants in the first round of the 1964 draft, he did not see eye-to-eye with head coach Allie Sherman, whom he called a "little Napoleon."

When Coach Sherman would not let Looney cut his tight pants, Looney said he would no longer punt for the team. When Sherman told Looney to follow his blockers, Looney theorized, "A good football player makes his own holes."[62]

The rookie runner refused to go to meetings, cut practice, and wouldn't talk to the press. Looney was late for team meals, missed team buses, and at one practice, he simply walked away from the team and began to toss a football back and forth with a little boy who happened to come walking by. One night when he was 10 minutes late for bed check, he deemed the $50 fine unfair because he had gone to bed an hour early the night before. "They still owe me 50 minutes," he reasoned.[63]

Sherman had it, and before the Giants had even finished camp, traded Looney to the Baltimore Colts where Don Shula, with his reputation for order and discipline, felt he could shape him up. Out of respect for Shula, the running back put on some awesome power/speed displays and with looser pants showed he could punt in the pros.

It wasn't long, however, before he was charged with assault after getting into a political argument with a stranger the night Barry Goldwater lost the 1964 presidential election (the running back was a huge supporter); Looney was traded to the Detroit Lions.

Though head coach Harry Gilmer described him as the player who would "save the franchise," that dream died during the third game of the 1966 season when Looney curtly refused to carry a message into the game against the Atlanta Falcons. "If you want a messenger, call Western Union," Joe Don told the coach.

Mr. Looney came to Washington for a draft choice. But like Allie Sherman, Looney had little respect for the great quarterback-turned-coach Otto Graham.

Four games into the 1967 season, Looney's second with the Redskins, the next team that came calling was Uncle Sam's. His Army Reserve unit was activated, and off Looney went to Vietnam where he spent nine months guarding an oil-tank farm in the combat zone.

Back in the States after his military service, Looney said all the right things in claiming to have a new attitude to give his best effort on the playing field. So, the man with a history of devilish behavior became a Saint under their head coach, Hall of Fame receiver Tom Fears.

While the coach had dreams of Looney leading his team in rushing, Looney's ongoing demons expanded in adding psychedelic drugs to his use of marijuana as part of a lifestyle that included extramarital affairs. In less than a year, the Saints placed the 27-year-old Looney on waivers, and his wife filed for a divorce.

The No. 1 draft pick of the New York Giants in 1964, one of the most physically gifted players to ever wear a uniform, Looney left pro ball three years and four teams later. In all of football there was no bigger problem child, nor more unfulfilled potential.

DOUG ATKINS

Similar to Looney, Atkins did not have a high regard for authority. Cleveland had made him their No. 1 pick in the 1953 NFL draft, and while Atkins immediately became an important factor on the Brown's defensive team (helping them to a divisional title in 1953 and the NFL championship in 1954), Atkins didn't take to Paul Brown's authoritative ways.

George Halas thought he could handle the giant defensive end, so he traded third- and sixth-round draft choices for him in 1955. Atkins was selected for eight Pro Bowls in 12 years in Chicago.

"Atkins was a freak of nature," said Don Pierson, a veteran reporter for the *Chicago Tribune* who covered the Bears for nearly four decades. "He was six foot nine and had collegiate high jumping titles. He played basketball. He did everything. He was also incorrigible. He'd often say whatever came to his mind at meetings. He was not very reverential to coaches."

The native of Tennessee was one of the first great defensive players in professional football who often batted passes down at the line of scrimmage and used his skills as a high jump champion (he once owned the SEC title) to leapfrog blockers and get to the quarterback. One of his patented moves was to literally throw a blocker at the quarterback. He was that strong.

"You didn't mess with him," recalled Mike Ditka, his teammate at the time. "When I was on the College All-Stars, we scrimmaged the Chicago Bears in Rensselaer, so I had an angle block on Doug. He was kind of moving away from me, so I grabbed his leg with my left arm. He knew I was coming to the Bears, but he picked me up by the back of my shoulder pads and said: 'Kid, I don't care if you block me, but if you ever hold me again, I will break your neck.'

"I quickly responded, 'Yes sir.'"

That respect extended from his competitors as well because Atkins wreaked terror for 17 years and more than 200 games on National Football League quarterbacks, inflicting the kind of devastation upon opponents that seldom, if ever, has been equaled on any football field. Including on himself. He played through pain and injury, a list that includes a broken collarbone, two damaged knees, a ripped groin muscle, a torn bicep, numerous cracked ribs, two hands broken twice each, both ankles sprained, and finally a broken leg in 1968.

"Doug could have played in any era. He was huge and athletic, and I would not believe this if I didn't see it," recalled Colts center Bill Curry. "It was late in Doug's career when he is with the New Orleans Saints, and we had a terrific left tackle with the Colts named Bob Vogel. Bob, who was six foot five, drops back in pass protection, and Doug leaps over him and lands on Unitas, sacking him. He was like Superman. Bob comes back to the huddle and says, 'Well, what do I do with that?' On the next play, Atkins throws Vogel ten feet like a rag doll to get at our running back. He was amazing."

He also was capable of devastation off the field.

During one practice at Wrigley Field, Coach Halas was freaking out about spies, and Atkins started blasting his shotgun to the top of the stadium yelling, "Spies!" while actually aiming at pigeons. (What was he doing with a shotgun at practice anyway?)

"Doug was a throwback," Ditka said. "We'd practice in St. Joe's out in Indiana, and Doug would be out late at night, and he'd come in way after curfew and walk right into Halas's room, lock it, and read the coach the riot act. We could hear Doug: 'Listen, you SOB! You're gonna sit there and listen about the things I don't like about you!' It was the greatest thing players had ever seen."

Halas apparently accepted the irreverence as part of the price realizing Doug could help the team, a price Paul Brown would not accept when he let Atkins go from Cleveland. With the Bears, Atkins forced Halas to hire a private detective to track player shenanigans, most of them victimless. Meanwhile, coaches refused to bed-check his room at training camp because he kept a pit bull named Rebel that was trained to kill.

Atkins himself was trained to kill quarterbacks (legend has it in their championship year of 1963, Atkins knocked eight quarterbacks out of the game) and one, Fran Tarkenton, famously offered this commentary about what it was like to see number 81 bearing down on you.

"He is the strongest man in football and also the biggest," 18-year veteran quarterback Tarkenton once said. "When he rushes the passer with those oak tree arms of his way up in the air, he's 12 feet tall. And if he gets to you, the whole world starts spinning."

KENNY STABLER

In "studying the playbook by the light of the jukebox," Raiders quarterback Kenny Stabler was a throwback in the vein of Bobby Layne in terms of being a charismatic leader of men (and a leading ladies man) and doing whatever it took to help his team win then insisting on buying the first round of drinks.

"There was a real belief in him," said Stabler's close friend Tony Cline, a Raiders defensive end. "When the team was down, he'd be in the huddle and reassure his teammates that 'Hey we got this. No problem.' There was a self-confidence that bounced onto the other guys. He certainly did not have the strongest arm going. But I can clearly remember, we could be down a couple touchdowns with just seven or eight minutes left in the game, and he dropped back, and he would not even have his arm in the passing position, but rather he'd be standing there with the ball at his side, like a gunslinger, and not moving as he analyzed the field until he saw what he liked. That was the belief in himself that he had, and it permeated the rest of the team."

That Stabler aura translated into victories, championships, and a Super Bowl title, all while leading the league in terms of the amount of fun they had doing it.

But things did not start out that way for Stabler in the NFL. Part of Alabama's 1965 National Champion team under Bear Bryant and an all-American in 1967, Stabler was drafted in the second round by the Oakland Raiders in 1968, where he languished behind the Mad Bomber, Daryle Lamonica, but learned a heck of a lot from legendary quarterback George Blanda as they watched from the sidelines.

"Kenny always wanted to prove himself. I think he felt he was always being challenged. Al Davis brought him up the hard way. Al made him sit there and watch Lamonica play," said Raiders veteran running back Pete Banaszak, a confidant of Stabler's. "If he were alive today, Kenny probably would point to George Blanda as the person he learned the most from. How to stay calm and just watch and learn, and he'll be ready when his chance came. George was such an asset, as he knew the game better than anybody. An intense competitor and leader. He was a man's man and a mentor to many of us on and off the field."

The southpaw quarterback first attracted attention in the NFL in a 1972 playoff game against the Pittsburgh Steelers. After entering the game in relief of a flu-ridden Lamonica, Stabler scored the go-ahead touchdown late in the fourth quarter on a 30-yard scramble. The Steelers, however, came back to win on a controversial, deflected pass from Terry Bradshaw to Franco Harris, later known in football lore as the Immaculate Reception. (See chapter 31, "The Immaculate Reception, Hailing Mary, and the Epic.")

In 1974 Stabler put it all together, despite bad knees, leading the Raiders to the top-ranked offense in pro football and was the NFL's Most Valuable Player. And it was a divisional playoff victory over the defending champion Miami Dolphins that season which cemented the Snake's reputation as the team's leader with his never-say-die attitude.

On a Saturday-afternoon game on December 21, at the Oakland Coliseum, the Raiders were up against a team that had dominated the early 1970s as Miami had reached three straight Super Bowls, winning the latter two. And in 1974, under brilliant coach Don Shula, with a crushing running game and a stellar No-Name defense that rarely made mistakes, the Dolphins appeared poised to retain their throne.

Nat Moore took a kickoff 89 yards and the Dolphins were up 7–0 in the blink of an eye. Stabler evened things up at 7 in the second quarter with a 31-yard touchdown play to running back Charlie Smith. The game see-sawed back and forth throughout the second half with Stabler connecting on a pair of touchdown passes, one for 13 yards to Fred Biletnikoff and a 72-yarder to speedster Cliff Branch.

The latter play had given Oakland the lead 21–19. However, Miami quickly retaliated as Benny Malone's 23-yard rumble for a score put the Dolphins back up, 26–21.

With just two minutes remaining, Stabler calmly marched his team downfield. Following a 20-yard kickoff return by Ron Smith, the Raiders had the ball on their own 32-yard line with 2:00 left to play and all three time-outs left. After a 6-yard completion to tight end Bob Moore and a short run, Stabler connected with Biletnikoff twice and two more completions got the ball down to the Miami 14-yard line. Clarence Davis then ran the ball 6 yards to the 8-yard line, where the Raiders called their final time-out.

On the next play, Stabler dropped back to pass and looked for his go-to, sure-handed receiver Biletnikoff in the end zone, but Biletnikoff was well covered. With Miami's Vern Den Herder dragging him down from behind, Stabler heaved a desperation toss into a "sea of hands" in the left side of the end zone, where Davis, well known for *not* having sure hands, fought his way through three Dolphins defenders to make the catch. After enduring a late hit by Miami's Manny Fernandez, the running back held on to the ball for a touchdown.

Oakland linebacker Phil Villapiano's subsequent interception of a Bob Griese pass allowed the Raiders to run out the clock and earn the win. Though they'd lose the AFC title game to the Steelers, the Raiders were on their way with Stabler at the helm.

The "Sea of Hands" exemplified Stabler's ability to lead late, come-from-behind drives.

"Kenny would become the greatest clutch player I ever saw," Banaszak said. "On the sidelines Coach Madden would have chewed his fingernails off, shaking his head, asking Kenny, 'What are we going to do?' And Kenny would calmly reply, 'Ah, we got it.' John would say, 'Oh yeah? Really? Well, okay, let's do it.' Kenny was smooth.

"It could be very tense, pivotal moments in a game, but he was a very calming influence to have in the huddle. There were times I'd excitedly say to Kenny, 'Snake, we gotta get this!' And he'd turn and calmly say, 'Don't worry, Rooster, we'll get it done.' He was at his best when the stakes were highest."

Though he was unable to scramble like he used to due to bad knees, and did not have a strong arm, (but somehow was brilliant on intermediate routes that often resulted in long pass plays to Biletnikoff, Branch, and tight end Dave Casper), teammates rallied around his leadership, often done with a wink and a smile.

"To keep things light at the same time, he'd often say something funny in the huddle," Banaszak remembered. "One game, we had a few beers the night before at a local bar talking about the next day's game, so in the late stages, he said, after calling the play, 'Now, Rooster, you gotta keep your feet steady when you block this guy, you can't be staggering around like you did last night leaving the bar...'"

The Raiders' quarterback called going out on the town with fellow players a way to achieve team unity.

Training camp was the time when one got closest with their teammates because they were stuck together. In Northern California the Raiders' camp took place during really hot days in Santa Rosa where the Snake and Company would make the nights even hotter.

Tony Cline explained what became known as "the Circuit": "[Coach] Madden was never a stickler for fines, and he was also aware about the importance of the players building a camaraderie. There used to be a couple of cliques. Before going out on the circuit, me, Banaszak, Biletnikoff, Dan Conners, and Kenny would huddle up as team meetings ended at about eight forty-five and curfew was at eleven, and we put our hands in and say, 'One, two, three— circuit!' Then we'd see how many bars we can hit in the two hours before curfew. It was a lot of fun. Everybody was sore and tired; it definitely was a way to blow off a lot of steam. And Stabler's famous quote, 'studying the game plan by the light of the jukebox,' came from these adventures. He'd be buying everybody drinks and telling stories, but then we'd have to race to get back before curfew. You can imagine all the stuff that was going on."

Though Madden and owner Al Davis must've known something was going on, what really mattered was that the players produced come game time.

And Stabler's party boys did, cementing their way to the playoffs again in 1975 and 1976. Stabler was AFC player of the year and led the league in passing as he took the Raiders all the way. They won the divisional round 24–21 versus the New England Patriots; then the conference championship 24–7 against the Pittsburgh Steelers, and ultimately swatted away the Minnesota Vikings, 32–14, in the Super Bowl.

"Kenny held a football camp every year during the off-season in Alabama, bringing kids in from all over. It was after practice one day, and I was with Otis Sistrunk, and Kenny was like a God down there. It was amazing. Conners and Banaszak were there. We were in a small town outside of Foley," recalled Cline. "After so many drinks, I was the only one that could drive. I had three guys who were, let's call it 'sleeping [it off]' there in the car. I am completely lost on the backcountry roads. I am the only one awake, and we come to this one-horse town, and there was this one cop car. I pull up to him, and it was one of those typical big-bellied southern sheriffs.

"I said, 'Sir, we got a problem here. I've got Kenny Stabler—' And I couldn't finish my sentence when he blurts out, 'You got *Keeeny*? Can you wake him up and have him sign something for me?' I said, 'You betcha!' and I was surprised that I did not knock the guy down with my breath.

"The sheriff was so excited to meet 'Keeeny' that we walked around to the backseat and as he opened the back door Keeeny practically rolled out. We managed to wake him up, and I think he signed the sheriff's tie. So, he is happy and said to 'follow me.' He did not turn on the siren, but he turned on his light and we basically had our own private escort through these backwoods country roads. He was right out of central casting like Buford T. Justice."

Kenny Stabler as a good ol' boy was right out of central casting himself and would be right at home carrying on in much the same way when he was traded to the Houston Oilers and then New Orleans on his way to Canton and the Pro Football Hall of Fame.

CHAPTER THIRTY-ONE

THE IMMACULATE RECEPTION, HAILING MARY, AND THE EPIC

T hree games during the NFL's third quarter have grown so biblical in proportion through the years that each bears a name worthy of their grand scale.

THE IMMACULATE RECEPTION

Every December 23, former Oakland Raiders linebacker Phil Villapiano receives a phone call from Franco Harris that begins with the following question: "What were you doing on this day X years ago?"

"He'll call around 4:07 p.m. or 4:08 p.m. because the game ran late. He's relentless with this phone call," Villapiano said.

Villapiano played a central role in the play that is known as the Immaculate Reception, where Harris made a shoestring catch off a deflected ball that gave Pittsburgh a last-second victory in the 1972 AFC playoffs.

The play was immortalized after the Heinz History Center, home of the Western Pennsylvania Sports Museum, installed a life-size figure of Harris in the grand concourse of Pittsburgh International Airport in 2006.

"I told him this year, 'Franco, my last tackle that I make before I die, that statue comes down!'" Villapiano said. "That is exactly right. That statue at the airport is going down. And the statue and I are going over the top, and down below it there is a dinosaur. And I'm going to impale it on one of those dinosaur tusks." The former linebacker roared with laughter.

But neither he nor his teammates were laughing after that play on a cold, blustery Saturday afternoon at Three Rivers Stadium. The December 23, 1972, game would be the start of a brief but intense rivalry between two very talented and determined teams. Before coach Chuck Noll arrived and began to turn the team around, the hapless Pittsburgh franchise had reached the playoffs just once, way back in 1947. The Oakland Raiders, behind their shrewd owner Al Davis, always seemed to be in the playoff hunt.

The game turned out to be a defensive battle. The game's first touchdown was not scored until late in the fourth quarter when Oakland stunned the Steelers' defense as quarterback Kenny Stabler (who had replaced an ill Daryle Lamonica) managed to scramble for 30 yards all the way into the end zone. Oakland had a 7–6 lead with about 1:17 left in the game.

Even though Pittsburgh only needed a field goal, things were looking as bleak as the weather. With twenty-two seconds left, the Steelers faced fourth-and-10 from their own 40. Pittsburgh's emergence with a fabulous 11-3 regular-season record was about to come to a close. Then came one of the most famous and most controversial plays in NFL history.

Narrowly evading the clutches of several Raiders, then ducking out of the pocket, quarterback Terry Bradshaw threw a desperation pass intended for running back John "Frenchy" Fuqua. Given the pressure on him, it was a terrific heave, right on target. However, safety Jack Tatum, thinking the ball would beat him there, was intent on jarring the ball loose by hitting Fuqua full force. He did with a forearm to the head, sending the Steeler to the ground. As he did, the ball ricocheted back toward the line of scrimmage. While Tatum celebrated, the ever-alert running back Franco Harris plucked the ball off his shoe tops in full stride and sped 60 yards for the winning touchdown. In an instant, the 59,000 Steelers fans jammed into Three Rivers Stadium went from deafening silence to a mighty roar of euphoria.

"I had taken my eye off of Franco to look back at Bradshaw and then saw the ball fly over my head after it made contact with Frenchy," recalled the Raiders linebacker. "And then Franco traps the ball on the ground. (Incomplete pass.) I have a good angle on Franco, but the tight end dove on the back of my legs, and once Franco has one step on you, it is over."

But Franco won't let it be over for the four-time Pro Bowl linebacker. Forty-six years later, to the week, Villapiano said, "Franco sends me a message, and it shows he is kissing the Pope's ring in Rome. And the Pope said, 'It was immaculate.'

"Now that he's been blessed by the Pope, I can't call Franco a liar."

HAILING MARY

Another devout Catholic, Dallas Cowboys quarterback Roger Staubach, was blessed when his prayers were answered in another divisional playoff game. One that would be forever referred to as the Hail Mary game.

On December 28, 1975, two great teams, the Minnesota Vikings and the Dallas Cowboys, led by two future Hall of Fame coaches, Bud Grant and Tom Landry, were facing off at Metropolitan Stadium.

Cowboys wide receiver Drew Pearson recalled the environment.

"It was overcast weather, cold. Everybody was saying this was the best Vikings team including all those that went to the Super Bowl. All smart veterans. Both teams are standing on the same sideline in that old Metropolitan Stadium. Vikings under Bud Grant would try to intimidate you coming out onto the field with short sleeves in the freezing weather. Here come Carl Eller, Alan Page, Jim Marshall, out of the tunnel and onto the field, and you are like, 'Whoa!'

"It was a knock-down, drag-out heavyweight title fight the whole game. It was very physical. We were the wild-card team, so that is why we had to go up there. But we played them tough. They scored late in the second half, making it 14–10. I was upset because they had shut me down. I only had one pass my way, and it was incomplete."

Dallas now needed a touchdown. Could Captain Comeback do it against the heralded Purple People Eaters, who had played tough and brilliantly all game?

As Staubach drove his team down the field, another play occurred that has been somewhat underreported.

"Now we were in the two-minute situation, and that's when Roger and I click. That is when Roger and I go to work," revealed Pearson. "And that is when Roger usually asks me what route I can get open on, not based on emotion of being angry that I can get open on anything after being shut out, but rather being a former quarterback that I had been surveying the field and saw what would work best."

It was fourth-and-long, game on the line. Staubach, his sore ribs aching in the Minnesota cold, winced as he zipped the ball to Pearson.

"I told him to run a post corner," Staubach recalled. "He made a great catch on the sidelines, then got knocked out-of-bounds. An usher went over and actually kicked Drew while he was down."

Pearson, who would make many clutch catches in high-pressure situations, including a 1980 playoff win over Atlanta and the 1973 playoff game-clincher against the Rams, explained what happened on this crucial play that would make the Hail Mary even possible. "I believe it came down to the fourth and eighteen. I felt [CB] Nate [Wright] bite on the fake then went to the corner. I did not beat him by much, just a step or two, but Roger had such a great arm and never got enough credit for his accuracy, but also threw the ball tremendously hard. So, the play was good for twenty-two yards and a first down. Back then it was a force out rule. If the defensive back knocks you out-of-bounds to prevent you from getting your feet in-bounds, it is still a catch."

But it was what happened next that was against the rules, in any era.

"I slid into the snow bank on the side of the field, and then the security guard comes over and kicks me while I'm lying on the ground! Yes, he's in a full security uniform with a little hat on and everything. If that happened today in an age of social media, it would've gone viral right away. Minnesota was penalized for that."

The security guard's blunder kept Dallas in the game. Bud Grant must have felt cursed—or at least felt like cursing.

"With one play left, I basically told everybody to block and for Drew to go deep. It was the old wish and a bomb," Staubach said. "Drew made a heckuva catch. As I tried to keep safety Paul Krause away with a pump fake, my throw was a little short, and Drew caught it on his hip. Of course, Minnesota fans felt he pushed off on Nate Wright, but Nate really slipped. You look at the film and there's no obvious interference. We scored a touchdown. Go ahead."

But even after that historic score (which included a bullet from the stands in the form of an orange whizzing by Pearson as he crossed the goal line), the game was not over, and another incident had Coach Landry wishing it was.

"After the Hail Mary, they bobbled the ball on the kickoff and were back around the 10-yard line. Then somebody threw a full bottle of Jack Daniels from the end zone stands hitting one of the officials square in the head and knocked him clean out and blood was all over the place," recalled Dallas defensive back Charlie Waters. "Earlier that year there was a soccer match where people were all over the field and there were some deaths. As they were tending to the ref, Coach Landry calls us all over and says, 'Okay when this game is over sprint to the locker room.' He was very concerned that the fans were going to go crazy because it was bedlam."

After the game, sportswriters asked Staubach for details of the game-winning pass under the ruthless pressure of the Vikings defense. His response, based on his Christian upbringing, gave the play eternal life. "Well, I guess you could call it a Hail Mary. You throw it up and pray," said Staubach. And thus, a new football belief system was born.

The Cowboys went on to defeat the Los Angeles Rams in the NFC championship game, but would lose, 21–17, to the Pittsburgh Steelers in Super Bowl X.

Roger Staubach won two championship rings, appeared in five Super Bowls, led the NFL in passing four times, was a six-time Pro Bowl quarterback, and was enshrined into the Hall of Fame, but that one play reaches far beyond the gridiron for it helped turn "Hail Mary" into a cliché of hope for all things desperate.

THE EPIC

Hope was something Miami Dolphins fans always had when Don Shula was roaming the Orange Bowl sidelines. His team found itself down, 24–0, in the first quarter to the San Diego Chargers in the AFC divisional playoff game held January 2, 1982.

Even though it was a late afternoon kickoff, the weather that day was very humid. But the Chargers were on fire anyway, averaging nearly 30 points a game as quarterback Dan Fouts was in the midst of directing one of the greatest offensive machines in NFL history.

With Don Coryell as the master offensive composer (with help from offensive coordinator Larrye Weaver, Ernie Zampese, and Dave Levy), San Diego had led the NFL in scoring and yardage in 1981, with Fouts setting a record by passing for 4,802 yards.

Getting time behind a stingy wall of veteran blockers like Ed White and Don Macek, Fouts could hand off or throw to brilliant running backs Chuck Muncie and James Brooks, on the ends he had a pair of All-Pro receivers in Charlie Joiner and Wes Chandler and in that mix was mold-breaking tight end Kellen Winslow, who would have a career-making day (he had also led the league in receptions for the second straight year) and would be the key figure in a game that would be forever known as the Epic.

Typical for a Shula-coached team, Miami fielded a top five defense led by end Vern Den Herder (a veteran of the No-Name unit) and the Blackwood brothers, Glenn and Lyle, as the safeties.

"I remember a lot of those things about the game, but the one thing that sticks out in my mind is when we are leading 21–0, and our sideline is celebrating," Winslow said. "I come off the field, and there is Charlie Joiner sitting on the bench. He has his helmet in his hands and is looking gloomily down at the ground. So, I asked, 'What is wrong?' I thought he was hurt or something. Charlie says, 'You do not do this to a Don Shula–coached team. He is going to take out Woodley and put in Don Strock. They are going to start throwing this football, and we are going to be here all day.'

"I got mad as I looked around and saw that we were celebrating. And I think that is one of the things that kept me going throughout the game. Veteran Charlie was absolutely correct," said the Chargers' tight end. "I remember the press belittling us as a West Coast team, soft. I remember saying clearly, 'Not today.' That fueled even me further. We are not going to be part of NFL lore on the downside of that."

But sure enough, things were heading in that direction when Miami took possession with 12:05 to go in the second. Looking for a spark, Shula pulled Woodley and replaced him with Strock.

"We were fortunate to get off to an unbelievable start. But the fight the Dolphins put up, coming back with the unbelievable play of Don Strock, it was just amazing," Fouts recalled. "I remember when Miami ran that hook-and-ladder play. I was standing on the sidelines with Charlie Joiner, and I said, 'Well, game's on now.' And so it was."

The six-foot-five former Virginia Tech quarterback, an eight-year veteran backup, rolled up his sleeves and went to work. With 8:31 left, it was 24–3. With 2:46 left in the half, it was 24–10. With six seconds left in the half, Miami had a first-and-10 at the San Diego 40. Strock passed to Duriel Harris, who then lateraled to Tony Nathan, who raced into the San Diego end zone. Miami was now down only 7 at the break.

Strock then picked up right where he'd left off. His 15-yard touchdown pass to Joe Rose tied the game at 24. And after Fouts hooked up with Winslow for a 25-yard scoring play, Strock answered with a 50-yard touchdown pass to tight end Bruce Hardy. Heading into the fourth quarter, with the game tied at 31, Miami finally took the lead on a Tony Nathan 12-yard run.

However, Fouts kept Miami on its heels, mixing runs and passes with equal success, and his 9-yard TD toss to Brooks knotted the game at 38.

"Well, the Dolphins had to make a decision in that game," the Chargers' quarterback stated. "If I'm not mistaken, I believe Joiner, Chandler, and Winslow all had over a hundred yards receiving. My job was to find the guy who had single coverage. And in that game, it was Kellen who was most often that guy. That was due to the threat of Joiner and Chandler on the outside. Also, the pass protection for me in that game was phenomenal. You put those elements together, and, in my mind, any one of those three in single coverage, they're gonna win that battle, especially Winslow with that size and speed."

Not only did Kellen have 13 catches for 166 yards (both playoff records) and a touchdown and produce some key openings for his running mates, but he also starred on special teams. Veteran TV reporter Chris Myers explained what he observed on that record-setting day. "There was a lot of star power on the Chargers side, but in regard to Kellen Winslow, I never saw a receiver take over a football game like that. I mean, as the receptions piled up, he looked more and more drained and worn down but kept delivering. And to be able to do all that and then also deliver on the special teams, blocking a field goal, that was a signature moment for him, the Chargers, and that game."

That signature moment came when the spent Winslow blocked Uwe von Schamann's 43-yard field goal attempt on the final play to force overtime.

Heavy with fatigue, the teams traded possessions six times in the extra period. Each kicker missed a clinching field goal, but, finally, no one blocked Rolf Benirschke's 29-yard effort, and after 13:52 of overtime, San Diego was victorious, 41–38. The Epic had finally concluded. The game resulted in NFL playoff records for points, 79, and total yards, 1,036.

The Chargers tight end was wore out from the heat and humidity and feeling numbness in his arm related to a shoulder injury. He broke two sets of shoulder pads. The Dolphins' D also delivered some blows. They gave Winslow a swollen eye, cut his lip, and left him with a pinched nerve in his left shoulder that delivered a jolt of searing pain each time he took a hit. Having laid it all on the line, when the game was over, the tight end had to be helped to the locker room by teammates Billy Shields and Eric Sievers; the cramps in his thighs, shoulders, and back were that intense.

Winslow talked about how part of that was the result of his role in the Chargers' game plan.

"Our coaches had made excellent adjustments, and I was our move guy," he explained. "Early in the game, we were doing fly, zip, zoom plays. Many of those involved me running past the formation going across the field. That takes its toll. So, after a while, we went from longer movement to shorter movement before the snap. Those were our indicators. That is where our reading came from. Making a presnap read, watching the defense move, by the time Dan is on his second step, he knows where he is going with the ball. Boom. Rhythm."

One week after their victory over the Dolphins in Florida's draining heat, the Chargers traveled to Ohio to face the Cincinnati Bengals in the AFC championship game in the coldest game in NFL history based on wind chill. (The air temperature was minus 9 degrees; factor in windchill, and you were looking at minus 59.) This game, too, ended up becoming part of NFL lore, and has since become known as the Freezer Bowl. But this time it did not end well for San Diego. The Chargers were defeated, 27–7, ending their season one game short of the Super Bowl for the second consecutive year, as they had lost, 34–27, to the Raiders in the 1980 AFC title game.

A blown-up photo of Winslow being helped off the field by teammates after the Epic covers an entire wall at the Pro Football Hall of Fame in Canton. Winslow himself expressed no doubt where that game ranks in his career: "It is number one. It is the reason why I am in the Hall of Fame.

"Over the years I have probably met over two hundred thousand people who've told me they were at the game," the tight end said, laughing. "I believe the Orange Bowl held only sixty thousand at the time."

CHAPTER THIRTY-TWO

THE CHESS MASTERS:
THIRD QUARTER

Two of the greatest coaches who ever paced an NFL side-line, Vince Lombardi and Paul Brown, reigned during the league's second quarter; however, it was the third quarter that produced the greatest depth of coaching talent pro football has ever seen.

The time period is rife with examples. John Madden and Tom Flores led the Raiders to three Super Bowl titles between them. With his success at the collegiate level, Jimmy Johnson's keen eye for developing young talent was the impetus behind the Dallas Cowboys dynasty of the 1990s. Art Rooney's patience with Pittsburgh head coach Bill Cowher yielded a Vince Lombardi Trophy. The amazing Joe Gibbs took the Redskins to Super Bowl crowns in two different stints. After Bill Walsh left, George Seifert picked up the baton and led the 49ers to a second straight championship. Bill Parcells had a magic touch with every team he took over. Marv Levy, Mike Ditka, Dick Vermeil, Marty Schottenheimer, and Mike Shanahan are tremendous talents, among many more.

And one trait they all shared is a great ability to relate to individuals and draw out the very best of their skills and to do so despite being in a pressure cooker week after week. As Don Shula once stated about his profession: "You don't win with *x*'s and *o*'s. What you win with is people."

CHUCK NOLL

As a guard and linebacker for the Cleveland Browns, Noll applied much that he learned from Paul Brown to achieve a tremendous amount of success as head coach of the Pittsburgh Steelers. In 23 seasons at the helm, he had 15 winning seasons, made the playoffs 12 times, winning four Super Bowls in six years. Noll remains the only coach in history to lead his team to two different back-to-back Super Bowl runs, in 1974 and 1975 and again in 1978 and 1979.

Noll's keen sense for talent was evident in his very first draft pick: Joe Greene in 1969. What Coach saw in Mean Joe, a defensive tackle out of tiny North Texas, was a player who provided leadership, fierce competitiveness, and an intimidating style of play that became the foundation for Noll's Steel Curtain. A two-time NFL defensive player of the year, 5 first-team All-Pro selections, and 10 Pro Bowl appearances, Greene is widely considered one of the greatest defensive linemen to play in the NFL.

Additionally, Noll is also responsible for the only draft class to yield four Hall of Famers: in 1974 Pittsburgh selected Lynn Swann, Jack Lambert, John Stallworth, and Mike Webster.

More than anything Coach Noll considered himself a teacher.

Steelers veteran Andy Russell, feeling pretty good about his own abilities after an all-star season, got a direct dose of Noll's penchant for instruction. "He was also the linebackers coach in his first season. Noll tells me, 'When you line up against these tight ends who are six foot five and two hundred sixty pounds, I want you to get into your stance and move your right foot three inches to the right.' I responded, 'Are you kidding me? I can stop these huge guys by moving my foot just three inches?' And Coach says, 'Success is in the details, Russell.'

"That was his mantra."

Noll's passion for education might have stemmed from the fact that he was a high school teacher before he ever became a coach.

Safety Mike Wagner recalled an individual lesson. "Coach Noll was extremely confident without being arrogant," he said. "He prided himself on being a teacher. He'd think nothing of pulling a player aside and give him a quick lesson. Like 'same foot, same shoulder.' He'd demonstrate how to take on pulling guards or fill a hole, among other things. I was just trying to make an impression, and something must've happened, because he kept me around for ten years."

Noll would talk football with his players, and at the same time quote Ralph Waldo Emerson or Emily Dickinson; this high-low approach was his method for relating to everyone. But the quotes that became memorable were Noll originals, scrawled in a small notebook he kept around: "Whatever it takes." "If you think you've arrived, you haven't." "Don't waste away." "Be a tomorrow person."

"'Be a tomorrow person.' If I had a nickel for every time I heard him say that," said defensive tackle John Banaszak. "Coach Noll was always looking ahead. His mind must've been going a hundred miles an hour all the time, because even after the Super Bowl win, he was already on to the next season before the champagne bottles were opened. It was always about the next step to be successful." Noll achieved great success coaching his way, reaching the Hall of Fame in 1993.

But for all those years he endured his coach's slogans, linebacker Russell got a measure of revenge one afternoon. "He had a line that he used when he cut players: 'You are no longer going to be with us because it is time for you to seek your life's work.' Well, when I decided to retire from football after the '76 season, and was making more money in my business than the Steelers were paying me, I made the announcement.

"I get a phone call informing me that Coach Noll wants to talk to me," Russell remembered. "So, I go to the stadium, curious as to what he is going to say. He was working at his desk and was in the middle of a phone conversation. He hangs up the receiver and looks at me. He says, 'I want you to play two more years. I'll make sure you get a nice bump up in salary.' I say, 'No sir. That is not going to do it, because I'm going out to seek my life's work.'"

Noll started laughing.

BILL WALSH

It seemed like Bill Walsh's life's work was destined to be coaching. After graduating from San Jose State with a bachelor's degree in physical education in 1955, followed by a two-year stint in the US Army, he began his coaching career in the Bay Area by building a championship team at Washington High School in Fremont before becoming an assistant coach at the University of California, Berkeley; then at Stanford; and then the Oakland Raiders in 1966. He followed that with a brief stint with the San Jose Apaches of the Continental Football League before joining legendary coach Paul Brown's staff with the new NFL franchise the Cincinnati Bengals in 1968.

During his eight years with the Bengals, based on the skill sets of Virgil Carter then Ken Anderson, a pair of accurate and mobile quarterbacks who lacked the arm strength for the deep vertical game, Walsh developed what became known as the West Coast offense. It is essentially a horizontal passing system that relied on quick, short throws, with the goal of spreading the ball across the entire width of the field. It was comprised of underneath crossing patterns, flooding an area and putting pressure on linebackers, use of the fullback as a possession receiver underneath, option reads by the receivers, and breakout patterns at the end of routes.

The West Coast offense was the nucleus of an ideal pairing when Walsh became head coach of the 49ers and drafted Notre Dame's Joe Montana. In 1980 Steve DeBerg was the starting quarterback who got San Francisco off to a 3-0 start, but after a 59–14 blowout loss to Dallas in Week 6, Walsh promoted Montana to starting QB. In an early December tilt versus the New Orleans Saints, Montana brought the 49ers back from a 35–7 halftime deficit to win, 38–35, in overtime. The 49ers improved to 6-10, but, more important, Walsh was making great strides and they were getting better every week. Quick feet, mind-numbing speed in reading defenses and going through his progressions, Montana had superb timing and a fine talent for throwing on the move as well as in the pocket.

Like Noll, Walsh as a great evaluator of talent, scored through the draft (including future Hall of Famers Joe Montana, Ronnie Lott, and Jerry Rice). He had seven winning seasons in his 10 years and reached the playoffs in all seven of those seasons. He'd earn three Super Bowl rings and would be inducted into the Pro Football Hall of Fame in 1993.

But unlike Noll, Walsh had a bit more flair and could, when he felt the time was right, keep things light. 49ers owner Eddie DeBartolo talked about why he hired Walsh as well as an example of the coach's humor on display. "Bill Walsh had a magical touch. Intelligent. A great motivator. A genius. I don't throw that word around, but he really was," DeBartolo said. "I remember also his sense of humor, like dressing up as a hotel bellhop, and as he tried to take one of the player's bags coming off the bus, they ended up yanking it back and forth. It was funny. He was effective in trying to keep the edge off and loosen things up a bit."

But when it came to designing plays, of which he had few peers, Walsh was all business, applying the same expression he used on his players, "you have to put the time in."

And it didn't stop just because one happened to have a good game or season. For Walsh, "putting in the time" was ongoing all the time.

Jerry: You knew he was going to get everything out of you. I remember it was my coming out game, like the third game of the year against the Rams. I think I had like 11 catches and maybe three touchdowns and I think Bill is calling me up to his office to congratulate me. I go up there expecting a pat on the back. Instead, he sternly advises me that he is expecting more from me, a lot more. As I start walking back down the stairs, I have this look on my face, thinking, "Huh, I can't believe that just happened." And as I was leaving his office, I noticed Joe Montana and Ronnie Lott were going up and were about to be told a similar thing. Coach Walsh never allowed you to get complacent. You could never feel that you've arrived. He always wanted to keep you on edge. He wanted you to be exceptional in the field.

TOM LANDRY

Bill Walsh was primarily known for his offensive creativity, but what made Tom Landry of the Dallas Cowboys so distinctive was that very few head coaches could match his skills for both offensive and defensive schematics. Multimotion offense, reviving the shotgun, and creating the flex defense, Coach Landry was an innovator on both sides of the ball.

Dan Reeves, who was a Dallas Cowboys running back for eight years under Landry, and who would go on to a long coaching career in the NFL, was in awe regarding that dual-ability of his mentor. "In all my thirty-nine years associated with the National Football League, I never saw anybody with the amount of knowledge of both offenses and defenses than Coach Landry. It was amazing how he can make us understand what both sides of the ball were trying to do with all that he knew. He was constantly looking for something different; otherwise he felt we were going to get beat. He'd be open to suggestions, but you better have a reason for it."

Educated as an engineer, Landry was all about devising a sound game plan and having his team prepared. He was among the first to hire a coach just to watch film and figure out tendencies of opposing teams (now a regular fixture among NFL teams).

There were reasons for everything he devised yet sometimes in the heat of a game, somebody like quarterback Roger Staubach would have to break off the called play and become Roger the Dodger, or there'd be running back Tony Dorsett whose instincts would often take him against the grain of Landry's play flow.

Even though he'd tried to maintain that stoic demeanor under his famous fedora, the engineer-turned-coach nevertheless had a hard time with deviations from his carefully crafted plans. In his own quiet way, the coach was as fierce a competitor as any of the players.

Landry had a hard go of it at first, suffering five straight losing seasons. Even though he had the right game plan, he simply did not have the personnel to execute it. But the pragmatic man would persevere: during his 29-year tenure, the Cowboys enjoyed 20 straight winning seasons (which included 270 career wins), finished first in their division 13 times, placed second 7 years, went to the playoffs 18 different seasons, and visited the NFL championship or the Super Bowl seven times, winning it all twice.

The roots of Landry's offensive philosophy actually came from his military experience. As a bomber pilot during World War II, Landry led a crew on more than 30 missions across Europe.

According to Hall of Fame receiver Raymond Berry, who got his first coaching assignment from Landry, he "told all the coaches the story that the Allies before they invaded Europe to take it back from the Germans, their approach to invading the European continent was to make a lot of feints up and down the coast to keep them off balance when the attack came at Normandy. He said his offensive philosophy was the same. It was about confusing the defense as to where the point of attack would be. He did it with multiple formations. He'd come out in an I-formation, then split the backs and have the tight ends in motion line up a double wing, go to spread formation. Giving the defense all these different looks was designed to create uncertainty for them as to where the play was going."

One of the keys to that success and one of Landry's many innovations was creating a motion offense all predicated on gaining a split-second advantage on the defense.

Roger Staubach, who played his entire career under Landry, explained. "The worst thing that can happen is the offense being in a formation that defenses can recognize, so he wanted to create an offense that would make it more difficult for the defense to make adjustments in time. A small example was the offensive linemen readjusting and that pause would cause the linebackers to briefly be unable to see the running backs. Another [example] we were using the shotgun formation when no one else was. That was in '75. Coach had a lot of people scratching their heads, but we use it on third down and the two-minute period and it has since become a big part of football. Putting people in motion because you can really hit receivers when you are right on top of them. So, motion made it more difficult for the defenders. And a split second could be all the difference needed in making a big play."

Another aspect of Landry's brilliance was acquiring personnel who created mismatches for the defense.

A quarterback in college and cornerback in the pros, Landry had developed a deep understanding of both sides, of every single position in extraordinary detail. A good example was his work on situational offense where he got "tweeners."

These were players who combined running back and receiver skills such as Billy Parks, Mike Montgomery, and Preston Pearson brought in to confuse the defense and create advantageous match-ups. For example, in that split second behind the wall, when the offensive linemen hitched, Landry would shift a running back out to wide receiver. That then became a mismatch of the linebacker at about 250 with a player like Montgomery who was six foot four and 220 pounds and could absolutely fly. It was an example of a matchup advantage the defense did not think about. And Preston Pearson ended up being the prototype of that tweener.

Having played as a defensive back then working as the defensive coordinator for the New York Giants (at a time when Vince Lombardi was the team's offensive coordinator), Landry was equally adept as a defensive strategist. Combining that direct experience with his fluidity involving complex concepts as an engineer led to his creation of a very successful defense, one that would yield not one but a pair of the best defensive units of all time, Doomsday Defense I and II. (See chapter 28, "D!")

However, that complexity also meant it would take time to fully reach fruition, but Landry was very adamant in demanding his players know their assignments inside out.

"It was an in-depth defense, and we studied, studied, studied. We had tests every week, and if we didn't get a certain grade, he'd make us watch about four more hours of film," said defensive tackle Bob Lilly. "Mistakes were run back and forth on film, and all of us hated it, but he wanted to hold us accountable. And we were. He wanted us to know how to play our positions, and the best way to teach us that is to show us our mistakes."

There is no mistaking that Landry was a demanding leader, but just about every player and coach associated with the man in the fedora have stories about his compassion. Hall of Fame defensive lineman Randy White, who spent his entire career in Dallas, perhaps best illustrates this:

"I will never forget one moment with Coach Landry. My father had passed away the night before a game. I did not tell anybody except for my roommate, Bob Breunig, who must've told Coach Landry. The next day as our defense was being introduced to the crowd, I was a bit teary-eyed thinking of my dad, and as I shook hands with Coach Landry, I looked at him, and he was a bit teary eyed, and he said, 'Randy, I know you are hurting, so after the game, you take all the time you need to be with your family.' That was a moment I will never forget. He was the real deal. Nobody's perfect. But if anybody comes close, it was Tom Landry."

DON SHULA

During a head coaching career that started with the Baltimore Colts (1963–1969) and ended after more than a quarter century in Miami (1970–1995), Shula won 347 games. In his 33 years as a head coach, Shula led his teams to 27 winning seasons, 19 playoff appearances, six Super Bowl appearances, and two Super Bowl victories. Inducted into the Pro Football Hall of Fame in 1997, Shula is the only coach in NFL history to have completed a perfect season.

At his core, what made Shula great was a laser-like focus on his personnel.

"From the moment he stepped onto the practice field he was all business. Very rarely was a smile cracked or a joke told. He was all about hard work and if you could not cope with that, you were gone. That was the choice," said Miami running back Larry Csonka. "You want to piss Shula off, don't worry about coming in late or make weight, all that stuff was standard. If you wanted to infuriate him, just act like you were not paying attention on the practice field. He'd trade your ass to Buffalo in the middle of a blizzard. Rookies learned that lesson in a brutal manner very quickly."

Selected in the ninth round of the 1951 draft by defending champion Cleveland Browns, defensive back Shula would make 21 interceptions over a seven-year career that included stints in Baltimore and Washington. He had a few collegiate coaching gigs until landing his first NFL coaching job as the defensive backfield coach for the Detroit Lions in 1960. After a couple seasons helping Detroit build one of the game's best defenses, Shula was hired as the head coach of the Baltimore Colts after owner Carroll Rosenbloom fired Weeb Ewbank (who'd get some measure of revenge against both, winning Super Bowl III). But in 1963, at thirty-three years old, Don Shula became the youngest coach in league history at the time.

The young man, aided of course by quarterback John Unitas, running back Lenny Moore, and a vicious defense made Baltimore very competitive. Shula earned coach of the year honors in 1964 despite losing to Cleveland in the NFL title game that year. He compiled a 71-23-4 record in seven seasons with Baltimore, but was just 2-3 in the postseason. And after the Super Bowl loss, Shula spent one more season as the head coach of the 8-5-1 Colts and missed the playoffs, before joining the Dolphins in 1970.

Right away Shula rolled up his sleeves, and despite their initial grumblings, the Miami players came to see what made him such a good coach.

From the first day, everything Shula did had a specific purpose. Miami practiced four times a day. Two normal practices at ten in the morning and three in the afternoon. But also one before breakfast and another after dinner. Both walk-throughs. He wasn't doing this to punish his players or prove he was a tough guy, but rather what they observed was that something was getting done. It really helped going over the plays and the system night and day as the Dolphins went from a 3-10-1 year to 10-4 in Shula's initial campaign in Miami, reaching the playoffs for the first time in the franchise's young history.

"His intensity was overpowering. At first, I resented it, because I didn't believe it. Then I realized that is who he was, and that is how we are going to play," Csonka said. "So, between the times you reported to the locker rooms prior to practice to the time you walked out of the locker room after the practice, you knew you had to have total concentration. If you messed up during practice, he'd rain havoc on your head in front of the team, so it was not worth it to become lackadaisical at practice and incur his wrath, because he would not let it die. He would wear you out with it. He'd be reminding you of it three days later. To be that possessed, that in tune with the pursuit of perfection, is not something I have seen in many coaches."

Shula was not a one-man band. He brought in great assistant coaches. Bill Arnsparger, Howard Schnellenberger, and Monte Clark. All three went on to become head coaches. But there was no doubt who the boss was.

"Don Shula was the savior of the Miami Dolphins," stated safety Dick Anderson. "When he arrived, the attitude in Miami changed one million percent. He had every minute of every day planned. It was all done with purpose. The coaching, the discipline, the intelligence, the transformation that was going on in Miami at that time was just amazing."

There's no secret why he was on his way to becoming the winningest coach in football. Shula had a way of getting the most out of a player. Players saw how hard he worked and how intense he was. And after that brilliant first season turnaround, it was then that the Dolphins' players were convinced Shula was a very good coach.

"Coach Shula at times could be a yeller and a screamer. He'd treat every player consistent but different. That is not a negative comment. He did what he thought he had to do to motivate that individual," said Anderson. "So, he treated players differently, but the same. It is a tremendous skill to have. He was very demanding and as a result that team probably made the fewest mistakes of any in pro football."

Ah yes, if there's one thing that could drive the intense coach into a rage it was mental errors. But luckily for the players, one thing that came with dedication of purpose and doing things over and over in four-a-day practices was that they would often become second nature in the heat of the action.

That was perhaps best exemplified by the consistent excellence of Miami's No-Name Defense, which was crucial in the Dolphins's back-to-back Super Bowl wins in 1972 and 1973.

But again, that focus by his Miami players was simply a reflection of their coach's persona going back to his own playing days.

"Don Shula was probably one of the most intense, fierce competitors that I've ever been around in the game of football. One of his strengths was communicating that competitive spirit to his team. Whenever we went out onto the field, we tapped into that belief that we can go out there, get after them, and win games. He was a competitor with a capital C," explained Baltimore's Hall of Fame receiver Raymond Berry. "He was my teammate the first couple years, and I practiced against him every day. He gave me a lot of tips and was a big help in my playing career. There is no question that even as a player you could see his coaching abilities. He was a limited ability player himself, but his great strength was knowing the game and realizing what the opponent was going to do before they did it. And that carried over into his coaching."

Another great trait Shula had was the ability to adapt to his personnel, not the other way around, which many less-successful coaches have insisted on.

For example, Shula's Super Bowl teams in 1971, 1972, 1973, and 1982 were all keyed primarily by a run-first controlled offensive strategy and a dominating defense. Then in 1983, shortly after losing Super Bowl XVII to the Washington Redskins, Shula drafted quarterback Dan Marino out of the University of Pittsburgh. Marino won the starting job halfway through the 1983 regular season, and by 1984, the Dolphins were back in the Super Bowl, due largely to a pass-oriented offense led by Marino's record 5,084 yards through the air and 48 touchdown passes.

The earlier line from the NFL's all-time winningest coach is worth repeating:

"You don't win with *x*'s and *o*'s. What you win with is people."

THE THIRD QUARTER ALL-TIME TEAM

OFFENSE

WRs	Cris Carter	Minnesota Vikings
	Jerry Rice	San Francisco 49ers
TE	Kellen Winslow	San Diego Chargers
G	Larry Little	Miami Dolphins
	John Hannah	New England Patriots
T	Anthony Munoz	Cincinnati Bengals
	Rayfield Wright	Dallas Cowboys
C	Jim Langer	Miami Dolphins
RBs	Earl Campbell	Houston Oilers
	Walter Payton	Chicago Bears
QB	Joe Montana	San Francisco 49ers

DEFENSE

DE	Bruce Smith	Buffalo Bills
	Reggie White	Philadelphia Eagles
DT	Joe Greene	Pittsburgh Steelers
	Alan Page	Minnesota Vikings
LB	Lawrence Taylor	New York Giants
	Jack Lambert	Pittsburgh Steelers
	Derrick Thomas	Kansas City Chiefs
DB	Lem Barney	Detroit Lions
	Jimmy Johnson	San Francisco 49ers
S	Ken Houston	Washington Redskins
	Ronnie Lott	San Francisco 49ers
P	Ray Guy	Oakland Raiders
K	Morten Andersen	New Orleans Saints
HC	Don Shula	Miami Dolphins

PART FOUR

Fourth Quarter

★ ★ ★ (1995–2019) ★ ★ ★

CHAPTER THIRTY-THREE

PLAYHOUSE: FROM RICKETY VENUES TO HIGH-TECH PALACES

Even though the NFL has branched off to football on Monday and Thursday nights, in essence it is the only pro sport to have its own day, Sunday. Sundays are the most sacred for football fanatics, and the expression "football as religion" can be taken to heart when it comes to stadiums.

In many fans' minds, football stadiums loom larger than other sports venues with mythical proportions linking back to the Roman Colosseum. (The word *Colosseum* has its own roots in the word *colossal*.) And we often hear football players referred to as gladiators.

But whether it was die-hard Bills fans freezing in weathered old War Memorial Stadium or the sleek, new, massive Mercedes-Benz Stadium now enjoyed in comparative luxury by the Falcons faithful, regardless of the size and assorted amenities, what these steel and concrete fixtures represent is a church of sorts, a gathering of a congregation where true believers come together week-in and week-out, year after year pouring out a lot of energy and emotion (and prayers) in support of their team.

Of course, that devotion is certainly affected by how well the home team performs overall. Conduct your own survey and you'll find it quite interesting to see how fans' memories put a different spin on a lack of parking, or insufficient restrooms, or bad sight angles, or rotten hot dogs and lukewarm beer if their gladiators down on the field were successful.

Back in the day, there were no stadiums with luxury anything; as a matter of fact, the venues in the first few seasons of the American Football League, in particular, tested everyone's limits.

"Many stadiums we played in the early days of the AFL were basically glorified high school fields," declared All-Pro guard Bob Talamini. He should know: his home field in Houston *was*, in fact, a high school facility.

JEPPESEN

The Oilers played on a ramshackle high-school-caliber stadium called Jeppesen (later renamed Robertson Stadium) on the University of Houston campus. Originally constructed in 1941 as a joint venture of the Houston Independent School District and the Works Progress Administration (WPA), part of FDR's New Deal, it was used as the home football field for all of the city's high schools.

Players complained that it not only smelled like a septic tank, but also the thin grass field was so hard that it was like playing on cement. Though there is no evidence that he fixed the odor or field conditions, Oilers owner Bud Adams did expand the seating capacity from 24,000 to 38,000 seats at a cost of $30,000 (more than $250,000 today).

In the AFL's first two seasons, 1960 and 1961, the Houston Oilers were the champions of the league and one of the most productive offensive units in pro football history. By the next year, Jeppesen was the site of the game that put the fledgling league on the national map when, on December 23, 1962, the Houston Oilers would host the Dallas Texans in the AFL championship game.

On that day, Jeppesen was overflowing with boosters, totaling more than a thousand above the park's capacity, so many of those sat on folding chairs around the running track that ringed the field. Though the home team lost in an exciting overtime contest, the franchise experienced a lot of success in those early years playing on a high school field.

WAR MEMORIAL

While Houston enjoyed success in a stadium used primarily for high school football, the Buffalo Bills were also able to produce back-to-back championships a few years later despite deplorable conditions with their stadium.

Whether they were steeped in soot, buried in snow, or consuming mass quantities of adult beverages to ward off the murderous wind blasts off Lake Erie, spectators at War Memorial, home of the Buffalo Bills from 1960 to 1972, was a stadium of unfriendly confines that provided no respite for fans (or players) from the dirty environment of the Buffalo area (laden with heavy industry: steel mills, chemical firms, refineries, and auto assembly plants). You'd think season-ticket holders would be better off taking a ride in a barrel over nearby Niagara Falls. Its nickname, the Rockpile, says a lot.

Like Houston's Jeppesen Stadium, it too was built by the WPA. Completed in 1938, War Memorial was located in a seedy part of the city where even the local team's star felt uneasy.

"I remember Cookie Gilchrist [Buffalo's All-Pro running back] paying somebody to watch to make sure his Cadillac did not get stolen. It was a distinctive car. He had written backward across the front of his hood, 'Lookie, Lookie, Here Comes Cookie,' so drivers could see it in their rearview mirror," laughed New York Jets kicker Jim Turner.

But visiting players did not enjoy many laughs when they shuffled off to Buffalo to play. "To get in and out of the field you had to walk up through the stands! Then onto the concourse, then up rickety metal steps leading up to the locker room. It was a real trap as you had to walk right by the fans yelling at you," recalled Chris Burford, a receiver for the Kansas City Chiefs.

Oh, yes, the Buffalo fans. They had a reputation for being exceptionally rowdy and aggressive.

Linebacker-punter Paul Maguire, who played his first four seasons in Los Angeles-San Diego, provides an example by relating a fan experience he never had at any other stadium.

"As a Charger, I remember coming to Buffalo, and first thing Coach Gillman says is, 'After we beat their ass today, when we are leaving the stadium, put your helmet on, because you're gonna get whacked with a brick,' because you had to go through a tunnel leaving the field to get to the locker room," he recalled.

"So, I'm leaving the field, heading toward the tunnel with teammate Dave Kocourek, and I'll never forget this the rest of my life. I hear a fan yell, 'Hey, Maguire!' I looked up just as he is throwing a full beer at me, and I caught it, popped the top, and drank it on the way in. I got a standing ovation from those in the end zone.

"Genesee," he specified. "Nobody drinks that stuff. Horrible beer."

Bills guard Billy Shaw experienced both ends of the spectrum during a brilliant nine-year Hall of Fame career in Buffalo.

"On the one hand, it was fun playing there because fans were in your back pocket. The season-ticket holders behind the Bills bench, we knew them by name. It would be like, 'Hi, Ralph. Where's Nancy?' And Ralph would say, 'Nancy had something to do today, but here's my friend Chester who came with me.' You interacted with the fans a lot more.

"But when we were not performing well, fans would let us know; they'd throw beer cans as we headed for that little bitty tunnel for the locker room. The fans disliked Boston more than we did, so if you lost to Boston at home, you never took your helmet or your pads off, as you'd be showered by fans with all kinds of debris."

Adding to the list of surprises were the physical defects of the stadium.

"To take a shower, we had to go up to the second floor and we had to wear towels because people could see us walk over the facilities from the locker room," recalled Bills kicker Pete Gogolak.

And once you got there a few more surprises awaited. Oftentimes they found showerheads with icicles hanging from them. There were only six showers for the entire team, and on too many occasions, a couple of them did not work at all.

"The first few players got hot water. So, it became a race. It got to the point, where we had guys faking an injury so they can get to the locker early and grab that hot shower," said Shaw. "And there were just two toilets. There was no real training room so one got taped in the locker room and there was only room for one person to get on the table at a time. You didn't feel like it was pro football."

KEZAR

Another "quirky" venue was Kezar Stadium, home of the 49ers (and Raiders for one season before they moved to Frank Youell Field, named after a local undertaker, while their Coliseum in Oakland was being constructed).

Completed in 1925, the multiuse stadium with a seating capacity of nearly 60,000, initially hosted many different sports: boxing, high school football, track meets, cricket, baseball, car races, lacrosse, and rugby. When the 49ers were formed in 1946 as part of the All-America Football Conference, Kezar became their home.

Built in the city of San Francisco about a mile from the Haight-Ashbury district and a mile from the Golden Gate Bridge, it was a cozy neighborhood stadium, where, like Chicago's Wrigley Field, fans would watch from the rooftops of their apartment buildings while others would make the short walk from other parts of the city to attend the game.

Former San Diego Chargers quarterback Dan Fouts has many memories of the stadium as his father, Bob, was the 49ers' announcer there for quite a few years. "I spent many games in the stands watching the 49ers at Kezar where you have fans, three guys on your left smoking cigars and three guys on your right smoking cigarettes," Fouts laughed. "Getting all that secondhand smoke and never buy a hot dog, because by the time it gets to you in your row, three people have taken a bite out of it, and somewhere along the line as they hand it down, you lose some of your change too."

The Hall of Fame quarterback's greatest thrill came from being hired as a ball boy for a few seasons, where he got to see players like Johnny Unitas, Dick Butkus, Bart Starr, and Roman Gabriel up close.

One of the unorthodox designs of Kezar was a lone, small dark tunnel where players from both teams had to go through.

"The tunnel is probably the most famous part of the stadium. When tempers would get raw out on the field, they often got settled in the darkness of the tunnel on the way back to the locker rooms," Fouts said. "I also remember John Unitas telling me the first time he was walking back to the tunnel, he was with John Brodie, the 49ers' quarterback. He did not have his helmet on, and Brodie quickly reminded him, 'If you're going on the field with me, you better have your helmet on.'" The throwing of cans of beer and soda got so bad that stadium management had to build a thick wire overhang at the tunnel entry.

DUAL-PURPOSE STADIUMS

Like the early days of the AFL, for many seasons NFL teams could not afford their own stadiums, and iconic baseball fields like Tiger

Stadium, Wrigley Field, and Yankee Stadium served as homes for the local NFL team too.

"There were very few football-only stadiums. Baseball was happy to share their stadiums with football because otherwise their stadium sat empty for months," said Joe Horrigan, executive director of the Pro Football Hall of Fame. "They were happy to have tenants from pro football. That was an easy fix for football."

However, in order for sports team owners to expand their economic base, a trend emerged in the late sixties and early seventies. The multipurpose stadium. They were primarily designed for major league baseball and pro football tenants. Shea Stadium was home to both the Jets and Mets. Veterans Stadium was the home of the Eagles and Phillies. The Oakland Coliseum hosted the Raiders and Athletics. Busch Memorial Stadium in St. Louis housed the Cardinals of MLB and the NFL. The Cincinnati Bengals moved into Riverfront Stadium to share with MLB's Reds. The Pittsburgh Steelers called new Three Rivers Stadium home along with baseball's Pirates.

While stadium facilities and operations improved as a result of this wave of modern construction, several problems emerged, particularly on the football side of things. Many of the new stadiums had artificial turf, making the players feel as if they were playing on carpet. This created new types of injuries such as turf toe and more concussions as a result of the harder surface. Over time, solutions like implementing new technological advances that allowed for better, more grass-like turf in places where natural grass wasn't suitable came into play.

But what began the next trend was the inescapable fact that dual stadiums ended up doing an injustice to both sports. NFL fans complained they were just too far away from the action.

RISE OF THE MODERN FOOTBALL-FIRST STADIUM

As the world knows, they love their football in Texas, and though (as the name suggests) it was originally built for their local baseball team, when the Houston Astrodome opened in 1965, it instantly became an architectural icon, and a few years later the NFL's Oilers called it home. In 2002, five years after the Oilers had moved to Tennessee, Houston's new NFL franchise, the Texans, began a trend by building a multipurpose, football-first home, one topped with a retractable roof and lots of bells and whistles.

Dallas Cowboys owner Jerry Jones would not be outdone by his Texan counterparts. His AT&T Stadium, opened in 2009, continued the movement to massive, yet sleek, structures that house monster LED video screens, fine restaurants, museum-quality art, cozy bars, pools, technology lounges, and, oh, yes, something for the players too, like cavernous locker rooms and state-of-the-art training rooms. The horseshoe-shaped venue (80,000 to 105,000 seats) hosted Super Bowl XLV in 2010.

VIKINGS' US BANK STADIUM

The builder behind such facilities as AT&T in Dallas, Lucas Oil Stadium in Indianapolis, and the US Bank Stadium that is the new home of the Minnesota Vikings is HKS Architects, a Dallas-based global design company. The $1.1 billion, 66,200-seat stadium occupies the site of the Vikings' former home, the Hubert H. Humphrey Metrodome, built in 1982.

One of the reasons HKS has become a leading designer of NFL facilities (their current project includes the new Los Angeles Rams/ Chargers stadium), is that it doesn't approach it from a pure architectural point of view. The company starts each project with a team of researchers. Some are sociologists, some are anthropologists, some have psychology backgrounds. They conduct a huge amount of research on the city, its culture, the people who live in the area, and their values.

"How they prioritize their values is what helps us create an iconic image that is represented in that culture," explained Bryan Trubey, the chief architect of the Vikings' stadium. "That is why we can stop somebody in the area and ask him about US Bank, and he will say something like 'That is perfect for us; it would not work anywhere else.' It is a pretty radical look, but it is derived from the things that we learned from our research about the area. It is sort of an iconic expression of their culture. It is a combination of a lot of things. Some people say it's a Viking longhouse. A Viking ship or an iceberg. All that is good. People see it the way they want to see it, and it's always positive, as it is representative of what they think and how they feel."

Never before has it been clearer that sports is entertainment, and to draw fans to a venue in an increasingly competitive fight for the consumer's disposable dollar, NFL executives and stadium architects have recognized how the times have changed in terms of how new generations prefer to even view a game in person.

For example, many fans today experience a game differently than the old-schoolers who would be glued to their seats until a halftime food and/or bathroom break. Millennials walk around and dabble with social media on their cell phones . . . get up and go have a cocktail at a bar . . . watch a touchdown standing at a different part of the stadium while describing the action to a buddy on the phone . . . or perhaps take an escalator to a restaurant and watch the game on a monitor while they recharge their portable devices.

FALCONS' MERCEDES-BENZ

All football executives know, in addition to catering to different age groups attending an NFL game, whatever stadium becomes their home, it also has to be able to draw revenue from a wide variety of events throughout the year. That was the thinking that drove the Atlanta Falcons' new Mercedes-Benz Stadium, but they have taken it a step further.

The $1.5 billion, 71,000-seat stadium, inspired by the Falcons' winged logo with a distinct exterior that includes eight retractable roof petals that open like a camera aperture (in less than eight minutes), and a five-story-tall, 360-degree HD video halo board, the world's largest, was designed with flexibility and intimacy in mind.

Primarily a football venue, with the help of a mechanized curtain system for mid- or upper bowls, the Mercedes-Benz Stadium can expand or contract seating capacity depending on whether it is hosting a music concert, NCAA basketball game, MLS soccer match, or Super Bowl.

"On the inside of the bowl, we developed the curtain system, where we could reduce the capacity by twenty-five thousand, and you would not notice that we reduced it by not covering seats but

AMB Sports + Entertainment

AMB Sports + Entertainment

rather by implementing a draping system that makes the volume of the building seem smaller," explained Falcons president Rich McKay. "We tried to make it a venue that could host many different types of events, and all of them would feel like the stadium was designed specifically for them. There is not one sign in the inner bowl. Everything is digital. We have eighty-three thousand feet of LED in the bowl. I think the second most in the world is fifty-five thousand. That gives you the ability to brand it anyway you want."

As for the main event—Atlanta Falcons football—the executives did something revolutionary, and it had nothing to do with technology. When the Atlanta Falcons announced throwback food prices at their new stadium—$2 hot dogs, popcorn, and sodas, $3 nachos and peanuts, $5 beer—fans loved it, and people in other cities started pushing their local ownership groups to follow suit.

"If they can get a hot dog on the street for two dollars, why can't they get that in the stadium for the same price?" McKay asked rhetorically. "We do want to change the game. We think fans deserve this. Listen, we ask a lot for our tickets. We ask a lot of the fans' time. They give us their emotional buy-in. So why not have a family come in and spend twenty-eight dollars on Cokes, hot dogs, and popcorn instead of a hundred dollars?

"We were finding in surveys over time that many families were, number one, no longer bringing their kids because they felt they could not afford it," he continued. "Number two, they were stopping on the way before the game to have their meals. So, Arthur [Blank, the Falcons' owner] made some adjustments to the plans, and now, for example, a fan can get a two-dollar cup that includes endless refills of soda. Guess what? You want to bring the cup back next week? Be our guest."

Though sales were up more than 50 percent, it didn't offset the drop in prices; however, subsequent surveys showed it did have an amazing impact on Falcons fans' satisfaction, and, as a bonus, spending per person did go up. With a twist on an old adage—"The way to a fan's heart is through his stomach"—the team is looking to expand its menu and throwback prices, and it has other NFL executives closely monitoring that plan.

While it will be fairly easy for team executives to swallow reducing food menu prices, what they will have a tougher time with, especially with those operating out of older stadiums, is how to attract new generations of fans who are determined that how they interact with the sport is going to be on their own terms.

"The building is being asked to do so much more on so many different levels and create the spectacle of the game-day experience in person that affects whatever is before kickoff, after the game-winning pass, and what happens during the half-time presentations," explained Bill Johnson, senior vice president of HOK Architects and the principal designer of the Falcons' new stadium.

"All those things are now a part of an entertainment experience, and the old buildings are having a real hard time keeping up with that. Now what the venues are being asked to do, and people like me that design them, is to create spectacle. It is on us to create something that is so compelling, that drives the fan to say, 'I want to get off the couch, fight the traffic, spend fifty bucks for parking, and brave the weather because I can't not be there.'"

He went on to say, "It is a huge issue that we are grappling with. We are trying to pull the league along into this because they created this issue for themselves. They have made the broadcast and online content so good and compelling that they have kind of cannibalized the game-day experience in person. So, this is a monster that they have created."

CHAPTER THIRTY-FOUR

A TUCK, A TACKLE, AND A MIRACLE

History has shown that a team's fortunes in the National Football League can change on a single play. Pittsburgh's domination of the 1970s took root when Franco Harris picked a deflected ball off his foot and raced in for a game-winning touchdown. In San Francisco, the 49ers' dynasty began when Joe Montana, unable to see through defenders bearing down on him, threw the ball to the back of the end zone where out of nowhere, receiver Dwight Clark, at the limit of his leaping ability, pulled it down with his fingertips, producing a come-from-behind win over America's Team, the Cowboys.

Among the iconic games and plays of the NFL's fourth quarter, the New England Patriots literally kicked off their amazing run with the help of a controversial call forever known as the Tuck.

THE TUCK

The New England Patriots' reign in the twenty-first century began after a 5-11 season in 2000. Coach Bill Belichick realized a swift change was needed. He reversed things the following year, finishing 11-5 and heading to the playoffs.

Their opponent in the divisional playoff game on a cold, snowy January evening in Foxboro was the Oakland Raiders. The visitors enjoyed a 13–3 lead midway through the final quarter. With snow making the footing perilous and the whipping winds affecting the flight of the ball, it appeared that the 10-point lead would be insurmountable.

New England quarterback Tom Brady, in just his sophomore season, had taken over when Drew Bledsoe was seriously hurt in the second game of the 2001 season. (Bledsoe was hit by New York Jets linebacker Mo Lewis and suffered a sheared blood vessel in his chest.) Though he had played inconsistently to this point in the season, throwing twice as many interceptions as touchdowns over the last five games, he rallied his team. Surprisingly, it was his legs that cut the deficit, as his 6-yard running touchdown reduced the Raiders' lead to 13–10, with under eight minutes to play.

The Patriots defense got the ball back, and Brady began another march down the field, but it appeared their season came to a crashing close on one play, because with under two minutes left, marching into Oakland territory, Raiders cornerback Charles Woodson blitzed and nailed the quarterback just as he finished a pump-fake.

It would wind up a controversial game-changing play. The result of Woodson's efforts initially appeared to cause a fumble that was eventually recovered by linebacker Greg Biekert, and, if it was a fumble, would have almost certainly sealed the game. However, officials reviewed the play and eventually determined that even though Brady had seemingly halted his passing motion and was attempting to "tuck" the ball back into his body, it was ruled an incomplete pass and not a fumble under the then-effective NFL rules.

The original call was overturned, and the ball was given back to the Patriots. Unsurprisingly, Raiders head coach Jon Gruden and his players complained vehemently.

With new life, Brady brought his team into field goal range.

With under a minute remaining, New England kicker Adam Vinatieri suddenly now had a chance to tie the game in regulation.

Like most occasions late in a close game, Vinatieri was on the sidelines kicking into a net.

Here's what the Patriots' kicker faced. He had missed four of his last five in other games from 40 to 49 yards, and none of those had been in a snowstorm. Now, with no time-outs, the Patriots didn't even have a chance to clear a spot. Down by 3, and facing a 45-yarder, the pressure mounted.

"Now I am thinking I have to make the best kick of my entire life just to go into overtime," Vinatieri recalled. "I don't know how much snow was on the ground, but it had to be four or five inches. There were very few games I played in with conditions like that. With so much snow on the ground, I reminded myself to take short steps because it is like running on ice; if you are not careful, you're gonna fall on your butt, and your kick is gonna shoot straight out to your linemens' rear ends, and you have lost the game. So, don't fall down, get the ball above the line of scrimmage, hit it straight, and still it has to go forty-five yards in a blizzard. Those two to three seconds it took to get through the uprights felt like an eternity. But when I saw the refs raise their arms straight up, there aren't words I can use to express how happy I was. Looking back, that is the kick I am most proud of just because of sheer difficulties and what it meant and what had to happen for it to be good."

Both teams had a couple possessions in overtime and then Brady found a rhythm and had worked his team down far enough to present Vinatieri the chance to drive through a 23-yard game-winning field goal.

"Though it was shorter in distance I don't think there is such a thing as an easy game-winner, especially in a snowstorm but after making the first one, it just felt at that point we were meant to win," Vinatieri said.

A couple weeks later Vinatieri would kick a game-winning field goal at the end of regulation to give New England a 20–17 upset victory over the St. Louis Rams in the Super Bowl. The Patriots would win two more Super Bowls over the next three years.

THE TACKLE

The Pittsburgh Steelers' road to the Super Bowl in 2005 did not come via a quarterback tuck but rather a quarterback tackle.

Like Tom Brady in the Tuck Game, Ben Roethlisberger was in his second season in the NFL. But he was in Indianapolis up against future Hall of Famer Peyton Manning, whose quarterback rating of 104.1 led the league that season.

In the divisional playoff game at the RCA Dome, Roethlisberger took it to the Indy defense right from the start.

The Steelers, the number six seed, stunned the home crowd by driving 84 yards and scoring on their opening possession. Roethlisberger completed six consecutive passes for 76 yards, including a 36-yard completion to tight end Heath Miller and a 6-yard touchdown pass to Antwaan Randle El. Later in the first quarter, Roethlisberger's 45-yard completion to Hines Ward moved the ball to the Colts' 8-yard line, and they scored another touchdown with his 7-yard pass to Miller, increasing the Steelers' lead to 14–0.

Late in the third quarter, after a sack of Manning followed by a fine punt return by Randle El, Roethlisberger took just five plays to get the Steelers on the scoreboard again, as Jerome Bettis's 1-yard touchdown run made it 21–3.

But Manning brought the Colts back. Two fourth quarter scores, one a 50-yard touchdown pass to Dallas Clark and a TD run by Edgerrin James followed by a two-point conversion brought the home team to within a field goal, 21–18.

And with 1:20 left in the game, after Manning was sacked on fourth and 16 at the Colts' 2-yard line, and the ball was turned over to the Steelers on downs, it looked like Pittsburgh was advancing in an upset.

But due to the fact that the Colts still had all three of their time-outs remaining, Pittsburgh chose to advance the ball toward another score instead of taking a quarterback kneel.

On Pittsburgh's first play, as sure-handed Bettis tried to run it in for an insurance touchdown, he fumbled for the first time all season as linebacker Gary Brackett popped it from the running back's hands with his helmet.

Indianapolis defensive back Nick Harper recovered the ball and had a convoy of blockers going the other way and appeared to be on his way for an Indy touchdown that would have given the Colts the go-ahead lead. In an instant it appeared the Steelers would suffer one of the worst playoff collapses in NFL history. Instead, Roethlisberger, who never quit on the play, and while doing a slow back pedal made a season-saving tackle at the Colts' 42-yard line, by spinning around and grabbing Harper's ankle.

Though the Colts were still able to advance to the Pittsburgh 28-yard line, Mike Vanderjagt, who had been perfect at home in the playoffs, missed a 46-yard game-tying field goal attempt wide right with 17 seconds left, and the Steelers ran out the clock.

Pittsburgh would go to Denver the following week and take the AFC crown, then defeat the Seattle Seahawks in Super Bowl XL. Roethlisberger, on a path to the Hall of Fame as well for his offensive prowess, could very well say it was a defensive play, that shoestring tackle, that was one of the most important plays of his career.

THE MUSIC CITY MIRACLE

In a wild card matchup on January 8, 2000, in Nashville between the Buffalo Bills and the Tennessee Titans, a special teams play would live on long after the season concluded.

With under two minutes to play, Titans kicker Al del Greco nailed a 36-yard field goal to give Tennessee a 15–13 lead. However, after his counterpart, Steve Christie, placed a 41-yarder between the uprights with just 16 seconds remaining, the Titans' dreams of glory seemed dashed as Buffalo went ahead, 16–15.

But the game was not yet over.

On a play the Titans practiced regularly (called the Home Run Throwback), after Christie made a short, low kickoff, Lorenzo Neal caught the ball near the Tennessee 25-yard line. Running to his right, he handed off to tight end Frank Wycheck, who spun and threw a low toss over to receiver Kevin Dyson.

Dyson proceeded to head down the left sideline, completely fooling the Bills' defense, and galloped 75 yards into the end zone.

As the Titans celebrated, the game officials huddled to determine whether Wycheck's pass to Dyson had in fact been a lateral and not a forward pass, which would have made the play illegal.

After studying the play at the sideline replay booth for what seemed like an eternity, referee Phil Luckett emerged to confirm that the call on the field would stand, and the touchdown was good. The Music City Miracle gave the Titans their first playoff win since 1991 and capped one of the most exciting finishes in NFL playoff history.

The Titans made it to the Super Bowl that year, coming from behind to tie the St. Louis Rams in the fourth quarter before bowing, 23–16.

Bills kicker Christie explained what happened from his perspective: "The call is Pooch Kick Right. You want the ball to land by the twenty-yard line. By the numbers. So, the idea is your coverage unit converges on the right side. Well that is when Tennessee pitched the ball back. And then Wycheck threw it back again. Well what happened was when Dyson got the ball back on the left side, Donovan Greer and I were the only safeties over there. So, everyone else got caught. Everyone else went to Wycheck, which is a mistake. Guys broke their lanes and there was no one on the right side of the field. So, what are you going to do? I wasn't going to be able to catch him."

A Pro Bowl kicker, known for his ability to connect on clutch kicks, particularly in bad weather, the Music City Miracle was the low point of Christie's 15-year career. But Christie, a cancer survivor, looks back at the play (sometimes) with a sense of humor. "Interestingly Alan Lowry, the Titans' special-teams coach, was my special-teams coach at Tampa. We never practiced that with the Bucs because we were never in a position to need it," he said laughing. "You've got to be close in a game to pull off tricks like that."

CHAPTER THIRTY-FIVE

THEY WORE OUT THE CHAIN GANG

Formidable defenses, like great pitching, can help keep teams in a given ballgame, but offensive units that keep the chains moving down the field with a certain flair and swagger, like home run sluggers, it could be argued, are responsible for the lion's share of fans coming through the turnstiles in an industry that, after all, is show business.

Today's version of the NFL is still riding a cycle of high-powered offenses. In Kansas City, record-breaking young quarterback Patrick Mahomes is thrilling Chiefs fans with his playmaking skills, finding incredible ways to win both with his feet and a lively arm that delivers from a variety of angles to the likes of tight end Travis Kelce and speed demon receiver Tyreek Hill.

In Los Angeles, with the arrival of offensive guru Sean McVay as head coach, former NFL number one draft pick quarterback Jared Goff along with 2017 offensive player of the year running back Todd Gurley, the venerable Coliseum is now packed with excitement week-in and week-out. And being in the entertainment capital, the Rams offense is the leading attraction being showcased to sell tickets when the franchise moves into a state-of-the-art stadium in 2020.

How much does offense dominate the current game? For a storied franchise long-known for defense and even in possession of one of the best linebackers in Khalil Mack, the Chicago Bears have climbed back into contention largely due to an offense that features an emerging quarterback in Mitchell Trubisky and an inside/outside running duo of Tarik Cohen and Jordan Howard.

But perhaps the best example is down in New Orleans where quarterback Drew Brees is a modern link to all great offenses of the past as he continues to collect records and lead his team to the postseason.

In the NFL, some of the most potent offenses through the decades achieved terrific results by doing it in a variety of ways. Most for one super season, but others sustained that success over a course of a few years (defenses always seem to eventually catch up).

There were those that effectively juggled quarterbacks ('50 Rams). Others did it more on running than passing ('41 Bears, '62 Packers, '72 Dolphins). Some loaded up on tight ends and a dominant back ('83 Redskins, '90 Bills), while others came at you in every possible direction ('81 Chargers, '99 Rams).

Of course, most had fine offensive lines to provide the inches and split seconds that made it even possible.

All had brilliant quarterbacks. Some of the very best include:

- Matt Ryan's '16 Falcons.
- Drew Brees's '11 Saints.
- Tom Brady's '07 Patriots.
- Peyton Manning's '04 Colts.
- John Elway's '98 Broncos.
- Randall Cunningham's '98 Vikings
- Brett Favre's '96 Packers.
- Troy Aikman's '92 Cowboys.
- Dan Marino's '84 Dolphins.
- Y. A. Tittle and the '63 Giants, and, in the same year over

in the AFL, the San Diego Chargers under the "Father of the Modern Offense," Sid Gillman.

- Johnny Unitas and the '58 Colts.

While admittedly it's difficult to compare offenses from different eras, with changing rules and defenses dominating in given cycles over the league's long history, here's a look at some of the very best offensive units representative of the different ways to achieve success.

PEYTON'S PLACE

Peyton Manning ran a brilliant Indianapolis Colts offensive unit in 2004, but even topped that with his play for the Denver Broncos in 2013.

You knew it was going to be a special year when Manning opened the season firing seven touchdown passes in a win over the defending Super Bowl XLVII champion Baltimore Ravens.

Denver built on that, averaging nearly 38 points a game, going 7-1 before their bye, then finishing the regular season at 13-3.

Running back Knowshon Moreno ran for more than 1,000 yards and caught 60 passes while totaling 13 touchdowns. All the receivers—Eric Decker, Demaryius Thomas, Wes Welker, and Julius Thomas—benefitted from a record-setting year by Manning. In earning his fifth NFL MVP Award, the quarterback finished the regular season with 55 touchdown passes, in addition to throwing for a league-record 5,477 yards, breaking Drew Brees's mark by a single yard. His 450 completions were, at the time, tied for second-most all time.

Welker, who also played with Tom Brady, compared the two:

"It is the same type of deal for Peyton as Brady. His preparation and understanding of defenses are amazing. All the checks he made at the line of scrimmage. The game-time intensity he brought to practice. Really understood about protections and what the defense was trying to do. He knew where to attack off a blitz. Putting the offense in the best call to be successful."

And the 2013 Broncos' offense was very successful. They tallied an NFL record 606 points, becoming the first team ever to eclipse 600 points in a season (though they'd score only 8 in a Super Bowl loss to Seattle). They had more 50-point games in a season than any other team in NFL history, with three. Four Broncos receivers recorded at least 10 touchdowns—an NFL record—and Manning set a season record with nine games with four or more touchdown passes.

THE GREATEST SHOW ON TURF

The year 1999 would be the first of three in which the St. Louis Rams produced "the Greatest Show on Turf," mesmerizing all fans of offensive football.

Third-string QB Kurt Warner came out of nowhere to throw 41 touchdowns, and the brilliant Marshall Faulk ran for 1,381 yards and had 1,048 yards receiving. Playing in a system devised by head coach Dick Vermeil and offensive coordinator Mike Martz, the Rams spread out their weapons to include a host of great receivers in Isaac Bruce, Torry Holt, Ricky Proehl, and speedy Az-Zahir Hakim (who had his breakout season in the NFL, averaging 18.8 yards per catch, 677 yards, and eight touchdowns), but along with Warner and Faulk, they will all tell you it was anchored by the Big Man.

"First off, that team was built before 1999. It takes time to build an offense. One of the first things I did when I had a good draft choice was to select Orlando Pace," stated Vermeil. Pace, a six-foot-seven, 325-pound offensive tackle, came from Ohio State. "We traded to move up from the sixth pick to the first. Watching him play in college, I felt Orlando was a future Hall of Famer. That is where it all started for us. He was our anchor. And from there we went on."

The ringmaster, Kurt Warner, who arrived in a well-documented Cinderella Story that included playing in Europe and working the nightshift stocking shelves at an Iowa grocery store, tore up the league after starter Trent Green went down with an injury.

He was a rookie in name only. Warner took advantage of all the reps he had in the arena league as well as Europe, and he was the MVP in both leagues.

In his first four years in the NFL, he threw 65 percent or better. Warner threw 98 touchdowns in his first three years in the NFL. No one in the history of the game had done that before.

Vermeil talked about what he observed when he brought him in originally.

"First off, Kurt was naturally accurate. He did not have to be in a perfect setup to throw the ball accurately. He could hold the ball in a crowd and hit the second and third receiver options accurately. Kurt had a tremendous ability to keep his focus downfield and strike accurately," explained the Rams' head coach.

"And when it came down to the final cut, we decided to keep him. We already had a backup quarterback from the year before, but we wanted to see what Kurt can do. I just had a hunch about Kurt. All year long as our scout team, quarterback Kurt threw the ball brilliantly against our own defense. I can remember walking off the field many times saying, 'either our defense stinks or this kid can really throw the ball.' Kurt could really throw the ball."

Right from the 1999 season's first possession, Warner threw it to everybody who was legally able to catch it. The Rams began by winning their first six games. Then after dropping a pair, they'd take seven of their last eight to finish at 13-3.

With players like Isaac Bruce, who had all the skills—speed, concentration, great hands, and could make the difficult catch and run well after he caught it, the Rams easily outscored opponents and are one of only four teams in NFL history to score 30+ points on 12 separate occasions during the regular season.

But at the core of the historic success of the 1999 Rams, who'd go on to defeat the Tennessee Titans in the Super Bowl, was the dual threat abilities of running back Marshall Faulk, who produced more than 1,000 yards both rushing and receiving.

"Marshall was just a raw, unique athlete. He was probably the finest player I have ever been around," Vermeil said. "He was so special in everything he could do. He was very bright. A gifted runner and a gifted receiver with a tremendous understanding of the game. Just a tremendous feel, Marshall had no limitations. The only limitation was when you did not call his play."

SHINING DESPITE THE LONG SHADOW

Very few franchises can boast producing back-to-back Hall of Fame quarterbacks, however, Steve Young followed admirably in the shoes of Joe Montana at San Francisco.

Nineteen ninety-four was a young man's year. Earning his second NFL MVP Award, the southpaw slinger from BYU had one of the greatest seasons ever for a quarterback. Young threw for 3,969 yards, a then-franchise record 35 touchdown passes with just 10 interceptions, completed 70.3 percent of his passes while breaking Joe Montana's single season mark with a then-record 112.8 passer rating, and also once again demonstrated his outstanding scrambling ability, accumulating another 289 yards and seven touchdowns on the ground.

Jerry: I caught 112 of Steve Young's throws for nearly 1,500 yards. What made him such a special player was his command of the huddle. A very, very intelligent guy. And he was such a double threat with his legs and arm. I'd say Steve was one of the fastest quarterbacks ever. Like Robert Griffin III. Opposing defenses had to respect that added dimension. Now, when he first came in the league, he was more of a running QB. But he worked hard and earned one of the highest passer ratings of all time. For a guy that wanted to become a pocket passer, that record shows he was able to accomplish that.

Steve was like Joe Montana in that both had this aura about them. You knew they were born to lead. From the second I stepped into the huddle with Joe, I could just feel it, and it was the same feeling with Steve. You knew these guys could lead you to the promised land. Neither was very vocal or animated. But you observed their intensity at practice, and you just knew they were intent on getting the job done.

With help from tremendous coaching, great support on both offense and defense, Young got the job done.

Under head coach George Seifert, Young's offensive handlers included Mike Shanahan and Gary Kubiak, both of whom would go on to very successful careers as head coaches themselves.

Young benefitted from a veteran offensive line that included all-stars Bart Oates at center and guard Jesse Sapolu, as well as tight end Brent Jones. Behind him, Ricky Watters was a dual threat, rushing for 877 yards while catching 66 passes. It was a deeply talented team that included 10 Pro Bowl players anchored by a defense that featured the NFL's defensive player of the year in cornerback Deion Sanders as well as the NFL's rookie of the year, defensive end Bryant Young.

With rookies producing and free agents coming through, the 49ers were poised to get their first Super Bowl title since 1989.

Taking six of their first eight games, after a bye during Week 9, San Francisco rolled on, winning seven of their final eight regular-season games to finish at 13-3.

Riding that powerhouse offense, the 49ers scored 44, 38, and 49 points in playoff wins over the Bears, Cowboys, and the Chargers to win the Super Bowl title.

Young completed 24 of 36 passes for 325 yards and six TDs and led all rushers with 49 yards on five carries in the finale.

After the game, the quarterback was ecstatic. "Is this great or what?" he enthused. "I mean, I haven't thrown six touchdown passes in a game in my life. Then I throw six in the Super Bowl! Unbelievable."

The southpaw was part of an offensive system that was recognized by its peers as one of the best of all time.

When asked what was the best offensive unit he faced in a standout 10-year career, defensive end Bill Maas did not hesitate.

"For me it was the San Francisco 49ers. Hands down. There was an ebb and flow of a National Football League game in the eighties and nineties that if you watched film and studied hard enough you knew generally where and when they were going to run out of different formations. Down and distance, field location. Not with them. They did the best job of keeping a defense on their heels instead of on their toes rolling forward, which defenses do. You did not know what they were gonna do," the former NFL defensive rookie of the year explained.

K-GUN

Though the Bills fell short in the Super Bowl, more than a quarter century later, analysts still consider Buffalo's K-Gun offense one of the best of all time.

Swashbuckling quarterback Jim Kelly, who had a tremendous knack for reading defenses on the fly, directed a unit that scored 428 points, good for first in the league, while averaging over 5.6 yards per play. By calling out plays in formation to his team at the line of scrimmage, Kelly prevented opponents from bringing in specialists and that created favorable mismatches for the Bills. It also had a tendency to leave defenses exhausted.

Its scary capabilities were on full display in the 1990 playoffs. After going 13-3, in just two games, the Bills scored an amazing 95 points and gained 995 yards.

In defeating the Raiders, 51–3, in the AFC title game, Buffalo set an NFL playoff record by scoring 41 points in the first half. They would have won it all save for a missed field goal in a 20–19 loss to the Giants that season in the Super Bowl.

The five-time Pro Bowl quarterback explained how today as yesterday executing the no-huddle offense still comes down to the same thing—a confidence game.

"I was fortunate because I had a center by the name of Kent Hull who directed his own line where to slide. I was in charge of all the skilled players. Even though they are running no huddle offense these days, they are still getting plays sent in from the sidelines. Peyton Manning called most of his own. Even in the two-minute drill, many today are still getting plays from the sidelines. We had to think so fast to get things in formation, and I told Tyrod Taylor and E. J. Manuel, two recent Bills QBs, that if they don't like a play coming from the sideline, you need to call your own, and that is something that you need to cover with your offensive coordinator prior to the game.

"If you don't like the first play, for example, you're gonna be defeated from the start because you won't have the confidence. You have to feel comfortable about the plays you are directing," Kelly explained.

One compelling fact was that despite having outstanding wide receivers in James Lofton and Andre Reed, as well as Keith McKeller, Don Beebe, and Pete Metzelaars, unlike most prolific offenses, the Bills did it by running comparatively fewer plays and by actually running the ball (479 attempts) more than throwing it (425). Thurman Thomas, who led the NFL in scrimmage yards (1,829), was the main runner in the K-Gun offense, one that did not have to run a lot of plays because with the no-huddle, it was able to put up points quickly.

And that hurry-up-and-win approach was well suited to its leader's temperament.

"That system fit Jim's personality perfectly," said receiver Don Beebe. "He just wanted to go out and have fun. Growing up in a family of six boys, I'm sure it was a lot like backyard football to him. Using the analogy of golf, sometimes you see a golfer out there analyzing every single thing for every shot. Then you have others that just step up and swing. Kelly was a lot like the latter. Let's not over-analyze. Instead, let's just go out and run them into the ground. We were conditioned and trained to get a play off every fifteen to seventeen seconds. And that was a great advantage for us then because particularly the defensive line would get so tired that they could not come off the ball very well in the third and fourth quarters. They were so exhausted."

Kelly's head coach Marv Levy was quick to point out that while Jim was a really good fit to run the offense, he got a lot of help from his defense.

"If you don't have a good defense, your quarterback becomes predictable and is going to get rushed, as he is forced to throw constantly playing catch-up. And we certainly had that: Darrell Talley, Shane Conley, Bruce Smith, Cornelius Bennett, and our free safety, Mark Kelso, who was one of the most underrated players. The K-Gun would not have been as successful as it was if it wasn't for the fact that our defense was so good. It all worked together."

Still, at its center was the charismatic Kelly. He was the uniting force that helped get Buffalo to four straight Super Bowls.

"Jim was a quarterback/linebacker," said Coach Levy. "He was tougher than fourteen miles of detours. He was well prepared and well respected by his teammates."

THE HOGS

Coming off a strike-shortened season in 1982, where the Washington Redskins won it all (the franchise's first title in 40 years) and had the rare honor of a kicker, Mark Moseley, named league MVP, they rolled to the title game the very next year behind a famous offensive line known as the Hogs. Led by Pro Bowlers Russ Grimm, Jeff Bostic, and Joe Jacoby, the Hogs helped running back John Riggins rush for 1,483 yards and break an NFL record with 24 touchdowns. Their play in the trenches contributed to quarterback Joe Theismann's completing 60 percent of his passes for nearly 3,800 yards and 29 touchdowns, earning NFL MVP honors. Charlie Brown led all wide receivers with 1,225 receiving yards on 78 receptions for eight touchdowns.

Under head coach Joe Gibbs, who'd gained some offensive wisdom serving on the Air Coryell staff in San Diego, the Redskins smoked defenses for 541 points, the second highest point total in NFL history. They dominated the 1983 season, finishing 14-2.

One of the keys was that they had specialized tight ends: Don Warren, Rick Walker, and Clint Didier. Each brought a different skill set to bear, and it added up to the team scoring more points and winning more games.

As Theismann explained, they could beat you anyway you wanted to play it.

"We became a very balanced offense. Back then, they had true strong and free safeties, strong being primary run stoppers and free being center fielders. Our aim was to make the safeties have to do both," the MVP signal caller said. "I remember it got to a point during the season where we were so confident when we walked out onto the field that we were never worried against any defense." Being on your way to a 14-2 record will have that effect.

And despite a shocking loss in the aforementioned Super Bowl, the Washington Redskins of 1983 were truly one of the dominant offensive forces of all time.

AIR CORYELL

Starting in 1979, like the Rams of the fifties and the Oilers of the sixties, the San Diego Chargers offensive juggernaut would not become a one-season wonder. And though they did not win it all, in coming close between 1979 through 1982 they sure made it exciting.

Surrounded by a bevy of brilliant coaches such as Ernie Zampese, Joe Gibbs, Larrye Weaver, and head coach Don Coryell, the Chargers would utilize personnel over the next few seasons like never before including a game-changer in the form of tight end Kellen Winslow. But it all was orchestrated by a tough, savvy gunslinger out of the University of Oregon, quarterback Dan Fouts.

Fouts was the first NFL player to surpass 4,000 passing yards for three consecutive seasons (1979–81). His career high of 4,802 passing yards during the 1981 season was an NFL record at the time. A half-dozen times he surpassed the 20-touchdown mark with a ca-

San Diego Chargers quarterback Dan Fouts (left), coach Don Coryell (second from right), and receiver Wes Chandler (right) were part of one of the most potent offensive units of all time: Air Coryell.

reer high 33 in 1981. The six-time Pro Bowl star who led the NFL in passing yards in four consecutive seasons was the league MVP in 1982.

The Hall of Famer is the first to credit his head coach for his good fortune.

"Don was a football guy to the core. He slept and lived football. Long, long hours at the stadium, or a training camp. This was nothing new to him. I'm sure instead of counting sheep, Coach counted footballs in the air to fall asleep," Fouts said. "You've heard the term 'players coach,' that was Don Coryell. He really cared about his players. He disliked front office politics. All he wanted to do was get better on the field. We would laugh a lot on the field. Coach just loved the game and it showed."

What the incredible numbers that were put up showed was that Fouts, his running backs and receivers had one very effective offensive line that made it happen. It included four-time Pro Bowler Ed White, five-time Pro Bowler Russ Washington, three-time Pro Bowler Doug Wilkerson, Billy Shields and Don Macek. One of their secrets was the longevity of playing together. In no small manner, it was their work that allowed the Chargers to lead the league in passing yards an NFL record six consecutive years from 1978–1983 and again in 1985 as well as leading the league in total yards in offense 1980–1983 and 1985.

"Yes, the first key move among many was the trade to acquire Ed White, a veteran All-Pro guy that was feared by defensive players. That allowed us to move Don Macek to center. Ed was a defensive all-American nose tackle at Cal. So, he had that kind of defensive mentality to attack. A unique personality that really made our unit gel. I look today at offensive lines that are in flux and all the injuries, and I look back on those five guys Shields, Macek, Wilkerson, White, and Russ Washington and it seemed like we played together every game for years. They were never hurt. They were always there. And that was good for me," said a grateful Fouts.

What was good for the quarterback as well was not only having great running backs in James Brooks and Chuck Muncie, who had speed, power, and great hands, and first JJ Jefferson then Wes Chandler and Charlie Joiner to throw to on the wings, but Fouts utilized a tight end like no one had ever done before.

As part of Air Coryell, Winslow led the NFL in receptions in 1980 and 1981. The key was moving him around and finding a mismatch. At six foot five and 260 pounds, with the speed and moves of a receiver, defenses would cover the all-American out of Missouri with a strong safety or a linebacker, as zone defenses were not as popular. Strong safeties in that era were almost like another linebacker, more of a run defender that could not cover a tight end as fast as Winslow.

In 1980 Air Coryell produced three receivers with more than 1,000 yards. Kellen Winslow had 89 catches for 1,290 yards, John Jefferson 82 for 1,340, and Charlie Joiner 71 for 1,132. They ranked first, second, and third in the AFC in receptions.

There were many dimensions to the Coryell offense; one of them was to have players that can do more than just one thing. Winslow was a perfect example, moving around and finding a mismatch. With his size and strength and speed, they would try to get Chuck Muncie out into space as often as possible. San Diego took flight all season long and didn't come down until falling just short of reaching the Super Bowl, losing a tight one, 34–27, to their rivals the Raiders in the AFC championship game.

The next season, averaging nearly 30 points a game, the league's leading offense carried on in record-setting fashion.

Fouts threw 609 times, completing 360 passes for 4,802 yards—all NFL records. The Chargers also set a record for total yards. Winslow caught 89 passes for 1,290 yards to lead the league; Charlie Joiner had 70 catches for 1,188 yards, and Wes Chandler added 52 grabs for 857 yards. Running back Chuck Muncie rushed for 1,144 yards and 19 touchdowns.

Despite having to compete with one of the NFL's worst defenses (ranked 26th of 28), San Diego went deep into the playoffs. Traveling to Miami they came out on top in one of the most exciting games of all time in defeating the Dolphins under taxing humid conditions. (See chapter 31, "The Immaculate Reception, Hailing Mary, and the Epic.")

Unfortunately, their season would end in the deep freeze the following week. In Cincinnati, facing the Bengals in the AFC championship game in the coldest game in NFL history based on the wind chill (the air temperature was minus 9), and the windchill was minus 59, most of Fouts's tosses fluttered in the whipping wind and in losing, 27–7, the team once again fell a game shy of the Super Bowl.

ALL HAIL THE FIERY OLD MAN

Right from the start, passing and scoring were the ticket to success in the American Football League when it debuted in 1960. And nobody did it better than George Blanda. The wily veteran quarterback, who played 10 years in the NFL, mostly riding the bench with the Chicago Bears, never really got a shot under George Halas. During his rookie season, he played behind the great Sid Luckman, then was lost in a mix of rotating QBs, leaving him quite frustrated and unfulfilled.

The AFL was the shot in the arm that led him to a great career. Blanda took the Houston Oilers to three straight title games, winning the first two. The 1961 offensive unit was exceptional, and with a leading defense, they were well positioned to defend their crown. Behind an offensive line that included Bob Schmidt at center, Al Jamison at tackle and Bob Talamini at guard, the Oilers mixed up the run with the pass very successfully, averaging more than 36 points a game, a lot even for the AFL.

At running back was Heisman Trophy winner Billy Cannon, who'd been instrumental in winning the 1958 national collegiate championship for LSU. The Tigers went undefeated and beat Clemson, 7–0, on Cannon's touchdown pass in the Sugar Bowl. In his senior season, he guided LSU to a return visit to the Sugar Bowl. Joining him in the Houston backfield was tough yard man Charlie Tolar, who combined speed, strength, and excellent balance in a fireplug frame. On the outside, wide receivers Bill Groman and Charlie Hennigan, each totaled more than 1,000 yards in the 14-game regular season.

However, there was no doubt who the leader was. The Houston quarterback had a well-earned reputation as one of the most driven athletes on the planet.

"Nobody was more competitive than George Blanda. He was a dominant figure in our huddle," explained Talamini. "But we needed that because we were a very young team, and he was a veteran in his early thirties. He had been around and seen a lot.

"He would not let a missed block go by. In the next huddle, before calling the play, he would say, for example, 'Which one of you guys let number seventy-three by?' And one of us would have to fess up, and George would snap back, 'Well, don't let that goddamn thing happen again. That guy kicked the s––t out of me!' He was a great leader—really, a coach on the field—and knew so much about the game. Frankly, he knew more than most of our coaches on the team."

Blanda was not the only feisty person on the team. Head coach Lou Rymkus, who had taken the team to a championship, didn't last the season. The 17-year veteran, whose coaching career included stints as an assistant with Green Bay and the Rams, and who was an all-American at Notre Dame during the 1940s, was an advocate of strict conditioning and stern discipline.

"Lou was a great coach," said Talamini, a six-time AFL All-Star, "but he was let go because he got sideways with owner Bud Adams. Lou was not very diplomatic. He'd rail against anybody, including the owner. When you do that so many times to the man who writes the checks, you're gonna be shown the door. So, they brought in Wally Lemm from the St. Louis Cardinals."

Lemm went 9-0, and one of the keys to his success was Billy Cannon. Fast and very powerful, the former LSU star also had terrific hands and was a tremendous receiver coming out of the backfield.

Receivers Hennigan and Groman, both somewhat undersized, were aided greatly by the tutelage of Mac Speedie, the onetime great wideout for the Cleveland Browns. They had to be, because Blanda put the pigskin up for grabs often. "Of course, that style of play mandated all the offensive lineman to be on their toes with so much pass protection required," Talamini pointed out. "The defensive linemen were not as restricted back then either. They could head rake, grab your mask, and place their fists under your chin, so pass protection was of the utmost importance in those years. And we practiced it over and over and over because we knew the quarterback needed extra time to find the open receiver. The defense would also use a lot of stunting to try to confuse us."

There was no confusion as to how the Houston Oilers became champions again in 1961. They had averaged a brilliant 443.5 yards per game. Cannon led the league in rushing, and Hennigan in gaining 1,746 yards receiving set a pro-football record that stood for more than 30 years. Winning AFL player of the year honors that year, Blanda led the AFL in passing yards (3,330) and flung an NFL record 36 touchdown passes.

And he was just getting started. In a career that spanned 26 seasons, the NFL's version of Father Time would play until he was 48, when he retired owning two dozen pro records.

DUAL QB STARS

Led by a pair of future Hall of Famers, Norm Van Brocklin and Bob Waterfield sharing the quarterback duties, the 1950 Los Angeles Rams averaged almost 39 points a game.

Throwing to the likes of receivers Tom Fears and Crazylegs Hirsch (another pair of future Hall of Famers), and Dan Towler, Glenn Davis, and Tank Younger, among others, while applying a fearsome ground game, they averaged 13 more points than their opponents. Among those providing the time and space were three All-Pro linemen: Dick Huffman, Bob Reinhard, and Fred Naumetz.

In scoring a record 466 points, Fears led the league and set an NFL record with 84 receptions while Van Brocklin and Waterfield finished one-two in passer rating. They rolled up more than 5,000 yards and knocked off the mighty Bears in the playoffs before being edged out by Cleveland, 30–28, in the 1950 championship game.

Under head coach Joe Stydahar, the Rams' record-shattering offense would carry on in 1951. This time Van Brocklin and Waterfield kept finding Elroy Hirsch open even more. Crazylegs caught 66 passes for a league record 1,495 yards and tied Don Hutson's mark with 17 touchdown receptions.

With three of the best fullbacks in the league in Younger, Towler, and Dick Hoerner, throughout the season the Rams would occasionally employ all three in the same formation during a few games. Using this "bull elephant backfield" along with the aerial show, the Rams racked up over 5,400 yards.

As if their arms and leadership weren't enough, Rams quarterbacks Bob Waterfield and Norm Van Brocklin were both accomplished punters. Playing out of nearby UCLA, Waterfield was among the punting leaders during his college days while Van Brocklin led the NFL, twice, in punting.

With all these weapons, the Rams made it all the way back to the title game in 1951. This time they won the NFL championship, defeating Cleveland, 24–17.

Some may argue the Rams' numbers were enhanced by facing some very porous defenses against the three teams that had come over from the AAFC: the Colts, 49ers, and Yanks. Nevertheless, it remains one of the most explosive offenses in the history of the National Football League, one that set all kinds of records: among them, producing 735 yards in a game, and Van Brocklin's passing for 554 yards in one game. Another, 29 consecutive games with 300 or more yards of offense, stood for nearly 50 years.

CHAPTER THIRTY-SIX

THE CHESS MASTERS:
FOURTH QUARTER

Though staffs are bigger these days and assist in a range of responsibilities, from skill training, to scouting, to conditioning, to game planning, NFL head coaches still must endure one of the highest-pressure work environments in sports. At the same time that one NFL season is winding down, another is just under way. And that is the coach-hunting season.

Even for those who get to experience the rare glory of winning it all, that feeling is even more fleeting when compared with the hours they claim to put in. But for most, the years of a gypsy existence trying to climb the next rung on the ladder to reach the pinnacle of their profession (for most, that is becoming a head coach in the NFL), it has become part of their DNA. And while they may seek to reduce their skyrocketing blood pressure by retiring or seeking temporary relief as a broadcaster, most come to find nothing else comes close to offering the same measure of satisfaction as the challenge of overseeing a successful football team.

Ask Dick Vermeil. After taking the Eagles to the Super Bowl, the head coach, known for putting in long hours, retired in 1982, citing burnout—only to return 15 years later to win a Super Bowl with the St. Louis Rams

Ask Joe Gibbs. The three-time winner of the Super Bowl as head coach of the Washington Redskins headed off to another profession that is close to his heart—overseeing a NASCAR race team—only to return to the NFL sidelines 11 years later.

Ask Bill Parcells. Giants, Patriots, Jets, Cowboys—everywhere he went, he took a struggling franchise, turned it around, and made it a playoff contender, but even retiring citing health concerns seemingly took a backseat to the lure of that challenge of coaching.

Ask Jon Gruden. The former Super Bowl–winning coach of the Tampa Bay Buccaneers enjoyed a very successful broadcasting career, but his heart and soul is being down on the field with a whistle and in the film room studying the Raiders' next opponent.

So, to have that desire it takes a special person.

JON GRUDEN

For Jon Gruden it is an ability to convey his enthusiasm for the game that comes across well as a motivational tool.

"Jon brings energy and passion. It is not phony, it is real. He loves all the various aspects of football and that is infectious to the players," said Falcons President Rich McKay, recalling their days together winning a Super Bowl in Tampa Bay. "In our case, he was brought into an environment where we had a really good football team. But we had some issues to deal with. He was the right guy for that, and he energized a franchise that had hit a wall. We were going to the playoffs, but we were not advancing. Jon's energy helped us tremendously."

Before that, Gruden worked his way up to offensive coordinator of the Philadelphia Eagles in 1995 after various offensive assignments with the 49ers and Packers. Developing a reputation working with quarterbacks, Gruden enjoyed success as the head coach of the Oakland Raiders when Rich Gannon arrived. They helped each other.

Under Gruden's tutelage, Gannon had his first All-Pro season after a dozen years in the league, and the coach had a leader on the field who would propel the team to the playoffs over the next couple seasons.

"Jon had an infectious personality and a ton of energy," said Gannon. "I've never been around a coach with such passion, not just for the game but even practice. Nobody prepared me better to play the games from our conversations during the week to his coaching the quarterbacks to his coaching quarterback tip sheets. He was with us all the time. Having him on the sidelines was a great benefit. We had hand signals, adjustments, code words, and tremendous communication all the time. It was amazing. It was a very productive relationship."

TONY DUNGY

While Gruden has his own kinetic style, the man he replaced in Tampa Bay, Tony Dungy was subtler.

With a calm demeanor and a focus on the positive, Dungy built a reputation demonstrating an ability to turn things around in the inevitable storms every franchise faces.

Dungy took over the Buccaneers in 1996 and had only one losing season with the team. However that was deemed inadequate by management, and he was fired following the 2001 season (losing a wild card playoff game to Philadelphia). In 2002, when he became head coach of the Indianapolis Colts, Dungy installed the Tampa 2 style defense he created, and he then never had a season with less than 10 wins and won Super Bowl XLI during his tenure.

The other component to Dungy was his compassion and faith.

"It doesn't get much better than Coach Dungy," said Colts quarterback Jim Sorgi, the backup to Peyton Manning. "Going into my second season, I learned that I had a torn labrum in my shoulder. I found out because all my balls kept hitting the turf throw after throw. I knew something was wrong. Doctors told me I had to sit out the summer training and I was worried because I wasn't guaranteed nothing. I had played well in my limited time during my rookie season, but not great enough to have them tell me I was the lock as the backup. I remember sitting in the training room, Coach Dungy comes up and tells me, 'God put you in this situation for a reason. Take care of the physical parts, and we'll have you ready for training when you're able.' That lifted the weight off my shoulders."

BILL BELICHICK

Under his famous "Whatever it takes" mantra on his way to winning four Super Bowls, Pittsburgh Steelers coach Chuck Noll convinced every player on his roster that their role was important for the team to be successful.

With Bill Belichick, his own well-documented mantra of "just do your job," is based on the head coach's superb ability to fill positional holes with the exact type of player he envisions for that role.

His tremendous success during his head coaching tenure with the New England Patriots really had its roots in the long hours spent helping New York head coach Bill Parcells, working his way up to eventually becoming the Giants' defensive coordinator. But even that was a trial, because superstar linebacker Lawrence Taylor was more than skeptical of the young man's promotion at first.

"We used to call him 'Doom.' Because every time there was a mistake, it was the end of the world. And he would just go off. And we said he just needs to settle down. I think Coach Parcells was a great mentor to Belichick," said Taylor. "From what I heard, his father was a coach, but when I heard Bill was hired as defensive coordinator, I was pissed and swore at Parcells wondering how an assistant special-teams coach was going to direct our entire defense.

"But Coach convinced me saying that most of the defenses we run come from Belichick. He gave Belichick the confidence, so we rolled with him, and he turned out to be a fabulous defensive coordinator. Personality-wise, he's got a whole lot of work to do," said Taylor laughing, "but as far as knowing football, *x*'s and *o*'s, ain't nobody better."

One of the reasons was that coming from a football family, Belichick became a real student of the game and immersed himself in its roots and nuances.

"Bill is the greatest historian I've ever been around in the NFL. Not even close. If I mentioned something about the Wing T, he'd tell me he read the book on it. He'd proceed to tell you many details about a given topic and was always searching for knowledge. To say he is a smart person, is like saying LeBron James is just an okay basketball player," said former New York Giants quarterback Phil Simms.

Belichick and quarterback Tom Brady have made history as they've combined to form the most successful quarterback-coach tandem in the NFL.

And it is all done with a look to tomorrow.

"You may have a big victory, but the next day it's almost a 'who cares' attitude. Bill is already on to the next game," explained former Patriots running back Danny Woodhead. "It doesn't matter to Bill if you're playing a team that is three and ten, or ten and three, the most important game is the next one."

At its core, it has been Belichick's willingness and diligence to look everywhere possible to put players in a position to succeed that has propelled him to greatness.

For much of the twenty-first century, Bill Belichick has been putting his New England Patriots in a favorable position. But even after nine Super Bowl appearances and six world titles, he can't wait for tomorrow.

CHAPTER THIRTY-SEVEN

THE INTIMIDATORS

Football will always be a violent sport—but who will be left playing it?
—*NEW YORK DAILY NEWS*, 2017

CTE found in 99% of studied brains from deceased NFL players.
—CNN, 2017

Football Wrestles with its Violent Nature—is the NFL Doing Enough?
—*SAN FRANCISCO CHRONICLE*, 2018

Would You Watch Football Without All the Violence?
—*WALL STREET JOURNAL*, 2018

Media headlines in recent years have helped draw attention to the serious health risks involved in playing football, and while the National Football League is one of the leaders in health and safety research and is constantly revising rules to try to limit the long-term damage done to players, football and ferocity are nothing new whatsoever.

Let's face it, the power and the fury have been part of its appeal from the beginning. (See chapter 4, "Head and Shoulders.") And with today's pro football TV contracts worth billions and broadcast ratings still impressive, it confirms the NFL's ongoing popularity.

Its appeal has long been to our most primitive instincts. A sport that is a combination of raw caveman strength and physical grace locked in gladiatorial combat that involves one of the most complicated chess matches one could imagine. And professional football, like no other game, has clearly represented America—the good, bad, violent, loud, ugly, and beautiful since the first kickoff.

Through the many years, what fans paid to see and tune in to watch are the actual collisions. In this world of violent impact, some of the very best include: Redskins linebacker Sam Huff, Eagles tackle Reggie White, Packers linebacker Ray Nitschke, the Colts' MLB Mike Curtis, the Chiefs' Willie Lanier, and a bevy of safeties who often get a running head start like Jack Tatum, Kenny Easley, Larry Wilson, Chuck Cecil, John Lynch, and Kenny Houston. In addition to the countless players on special teams, there have been a fair share with a reputation for physicality on the offensive side of the ball as well, including Hall of Fame tackle Bob Brown and running back tanks Larry Csonka and Earl Campbell. (See chapter 27, "The Workhorse.")

To better understand where we have come today, it is informative to understand the style the National Football League (and colleges and high schools too) had been played in for many decades by examining some of the hardest-hitting players

Colts linebacker Mike Curtis demonstrates the particularly aggressive style of play during the sixties and seventies as he takes down Rams quarterback Roman Gabriel.

Courtesy J. Michael Curtis

who dominated in an era(s) where that was the name of the game. Remember, too, about the psychological aspects, because as part of that ongoing chess match, much of the arsenal of a hard-hitting player was his reputation. It is a mind game out there as well.

THE CLAW

Take a look at the Chicago Bears' Ed Sprinkle. Spanning his playing days from 1944 to 1955, Edward Alexander Sprinkle was known to many as "the Meanest Man in Pro Football" and was nicknamed "the Claw"—a reference to an illegal clothesline tackle in today's game. Come on, the dude was a defensive end at just six foot one and barely 200 pounds. Do you honestly think he had players such as massive running back Marion Motley quaking in their cleats? If anything, Sprinkle's famous response to his nasty reputation was the real truth. "We were meaner in the 1950s, because there were fewer positions and we fought harder for them. It was a different era." In other words, he was doing what everyone was doing in a dog-eat-dog environment, only having that reputation apparently had more advantages than disadvantages, as he enjoyed a long career.

If Sprinkle was known as an intimidator, then what would you call his much bigger and more athletic replacement Doug Atkins? A good ol' boy from Tennessee who was more than a half foot taller and 75 pounds heavier, and who, if provoked, would knock you into next week, the future Hall of Famer could play anyway you wanted to go at it. (See chapter 30, "He's Got Character.")

JACK SPLAT

A middle linebacker whose quickness and intelligence were over-shadowed by a toothless snarl and mean disposition was two-time

NFL defensive player of the year and nine-time Pro Bowl player Jack Lambert of the Pittsburgh Steelers.

"When Jack stepped on the field, he was nasty," explained his fellow Hall of Fame teammate Joe Greene. "His size was perfect for our defense, especially the pass coverage. He got down in the middle zone quickly, and it was very difficult to get the ball over him. Jack also had the tenacity to overcome players much bigger than him, since he weighed only two hundred eighteen pounds. He just had a ferocious personality. He could bend his knees and get down, getting the leverage when he had to. Jack was a very good blitzer. And Jack was very, very smart. He called the defense for us, setting the coverages."

On top of his smarts, Lambert was a fearless, fearless hitter. And he didn't accept excuses for himself or anybody else.

The term "fearless hitter" is often associated with safeties, and more than a few have thrilled fans and rattled bones of opponents with their savage tackling. During a productive nine-year career that ended in 2017, running back Danny Woodhead, despite being undersized (listed generously at five foot nine and 200 pounds), showed no fear and earned a reputation for being resilient. He explained why safeties, also not among the biggest players, could make a ball carrier see stars.

"There are lots of hard-hitting linebackers, but sometimes the toughest hits come from safeties that you can't see. Plus a lot of times they are coming downhill and have more distance to build up speed at impact. So those are the hits that you remember." Or don't remember.

CAPTAIN CRASH

One of the most effective safeties who maximized his not particularly big frame so well that he became known as Captain Crash, was

Dallas Cowboys safety Cliff Harris, named to the NFL 1970s All-Decade Team.

An anchor of the Doomsday Defense, Harris approached tackling with a combination of science and martials arts philosophy.

"I had a degree in math and a minor in physics, so I understood force equals mass times acceleration. So, I knew how to hit," said Harris. "I played between a hundred ninety and two hundred pounds. And my knowledge of the science of hitting certainly helped me, especially with the bigger players in the two hundred forty to two hundred fifty Csonka range.

"I think there's several things that were really important. One is knowing how to explode with force. My dad was a fighter pilot in World War II. He was trained in judo. So, from that martial art discipline, my dad taught me how to use that other person's speed, weight, and momentum against them. In other words, you hit a guy you spin the way he is going and smack him down using his own speed and strength and knowing where to do that. It is kind of like a wrestler, whether they grab low or high, they use leverage to put their opponent on the ground," the two-time Super Bowl champion explained.

"I think the other thing that helped me was my mathematical-oriented mind, knowing the physics and understanding instinctively where the weak spot would be in the most pivotal part in motion where you can utilize your speed and angle that you are hitting the opponent with, knowing that it was their weakest and most unbalanced point. The other important point was to take what my dad taught me from his judo experience, which was to take the opponent and use their size and speed to spin and flop him hard onto the ground. I had a lot of power for my size, which was enhanced by technique."

The six-time Pro Bowl safety was an avid weightlifter who could power clean nearly 350 pounds, a lot for someone who weighed only 190.

At the same time, playing in a position that is physically the last line of defense, it also demands a strong cerebral approach.

"That is exactly right," said Harris, "because in a sense you are playing a mental position. You are jousting with the quarterback and the offensive coordinator up in the booth trying to beat you mentally, not physically. What I tried to do and that was what Coach Landry taught all of us, was to anticipate not react. That is the way you win. If a quarterback can anticipate your move, chances are he is going to beat you. If he can't, and he has to react, you can beat him."

RONNIE LOTT

Cowboys coach Landry also had a lot of respect for another safety. He once stated that San Francisco's Ronnie Lott was "like a middle linebacker playing safety. He's devastating. He may dominate the secondary better than anyone I've seen."

Lott's autobiography was certainly aptly titled: *Total Impact*. For 14 seasons, he struck fear into the opposition, but was held in high esteem as well.

"Ronnie Lott, let's not argue the point, he might be the hardest hitter of all time. He was absolutely relentless. There was absolutely no fear in this man," said wide receiver Don Beebe. "When you watch him on film, some guys would make choppy steps and slow their feet down before contact, but Ronnie would actually tackle you as if you were five yards after contact. He was like the good sprinter that runs through the tape at the finish line."

And Lott did it from every position he played. He earned 10 Pro Bowl invitations at three different positions.

His sustained excellence stemmed from an attitude he developed early on.

"The way I play is important to me, because I know I'm not gifted with great athletic ability or speed. But God always gives you the ability to do one thing, and that's to try hard. That was my attitude. If that means going out and running into somebody who's bigger or faster or tougher than you, you just do it."

John Lynch, now the GM with the 49ers franchise, made the Pro Bowl nine times as a thunderous-hitting safety. He said he owes a lot of it to conversations he'd have with Lott, who'd visit practices when Lynch was playing under coach Bill Walsh at Stanford.

"Ronnie was very impactful to me regarding my approach to tackling. I had only moved over to safety in my junior year at Stanford. He spoke to me about the mentality of the position. It was a different era, and this sounds cruel now, but it was the way the game was played then. I remember Ronnie telling me, 'Your job is to let people know that if they enter your area, it will be under their own peril. And it is not going to be comfortable,'" recalled Lynch.

"We would have more conversations, and he talked about this idea—and it is something that I will never forget and something I carried with me throughout my career. He said, 'Ninety-nine-point-nine percent of the players in the NFL hit *to* the contact. It is only a very few who hit *through* the contact. You have that ability, but you have to envision it.' Ronnie said when he saw a ballcarrier that he'd envision four of them and aimed to get to that fourth dimensional figure behind the other three. So, I always had that in my head, and it came straight from Ronnie, who did it better than anyone."

DICK BUTKUS

No one could ever get into the head of Chicago Bears linebacker Dick Butkus, but you can be sure he got into the minds of his opposition. This was a player who was a natural. A natural-born killer on the field. His impact on professional football is as subtle as a sledgehammer.

At six foot three, 250 pounds, Butkus was a one-man wrecking crew in the middle of the field whose controlled fury struck fear into opposing players for years. There were others like Chuck Bednarik and Dick "Night Train" Lane with hard-hitting reputations, but ever since his rookie season of 1965, most opponents called him the hardest hitter they faced.

Hall of Fame running back Floyd Little gives a good example with this story.

"We were playing in Denver. The weather was bad, the game was tight, and nobody was really moving the ball. On one play Butkus hit me so hard everything in my nose came out, blood all over my jersey, but my philosophy was never let them know they hurt you. If they find out, they're like sharks, they'll attack with greater intensity.

"Well Butkus hit me so hard, I jumped up and said":

Little: "Hey man, you can still roll."

Butkus: "You okay?"

FL: "They told me you were slowing down."

DB: "You okay?"

FL: "You are playing like lights out."

DB: "You okay?"

FL: "Why do you keep asking me that?"

DB: "Because you are in the wrong huddle."

"I'm looking over at my teammates who have their hands on their hips shaking their heads as was the ref. It was the first time I ever had to come out of the game."

Little was not the first to suffer that experience.

In arriving with such a distinct force, Butkus often prided himself saying his mantra was making a play where, "as a player got up, he didn't have to look around to know who tackled him."

Over a nine-year marauding career, Butkus made a lot of players see stars.

Before a brilliant career was cut short by injury (a shredded right knee forced him to retire in 1973), one of the underreported skills that made the University of Illinois product so good was his range for a big guy. With his tremendous anticipation and instincts, there is no doubt that the number of interceptions and forced fumbles are a testimony to how good this guy really was.

"One thing people forget about Dick Butkus was that in addition to being such a physical presence, was he was as quick as a cat, strong or weak side he can get there in a heartbeat. Could he run somebody down thirty or forty yards away? No. But that was not his job either. Butkus had amazing instincts. When that ball was snapped, he had a really good idea where the ball is going. And he arrived there in a big physical way. Butkus was a student of the game who rarely made mistakes," explained his longtime teammate, defensive end Ed O'Bradovich.

"You look at game films and it would be a rare play to see him out of position. Butkus had unbelievable timing about arriving at the play, instinctively knowing from what angle and when to make contact. He was superb at how to drive through the ballcarrier and how to take him down. He was unbelievable."

Another teammate, tight end Mike Ditka, an intimidating figure in his own right, talked about the unheralded skill set of Butkus.

"I played with Bill George, the Bears' All-Pro linebacker, and thought he was fantastic, but Dick was a whole other animal. He was the real deal. He even beat up his teammates; he took no prisoners. I don't think he got enough credit for how well he moved. He was tremendous in anticipating and filling holes, plus he was a big guy that could really motor from sideline to sideline. And he arrived with a thud," Ditka said. "One other thing I believe about Dick that was overlooked was his ability to strip and force fumbles in general. I don't know how many fumbles he forced in his career, but it was a lot."

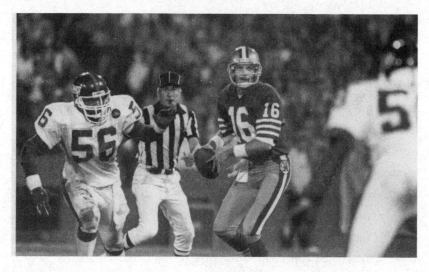

The referee is in a good position to see which is quicker on this play: Joe Montana's release or Lawrence Taylor's legendary swat.

Copyright Michael Zagaris

LAWRENCE TAYLOR

The ability to strip and force fumbles was a skill that was not overlooked when talking about one of the greatest intimidators of all time—New York Giants linebacker Lawrence Taylor.

In fact, it was precisely that ability, never seen before to such an extent, that was part of Taylor's talents that simply changed how the game was played.

Drafted number two overall in the 1981 draft out of the University of North Carolina, the six-foot-three, 240-pound Taylor transformed the position of outside linebacker from read-and-react to attack mode. His speed and strength combined with an off-the-charts aggressiveness and intensity, made him a dominant defensive player and one of the most feared players in football. Taylor was not only a three-time NFL defensive player of the year, a 10-time Pro Bowl star, a member of the NFL's 75th Anniversary All-Time Team, but was also honored as the NFL's Most Valuable Player in 1986.

Before Taylor arrived in the NFL, the 4-3 defense was the dominant formation. The four defensive linemen were backed by three linebackers, with the middle linebacker anchoring the entire unit. The best middle linebackers Butkus, Nobis, and Nitschke controlled the action primarily by stopping the run. But rules changes allowed the offenses more freedom and by the early 1980s more and more were using running backs and tight ends in the downfield passing game. Defenses countered by employing the 3-4, which featured two inside linebackers to handle the run and two outside men to join coverage—and apply pressure to the quarterback. Enter Taylor. For the next decade plus, with his freakish athleticism and sheer relentlessness, no one rushed the quarterback like Taylor.

His talents forced the creation of new offensive formations, changed blocking schemes, and revolutionized modern defensive thinking.

"I believe that Lawrence saw the game differently. He practiced at a speed that was equal to or greater than game speed. Certainly faster than anything I had experienced coming into the NFL. Essentially, he could see things and anticipate how plays would unfold much quicker than any player could even get an idea that I observed in the NFL," explained his longtime linebacking teammate Carl Banks, a member of the NFL 1980s All-Decade Team. "He watched very limited film but could diagram how you would want to attack the opponent. That is how good he was. Like those other few all-time greats, Lawrence had tremendous, tremendous instincts. They just understood the game at such a unique level."

He changed the game because before he arrived, teams would pull out guards to hit the outside linebacker, but there was no guard good enough, fast enough, athletic enough to get to Lawrence Taylor. He changed blocking patterns, and it is now a regular part of playbooks at all levels of the sport. This slide to protect against people like Lawrence Taylor. Lawrence was the first to force it because he was unblockable.

"I believe Lawrence Taylor is the greatest player in the history of the National Football League. I think he changed the game radically. Forget about blocking him, you could not block him," explained long time NFL executive Ernie Accorsi.

"In the eighties, there was the emergence of the cocked-left tackle at an angle. You do not see that anymore because Lawrence Taylor is not playing anymore. All of a sudden, the left tackle used to take a forty-five-degree angle with his left foot, and the whole league would play that way. You may have a chance of chipping him on a wet, muddy field, but on Astroturf you had no shot."

When asked why, in a passing era when teams were playing two, three, and four wide receivers, he'd line up three tight ends instead, Redskins coach Joe Gibbs quipped famously, "We had to figure out a way to stop Lawrence Taylor. I'd put a tight end on that side. I put a tight end in the slot on that side, and I motioned a tight end over to that side. If we didn't, we could not win the division."

Great intensity, speed, and strength that fueled an attacking style unlike any other, Taylor could run around you or over you. With his quickness, the big linebacker was full speed after two steps.

"A transcendent one-of-a-kind athlete. I don't recall ever seeing him doing a push-up or lifting a weight but once the game started, he played as if his hands were on fire. He played every play as if it was his last one. He left it all on the field every play," said New York Giants receiver Phil McConkey. "So, when your best player in one of the best teams in the history of the league is doing that, you better be doing the same thing. That is the reason why we were Super Bowl champions."

There are exaggerations and clichés all over the place, but when you have players telling you about Taylor's ferociousness on every single snap in practice, that is the way he was.

Taylor was not the senior vocal leader that his defensive cohorts George Martin and Harry Carson were. But even the veterans who were watching him had to get in gear because if a surefire Hall of

Famer was doing it, you'd better also. Lawrence was a tremendous motivator through example. It really stemmed from a fierce determination to be dominant, a player willing to risk failure to change a game.

Taylor talked about how he developed his intimidating approach to the game including where the trademark hammer swing came from in stripping the ballcarrier.

"In my last two [college] seasons I started to pick up the pace and become a better player. And it happened in a game against North Carolina State. I was rushing the quarterback, and the ball was sitting out there, so I went to strip it. I did, and a teammate picked up the ball, went in for a touchdown. I learned from that point on: 'Hey, it is all right to tackle, but it is something special to make a play.'

"And, hell, if I'm rushing the quarterback, you can't see me anyways, so what the f‑‑k, I just want to knock the ball out of his hands," Taylor said, "So I started to realize in the course of the game, there were only seven or eight plays that make a difference in the outcome. Changing the tide, changing the direction of the game, changing the flow of the game comes down to just a handful of plays.

"So, if you can make or be around those seven or eight plays, you don't have to make a hundred tackles, you can make the two or three that will change the course of the game. And you're going to be the hero. I am always looking for those opportunities. When the game is hanging in the balance, and the captain gets down on their knees in the huddle and calls the play and says 'hey, somebody's got to make a play,' I want to be able to raise my hand and say 'hey, over here.' That is the difference between me and a lot of other players. [Some shy away] I will make the last play. I will get the last shot. I don't care. [You] can't be afraid to fail."

While Taylor had a lot of talent surrounding him as part of the Big Blue Wrecking Crew, teammate Banks offered an illustration of how naturally gifted this guy was.

"Classic story I tell about Lawrence is a bit comical. He is known for his nightlife and showed up late for one meeting. He fell asleep during the morning film review. One of our defensive coaches was getting frustrated and yelled at Lawrence. So, Lawrence says, 'okay what is it that you want?' Coach says, 'I want you to pay attention,' so Lawrence says, 'okay turn off the lights and turn the film back on.' So, after just one play. Lawrence says, 'stop the film.' Lawrence walks over to the chalkboard, draws up an entire plan for how to rush the Redskins in our next game. We went with it, and it was very successful. Coaches just scratch their heads and wonder why they didn't think of it. Again, Lawrence saw stuff that most of us did not."

What a whole nation saw on a *Monday Night Football* game on November 18, 1985, when NFC East rivals the New York Giants faced off against the Washington Redskins, was coming up on the downside when going up against Taylor. (See chapter 24, "Prime Time.")

With his well-honed instincts, the linebacker anticipated where Washington's Joe Theismann was going to try to run and beat him to the point, but the Redskins quarterback was almost immediately trapped between Taylor and fellow linebacker Harry Carson. But it wasn't clear until the reverse angle of the play was shown why the tough Redskins quarterback wasn't getting up after the sack and why Taylor was frantically signaling to the sideline for medical help.

The blow caused a gruesome break of Theismann's right leg between the knee and ankle. It eventually ended his career, but as a great competitor and sportsman, Theismann harbors no hard feelings toward the Giants' linebacker. In fact, in recalling their duels over the years and calling games as a broadcaster, Theismann has nothing but the utmost respect for Taylor.

"Lawrence Taylor stands alone at the top. Lawrence had an innate ability to dissect angles. He had great natural strength. He had speed that you just could not think somebody of that size could have. Lawrence had a relentless motor. He had the size, power, and strength to run over smaller people, and the quickness to get around bigger people.

"Taylor was simply a destructive force. If there ever was a Superman in the NFL, he wore number 56 for the Giants," the Redskins quarterback added. "He was the only defensive player I can remember who we had to design our game plan around. The first question at our meeting was, 'how are we going to handle Lawrence?'"

For most teams, not very well.

In a 13-year career Taylor produced 132.5 sacks, many of them savage, blind-side hits that often resulted in fumbles. Only Reggie White had more official sacks when Taylor retired after the 1993 season. Taylor was voted to the Pro Bowl in each of his first 10 seasons, an NFL record.

CHAPTER THIRTY-EIGHT

THE *FOOT* IN FOOTBALL

They've long been portrayed in movies and television as the butt of cultural jokes—frail, smokers, poor understanding of the game, heavy drinkers with unpronounceable names, hunkering under an oversize jacket standing alone behind the bench, spoke English poorly, and didn't fall in line with the rest of the team physically. But when soccer-style kickers proved the instep is mightier than the toe, at least more accurate and offering greater range (are there any other greater criteria?), every team eventually jumped on the bandwagon. In the late fifties, the straight-on kickers made just over 50 percent of their field-goal attempts, whereas in recent seasons soccer-style booters made better than 80 percent. The math is pretty straightforward even if the contact with the ball is not.

The last hurrah for the straight-on kicker after the twilight of George Blanda's 1970 season of miracles or Tom Dempsey's record 63-yard field goal that same year, was perhaps the Redskins' Mark Moseley, who won a very rare honor as league MVP in the strike-shortened season of 1982. Though it would take more than a few seasons, kicking in the NFL has now long belonged to the sidewinders.

Why the greater accuracy and distance? It comes down to two

concepts involving physics: surface area and angular momentum, respectively. The more force one can apply to the ball, the farther it will go. The greater contact area provides more margin for error.

There were a few soccer-style kickers in college football beginning in the late 1950s and early 1960s, but the position of kicking wasn't even a dedicated roster spot in the NFL in the early sixties.

A perfect example was the 1962 Green Bay Packers. In defeating the New York Giants in the NFL championship game, they had wide receiver Max McGee handling the punting chores. Safety Willie Wood booted the kickoffs, and guard Jerry Kramer, when he was not leading Jim Taylor around end with the sweep, attempted the field goals and PATs.

But changes were afoot. Just as baseball would employ specialty middle relievers, closers, and the designated hitter, and the NBA would sign on sharpshooters that could regularly nail the new 3-point shot, NFL teams began to make some changes after the success of one soccer-style kicker who helped lead the Buffalo Bills to back-to-back AFL championships.

THE PETER PRINCIPLE

Pete Gogolak was a Hungarian refugee who revolutionized professional football, not once but twice. First, following an All-Pro season in 1965, Gogolak had other NFL teams immediately searching worldwide for their own soccer-style kicker. Second, Gogolak was also among the first to play out his option and successfully test the market as a free agent.

Growing up playing soccer, young Pete fled to America with his parents (and future fellow NFL kicker, brother Charlie) to escape the Hungarian Revolution in 1956, which would be brutally suppressed by the Soviet Union. His family settled in upstate New York. The youngster had never heard of football or seen a game. To his disappointment, his high school did not have a soccer team. But then again, very few schools did.

"I saw the sport for the first time on TV here," he said "I remember this big guy Lou Groza kicking the ball straight on with his toe. I remember turning to my father and saying, 'What a funny way to kick a ball.' So even though there was little emphasis on the kicking game outside of PATs and kickoffs, I tried out for the high school football team."

His initial efforts were embarrassing failures.

"I remember vividly the first time I tried kicking this pear-shaped ball, it barely got off the ground. I almost took a few linemens' heads off, going well under the crossbar, with everyone laughing. However, I knew it was something I could succeed at and proceeded to work at it."

Gogolak practiced tirelessly, and he'd go on to a record-setting experience while attending Cornell University. He set a national major college record of 44 consecutive kicking conversions from 1961 through 1963. Overall, his conversion record was 54 for 55 during his three-year varsity career. His 50-yard field goal versus Lehigh in 1963 was the nation's longest in a major college game at the time. He also booted eight of 40 yards or more. But to his disappointment, no one in the NFL drafted Gogolak. No scouts were watching many Ivy League games then. Again, it was also a time when a team carried around just 33 players and no specialty kicker, as that person usually played another position as well. But after the AFL's Buffalo Bills sent a scout to observe him, they decided to take a chance, picking the Cornell kicker as a late-round novelty.

Much to their surprise, Gogolak was a booming sensation from his very first game. Playing the New York Jets down in Tampa, Florida, in an exhibition game, the Hungarian booted a 57-yard field goal, one of the longest ever to that point. And in their season opener against the Kansas City Chiefs, Gogolak accounted for a pair of field goals, one to open the scoring and one to end it, and had four PATs in between. It kicked off nine straight wins for the Bills on the way to a 12-2 record and then a victory in the title game over the San Diego Chargers. Gogolak was a big part of that success.

Old War Memorial Stadium was often packed. The media really built up this soccer-style kicker's impact. One newspaper headline read "It's a Bird, It's a Plane, No, It's Pete Gogolak."

As a key contributor in helping Buffalo win back-to-back titles the next season, Gogolak made the All-AFL team.

Gogolak laid out what happened that would go on to change the sport:

"Pro football is very much a copycat league, so following my success, teams like the Kansas City Chiefs and Dallas Cowboys (with their "Kicking Karavan"), staged cross-country clinics as well as try-outs in foreign countries in hopes of scoring their own sidewinder. Dallas found Toni Fritsch in Austria, and with the success of other foreigners, such as Bobby Howfield from England, Jan Stenerud from Norway, and Cypriot Garo Yepremian, suddenly everyone saw the potential.

"Straight-on kickers were steadily being replaced by soccer-style kickers because we were more accurate and from longer distances. So, I was amazed that no one had tried this before I arrived," Gogolak said.

An escapee from one revolution who adapted well to a foreign game in his new country, the New York Giants' all-time leading scorer and two-time AFL champion with the Buffalo Bills, Peter Kornel Gogolak played a significant role in revolutionizing the NFL, as both a sidewinding kicker and a pioneer in free agency.

THUNDERFOOT AND THE SKI JUMPER

One grew up in a place more known for winter sports: Norway. The other was a good ol' boy who excelled in athletics despite the suffocating heat and humidity playing in America's Deep South (born in New Orleans and attending colleges in Mississippi). As teammates with the Kansas City Chiefs for 11 seasons, from 1967 through 1977, Jan Stenerud and Jerrel Wilson formed one of the most consistently excellent kicking tandems in NFL history.

At a time when special teams were not given much consideration, Wilson's high, booming punts that sailed far down the field were a potent weapon in the battle for field position. His majestic trajectories made other people aware of how important the kicking game could be.

"Jerrel Wilson was a big man for a punter," explained Stenerud. "I remember the first time I saw him warming up, at the Orange Bowl. He was putting on a show for Hank Stram. Standing there with no helmet on, he was kicking these monstrous, soaring punts seventy to eighty yards. Keep in mind rule changes started like '73 and '74. Prior, the whole team could release and race downfield on the snap of the ball. Now only the two outside players could, as the others would have to wait for the ball to be kicked. That is about one and a half seconds. So, hang time became more important. Jerrel hit that ball hard."

The secret to Thunderfoot's style was to throw everything in his comparatively large body at the ball (he was a backup running back). The unprecedented power came from trying to snap everything— his hips, abs, knees, thighs, toes—into each punt.

Wilson retired with multiple team records including a franchise-record 1,014 punts during his career, highest average yardage in a career with 43.6, in a season with 46.1, in a game with 56.5. He owned the NFL record for most seasons leading the league in punting average, with four: 1965, 1968, 1972, and 1973.

Wilson's kicking colleague, Stenerud, experienced a less conventional route to success in the NFL. The native of Fetsund, Norway, who was in America because of a ski jumping scholarship, recalled how it began: "My junior year, I was running the stadium steps at

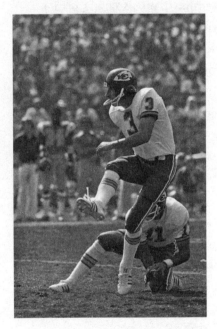

Jerrel Wilson (above) and Jan Stenerud of the Kansas City Chiefs produced one of the best kicking tandems in NFL history.

Courtesy Kansas City Chiefs

Montana State, and one day the guy kicking field goals was also the defensive back, Dale Jackson, a safety. I went down to the field, and he was kicking straight on. I was wearing tennis shoes. And I noticed I was kicking quite a bit farther than him, even straight on."

Over the next few days, word got out. One afternoon, the Norwegian ski jumper was in the middle of his running workout when a booming voice yelled out. "Hey, skier! Get your butt down here. I hear you can kick!"

It was the school's football coach, Jim Sweeney. Though Stenerud had a rough start, it was a day that would change his life.

"He had me try a kickoff. I had never seen a tee before," recalled Stenerud. "I didn't know how to place the ball on it, and the players and coaches are standing around wondering, 'What is this skinny skier doing?' I proceed to top my first kick. I heard muffled laughter. So, I try another. Kicking from the forty, I was nervous and all charged up, but I hit it perfectly. It soared high, went through the goal posts, and into the stands. They weren't laughing now."

After the next few attempts did the exact same thing, players started cheering.

"As we walked off the field, Sweeney asks me, 'Hey, kid, what are you doing tomorrow?' The first thing that went through my mind was, 'This is America,' where I always heard about 'This is the land of opportunity' and felt kicking this football might be mine."

The slender Norwegian jumped at the opportunity and had an amazingly successful career. Over 19 seasons, he converted 373 out of 558 field goals (67 percent) and 580 out of 601 extra points (97 percent) for a total of 1,699 points scored. Stenerud was voted to the Pro Bowl six times and was key in helping the Chiefs win their first Super Bowl, 23–7, over the Minnesota Vikings in 1970 with three field goals and two PATs. The Chiefs retired Stenerud's jersey number 3 in his honor. In 1994 he was selected to the NFL's 75th Anniversary Team, but even more significantly Stenerud was the first pure kicker voted into the Pro Football Hall of Fame.

However, the mind-numbing, constant pressures of the game left Stenerud plagued by anxiety, even now. "Throughout my career, and to this day many years later, I continue to have two recurring dreams," he said. "In one, I am in the mountains atop a ski jump. That is fun. You glide through the air for five or six seconds. But I never get to jump. I am putting my skis on but never get to go. I wake up wondering why? The other is that I am dreaming, and it is right before the football game. And I cannot seem to get out onto the field. It is always something: shoelaces, chin strap—something . . . I think 'I am going to be late for the kickoff!' I feel what that is telling me is that I was feeling even more pressure than I consciously thought during my career kicking in the NFL."

Even though he stood the test of time kicking for three different teams in three different decades and was so proficient that he was selected to the Pro Bowl at age 42, no matter how much success he enjoyed, Stenerud just couldn't shake the pressure that came with each attempt.

"I can remember standing on the sidelines many times since early in my career thinking, 'if I miss my next kick' there may be someone new on the roster Monday. That went through my mind countless times over the years. It is a part of the position. I just constantly fought with myself to get those thoughts out of my mind. 'You gotta make this next kick!'"

THEIR TEAM'S BEST ATHLETE IS THE PUNTER

There is a reason why Ray Guy was the first pure punter ever selected in the first round of an NFL draft. Whenever the Raiders dropped back into punt formation, the sky was the limit. It is that simple. No one in the history of the NFL kicked the ball as consistently high and as consistently well as the angular six-foot-three athlete from Southern Miss (the same school as Jerrel "Thunderfoot" Wilson).

Guy averaged 45.3 yards per kick as a rookie and earned the first of six straight Pro Bowl selections. Although he led the NFL three times and had a career average of 42.4, it was the height of his punts that raised them above the rest. Guy's skyscraper efforts served him well. Amazingly, he punted more than 1,000 times in 14 seasons and had only three blocked.

In a game of field position, Guy offered a special reliability to his teammates.

"Being the team's center that included snaps for punts and field goals, I knew that if we were buried deep in our own territory, it was a comfort to know that Ray Guy would punt it from here to the great beyond," explained Hall of Fame center Jim Otto. "Ray Guy was used so much to get us out of trouble. And he did. Time and again. So, we were able to get the ball back again from the opponent, and often times get a field goal or a touchdown. Ray was a tremendous athlete and very dependable. He would come into that huddle on fourth down and we'd look at each other feeling confident in our punter's ability as he got us out of trouble far more times than not."

A global audience saw his athleticism on display in Super Bowl XVIII. Head coach Tom Flores recalled a telling moment. Standing at the 45-yard line Guy leapt to pull down a high snap and delivered a 42-yard punt over a strong rush.

"It was one the key plays of the game," Flores recalled. "The snap was about 15 feet in the air, but Ray went up and caught it with one hand. And he did it effortlessly. As far as running, jumping, throwing, speed, and agility, Ray was probably one of the best athletes on the team."

Physically, Guy was well suited for the position. He had long legs. He was exceedingly flexible, and his follow-through always seemed to be two to three inches above his head.

One of the achievements in his career was the fact that being a number one draft pick showed young kickers coming up in high school and college how important punting had become to the game. Paul Maguire, a veteran punter-turned-broadcaster, just marvels at what the guy could do. "Ray Guy was just special. He could really put the air under it, and it is hard to remember when he had a really bad punt. He just did it so right for so long. He was a number one draft pick. And I remember Al Davis telling me, 'Paul, I never have to worry if our offense is not moving the ball, because Ray could always get us out of trouble. It is the best weapon we have.'"

The first pure punter elected into the Pro Football Hall of Fame, Ray Guy continues to be the standard by which all other punters are measured.

THAT JACKRABBIT HAS GOT A KICK

Ever since becoming the all-time leading scorer for the Jackrabbits of South Dakota State back in 1995, Adam Vinatieri, the human version of the Energizer rabbit, just keeps on kicking. As of the 2019 season, Vinatieri, 46, is the oldest active player in the NFL and is the league's all-time leading scorer. He is the only player ever to score 1,000 points with two different teams (New England Patriots, Indianapolis Colts).

In addition to his prodigious productivity over a long span, it is also the way he's done it that makes him a certain Hall of Famer. A four-time Super Bowl champion, it has been Vinatieri's winning boots in the waning seconds that helped his team hoist the Lombardi Trophy twice.

His brilliant kicks in deep snow in a playoff win over the Raiders in the famous "Tuck Rule" Game (one to tie it in regulation and one to win it in OT) have helped earn him the nickname Automatic Adam.

"What sticks out about Adam to me is to be able to produce at such a high level for such a long period of time. He was one of those players that really took care of himself from the beginning. Adam is like the proverbial 'getting better with age like fine wine,'" said Colts quarterback Jim Sorgi. "Game-winning kicks in the Super Bowl certainly put Adam on the map, but it's really been his commitment to consistency over a long period of time that has really helped make Adam one of the clutch kickers of all time. And it doesn't matter the distance; from the chip shot to the midfifties range, Adam has been trusted to do it. And he has for many years."

The secret to his coolness under pressure might be found in his bloodlines, as he is related to the late daredevil Evel Knievel. "Yes, he is like a second or third cousin on my mom's side," Vinatieri revealed. "But if he misses one of his attempts, he ends up all broken up or dead. If I missed one of mine, I can feel the same way, but not quite as big a deal, I suppose."

Given many names—among them, Money, Mr. Clutch, Iceman, Adam Bomb—the native of the Black Hills of western South Dakota will one day be given the title "the greatest kicker of all time."

CHAPTER THIRTY-NINE

THE ARTISTIC ARCHIVISTS

With a twist and a nod to the unofficial motto of the US postman—"Neither snow nor rain, nor heat nor gloom of night have prevented these cameramen from the swift completion of their appointed rounds"—for more than 50 years, NFL Films has played a major role in developing pro football as a core fabric of pop culture.

Its constant adaptation to new technology and imaginative storytelling techniques, including original music and distinctive narration combined with artistic camera shots and audio that captured the game from the inside, has built up players to mythic proportions.

"I truly believe they made football a pop culture phenomenon," said Joe Horrigan, executive director of the Pro Football Hall of Fame. "They created a mystique of football. They took it from a man's game on a field for a limited number of people to see it, to something you can see on TV highlights, feature film, up close with their helmets off. They just did so much for the game."

Winners of over 120 Emmy Awards, its body of work has produced a worldwide following, but there are no bigger fans than the players themselves, many who grew up watching NFL Films's highlights on television.

Prior to the company's creation by Ed Sabol in 1962 (then known as Blair Motion Pictures, named after his daughter), film in football had been used primarily as a strategic tool for scouting talent and devising game plans. Sabol was a World War II veteran who worked selling topcoats but had a passion for film. He'd imitate the style of John Ford, one of his favorite Hollywood directors, and shoot footage of his son Steve's football games from all kinds of angles.

After learning that rights were available and confident in his creative skills, Big Ed successfully bid $3,000 for the film rights to the 1962 NFL title game in Yankee Stadium where the Green Bay Packers would face the New York Giants.

However, at a time when the NFL was far from the most popular sports league in America, lagging behind major league baseball and college football, things were looking bleak when the game and Sabol's new career kicked off.

On a very cold and windy day, his battery of World War II–era cameras kept jamming up as film cracked and lenses froze.

But like the postman, the crew persevered and after editing the film, entitled *The NFL's Longest Day*, both league officials and not long thereafter, America, enjoyed their ability to tell a story, presenting artistic essays of the sport, including popular and telling slow-motion tributes to the talents and courage of the ballplayers, capturing all the great nuances of the game including personalities.

With humble origins that began in a few old, small offices just above a Chinese laundry in Philadelphia, NFL Films has since become a self-contained 200,000-square-foot state-of-the-art film and television production facility in Mount Laurel, New Jersey. It houses the world's largest sports film library, including over 100 million feet of football action stored in more than 50,000 cans. That massive inventory includes: every championship game since 1933; footage dating back to 1894 of Princeton versus Rutgers—shot by Thomas Edison—as well as the 1925 Pottsville Maroons. Ed's son, Steve, helped his father run the budding business after quitting football at Colorado College.

And business was good, especially when cable television really took off in the late seventies and early eighties. In addition to playing a significant role for *Monday Night Football* by packaging the prior day's game highlights for the popular halftime show with Howard Cosell, NFL Films flourished with a long-running program on HBO. Then *This Is the NFL* went on to become one of the longest-running syndicated sport shows in history. The key to success was having a crew comprised of personnel with intimate knowledge of the game.

Phil Tuckett was tailor-made. He was a young receiver struggling to crack the roster of the vaunted San Diego Chargers offense. As the owner of a college degree in English and in need of more than the wages from being on the Chargers' taxi squad to support a wife and young child, Tuckett applied his writing skills to produce stories for local publications about sports, including work based on his own football diary a la Packers guard Jerry Kramer. His journal landed stories in *Sport* magazine, a popular national publication. Everything would change for the better in the mid-1960s, when Ed Sabol came into his world.

One afternoon, seeing his coach Sid Gillman, a film aficionado, eating lunch with Ed Sabol, the writing receiver walked over, and with the magazine open to his article, handed it to Big Ed.

After reading the feature story entitled "How I Won My Lightning Bolts," it led to an exchange that would change the lives of both men.

"Ed looks at me and says, 'you are wasting your time playing football because you can write about it. Very few football players can write about the game they're playing. I have a company called NFL Films and I will teach you how to make movies. If you can write, you can make a movie. I will train you to do it. But I need you to resign from the team right now."

The receiver was hanging by his fingernails in a pro football career where every practice was a serious game for him. If he didn't come through, he might not be activated for the next game and when that happened, his already meager paycheck would drop by two-thirds. Still, it was not only his dream but his father's, so he turned Sabol down.

That all ended when he got cut two weeks later. Tuckett soon called Sabol, who agreed to give him a chance. He packed up the family and moved to Philadelphia where he became a cornerstone of NFL Films for 38 years.

The academic all-American from Weber State would go on to win 30 Emmy Awards for cinematography, writing, editing, and directing for shows like *Football America, The 100 Yard Universe, Autumn Ritual*, and *Lost Treasures of NFL Films*.

Tuckett likened Big Ed to Walt Disney, a good animator but better as a visionary that could inspire other artists to implement his grand plans. On the other hand, his other boss, Steve, was a filmmaker, much more hands-on in the physical production of achieving his father's vision.

"Every waking moment Steve's thoughts centered around how to make the best movie possible," said Tuckett. "And he only cared about football. He did not care about branching out into other areas. Big Ed was that way too. They had the vision of what NFL Films should be. It was NFL football one hundred percent. Ed only wanted to be in the position that he was in. Steve was the nuts and bolts and would've been the executive vice president even if he was not the son of the founder. He was talented enough and knowledgeable enough as a filmmaker that he would've risen through the levels anyway, but personality-wise, they were completely distinct."

While sports like baseball and boxing have long histories, they have not been chronicled as well because they did not have what professional football had with what Ed and Steve Sabol began and what the NFL embraced, capturing the game on film over time with key

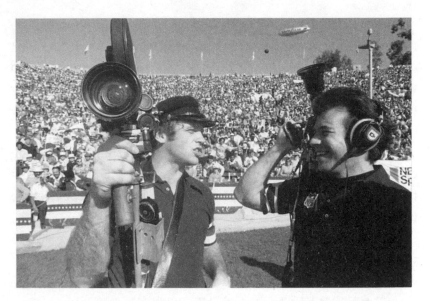

NFL Films's Phil Tuckett (left) and Steve Sabol covering Super Bowl XI at the Rose Bowl.

Phil Tuckett Collection

elements being a pair of giants in music and narration. The stirring compositions of the original music by Sam Spence and the "voice of God" narration by John Facenda, delivering dramatic lines such as, "It starts with a whistle, and ends with a gun," and "The autumn wind is a Raider," was supported by the use of montage and slow motion to capture the glory of the game.

Tuckett explained how Facenda came on to the scene and the impact he had.

"Legend has it that John and Big Ed were drinking buddies—or at least in the same bar with other drinking buddies. Facenda was a little tipsy and talking about the Philadelphia Eagles. He was doing a Shakespearean version of an Eagles' play-by-play. Ed heard that and immediately thought, 'I bet that would sound great against our footage.' Being a local guy, literally right around the corner from us, John came in and read a script, and it was so powerful. There was an instantaneous feeling in the room that this was the voice we needed," said Tuckett. "The voice of God. The voice from the burning bush."

NFL Films's work was so good that it was asked to consult on a number of Hollywood pictures, including *Invincible, Jerry Maguire, Rudy, Paper Lion, The Waterboy, Everybody's All-American, Unnecessary Roughness, Black Sunday, Semi-Tough,* and *Brian's Song.*

However, there was one particular motion picture experience that stood out above all for Steve Sabol. He was called in as a technical advisor for a 1969 film titled *Number One,* featuring legendary actor Charlton Heston as a quarterback for the New Orleans Saints.

"They had a couple problems," Sabol recalled. "Most importantly, they couldn't get Mr. Heston to throw the ball properly. I will never forget one of these old Hollywood union grips on the set who had been through countless movies. He was standing next to me and shaking his head as he muttered, 'They can teach the guy to ride a chariot. He can paint the Sistine Chapel. He's Moses able to part the Red Sea, yet the son of a bitch can't throw a spiral!' The old man gave me a whole new respect for how difficult it is to play quarterback in the NFL."[64]

In the early days of its operation it was difficult for NFL Films to get the respect of the players and coaches, who saw the wearing of wires for sound recording as a huge imposition, a violation of the inner sanctum.

"I think the fact that Steve was a jock and I played in the NFL, and we looked at it from the player's point of view, there was a trust factor that may not have been there otherwise," said Tuckett. "Seeing us as more like peers that enabled us to talk to some of these guys and convince more players and coaches to be wired for sound. When others saw the success of it, it became much more easily accomplished."

Even the best coaches eventually embraced it. NFL fans who grew up in the 1970s and 1980s won't forget watching such classic

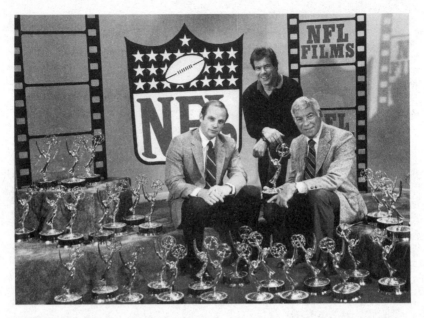

The NFL Films triumvirate of Phil Tuckett (l), Steve Sabol, and founder Ed Sabol (r) with their Emmy Awards.

Phil Tuckett Collection

highlights where Chiefs coach Hank Stram shouts encouragement—"Just keep matriculating the ball down the field, boys!"—or Vince Lombardi bellows, "What the hell is going on out here?! Everybody grabbing, no one tackling."

As a starter for the four-time Super Bowl dynasty Pittsburgh Steelers of the seventies, perhaps safety Mike Wagner put it best in modern context when he said: "I think it's spectacular what NFL Films has accomplished and continues to produce. What you see today when somebody tells a young person about a particular player or particular game, is they break out their cell phone and then look it up on Google. Hey, it's one way for us old guys to be remembered."

CHAPTER FORTY

MY TEAM

Professional football wouldn't be possible if not for the owners, and the recent selection of Jerry Jones into the Pro Football Hall of Fame is certainly a most apt honor for his contributions to the game. (See chapter 25, "Dynasty.")

"Jerry Jones is a perfect example of someone who is willing to risk it all," said Joe Horrigan of the Pro Football Hall of Fame. "A friend once defined an entrepreneur as 'someone willing to risk everything. Not most. Not little. But everything for what he is wanting to achieve.' And that is what Jerry Jones did. He was willing to risk it all. And he literally took a team that was going into bankruptcy and built it into an empire. People say that is an achievement in business, but football is a business."

Early owners operated with business mind-sets, too.

GEORGE PRESTON MARSHALL

One of the more controversial owners, yet one who made crucial contributions to the game beyond his own team, was Boston/Washington Redskins owner (1932–1969), George Preston Marshall.

Working from a firm philosophy that football was entertainment, Marshall was less an *x*'s and *o*'s owner than he was a flamboyant showman with a flair for promotion. He was looking to expand his fan base to include women, children, and casual football fans, which he did by pioneering gala halftime pageants (including circus acts and Hollywood performers) and creating a fight song, "Hail to the Redskins," the first of its kind. He wanted Sunday afternoons to be a more festive, family friendly affair.

More important for the league as a whole, however, Marshall sponsored many of the NFL's rule changes during the thirties and forties designed mostly to help open up the game. One was to allow a forward pass to be thrown from anywhere behind the line of scrimmage, rather than at a minimum of five yards behind the line, which was previously the rule. Another was the move of the goal posts from the end line to the goal line, to encourage the kicking of field goals. This change remained in place for nearly four decades until NFL goal posts were returned to the end line in the mid-1970s as part of an effort to decrease the influence on the game of kicking specialists. Marshall was also the main force behind splitting the league into two divisions and establishing a definitive annual championship game.

Despite his penchant for forward-looking adjustments to gameplay, the Redskins owner was, sadly, the last to integrate, infamously stating, "We'll start signing Negroes when the Harlem Globetrotters start signing whites."

Bobby Mitchell would become the first African American football player to play a game for the Redskins, and he played with the team from 1962 through 1969, initially at running back, but making his biggest impact at wide receiver.

SONNY WERBLIN

About the time Mitchell arrived in Washington, over in the American Football League, the floundering New York franchise was threatening to sink the entire league until an investment group led by Hollywood executive Sonny Werblin took over as owners and implemented major changes.

"As New York goes, so goes the league," was a popular saying in sports. In 1962, as Titans owner Harry Wismer was losing $2 million, he desperately pledged his share of income from the league TV contract as collateral against a $190,000 loan, but the money ran out before the team's early-season trip to the West Coast. The fans had all but disappeared, to be replaced by a growing army of creditors.[65]

Werblin, a vice president at MCA, the world's largest talent agency and president of MCA—TV a subsidiary, was familiar with the situation since it was his company that helped negotiate the league's first TV contract. Establishing a syndicate to avoid antitrust problems, Werblin's group of businessmen purchased the New York Titans club from bankruptcy court for $1 million. The sale became final in February 1963.

Using his influence and extensive show business acumen, Werblin instituted a whirlwind of moves. He changed the team's name to the Jets, their colors to green and white, hired a two-time NFL championship coach in Weeb Ewbank, and snatched coveted Ohio State University running back Matt Snell away from crosstown rival the New York Giants (he'd become the 1964 AFL rookie of the year). The only thing left to do was to recruit a potential superstar, someone to light up the marquee and dominate the media capital headlines.

By drafting and signing Alabama quarterback Joe Namath to an unprecedented $427,000 contract—nearly half the price Werblin and his partners paid for the entire franchise!—the Hollywood executive made a huge publicity score in finding the star he was looking for. That deal's impact reached well beyond Jets fans. Soon

Former 49ers owner Eddie DeBartolo is welcomed into the Pro Football Hall of Fame by a few of his HOF players: (l-r) Charles Haley, Steve Young, Ronnie Lott, Jerry Rice, and Joe Montana.

Courtesy Terrell Lloyd, San Francisco 49ers

"Broadway Joe" became the biggest attraction in all of football. And would culminate with the milestone win in Super Bowl III.

EDDIE DEBARTOLO

Super Bowl victories would be how Eddie DeBartolo, owner of the San Francisco 49ers beginning in 1977, would measure success. Under his tenure, the Niners averaged 13 wins per season, including the playoffs, from 1981 to 1998—not including the strike-shortened 1982 season. They made the playoffs 16 times and won five Super Bowls.

"Eddie DeBartolo set the tone as an owner who cared about every person, their job, and winning," David Baker, president of the Pro Football Hall of Fame said. "Before the season he would sit down with every person in the organization—groundskeepers, equipment manager and he'd ask each one question. What do you need to win a Super Bowl? Eddie didn't have the time to do that. He made the time to do it."

"I think the one thing Eddie did, was the best thing that he did and that is he cared so much," said San Francisco safety Ronnie Lott. "There are a lot of people that say they care and there are others that walk the walk. What I always thought was amazing was our owner's intensity. It could be the way that he walked in the locker room or the way he walked out of the locker room and being stubborn about moments. No owner cared like our owner did. Not even the great Paul Brown who was an owner that coached."

Growing up in Youngstown, Ohio, DeBartolo had access to the family's company season tickets to the Cleveland Browns games, and even though Pittsburgh was closer, he was always a die-hard Cleveland Browns fan. The teen enjoyed the likes of Jim Brown, quarterback Milt Plum and receiver Gary Collins. And despite not being able to land the deal with his father to purchase the favorite team of his youth when it became available, he ended up coming out West as a young man and making his own way as the owner of the 49ers.

Learning from his dad, who operated a very successful real estate business with the philosophy that he'd paid for the best but also expected only the best from them in return, the 49ers' new boss ensured that his teams always traveled in style and comfort, on large, wide-body planes, and each player had his own hotel room, when that mentality of luxury hadn't yet set in leaguewide.

After hiring Bill Walsh as head coach, the two fostered a competitive but nurturing environment.

"I think what made Eddie DeBartolo a great owner was that he was like a twelfth man," Jerry Rice said. "So supportive, he was going to get you everything that you needed. Travel and accommodations were first class. Excellent training facilities. The only thing he wanted in return: win Super Bowls. That was the bottom line."

AL DAVIS

Across the bay, the Oakland Raiders' Al Davis also prioritized winning. In fact, his mantra, "Just Win Baby," became the unofficial slogan of the team.

Driven, dedicated, and knowledgeable, a graduate of Erasmus High School in Brooklyn followed by college at Syracuse University, Davis committed himself at a young age to the sport and gained experience as a scout, coach, and executive (including a brief stint as Commissioner of the AFL), all of which served him well as the owner of the Raiders.

In 1960, Head Coach Sid Gillman hired Davis as offensive end coach of the newly formed Los Angeles Chargers. After two division championships in just three years there, it was on to meet the challenges with the Raiders of Oakland in 1963. Just 33, Davis was the youngest man in pro football to hold the demanding dual positions of head coach and general manager. He turned the franchise around.

Beginning that year and going to 1992, the Oakland/LA Raiders owned a winning percentage of .661, 285 wins, 146 losses, 11 ties, the best among all major sports teams. It was a reign that saw the Raiders make 18 postseason appearances and win three Super Bowls.

"You loved and hated him," said running back Pete Banaszak, who spent his entire career, from 1966 to 1978, playing for Davis. "I remember Fred Biletnikoff yelling at him with every cussword he could think of

Raiders owner Al Davis (middle) operated one of the most successful franchises in team sports history.

right to his face. Al just waved him off and, in that Brooklyn-esque accent, said, 'Ah, ya bastard, don't bring ethnics into this.' Fred retorts with more expletives. Then the next day, you see them walking arm-in-arm down the sidewalk. It was like *One Flew over the Cuckoo's Nest* there.

"I remember we'd be practicing on one end of the field, and Al would be all the way on the other end watching us leaning against the goalpost a hundred yards away. He has a hand up near his face so he could watch his Super Bowl ring shine in the sun. Al was eccentric, but you know what? He was a good man. I remember being at training camp one time, and my daughter got really sick. We thought she might have cancer. Long story short, it was some sort of infection. Al came up to me and said, 'I know it is bothering you. Why don't you go on home to see how your daughter is.' I never forgot that. Al was somebody special, and he always seemed to be able to push the right button with you."

Sometimes though, Davis could be very stubborn. One of the more notable instances, besides the saga of his fight with the league to move his franchise to Los Angeles, was his feud with star running back Marcus Allen. For reasons never fully explained, the former USC all-American—who won rookie of the year, Super Bowl MVP, and NFL MVP awards as the star runner in the Raiders backfield—had been dropped down in the depth chart and was wasting away gathering splinters on the bench.

"I never quite understood what made things go bad," Allen said in a 2012 documentary. In 1993 he signed with the Kansas City Chiefs, earning comeback player of the year, and played five solid seasons with the Raiders' hated rivals.

But the GM-owner also made some brilliant moves with personnel, reviving careers where others saw no possibilities.

For all intents and purposes quarterback Jim Plunkett's career should have ended after two mediocre years with the 49ers, who acquired him from New England in a trade before the 1976 season.

But the Raiders owner picked him up off waivers for $100 before the 1978 season. He then patiently worked on rebuilding Plunkett's health and confidence and by the time starting quarterback Dan Pastorini went down to injury early in the 1980 season, Plunkett stepped in brilliantly. He won NFL comeback player of the year after leading the Raiders to a victory over Philadelphia in Super Bowl XV. He won a second Super Bowl ring in 1983 after replacing an injured Marc Wilson.

Davis's keen eye extended to having the vision of how a fading star player could help him in a completely different position.

"One of the genius things of Al Davis was in acquiring Billy [Cannon] from the Oilers and converted him to a tight end," said Cannon's All-Pro blocker in Houston, Bob Talamini. "That was an unusual turn of events as the number one runner in the country for years, Billy, who could not maneuver as well in traffic, could now get the ball more often in the open field as the tight end, which had become more of an integral part of the offense by then. Billy became even more dangerous from that position."

In terms of positioning, the Raiders enjoyed a mystique as a bunch of thrashing renegades, a reputation the owner didn't mind (he loved to intimidate) and was enhanced by the popular "the autumn wind is a Raider" program by NFL Films. They were a polarizing franchise. Loved and hated. Like their maverick owner who took on the league alone, it was a team filled with outcasts who banded together against everyone else. Many in the media (and more than a few opposing players) called them thugs as they often led the league in penalties. But they also won . . . a lot.

"When you play for the Raiders, you play to win and you play tough. It's not something the coaches teach or talk about. It's just there, like in the air. It's an attitude—you are going to hit people and smash them if you are a Raider," said linebacker Phil Villapiano, who played nine years for Davis. "It is such a freeing feeling. So much fun."

THE EVERLASTING TEAM

Canton. The mere word conjures up football glory. From the sport's early roots when names like Jim Thorpe and words like "dynasty" first appeared, to the modern era when a player hears the words, "he's headed to Canton," there is no greater individual accolade in the sport.

Canton, Ohio, is the home of the Pro Football Hall of Fame. And of the 24,000 athletes who have played professional football since 1920, just over 300 are enshrined there.

As the culmination of a career that they gave their blood, sweat, and heart to, it is a very special feeling, clearly quite a distinctive one, for a player knowing they are now part of an everlasting team.

To get an understanding of what it means to receive this recognition, we've asked a few honorees to try and put it into words:

"It is about as personal as you can get. It is the ultimate compliment. And it is permanent. You don't have to explain anything. Someone calls you a Hall of Famer, that says it all," stated Kansas City Chiefs quarterback Len Dawson, a 1987 enshrinee who grew up and played high school ball in the Canton area.

Denver Broncos running back Floyd Little, who finished his career as the seventh all-time leading rusher, was known for his patience, waiting for his blockers to create a hole. But that was nothing compared with his patience and subsequent appreciation for being enshrined into the house of the sport's immortals.

"It is the greatest honor an athlete can receive in my opinion. My entire life has changed since I was voted into the Hall of Fame. Every player who has played this game, their whole desire is to get into the Hall. There is such disappointment when it does not happen. I was passed over for forty-four years." Ironically that was the former NFL rushing leader's uniform number.

Jan Stenerud was the first pure kicker enshrined and was greeted by his new teammates with tidings like—"you're in forever." "You can't get cut from this team." "You can't even die from this team." "Over the years

I have met many more and some of the greatest from a given position. They are so humbled by it. They have a number on the inside of the sport coat. When I got in, I was number one hundred sixty."

"Hard to describe, but it is one of those high honors that I cherish and value. It is one of those like a gift that keeps on giving," said Detroit Lions running back Barry Sanders. "You think about all the great players in there that had an influence on me that I grew up watching, then learn that I had influence on others who came after me. There is nothing like actually being able to play the game at that level. The Hall of Fame reminds me of that. And my appreciation for that honor increases in value with each passing year."

Barry Sanders's number one fan: his mother, Shirley Ann.

Courtesy Sanders Family Collection

CHAPTER FORTY-ONE

NOW, THAT WAS SUPER

Some of the NFL's most memorable plays have taken place in the sport's biggest game, the Super Bowl:

- New York Giants receiver David Tyree makes an incredible "helmet" catch to help ruin the Patriots' bid for a perfect season.
- The New Orleans Saints stun the world, opening the second half with an onside kick resulting in a score that would be significant in defeating the Colts.
- Just as Seattle is poised to come from behind and win on the game's last possession, undrafted rookie defensive back Malcom Butler's goal-line interception preserves New England's victory.
- Rams linebacker Mike Jones's sure tackle of Titans receiver Kevin Dyson at the 1-yard line in the waning seconds of regulation prevents Tennessee from at least tying the game and sending it into overtime.

There have also been entire Super Bowl games that have reflected all the excitement, drama, and thrills that the two best teams of that season can offer when they exchange heavyweight blows in an effort to complete a hard-fought season with the title of world champion. Here are a few of the best.

PLAYING THE STEELERS, IT'S CURTAINS

Down in Miami at the Orange Bowl on January 18, 1976, Super Bowl X marked the first time that two teams that had already won a Super Bowl would face each other. The defending champion Pittsburgh Steelers had to go through the Dallas Cowboys in order to retain their crown. Both were loaded with talent. Both had tremendous coaches.

Things however did not start out well for the champs. In Pittsburgh's first possession, punter Bobby Walden fumbled the snap and the 11-yard loss set Dallas up on the Steelers' 29-yard line. The Cowboys, the first wild card team to ever reach the NFL finals, wasted no time as Roger Staubach immediately connected with Drew Pearson on a 29-yard pass play for a touchdown. First quarter, 7–0 Dallas.

However, the Steelers' emerging young star, wide receiver Lynn Swann, hospitalized only two weeks earlier with a concussion and dropping passes in practice, began playing with defenders' heads. He delivered the equalizer moments later as Terry Bradshaw brought the Steelers right back. Key to the eight-play, 67-yard drive was Swann maneuvering his body to make an all-time great catch along the sidelines for 32 yards despite Dallas defender Mark Washington draped all over him.

"Not only were his body and the ball out-of-bounds, but also Lynn literally running down the sideline made the adjustments with his hands then contorts his body to get both feet in-bounds. My gosh, that was as incredible a catch as you will ever see, especially in a game of that magnitude," Bradshaw said.[66]

Steelers defensive stalwart Joe Greene, who'd felt a twinge in his neck earlier, was standing on the sidelines with a perfect view.

"After they scored a touchdown, I was moving very poorly and not putting any pressure on the quarterback. I left mid–first quarter and did not come back. I was a cheerleader. I was in a great seat to watch Lynn Swann levitate."

Despite tremendous firepower on both offenses, this game would be primarily a defensive struggle and points were going to be hard to come by.

That meant field position, and the kicking game would be crucial (evidenced by the blocked punt).

Dallas's Toni Fritsch's 36-yard field goal gave Dallas a 10–7 lead at the half, which stood up through the third quarter as both team's defenses continued to dominate.

His counterpart, Roy Gerela, was having an off-day. His first kickoff was returned by Thomas "Hollywood" Henderson for 48 yards, stopping only when Gerela tackled Henderson. The tackle left Gerela with cracked ribs, and the injury, combined with the swirling winds at the Orange Bowl, led to Gerela missing a 36-yard field goal attempt in the second quarter.

Things didn't get any better for the Pittsburgh kicker at the start of the second half. Though Steelers defensive back J. T. Thomas picked off Staubach to give Pittsburgh the ball at the Cowboys' 25-yard line, the Steelers came up short and Gerela was called in to kick a field goal that would even the game at 10. Gerela, who had only missed two field goals inside the 40 all year, proceeded to miss his second one of the game.

However, as Dallas defender Cliff Harris taunted Gerela about the missed opportunity, the kicker's teammate Jack Lambert stormed over.

"The wind was blowing pretty stiff straight across the field from my right to left, especially at the goal-line area. With the swirling wind, the ball made a quick fade just before the uprights and barely missed," Gerela recalled. "Cliff Harris watches the ball miss, then says, 'Hey, good kick; keep it going.' I push him with my forearm, trying get him out of my face. Then Jack saw that and reacted instantly, throwing Cliff to the ground."

In the ebb and flow of a tightly fought contest, the Lambert incident (which teammate Andy Russell said easily could have been called a penalty) was a momentum game changer. Lambert played like a man possessed, firing up his teammates, and Gerela found his footing.

Playing through the throbbing pain, Gerela nailed two fourth-quarter field goals, giving Pittsburgh a 15–10 lead. The Steelers made it 21–10 on a terrific 64-yard touchdown pass from Bradshaw to Lynn Swann. However, behind Staubach, aka Captain Comeback, the Cowboys drove 80 yards in five plays with under two minutes to play to make the score 21–17. On the drive, two passes of 30 and 11 yards from Staubach to Drew Pearson proved the key, leading to a 34-yard scoring pass.

Things were a bit out of rhythm for Pittsburgh because Bradshaw got knocked dizzy on his 64-yard pass to Swann. In stepped backup Terry Hanratty, who could not do much against the reenergized Dallas defense.

Facing fourth down and 9 to go on the Dallas 41 with only 1:28 left to play, coach Chuck Noll decided to gamble, his decision influenced by the fact that Dallas had no time-outs left. Rather than punt and risk the runback, he had the Steelers go for the run. Five plays later the game was over. Pittsburgh held on to win, 21–17.

Celebrating in the locker room, Steelers teammates reflected back on that play by their middle linebacker and his subsequent dominating impact.

"Lambert got us going, you could just feel it," Joe Greene said. "Lambert was feeling it as in between plays he was ranting and raving at everything psyching himself into a frenzy."

Lambert had 14 tackles that game, but it was a rather unusual inspirational lift (and throw down, a sort of uncredited 15th tackle) that unleashed the team's spirit that guided Pittsburgh over Dallas in Super Bowl X.

"That guy's gotta learn the Steelers don't get intimidated," said Lambert after the game. "So, I decided to do something."

The two teams faced off again three years later in Super Bowl XIII, once again at the Orange Bowl in Miami. This time the Dallas Cowboys were defending champions. However, both the Pittsburgh and Dallas players knew after the final whistle blew at the Orange Bowl this time, one franchise was going to become the first team to win three Super Bowls. One team would lay claim to being the team of the 1970s.

What had not diffused since their last meeting was the perceptions of the teams and how they viewed themselves. The Steelers were basic. Blue collar and smash mouth. The Cowboys high-tech and flashy. With a flex defense and motion offense, Tom Landry's schemes and playbook required a lot of study. Pittsburgh felt they hid behind a bunch of gimmicks compared with their straight-up intimidating approach that Dallas thought relied too much on brawn and less on brain.

As a matter of fact, motivated after Dallas Cowboys linebacker Thomas "Hollywood" Henderson declared to a group of reporters during the week of Super Bowl XIII, that "[Terry] Bradshaw couldn't spell *cat* if you spotted him the *c* and the *t*," the Steelers' quarterback did not fall for the bait and would let his play do the talking.

In 1978, rule changes preventing contact with receivers beyond five yards from the line of scrimmage opened up the passing game. Bradshaw adapted well. Throwing the ball often to new deep threats Lynn Swann and John Stallworth, he totaled 28 passing TDs, 10 more than his career best, and in guiding his team to a 14-2 record, Bradshaw was voted AP NFL MVP and went to his first Pro Bowl. And even though he preferred the controlled offense of rushing and short passes, the "whatever it takes" mantra of Pittsburgh coach

Chuck Noll overrode his own basic philosophy, feeling in this case it would be the deep ball that would be the difference in defeating Dallas.

Bradshaw struck pay dirt first. Taking advantage of a Dallas fumble, he hit John Stallworth for a 28-yard touchdown. But in a similar situation, the Cowboys evened things at 7 after they recovered a fumble and Staubach connected with Tony Hill up the left side for a 39-yard scoring play.

On Pittsburgh's first possession of the second quarter, linebacker Mike Hegman took Bradshaw's fumble to the house 37 yards away, but just two minutes later, things were even once again after Stallworth broke Aaron Kyle's tackle on a short pass and galloped to a 75-yard TD.

Following up on a Staubach interception by Mel Blount, Bradshaw completed a pair of passes to Swann for 29 and 21 yards. Then, with less than 30 seconds in the half, on third-and-1, Bradshaw rolled out right and connected on a 7-yard TD pass play to running back Rocky Bleier.

The 21–14 halftime score nearly duplicated the final score of their Super Bowl X encounter (21–17).

After both teams made adjustments to slow down the offensive show (at least for the third quarter), Dallas had a terrific opportunity to tie the game in the middle of that period. After several runs by Tony Dorsett, including a 7-yard run up the middle, Dallas had a third-and-3 from the Pittsburgh 10-yard line; however, in a play that will live in infamy, future Hall of Fame tight end Jackie Smith, alone in the end zone, dropped Staubach's pass, and the drive yielded only a field goal.

Players from both sides point to that dropped pass as a turning point.

"Yes, the score at the time was 21–14. If Jackie makes the catch, the game is tied," Steelers defensive tackle Joe Greene said. "I got blocked but saw the throw. It zipped past my head, but it was slightly low and behind Jackie. Jackie had the opportunity to catch the pass, and he'll tell you he'd make it nine times out of ten, but he didn't here, and that denied the Cowboys from gaining momentum."

"I went over to Jackie and said, 'I know how you feel,'" recalled Jethro Pugh, Dallas's veteran defensive tackle. "The thing about it, in the final practice, Coach Landry says, 'All right, let's do this one more time, because it is a sure touchdown.' When Coach Landry called that play in the game, everybody stood up from the bench just to watch. Because it was a sure touchdown, and everybody wanted to see it. He drops it."

Momentum seemed to swing Pittsburgh's way from there. First, a controversial pass interference call against Benny Barnes moved the Steelers deep into Dallas territory, leading to a Franco Harris 22-yard touchdown run. A special-teams fumble would lead to another Steelers score, as Bradshaw connected with a brilliant pass to a leaping Lynn Swann in the back of the end zone. It gave them a commanding 18-point lead with less than seven minutes left in the game.

"I am on the wedge as part of the kick return team. I have a broken thumb. Roy Gerela squib-kicked the ball. I pick it up and start running, get hit, and fumble it. Pittsburgh recovered it, and two plays later, they score a touchdown," Randy White explained. "Now, everybody blames Jackie Smith for dropping that pass in the end zone, but that fumble is a play that will haunt me until the day I die."

But as Bradshaw reminded his Steelers defense, Dallas had a leader with a relentless reputation.

"Staubach was deadly, and he had no quit in him. You always had to be on your toes against him, or he would tear you apart. He was very, very competitive, that is for sure," said Steelers safety Mike Wagner.

Sure enough, Captain Comeback scrambles for 18 yards, hits tight end DuPree and running back Dorsett with key passes, and, along with a 29-yard run by Dorsett, Dallas scores to make it 35–24. The Steelers' Tony Dungy touches Rafael Septien's onside attempt, and Dallas recovers. After the two-minute warning, Staubach, spreading the ball around to Dorsett and Drew Pearson, finds Butch Johnson for a 4-yard score to close it to 35–31.

But after Pittsburgh safely secured the onside kick, Bradshaw and his team could finally let out that much-needed sigh of relief. After taking a knee twice, Bradshaw completed his MVP performance, in which he threw for a career-high 318 yards and four touchdowns (a SB record at the time). It was one of the greatest games of his illustrious career.

Though Dallas won more games in the 1970s than any other franchise and appeared in five Super Bowls (its three losses were by a combined 11 points), it would be Pittsburgh who earned the title of the team of the seventies as well as the first team to win three Super Bowls.

Ever the competitor, Staubach still often thinks back about those two Super Bowl games.

"We had a tremendous decade, but Pittsburgh sent the message they were the team of the seventies. We would've been had we won that game. I'm grateful for the wins we've had, but yes I am very competitive and hate to lose," he said half-laughing. "To this day I still remember many details of those two Super Bowl losses to the Steelers. But Pittsburgh was a great team no doubt. It really was the best against the best, so what did it mean to not only lose another SB but to do so against the Steelers? And both games by only a combined 8 points!"

ONE MORE SHOT AT GLORY

Coach Noll was driving and squeezing a now aging, yet still deeply talented and more savvy Steelers club to one last hurrah.

In 1979 Pittsburgh suffered injuries early in the regular season to several offensive starters, but wide receiver John Stallworth picked up the slack, producing a tremendous All-Pro season with 70 catches for more than 1,100 yards. Steady Franco Harris rushed for more than 1,000 yards, as the Steelers had a 12-4 season, then knocked off the Dolphins and Oilers in the playoffs to face the unheralded Los Angeles Rams in Super Bowl XIV.

"Well, if you think of what we accomplished, we were the first to win three and we were staring at number four. And what about injuries? Just the odds to overcome seemed daunting to overcome all the obstacles and you get to the place you aim for at the end of the season and we are there," Stallworth said.

Despite winning five of their last seven, the Rams' 9-7 record was among the poorest of all the NFL playoff teams. Yes, they did upset Dallas in the playoffs, but their unimpressive 9–0 win over the Tampa Bay Buccaneers in the NFC championship game made them underdogs, as Pittsburgh was favored by 11.

The odds against Los Angeles were not helped by the fact that they were still slowed by key injuries—cornerback Rod Perry (knee and concussion), safety Dave Elmendorf (neck), linebacker Jim Youngblood (shoulder). Star defensive end Jack Youngblood would play with a fractured leg suffered in the playoffs. Offensively, starting quarterback Pat Haden was lost for the season with a broken finger. Super Bowl XIV would be just the eighth start for his replacement, Vince Ferragamo.

Ferragamo, a third-year pro, did not have impressive stats during the regular season (even dipping under a 50 QB rating at one point) and was even benched for a pair of games due to poor play. However, he did lead the team to wins in four of their last five games, including an overtime win over the rival 49ers. And thanks to outdueling Staubach with three touchdown passes including his 50-yard game clincher to wide receiver Billy Waddy, Ferragamo led a stunning playoff upset over the Cowboys in Dallas.

However, the Rams had only the sixth best record in the NFC (and the poorest record of any team entering a Super Bowl).

The Pittsburgh Steelers had won Super Bowl IX and X primarily on their superb defense, but that Steel Curtain was showing signs of rust heading into their tilt against the Rams.

Giving up 262 points during the regular season was the most a Steelers defensive unit had yielded going all the way back to 1971, which was the last season they did not qualify for the playoffs. Pittsburgh was good and sporadically great, but it no longer dominated opponents on a regular basis.

One advantage the Rams had was the fact their defensive coordinator, Bud Carson, had an intimate knowledge of the Steelers, having been their defensive coordinator for six years before coming to Los Angeles. They also had two other coaches that were formerly on the Pittsburgh coaching staff: offensive coordinator Lionel Taylor and defensive line coach Dan Radakovich. Combined, the staff had a detailed understanding of Pittsburgh's personnel and schemes, an asset that literally gave Terry Bradshaw nightmares leading up to the game.

"They knew we preferred basic fronts," he said. "Full right split. Open right. Flood right opposite. They knew our plays. They knew our audibles. They knew how we liked to attack certain fronts. They knew our adjustments on routes. And, frankly, all that got in my head. We were heavily favored, and nothing is scarier than facing upstarts. That is what we were in Super Bowl IX. Plus, we were playing in Los Angeles. It just seemed to me everything was against us. Everything. And I fought that feeling all week. It was mental torture the entire time. I'm tossing and turning: 'They know everything, they know everything, they know everything, they know everything.' And . . . they did!"

Come game time, Pittsburgh opened the score with a Matt Bahr 41-yard field goal. Ferragamo then led the Rams on an 8-play drive to score the game's first touchdown. Bradshaw would give Pittsburgh the lead back after a 9-play, 53-yard drive culminated in Franco Harris's 1-yard score, which would be the only touchdown for the Steelers in the first half. Carson's defense was familiarizing itself with Pittsburgh's patterns, even adjusting well to Bradshaw's audibles. The Rams forced a three-and-out, and on Pittsburgh's next possession, Bradshaw threw an interception that safety Dave Elmendorf took back to the Steelers' 39. On top of that, Ferragamo managed to get the Rams into position on a pair of drives that yielded two Frank Corral field goals, and Los Angeles went into the locker room at the half nursing a 13–10 lead and feeling very confident.

What took place at intermission in the defending champion's locker room was a bit out of character. "In all the years we played together, it was at halftime of Super Bowl XIV that Terry talked for the first time," said Steelers defensive anchor Joe Greene. "He spoke up, basically saying we have to be at our best to beat this team, and right now we are not there. We did not come here to lose this ballgame. He put forth a tremendous effort."

Upon returning to the field, Bradshaw indeed ignited a spark. A 47-yard touchdown bomb to Swann put the Steelers up early in the third, 17–13. But on LA's next possession, after Ferragamo connected with Waddy for a 50-yard play, running back Lawrence McCutcheon connected with speedy receiver Ron Smith on an option pass for a 24-yard score, and the Rams took back the lead, 19–17. Their defense kept Bradshaw and company in check, picking him off twice, and for the third time, the Rams ended a quarter holding the lead.

The Rams' knowledge of the Steelers' offensive tendencies led to one of their biggest opportunities late in the game. "We knew that if Bradshaw ever left the pocket, he always scrambled to his right— again, a key fact we got from Bud Carson's time in Pittsburgh. And whenever he scrambled, Terry always looked for his wide receivers," said Rams safety Nolan Cromwell, the 1980 NFL defensive player of the year, still wincing at the memory. "I was in a great position to make the play, and I flat out dropped it. It was a huge play, because if I would have caught it and kept on running, I looked up, and there was nobody to stop me from scoring." The play would have given the

Rams a 9-point lead in the fourth quarter and, quite possibly, an upset win.

But then Pittsburgh would prove why they had won three Lombardi Trophies in five seasons. Bradshaw, who was absolutely driven to never experience losing a Super Bowl, recalled what happened next.

"I remember being behind heading into the fourth quarter, and I'm standing on the sidelines and Chuck [Noll] says, 'we're not gonna beat these guys running. We're not gonna beat these guys on possession passes. We are going to beat these guys throwing the football deep.' I said, 'ok.' He said, 'let's go, open right 60 prevent, slot hook and go.' I tell Chuck, 'I haven't completed that since I don't when, but I will give it a shot.'"

On third and 8 from their own 27, Bradshaw connected on a perfect throw to Stallworth over the deep middle that resulted in a 73-yard scoring play. Pittsburgh went back on top, 24–19.

In front of a riveted, excited crowd of nearly 104,000 packed into the Rose Bowl, witnessing one of the most exciting Super Bowls of all time, the magical day Ferragamo was having looked like he just might bring his team back for a victory. With sharp running by Wendell Tyler and getting passes to his wide outs Preston Dennard and Billy Waddy, the confident quarterback, playing like a poised veteran, engineered a drive that broke into Steelers territory. It is then that the clock struck midnight.

With visions of taking his team in for the go-ahead and potentially game-clinching score, on first-and-10 from the Steelers 32, Ferragamo dropped back and saw Billy Waddy and Preston Dennard, but what he didn't see was Steeler Jack Lambert. The gap-toothed linebacker picked off the pass. Pittsburgh added an insurance touchdown and though the underdog Rams gave it all they had, Pittsburgh had won its fourth Super Bowl in six years.

The Rams' quarterback was philosophical about coming up short in one of the most entertaining Super Bowls of all time.

"Really the only difference in the game was that they made just one more big play than we did. We had chances, but when the chips were down, they came through and that was the difference. Everybody on the Rams played their heart out. Pittsburgh was just better. We were going up against the best of all time, the Steelers were really phenomenal."

In the waning moments of the game, knowing it was the end of a dynasty, Bradshaw reflected.

"I remember standing in the huddle I was almost giddy with relief. I remember just looking around the crowd and just took it in. I heard the roars, the screams because normally you block that out. I took it all in because I knew that this was it, that we will not be back again. I think that had a lot to do with me just savoring that precious moment. The first to win back to back, first to win three, first to win four in six years. It all flowed through me at that instant."

GOLD RUSH

While there were a few moments the Cincinnati Bengals' players could savor in their fine performance in Super Bowl XXIII, their memories would be forever tainted when, as their All-Pro quarterback Boomer Esiason would say: "It was well played and competitive; that is why it really came down to their ninety-two-yard drive. That is when Joe Montana and Jerry Rice basically took over, making plays to show why they were future Hall of Famers. Because they did it on the grandest of stages. And did it on a very high level."

On January 22, 1989, with more than 75,000 in attendance at Joe Robbie Stadium and a hundred million viewing on television, the 12-4 Bengals were facing the 10-6 49ers in the NFL finale.

Behind a talented front line led by Max Montoya and Anthony Munoz (Munoz was named the NFL offensive lineman of the year for the third time in his career and was selected to play in the Pro

Bowl for the eighth consecutive season), Esiason had an amazing season. The southpaw threw for 3,572 yards and 28 touchdown passes, with only 14 interceptions, making him the top-rated quarterback in the league with a 97.4 passer rating and earning him the NFL Most Valuable Player Award.

Tight end Rodney Holman was a Pro Bowl teammate, while Eddie Brown was the leading receiver. James Brooks, Ickey Woods, and Stanley Wilson filled out the backfield. Wilson, the team's key tough-yards guy, was found the night before in his hotel room by Coach Wyche in a drug-induced haze. He would be unavailable. Defensively, Cincy was led by Pro Bowl defensive backs Eric Thomas and David Fulcher (part of the Swat Team), who combined for 12 interceptions. A strong defensive line was keyed by Pro Bowl defensive tackle Tim Krumrie.

They'd need to be strong in taking on a 49er's offense featuring Joe Montana, Jerry Rice, and Roger Craig, with their own fine line, including Randy Cross and Jesse Sapolu. Charles Haley and an aggressive backfield led by safety Ronnie Lott anchored the defense.

Despite the two powerful offenses, in a very competitive first half, it would be defense that dominated. Each team, however, would suffer injuries to a starter. On the first series after the kickoff, 49ers OT Steve Wallace was sidelined with a broken ankle, a loss of one of their best blockers.

After an exchange of punts, the Bengals' All-Pro defensive tackle Tim Krumrie was injured on a freak play when he planted his foot and his left leg snapped in two places. The injury came on the first play of a 73-yard, 13-play San Francisco drive that culminated in Mike Cofer's 41-yard field goal.

"The heart and soul of our defense was instantly gone," said Esiason. "You really can't quantify how great a player he was to our team until he was out."

Krumrie, a team leader, explained what happened on the gruesome play that had the stadium gasping then sitting in stunned silence.

"Nobody hit me. I did not trip over anybody. I just planted. It buckled. I looked down and it was facing the other way. I try to get up. I couldn't, then said a few choice words. Everyone said it must have really hurt, and I said I don't really know because I was so pumped up with adrenaline. It was a self-inflicted situation.

"So, they put me on a stretcher took me to the locker room. The medical folks said they were going to give me some medication and then take me to the hospital.

"I said, 'no that is not going to happen. I wanted TV and some beer.' They talked about taking medication because they wanted to set my leg then. I said no. I asked the cop standing nearby for a bullet. He said no, they hand me a towel. While I bit it, they set it. No painkiller."

With an exchange of field goals, the game was knotted at 3 during intermission.

"When the players came in the locker room at halftime and saw me, they said, 'Wow, you still here?!'" recalled Krumrie. "I said, 'Hey, guys, I want to see you win a championship.'"

His teammates gave it all they had but ultimately would come up short. After another exchange of field goals in the third quarter, Cincy's Stanford Jennings took a kickoff 93 yards for the game's first touchdown, making it 13–6 Bengals. But on the following possession, Montana and Rice were finding their rhythm. Opening up the fourth quarter, Montana connected with Craig on a 40-yard pass play, and that set up a 14-yard touchdown pass to Rice. Game tied at 13.

But NFL MVP Esiason was finding his rhythm too. On a 10-play, 46-yard drive that took more than five minutes off the clock, the Bengals' QB took his team from its own 32 to the 49ers' 22, where Jim Breech put his team ahead by connecting on a 40-yard field goal.

Down 16–13 with just over three minutes left, and having to start from his own 8-yard line after an illegal block penalty during the kickoff, Joe Montana explained what he was thinking (that is, after he tried to lighten things up by asking his teammates during the TV time-out, "Hey, isn't that John Candy?" pointing to the crowd at the other end of the field).

"At that point, all we were thinking about was getting a field goal to tie. We had a lot of time to do that. It wasn't like we were staring at fifty seconds left. For good NFL offenses three minutes and twenty seconds is an eternity," Montana said. "So, our goal was to get to the twenty-five yard line for a field goal, and if we could reach that area with some time left on the clock, we could take some shots at the end zone."

Montana completed short passes to Craig, Frank, and Rice then a Craig run made it to their own 30 at the two-minute warning. That was followed by 17- and 13-yard passes to Rice and Craig that put San Francisco into Cincy territory on its 35.

He might have been Joe Cool on the outside, but Montana was fighting an internal foe at the most crucial time. On first-and-10, as he dropped back, the 49ers quarterback found himself suddenly hyperventilating and dizzy, with blurred vision.

"I don't know exactly what happened, but since I don't normally eat much before a game, I had tried some ginseng and stuff to give you energy, but in the end, I think I ran out of fuel," said Montana. "I was dizzy heading to the line, and, unfortunately, when I dropped back, I knew Jerry was wide open, and I tossed it away. If I know Bill, he was probably saying on the sideline, 'What in hell was *that*?' I remember one time I threw a really bad interception, and I walked over to him after the turnover, and he said, 'What was that?' with this attitude. I said, 'That was an interception, Coach.' I never walked by him again after an interception," the 49ers' quarterback said, laughing.

Joe looked to the sidelines and pointed in circles to his head to let Coach Walsh know he was dizzy on that play, but then quickly realized if Coach thought something was wrong, he'd take him out. So, Montana promptly staggered back to the huddle.

"Breaking the huddle, I started getting dizzier. Then, putting my hands under center, it seemed to go away, and I said to myself, 'Okay, I'm good.' But as soon as I started to drop back, the dizziness returned. So instead of taking any chances, I turned and just threw it away. What is weird was that that feeling never came back."

And the comeback continued. After an illegal man downfield penalty made it second and 20 from the 45, wide receiver Jerry Rice explained what happened next:

I run a square in route across midfield and was able to elude three defenders for a 27-yard gain. The play gave us a first-and-ten from the Bengals' 18-yard line. After Joe connects with a pass to Roger that goes for eight yards, we take our second time-out with just thirty-nine seconds left. It is second down and two from the Cincinnati ten-yard line.

Coach Wyche would later say that if it came down to one play, he thought that they'd go to me. And after three catches on that drive it would figure we'd try it again, but Coach Walsh knew Coach Wyche was likely thinking that way, so he decided to make me a decoy.

So, the play was called "twenty halfback curl x up" where Roger is the primary receiver and John the read receiver. I went in motion. Roger breaks outside splitting the safeties, then he cuts back inside while John runs underneath. Safety Ray Horton was not sure which receiver to follow and in that split-second Joe found a tiny space to deliver the game-winning pass to John. The 49ers were world champions for the third time (and my first) with a 20–16 victory.

HOLMES IS WHERE THE HEART IS

Just like most of the victories during their dynasty run of the 1970s, one of the most thrilling Super Bowls of all time would involve another Pittsburgh Steelers team. And in a tremendous see-saw battle that came down to the game's final moments, the franchise would come away with a record sixth Lombardi Trophy.

Despite a schedule that was the franchise's most difficult in the last 30 years, head coach Mike Tomlin, offensive coordinator Bruce Arians, and defensive coordinator Dick LeBeau helped lead Pittsburgh to a 12-4 record, took the AFC North crown and defeated the Chargers and Ravens to reach Super Bowl XLIII.

Down in Tampa on February 1, 2009, they would face the 9-7 Arizona Cardinals, who made it to the final contest primarily on the arm of quarterback Kurt Warner, he of "the Greatest Show on Turf" fame when he directed the St. Louis Rams to a nail-biting victory over the Tennessee Titans in XXXIV.

Pittsburgh had a star quarterback themselves with a Super Bowl win under his belt—Ben Roethlisberger.

The Steelers also had the best defense in the NFL. Linebacker James Harrison set a team record with 16 sacks, forced seven fumbles, an interception, and scored a safety. He became the first undrafted player to earn the league's top defensive honor as he was named the NFL's defensive player of the year. Harrison led a Steelers team that dominated just about every defensive category there was including total yardage allowed, first downs allowed, and points allowed.

It was the defense that kept Warner in check most of the first half, and like the Bengals-49ers of Super Bowl XXIII, the first half was tightly contested with both sides bending but not breaking.

With the Steelers ahead just 10–7, it appeared the Cardinals would grab the lead at the halftime whistle. After Arizona picked off Roethlisberger, Warner began the potential go-ahead drive from the Pittsburgh 32 at the two-minute warning. After several completions to Larry Fitzgerald, Anquan Boldin, and Tim Hightower, it was now first and goal with just18 seconds left. Out of the shotgun, Warner surveyed the defense; immediately pressured by linebackers LaMarr Woodley and Lawrence Timmons, he threw to Boldin, who had separation from defender Deshea Townsend.

Riveted to Warner's eyes, Harrison, who was supposed to blitz, instead faked and then dropped back, where he picked off the ball intended for Boldin.

"As soon as I caught the ball, I said to myself, 'All right, I am about to score!' I could not see anybody but Kurt. A split second later, I see a sea of red jerseys, and I said, 'I am *not* about to score!' All of a sudden, it felt like there were twenty red shirts on that field," recalled Harrison. "I am fighting with Deshea Townsend, our cornerback, as he is imploring me to give him the ball. Picking the ball off and dealing with Deshea seemed like it took forever, but we finally got it going, I have blockers, but we get into a small crowd, and I say, 'All right, I am about to go down here.' Somehow, I get through it, and I got a lot of help. I remember during practice that week that if one of us got a turnover, our defense would run the entire length of the field. It happened to actually take place, and the team effort turned out to be a significant play in our win."

Plenty of Cardinals had a shot at Harrison as he rumbled down the sideline, but by the time receiver Fitzgerald caught up to the gasping linebacker, they tumbled head-first into the end zone.

Harrison recalled: "After I beat the last lineman, I said, 'Okay, I got it.' I never saw Fitzgerald. Fitz went to swing at the ball. He actually missed the ball and hit my chest. That gave me an instant to clutch the ball because had he hit it, for sure that ball would have fell out of my grasp. When Fitz pulled me down, I got hit in my neck by Steve Breaston, Arizona's wide receiver, and everything just goes straight to the ground. My head hits first. I could hear nothing as I am running. I could hear the crowd only after I fell on my neck. I rolled over, then I heard fans yell."

The linebacker's 100-yard return for a touchdown was the longest play in Super Bowl history and, more important, gave Pittsburgh the momentum with a 10-point lead at halftime.

"Momentum shifts can be seismic in games," observed Boomer Esiason. "Most often, defensive plays, like jarring a ball loose and recovering it, a sack, or a pick go far in saving a game for a team or losing it for the team it goes against.

"Perhaps the greatest defensive play in Super Bowl history was the James Harrison hundred-yard pick-six," he said. "I was broadcasting that game," said Esiason, who moved to the booth after hanging up his cleats following the 1997 season. "There was no time on the clock, and I said, 'He better score; otherwise it is a waste of a lot of effort by the whole defensive unit.' James's play saved the game for the Pittsburgh Steelers."

The lead grew to 20–7 before Arizona mounted a brilliant comeback. Warner, who had been through this before, calmly and patiently brought his team back—all the way back—and after a safety, a long drive that resulted in 7 points, and then another touchdown after he hooked up on a 64-yard pass play to Fitzgerald, now with under three minutes to play, his team was leading the Super Bowl, 23–20. Warner would complete 31 of 43 passes for 377 yards, setting a record third Super Bowl 300-yard passing game, and three touchdowns.

With just 2:37 left in the fourth, Pittsburgh was behind for the first time all day. And while Harrison had "saved the game for Pittsburgh," it would be receiver Santonio Holmes who won it for them.

"A teammate came up to me and said, 'We need a play from you,'" said Holmes. "Watching Fitzgerald run free to that end zone to put Arizona ahead really sparked me. It was a call to action. I remember right before we went onto the field, I walked up to Roethlisberger. I looked at him and said, 'No disrespect to the rest of our guys, but right now I want the ball.' He did not look at me. He did not say anything. He just continued to stare onto the field. It let him know I wanted it as bad as he did."

After a holding penalty on the first play, Roethlisberger faced first-and-20 from his own 12. With the help of a pair of 13- and 14-yard completions to Holmes, Pittsburgh found itself on the 50-yard line with just over one minute left in the game.

Following a 4-yard gain, Roethlisberger and Holmes connected for a 40-yard pass-run play, getting all the way down to the Arizona 6. On the very next play, Holmes got open in the end zone, but Roethlisberger's perfect pass went right through his hands.

"I was gathering myself after dropping the game-winning touchdown. I was really upset with myself on that opportunity I just missed," recalled Holmes, "but I remember tight end Heath Miller coming up to me and saying, 'Don't worry, the next pass is going to come to you.'

"Roethlisberger came into the huddle, and I was surprised by the play call. It was something we had been working on since the start of the playoffs, but it was never successful. Overthrown, knocked down, incomplete, out-of-bounds. I stumbled but knew my job was to be at the back of the end zone and wait. I look back and see Ben point to me and then let the ball go. I didn't even see or feel the defenders near me—it was just me and the ball."

With not so much as an inch margin of error, arms extended fully above his head, Holmes picked the ball out of the air just beyond the reach of the defenders in the back right corner of the end zone, and landed with his toes barely inside the out of bounds line. Pittsburgh had a 27–23 lead with 29 seconds left. The Steelers forced a Warner fumble, and they were, yet again, Super Bowl champions.

THE FOURTH QUARTER ALL-TIME TEAM

OFFENSE

WRs	Randy Moss	Minnesota Vikings
	Terrell Owens	San Francisco 49ers
TE	Tony Gonzalez	Kansas City Chiefs
G	Bruce Matthews	Houston Oilers / Tennessee Oilers/ Titans
	Larry Allen	Dallas Cowboys
T	Jonathan Ogden	Baltimore Ravens
	Walter Jones	Seattle Seahawks
C	Dermontti Dawson	Pittsburgh Steelers
RBs	Barry Sanders	Detroit Lions
	Marshall Faulk	Indianapolis Colts St. Louis Rams
QB	Tom Brady	New England Patriots

DEFENSE

DE	J.J. Watt	Houston Texans
	Michael Strahan	New York Giants
DT	Warren Sapp	Tampa Bay Buccaneers
	John Randle	Minnesota Vikings
LB	Junior Seau	San Diego Chargers
	Ray Lewis	Baltimore Ravens
	Derrick Brooks	Tampa Bay Buccaneers
DB	Deion Sanders	Atlanta Falcons / Dallas Cowboys
	Charles Woodson	Oakland Raiders / Green Bay Packers
S	Ed Reed	Baltimore Ravens
	Troy Polamalu	Pittsburgh Steelers
P	Shane Lechler	Oakland Raiders Houston Texans
K	Adam Vinatieri	New England Patriots / Indianapolis Colts
HC	Bill Belichick	New England Patriots

OVERTIME

No doubt football and specifically the NFL have become a core fabric of pop culture, and despite the need to overcome the challenges of the next one hundred years, including concussions, drugs, pricing out the average fan, gambling, and the speed of the game, some of the most notable players and coaches that have made an impact offer their views as to why the sport has grown from humble beginnings to stunning and continuous extraordinary popularity across a broad social spectrum in America.

I think the team concept of the sport is very American. I think the hard work football players have to do to be successful is something people admire. It is a tough sport. It is a tough game. It carries a very American philosophy of getting up again and again after being knocked down. It is a very physical sport that not many other nations have really anything similar. So I think it is a very good reflection of the American mentality. **—Raymond Berry**

There is so much about the game that captures people's imaginations and draws them in. Communities and parents are involved in the game from an early stage. There is so much involvement beginning at the grass-roots level, so the NFL, being the pinnacle, it touches so many demographics. Also, when you think about the humble beginnings of the NFL, it has evolved tremendously through rules and equipment. It has great staying power.   **—Barry Sanders**

It is football's combination of grace and violence. The beauty of Warfield leaping over midfield to snare a pass, then the violence of him getting whacked. A guard pulling around end then demolishing a defensive back. Those things appeal to the sports fan that baseball doesn't have. Plus, football is an event because each one of those sixteen games has more importance than a 162-game baseball season.　　**—Bob Griese**

It is a great American game. I think pro football and football in general is as American as apple pie. From high school and college, it is a great tradition. Tailgating, camaraderie, and you simply learn a lot being a teammate. You learn from other perspectives.

It's not for everyone, as we have so many sports. But I think by being part of a team, they become better people in the long run. Working for the common good. I mean this seriously: that I consider myself very fortunate to as far as assimilation into American society, which I would have done anyways, but football provided a stepping-stone to being accepted. To do that through football means a lot.　　**—Pete Gogolak**

It is the greatest game in the world. It is so hard. It is so physical. It takes so much emotion. And you have to wade through miles and miles of torture to get one great feeling. And when that feeling comes, it is the greatest there is.

I can honestly say that, growing up, if I had a hundred experiences in sports, baseball was ninety-nine of them. But once I got old enough and really started appreciating football, there was something about this game that drew me exclusively to it.

Football is a game of constant adversity. And sooner or later, you go, "Wow, this is why I play, because that was good." It is a game of torture for everybody. And for quarterbacks, it is unbelievable. But you chase it for that one fleeting moment.

I was so lucky for so long to play on a team that won a lot of games, and whenever we'd be flying back home after a road win, it would be the greatest three hours of my life. You can forget about everything, enjoy the victory, and relax.

Why do you think coaches put in sixteen hours a day? Because they get to go out on the field on Sunday and feel the rush of game day. And if it all works and they win, that is why you do it. And I will never get that feeling again.

I never get that rush as a broadcaster. On a scale of one to ten, winning a football game is a ten and doing a great job as a broadcaster is a one. You can't even compare it. **—Phil Simms**

Men have a tendency to watch a boxing match or war movie, and football is war without killing each other. Women like it too. We're doing everything out there but kill, but there is a purpose to it. It is execution and athletic talent on display. I have a lot of admiration for both the players that came before me and the ones out there performing now. I got to meet many. Sammy Baugh was my dad's hero. So, I am thrilled to have been just a little part of it. **—Bob Lilly**

The country is in love with football. It is the number one sport in America. Also, the fact that the Super Bowl is a single game. It is not the best of seven. All the sweat and toil, weights, conditioning, and film study come down to that one game. It is the biggest game in the number one sport. **—John Stallworth**

Its popularity has now become 24–7, 365 days a year. Used to be, you look at the calendar and [it] was pretty much done after the Super Bowl. **—Rich Gannon**

You also have to give credit to today's players, as they are a significant part of the social media world. They are becoming stars sometimes before they even touch a football in the NFL. Get yourself goin' on a Twitter account, and you can be a star before you play your first pro game. There are more marketing opportunities today, and savvy players are taking advantage of them. Imagine if Deion Sanders and Michael Irvin were starting out today. **—Herschel Walker**

Every game matters. It is awesome. You have only eight home games a year. What else are you going to do on a Sunday afternoon, Sunday night, or Monday night that's more fun?   **—Drew Esocoff, TV director**

These days, I'm a fan like everybody else. I can't wait for the next season to start. It has become such a part of our lives that fans in making weekend plans often pore over their team's schedule before making a decision. Life is busy, and it is a challenge, and we all go through difficult times, so football and sports in general are an outlet to forget about issues for a while. It is something we look forward to.   **—Roger Staubach**

It is the best game to watch. TV has certainly helped promote the game. Even if you don't have a local team to root for, say in Maine or Wyoming, when a team is winning, everyone wants to watch them. Like the Packers, then that is how Dallas became "America's Team." . . . People want to watch the winners. They always have.   **—Paul Hornung**

The game is probably more entertaining today than it ever was. It used to be that only one or two teams had an innovative wide-open offense. Now it seems every team throws the ball more than they run it. At the same time, fans still enjoy the 10–7 defensive struggles because there's a lot of tension, as the outcome is still in doubt until the very end of the game. Generally speaking, however, fans love the wide-open game. That is why quarterbacks and wide receivers are being paid all that money. There are more things going on than just a slugfest.   **—Coach Dick Vermeil**

I think it is one sport that really embodies team and gives you the opportunity to root for the individual as well. It is also offers an exciting playoff format of single elimination.   **—Carl Banks**

We are like modern-day gladiators. Fans like the intensity of it. The drama, rivalries, and because each game is very significant, our Super Bowl is by far the most-watched championship.   **—Terrell Suggs**

Hopefully the NFL will continue its high level of play. It is a quick game. Four seconds, and the play's over. It is a six-inch game, played between the ears. **—Jim Taylor**

Clearly it is a very physical game, but it is also a highly skilled game. It is simply fun to watch, and it provides a lot of excitement. You have players of different sizes and skill sets, and they have to perform as a team to be successful. **—John Hadl**

I think gambling on it is one thing. The popularity of fantasy football allows you not to be locked into just one team. Fantasy football has increased the popularity of the NFL exponentially. Now you have people that don't really know the game but want to be in a fantasy football league. It has become a gateway to learn the sport.

I also think it is a great escape. Go back to the Depression. Football was extremely popular when things were not going well. It was a place for people to go to escape the problems they had. It was basically a fantasy world. Our world is a fantasy world. Let's face it, the adulation, the amount of money being made, the pedestal you're being put on, it is not the real world. **—Joe Theismann**

Super Bowl Sunday is the one time when our entire country is together. More so than at any other time during the year. We are having a shared experience. New Year's Eve and Thanksgiving are different on the East Coast and West Coast and Midwest time zones. The fact that Super Bowl day is the highest-rated day [for television programming] the kickoff or fourth-quarter whatever we are a united nation like [at] no other time. There is nothing like it. There is no other moment. You stop the United States in the middle of the fourth quarter in a close Super Bowl.

There are a 110 million-plus people watching. They are watching the game in Harlem. They are watching the game in Beverly Hills. They are watching the game in hospitals. They are watching at a polo match. Young and old, rich and poor, black and white, male and female, it has the appeal that reaches out to everybody. More than any other thing that happens in this country, for different reasons. Everybody finds their own reason.   **—Mike Weisman, TV producer**

It goes back to the gladiator days. The fans love it, and it is a way of life now. This game has been around for a hundred years now, and that is almost as old as my mom. Every week, Americans wake up and look forward to watching the game.   **—Willie Brown**

It is one thing to have the great players and the great minds that are coaching these great players, but you go to Europe, and their football fan base is humongous. The United States has its own form of that, and it is called the NFL.   **—Bo Jackson**

The mix of what makes the game, from the pomp and circumstance, to the primal violence, to the enthusiasm of the fans. There is so much of it that makes it sport.   **—Randy Cross**

People recognize that football is the ultimate team sport and identify with team success. And America loves violence—the NFL has mastered marketing violence.   **—Joe Kapp**

There is a kind of magic to the NFL. You build up to the game all week, then you take a few days after to talk about it, celebrate or complain, and every game matters. It is a big deal. Every Sunday, you live and die with that team. You do not skip a couple games, like baseball.

—Chris Myers, sportscaster

I think it is identical to the nature of the United States of America. It is sacrifice. It is hard work. It is teamwork. It is tough. To me, it personifies how this country was built. It is an event. It is what this country is really all about. I don't think the country can get enough of it.

I will tell you this: when I came in the league in 1970, it was already big. But I never could dream, nor do I think Pete Rozelle could have ever thought it would come to this. Other than two major religious holidays, the Super Bowl is the biggest day in America. This shows how big the sport has become. The Super Bowl is our biggest day. The draft has become the second biggest day, more than championship day games, and it shows you how incredibly popular all aspects of our game has become.

So many people have built their days and weekends around NFL games. And every game is important. In baseball, you can lose the first game and still win the next three and take a four-game series.

—Ernie Accorsi, NFL executive

Here's something one of my coaches said: "To know the game is great, to play the game is greater, but to love the game is the greatest of them all."

—Coach Marv Levy

Well, you hear a lot of talk these days about concerns that the human body was not made to play this game. I carry injuries with me every day. This August I am getting a new hip. I've been knocked out with concussions. All those things are being brought to awareness, but there is one thing not being talked about: there is no place that you can take people from different walks of life—different races, religions, socioeconomic levels—and bring them together and be brothers for life. *For life.*

To overcome common obstacles to reach a goal. All those differences go out the window because you want to do something collectively. Could you imagine if you could get all your office personnel to work together like that? The game itself is so amazing. It is such an eye-opener. There's nothing like it in the real world.

Yes, to put all your differences aside because now is the time to get something done. I have been in broadcasting, different forms of business, and really miss that. There's no place else where that unity comes together that exemplifies itself as a team more than a football team—specifically an NFL football team.

—Bill Maas

Every single player will tell you that when they announce your name when you are coming out of that tunnel, and you hear the fans yelling, that is the moment you never forget. The roar of the crowd.   **—Tim Krumrie**

What makes this game special is that a lot of people have to subjugate and sacrifice for the good of the team. In an abstract way, it is a microcosm of life. That is why it is the greatest game.   **—Dan Hampton**

It is the greatest team sport ever devised. Everybody has a role, and when you begin to respect everybody else's role, you begin to work together. It is the only sport where every teammate depends on each other on every play just to survive.

The concept of the huddle. Huddle up. The concept of crunch time, when you really have to perform. The fact that you will get knocked down and there will be times when you feel you can't go on.

I make frequent speech appearances, and I tell them I have yet to see one time where somebody went back to their calculus or chemistry teacher for advice, but every one of us goes back to our coach. Most times in the classroom, they are not learning the most important thing in life, which is how do you get back up after getting knocked down. And to keep going when you don't think you can go on. And that coach taught you that.

So, I think football is an incredible metaphor for life.

Players have to depend on each other, and there is a strategy to it. Sometimes you get tackled for a loss, and there is adversity on the other side of that line. All those things, I think, make it a metaphor, which is perfect for television, in that there are heroes and tragedies. And there is always an opportunity to come back.   **—David Baker, Hall of Fame**

To me, it is the greatest sport. It is hard, it is not easy to be successful, and I think that is what America is all about. It takes teamwork. It takes people from different backgrounds coming together, or else a play doesn't work.

I don't care if you have Jerry Rice, Barry Sanders, John Elway, and Joe Montana on your team; unless everybody is doing his job consistently, it won't work. I think that is part of the appeal, in that it brings people to-gether better than any sport.

Hard work, teamwork, not being concerned about who gets credit—to me football embodies everything that America is about.

—John Lynch

Let's hope we have one hundred more.

—Mike Ditka

NOTES

1. Tony Collins, *The Oval World: A Global History of Rugby* (New York: Bloomsbury Sport, 2015), 9.
2. Daven Hiskey, "Who Invented Baseball?," Today I Found Out, last modified March 20, 2012, www.todayifoundout.com/index.php/2012/03/abner -doubleday-did-not-invent-baseball/ as of 4-12-18.
3. Roger Treat, *The Official Encyclopedia of Football* (New York: A. S. Barnes, 1972), 17.
4. David Neft, *Pro Football Encyclopedia 1978* (New York: Grosset & Dunlap, 1978), 664.
5. " 'Pro' Football Moguls Form National Body," *Evening Repository* (Canton, OH), August 21, 1920.
6. Pro Football Hall of Fame archives. Akron's Frank Nied took down the minutes, which would later be typed up on the letterhead of the Akron Professional Football Team, and the two-page record of that meeting is on display at the Pro Football Hall of Fame.
7. "Potsy" Clarke, "Side Lights on Professional Football," *All-Sports* (November 1924), 44.
8. *Evening Repository* (Canton, OH), January 29, 1921.
9. *Birmingham (AL) News*, December 29, 1932.
10. Chuck Voorhis, "Pros Produce a Punch, Will Amateurs Match It?" *Charlotte Observer*, December 28, 1933.
11. *Philadelphia Daily News*, January 26, 2000, 100–101.
12. *Ibid.*
13. *Los Angeles Rams Vs. Chicago Bears*, Los Angeles Memorial Coliseum Official Program, November 1, 1959.
14. Mark Kram, "Making Some Headway?" *Philadelphia Daily News*, January 26, 2000, 100.

15. Dan Daly, *The National Forgotten League: Entertaining Stories and Observations from Pro Football's First Fifty Years* (Lincoln: University of Nebraska Press, 2012), 239.

16. *Ibid.*

17. Duncan, 95.

18. Chris Willis, *Walter Lingo, Jim Thorpe, and the Oorang Indians: How a Dog Kennel Owner Created the NFL's Most Famous Traveling Team* (New York: Rowman & Littlefield, 2017), 124.

19. Ralph Hickok, "On the Road Again and Again," *Sports Illustrated,* September 9, 1987.

20. Mike Rathet and the editors of *Pro Quarterback* magazine, *The World of the NFL: Pro Football* (Chicago: Henry Regnery, 1972), 68–69.

21. Greg Bedard, "An Anniversary Note," *Boston Globe*, April 24, 2011.

22. "#41, Guy Chamberlin: The Nebraska 100," *Omaha (NE) World-Herald* online, accessed March 27, 2018, http://dataomaha.com/neb100/player/41.

23. George Halas, "My Forty Years in Football," *Saturday Evening Post*, November 23, 1957.

24. *Ibid.*

25. Daly, *The National Forgotten League*, 52.

26. US Naval History, US Congressional Medal of Honor Society, http://www .cmohs.org/recipient-detail/2853/lummus-jack.php.

27. John Carroll, *Fritz Pollard: Pioneer in Racial Advancement* (Urbana and Chicago: University of Illinois Press, 1998), 134.

28. *Ibid.,* 137–38.

29. Charles Ross, *Mavericks, Money and Men: The AFL, Black Players and the Evolution of Modern Football* (Philadelphia: Temple University Press, 2016), 143.

30. Nathan Fenno, "Pressing Forward," *Los Angeles Times*, January 29, 2017, D5.

31. Woody Strode and Sam Young, *Goal Dust* (Lanham MD: Madison Books, 1990), 142.

32. *Ibid.,* 150.

33. Ross, *Mavericks, Money and Men*, 143.

34. Thomas Smith, "Civil Rights on the Gridiron: The Kennedy Administration and the Desegregation of the Washington Redskins," *Journal of Sport History* 14, no. 2 (Summer 1987): 191.

35. Ross, *Mavericks, Money and Men*, 148.

36. Jack T. Clary, *Cleveland Browns* (New York: Macmillan, 1973), 16.

37. Paul Brown, "I Call the Plays for the Browns," *Saturday Evening Post*, December 12, 1953, 112.

38. *Ibid.*, 113.

39. Daly, *The National Forgotten League*, 5.

40. Richard Goldstein, "Sammy Baugh, Top Quarterback and Key Figure in Early N.F.L., Dies at 94," *New York Times,* December 17, 2008, https://www.nytimes.com/2008/12/18/sports/football/18baugh.html.

41. Frank Litsky, "Don Hutson, Star Pass-Catcher, Dies at 84," *New York Times,* June 27, 1997, https://www.nytimes.com/1997/06/27/sports/don-hutson-star-pass-catcher-dies-at-84.html.

42. Michael MacCambridge, *Lamar Hunt: A Life in Sports* (Kansas City: Andrews McMeel, 2012).

43. Gerald Eskenazi, "Lamar Hunt, a Force in Football, Dies at 74," *New York Times* online, December 15, 2006, www.nytimes.com/2006/12/15/sports/football/15hunt.html.

44. George Sullivan, *Touchdown! The Picture History of the American Football League* (New York: Putnam, 1967), 112–13.

45. MacCambridge, *Lamar Hunt,* 99.

46. John Eisenberg, "A Football Interloper's First Gust of Success," *New York Times,* December 15, 2012, https://www.nytimes.com/2012/12/16/sports/football/in-1962-championship-spectacle-put-the-afl-in-the-game.html.

47. Ross, *Mavericks, Money and Men,* 11–12.

48. Leonard Shapiro, "A Typical NFL Training Camp: Sweating and Straining in Stifling Heat," *Football Digest,* July/August 1978, 50.

49. Jerry Rice and Randy O. Williams, *50 Years, 50 Moments: The Most Unforgettable Plays in Super Bowl History* (New York: HarperCollins/Dey Street, 2015).

50. *Ibid.*

51. *Ibid.*

52. *Ibid.*

53. *Ibid.*

54. Leonard Shapiro, "The Hit That Changed a Career," *Washington Post,* November 18, 2005.

55. Sullivan, *Touchdown!,* 57.

56. Rick Maese, "At NFL's Job Fair, Time to See the Doctor," *Washington Post,* February 27, 2017.

57. Art Donovan, *Fatso: Football When Men Were Really Men* (New York: William Morrow, 1987).

58. Daly, *The National Forgotten League,* 52.

59. Jack Murphy, "Looney Is Playing a New Tune," *Sports Illustrated,* August 4, 1969, www.si.com/vault/1969/08/04/610502/looney-is-playing-a-new-tune.

60. P. S. Ruckman Jr., "The Very Colorful Joe Don Looney," *Pardon Power* (blog), March 28, 2010, www.pardonpower.com/2010/03/very-colorful -joe-don-looney.html.

61. *Ibid.*

62. *Ibid.*

63. *Ibid.*

64. Randy Williams, "NFL Films: Football's Eyes and Ears," *Hollywood Reporter*, November 7, 2001.

65. Sullivan, *Touchdown!*, 149.

66. Rice and Williams, *50 Years, 50 Moments*.

BIBLIOGRAPHY

BOOKS

Jim Acho, *The Foolish Club*. New York: Gridiron Press, 1997.

Johnny Anonymous, *NFL Confidential: True Confessions from the Gutter of Football*. New York: Dey Street, 2015.

Jaime Aron, *Breakthrough Boys: The Story of the 1971 Super Bowl Champion Dallas Cowboys*. Minneapolis: MVP Books, 1971.

Jim Baker and Bernard Corbett, *The Most Memorable Games in Giants History*. New York: Bloomsbury, 2010.

Phil Berger, *More Championship Teams of the NFL*. New York: Random House, 1974.

David Boss and Bob Oates Jr., *The First Fifty Years: A Celebration of the National Football League in its Fiftieth Season*. New York: Macmillan, 1969.

Terry Bradshaw and David Fisher, *Keep It Simple*. New York: Atria Books, 2002.

John Brodie and James Houston, *Open Field*. Boston: Houghton-Mifflin, 1974.

Paul Brown with Jack Clary, *PB: The Paul Brown Story*. New York: Atheneum, 1979.

Bob Carroll, *When the Grass Was Real: Unitas, Brown, Lombardi, Sayers, Butkus, Namath and All the Rest: The Ten Best Years of Pro Football*. New York: Simon & Schuster, 1993.

John Carroll, *Fritz Pollard: Pioneer in Racial Advancement*. University of Illinois Press, 1998.

Kevin Carroll, *Houston Oilers: The Early Years*. Austin, Texas: Eakin Press, 2001.

Jack Clary, *Cleveland Browns*. New York: Macmillan, 1973.

Howard Coan, *Great Pass Catchers in Pro Football*. New York: Julian Messner, 1971.

Howard Cosell, *Like It Is*. Chicago: Playboy Press, 1974.

Howard Cosell with Peter Bonventre, *I Never Played the Game*. New York: William Morrow, 1985.

Larry Csonka and Jim Kiick with Dave Anderson, *Always on the Run*. New York: Random House, 1973.

Bob Curran, *The $400,000 Quarterback or the League That Came in from the Cold*. New York: Macmillan, 1965.

Dan Daly, *The National Forgotten League: Entertaining Stories and Observations from Pro Football's First Fifty Years*. Lincoln: University of Nebraska Press, 2012.

John Devaney, *Star Pass Receivers of the NFL*. New York: Random House, 1972.

Gregg Easterbrook, *The King of Sports: Football's Impact on America*. New York: St. Martin's Press, 2013.

Larry Fox, *Broadway Joe and His Super Jets*. New York: Coward-McCann, 1969.

Lew Freedman, *Football Stadiums: A Guide to Professional and Top College Stadiums*. Ontario, Canada: Firefly Books, 2013.

Joe Garner and Bob Costas, *100 Yards of Glory: The Greatest Moments in NFL History*. Boston: Houghton Mifflin Harcourt, 2011.

Bob Griese and Dave Hyde, *Perfection: The Inside Story of the 1972 Miami Dolphins' Perfect Season*. New York: Wiley & Sons, 2012.

Marc Gunther and Bill Carter, *Monday Night Mayhem: The Inside Story of ABC's Monday Night Football*. New York: William Morrow, 1985.

David Harris, *The Rise and Decline of the NFL*. New York: Bantam, 1986.

Jack Horrigan and Mike Rathet, *The Other League: The Fabulous Story of the American Football League*. Chicago: Follett, 1970.

Al Levine, *Miami Dolphins: Football's Greatest Team*. Englewood Cliffs, NJ: Prentice-Hall, 1973.

Frank Lodato, *But We Were 17 and 0*. Lake Worth, Florida: IQ Publications, 1986.

Vince Lombardi with H.C. Heinz, *Run to Daylight!* New York: Simon & Schuster, 1965.

Michael MacCambridge, *America's Game: The Epic Story of How Pro Football Captured a Nation*. New York: Random House, 2004.

Michael MacCambridge, *Lamar Hunt: A Life in Sports*. Kansas City: Andrews McMeel, 2012.

John Madden, *Heroes of Football: The Story of America's Game*. New York: Dutton, 2006.

Tod Maher and Bob Gill, eds. *The Pro Football Encyclopedia*. New York: Macmillan, 1997.

Alex Marvez, *Wild Ride! The Illustrated History of the Denver Broncos*. Dallas: Taylor, 1998.

Mike Mathet, *Dolphins 73*. Miami: Miami Dolphins, 1973.

Bob McGinn, *The Ultimate Super Bowl Book*. Minneapolis: MVP Books, 2009.

Joe McGuff, *Winning It All: The Chiefs of the AFL*. Garden City, NY: Doubleday, 1970.

Morris McLemore, *The Miami Dolphins*. New York: Doubleday, 1972.

Dave Meggyesy, *Out of Their League*. New York: Paperback Library, 1971.

Al Michaels with Jon Wertheim, *You Can't Make This Up: Miracles, Memories, and the Perfect Marriage of Sports and Television*. New York: HarperCollins, 2014.

James Miller and Tom Shales, *ESPN: Those Guys Have All the Fun*. New York: Little, Brown, 2011.

Jeff Miller, *Going Long: The Wild 10-Year Saga of the Renegade American Football League in the Words of Those Who Lived It*. New York: McGraw-Hill, 2003.

Joe Namath and Dick Schaap, *I Can't Wait 'Til Tomorrow . . .'Cause I Get Better Looking Every Day*. New York: Random House, 1969.

David Neft, Richard Cohen, and Rick Korch, *The Sports Encyclopedia: Pro Football, The Modern Era 1960-1995*. New York: St. Martin's Griffin, 1996.

Terry O'Neill, *The Game Behind the Game: High Stakes, High Pressure in Television Sports*. New York: Harper & Row, 1989.

Steve Perkins and Bill Braucher, *The Miami Dolphins: Winning Them All*. New York: Grosset & Dunlap, 1973.

Robert Peterson, *Pigskin: The Early Years of Pro Football*. New York: Oxford University Press, 1997.

John Pirkle, *Oiler Blues*. Houston: Sportline, 2000.

George Plimpton, *Paper Lion*. New York: Harper & Row, 1966.

Gary Pomerantz, *Their Life's Work: The Brotherhood of the 1970s Pittsburgh Steelers, Then and Now*. New York: Simon & Schuster, 2013.

Mark Ribowsky, *Slick: The Silver and Black Life of Al Davis*. New York: Macmillan, 1991.

Jerry Rice and Randy O. Williams, *50 Years, 50 Moments: The Most Unforgettable Plays in Super Bowl History*. New York: HarperCollins/Dey Street, 2015.

Susan Reyburn, *Football Nation: Four Hundred Years of America's Game*. New York: Abrams, 2013.

Charles Ross, *Mavericks, Money and Men: The AFL, Black Players and the Evolution of Modern Football*. Temple University Press, 2016.

Lou Sahadi, *Miracle in Miami*. Chicago: Regnery, 1972.

Don Shula with Lou Sahadi, *The Winning Edge*. New York: EP Dutton, 1973.

Jim Spence with Dave Diles, *Up Close and Personal: The Inside Story of Network Television Sports*. New York: Atheneum, 1988.

Hank Stram with Lou Sahadi, *They're Playing My Game*. New York: William Morrow, 1986.

Woody Strode and Sam Young, *Goal Dust*. Lanham, North Dakota: Madison Books, 1990.

George Sullivan, *Touchdown! The Picture History of the American Football League.* New York: Putnam, 1967.

Roger Treat, *The Encyclopedia of Football.* New York: A.S. Barnes, 1977.

Bill Walsh with Glenn Dickey, *Building a Champion: On Football and the Making of the 49ers.* New York: St. Martin's Press, 1992.

Pete Williams, *The Draft.* New York: St. Martin's Press, 2006.

NEWSPAPERS, WEBSITES, AND PERIODICALS

Akron Beacon Journal

Akron Evening Times

Atlanta Journal Constitution

Baltimore Sun

Bloomberg.com

Boston Globe

Boston Herald

Buffalo News

Canton Daily News

Canton Evening Repository

Charlotte Observer

Cincinnati Enquirer

Cleveland Plain Dealer

Daily Variety

Dallas Morning News

Dayton Journal

Denver Post

Espn.com

Football Digest

Ft. Worth Star Telegram

Hollywood Reporter

Houston Chronicle

Indianapolis Star

Kansas City Star

Life

Los Angeles Times

Miami Herald

Milwaukee Journal Sentinel

Newsweek

New Orleans Times-Picayune

New York Post

New York Times

Nfl.com

Oakland Tribune

Orlando Sentinel

Pittsburgh Post-Gazette

Pro-football-reference.com

Profootballhof.com

St. Louis Post-Dispatch

San Francisco Examiner

San Jose Mercury News

Saturday Evening Post

Si.com

The Sporting News

Sport

Sports Business Journal

Sports Illustrated

Sport World

Tampa Tribune

Time

USA Today

Washington Post

VIDEO

LA84 Foundation Research Library Film Archives

NFL Films

University of California, UCLA – Film Archives

YouTube

INDEX

Page numbers in *italics* refer to illustrations.

ABOUT THE AUTHORS

JERRY RICE is a Hall of Fame wide receiver and three-time Super Bowl champion. He is regarded as the best wide receiver ever to play in the National Football League. During a fifteen-year career with the San Francisco 49ers, Rice teamed up with Hall of Fame quarterbacks Steve Young and Joe Montana to win three Super Bowl championships ('88, '89, and '94) and a Super Bowl MVP award. Rice also played for three seasons with the Oakland Raiders and one season with the Seattle Seahawks before retiring from football in 2005. Rice was inducted into the College Football Hall of Fame in 2006 and the Pro Football Hall of Fame in 2010. He is now a television personality—in both sports and entertainment—and continues to grow his celebrity beyond the football field. He resides in the San Francisco Bay area.

RANDY O. WILLIAMS has written extensively on sports and entertainment for major publications such as *Sports Illustrated*, the *Los Angeles Times*, the *Washington Post*, NFL.com and ESPN.com. He previously teamed up with Jerry Rice for the *New York Times* bestseller *50 Years, 50 Moments*. He resides in Southern California.